HISTORY, APOCALYPSE,

and the

SECULAR IMAGINATION

New Essays on Augustine's *City of God*

Edited by

Mark Vessey
Karla Pollmann
Allan D. Fitzgerald, O.S.A.

Proceedings of a colloquium held at Green College,
The University of British Columbia,
18–20 September 1997

PHILOSOPHY DOCUMENTATION CENTER

This collection of essays is also available in the journal
Augustinian Studies 30:2.

Philosophy Documentation Center
Bowling Green State University
Bowling Green, OH 43403-0189 USA

Phone: 419-372-2419
Fax: 419-372-6987
e-mail: pdc@bgnet.bgsu.edu
http://www.bgsu.edu/pdc

ISBN   1-889680-04-4
Library of Congress Catalog Card Number: 99-066806

CONTENTS

III. The Secular Imagination

ACKNOWLEDGMENTS

From inception to completion, this volume has been the work of many hands. Its scheme of contents it owes in large part to Paul C. Burns and Harry O. Maier, whose respective interests in history and apocalypse shaped the Vancouver colloquium from which it sprang (the 27th Annual Medieval Workshop at the University of British Columbia). James J. O'Donnell and Eugene Vance, both participants in the colloquium, provided support and encouragement at a crucial stage. Gretchen Minton did the lion's share of the work of organizing that meeting, with notable help from Richard Unger of the History Department at UBC. Sheri Powell undertook the copy-editing and indexing. To all of them, and everyone else who has shared in this project to date, the editors wish to express their thanks. The expenses of the colloquium were met by grants from the Social Sciences and Humanities Research Council of Canada, and from the Offices of the Vice-President (Research) and Dean of Arts at the University of British Columbia, with further assistance from Green College and the Peter Wall Institute for Advanced Studies (both at UBC) and the Vancouver School of Theology.

M.V., K.P., A.F.

NOTES ON CONTRIBUTORS

Philippe BRUGGISSER is Privat-Docent in Sciences de l'Antiquité, Université de Fribourg.

Peter J. BURNELL is Associate Professor of Classics, University of Saskatchewan.

Paul C. BURNS is Assistant Professor of Classical, Near Eastern and Religious Studies, University of British Columbia.

Virginia BURRUS is Associate Professor of Early Church History, The Theological and Graduate Schools, Drew University.

Catherine CONYBEARE is Lecturer in Classics and Ancient History, University of Manchester.

J. Kevin COYLE is Professor of Early Christianity and Patristics, Faculty of Theology, Saint Paul University, Ottawa.

Paul B. HARVEY, Jr. is Professor of History and of Classics and Ancient Mediterranean Studies, Pennsylvania State University.

Michael J. HOLLERICH is Assistant Professor of Theology, University of St. Thomas, St. Paul, Minnesota.

Kevin L. HUGHES is an Arthur J. Ennis, O.S.A., Teaching Fellow in Core Humanities, Villanova University.

David LAMBERT recently completed a doctorate in History at Oxford University.

Harry O. MAIER is Associate Professor of New Testament Studies, Vancouver School of Theology.

Neil B. McLYNN is Associate Professor of Law, Keio University.

Gretchen E. MINTON is completing a doctorate in English at the University of British Columbia.

Gerard J. P. O'DALY is Professor of Latin, University College London.

Karla POLLMANN is Associate Professor in Greek, Latin and Ancient History, University of St. Andrews.

Joanna Vecchiarelli SCOTT is Professor of Political Science, Eastern Michigan University.

Thomas A. SMITH is Associate Professor of Religious Studies, Loyola University New Orleans.

Mark VESSEY is Associate Professor of English, University of British Columbia.

INTRODUCTION

———•◦•◆•◦•———

Perplexae quippe sunt istae duae civitates *in hoc saeculo* invicemque permixtae, donec ultimo iudicio dirimantur.

Augustine, *De civitate dei* 1,35

At the Paris congress of Augustinian studies in 1954, Henri-Irénée Marrou wondered aloud whether the time had come for a full-scale "scientific" commentary on Augustine's *City of God,* a task not performed since Juan Luis Vivès's edition of 1522.[1] Such an undertaking, he suggested, would now necessarily be collaborative; as a model, he mentioned current work toward a commentary on the *Historia Augusta*. The remarks were made at a session on "The Theology of History" whose very inclusion in the program of the congress Marrou interpreted as a sign of the favor newly accorded to this aspect of Augustine's oeuvre by scholars who, living through the political and military crises of the first half of the twentieth century, had more reason than their predecessors to pose the problem of the Meaning of History.[2] Fifty years on, our putatively modern or postmodern sense of crisis has evolved, and with it our ways of posing or disposing of that problem. Yet there has been no slackening of interest in the *City of God,* and it is safe to prophesy that when the sixteenth centenary of the Fall of Rome in 410 C.E. comes round, Augustine's response to the

---

1. Introducing another recent collection of papers on *Il De Civitate Dei: L'opera, le interpretazioni, l'influsso* (Rome: Herder, 1996), its editor, Elena Cavalcanti, regrets, "la mancanza . . . —per quanto riguarda le interpretazioni—di un lavoro sull'edizione e commento pubblicati da I. L. Vives, a Basilea nel 1522, opera che rappresenta un trapasso della ricezione del monumento agostiniano dal medioevo all'età moderna" (13).

2. *Augustinus Magister: Congrès International Augustinien, Paris, 21–24 septembre 1954,* 3 vols. (Paris: Études Augustiniennes, 1955) 3.195.

event, in twenty-two books, will still be a subject of widespread fascination. Meanwhile, commentary on the *City of God* continues to multiply, in many languages and genres, without yielding the work of formal synthesis envisaged by Marrou. Its absence, at this point, is unlikely to occasion much surprise or dismay. The classical age of the printed commentary, which began in the generation of Vivès and Erasmus, is all but over. For texts like the *City of God* which powerfully invite comprehensive "scientific" elucidation and have no less powerfully resisted it thus far, the future of interpretation lies in other, more flexible media. Flexible, but not exclusively electronic. By calling itself a collection of essays, the present volume announces a desire on the part of its contributors to continue exploiting the resources for reflection, argument, and exposition traditionally offered by the multi-authored book on a clearly defined theme.

History, Apocalypse, and the Secular Imagination gathers the first fruits of a collaboration begun, however modestly, in the spirit of Marrou's suggestion of 1954. Its origins lie in an informal consultation of about two dozen scholars, held during the Twelfth International Conference on Patristic Studies at Oxford in 1995. There it was proposed that a series of colloquia be arranged on the *City of God,* with a view to preparing the ground, if not for a formal commentary on that work, then for some future synthesis of scholarship and interpretation, presumably to include a web site or virtual Cityspace. The first meeting was convened at the University of British Columbia, Vancouver, in September 1997, under the title used for this volume. The particular choice of theme was dictated jointly by the interests of the local organizers and by a concern to mark out a field of study that would reflect the ambition of Augustine's work while also inviting concerted discussion. Forty papers were read over the three days of the meeting, seventeen of which appear in revised form below, together with one written separately.

In the event, it has proved possible to arrange these essays on an axis continuous with Marrou's research on the *City of God* during the 1950s and 1960s, which focused on what he called *le temps de l'histoire,* translating Augustine's *saeculum.* That research issued in lectures given in Montreal in 1950 and at Villanova University in 1964, and in a seminal paper at the Oxford patristics conference in 1955, before culminating in his 1968 book, *Théologie de l'histoire.*[3] By revealing the subtlety of Augustine's thinking on the condition

---

3. H.-I. Marrou, *L'ambivalence du temps de l'histoire chez saint Augustin,* Conférence Albert-le-Grand, 1950 (Montreal: Institut d'Études Médiévales, 1950) esp. 78, where he translates the passage cited as the epigraph to this introduction: "'jusqu'a ce qu'intervienne le jugement final, aussi

and ends of human life in time, Marrou opened the way for some of the most creative English-language scholarship on Augustine of the 1960s, including that of Peter Brown, who was among the first to catch the "new" sense of the Augustinian *saeculum*,[4] and of Robert Markus, who made it the basis of a far-reaching reinterpretation of Augustine's theory of history and society.[5] Without necessarily engaging directly with such earlier work or endorsing its more controversial claims, the essays collected here all seek in their various ways to expand and corroborate the kinds of readings of Augustine that this now "classic" modern scholarship on Late Antiquity has made possible. So far as they can be said to share a single subject, it is that of the action—in and as a result of Augustine's work—of what is here styled the *secular imagination*.

The phrase requires some explanation. The "imagination" for Augustine can be a snare, which is why he condemns the fictions of the poets. More neutrally, it

---

longtemps que dure *ce temps de l'histoire,* les deux cités sont entrelacées l'une à l'autre . . . et intimement mélangées' . . . si bien que seul le regard de Dieu peut les distinguer" (emphasis added); "*Civitas Dei, civitas terrena: num tertium quid?*" in *Studia Patristica* 2 (1957): 342–50;*The Resurrection and Saint Augustine's Theology of Human Values,* The Saint Augustine Lecture, 1965 (Villanova, Pa.: Villanova Press, 1966); *Théologie de l'histoire* (Paris: Le Seuil, 1968). For the course of Marrou's work, see A.-M. 'la Bonnardière, "La 'Cité terrestre' d'après H.-I. Marrou," in *Saint Augustin et la Bible,* ed. A.-M. la Bonnardière (Paris: Beauchesne, 1986) 287–398, who notes his longstanding interest in Augustine's reading of John's Apocalypse (cf. *Théologie de l'histoire* 39–42).

4. See, e.g., P. R. L. Brown, "Saint Augustine," in *Trends in Medieval Political Thought,* ed. Beryl Smalley (Oxford: Clarendon Press, 1963), repr. in his *Religion and Society in the Age of Saint Augustine* (London: Faber & Faber, 1972)) 25–45 at 37: "The object of [Augustine's] contemplation . . . is not the state: it is something far, far wider. For him it is the *saeculum.* And we should translate this vital word, not by 'the world,' so much as by 'existence'—the sum total of human existence as we experience it in the present, as we know it has been since the fall of Adam [sic], and as we know it will continue until the Last Judgement" (citing Marrou, *L'ambivalence*). Cf. M. Vessey, "The Demise of the Christian Writer and the Remaking of 'Late Antiquity': From H.-I. Marrou's Saint Augustine (1938) to Peter Brown's Holy Man (1983)," *Journal of Early Christian Studies* 6 (1998): 377–411.

5. R. A. Markus, *Saeculum: History and Society in the Theology of St. Augustine* (Cambridge: Cambridge University Press, 1970; 2nd ed. 1988)) 62: "Augustine saw the whole course of history, past, present and future, as a dramatic conflict of the two cities, that is to say, in terms of a tension of forces which will only appear in their naked reality beyond temporal history. From this point of view the sphere in which human kingdoms, empires and all states have their being is radically ambiguous . . ." (citing Marrou, *L'ambivalence*). See also the essays in his *Sacred and Secular: Studies on Augustine and Latin Christianity* (Aldershot: Variorum, 1994) and his *The End of Ancient Christianity* (Cambridge: Cambridge University Press, 1990). La Bonnardière (above, n.3) 396–97 reports the initial reaction to Markus's work. For a more recent critique, see the essay by Michael Hollerich in this volume

is the faculty by which the mind creates images for its own contemplation, especially but not only of objects of sense perception. Crucially, it is the faculty by which objects, scenes, or events in the past or future are brought into the present.[6] The central importance of Augustine's view of the imagination for the narrative of his *Confessions* is clear even from so summary an account as this. It will be argued below that it also has a special relevance to his enterprise in the *City of God*. To put the matter more straightforwardly than Augustine himself ever does: the apprehension and artistic representation of the reality of life in and beyond the *saeculum* require works of the imagination.[7] To describe heaven (*City of God* 22) is an imaginative act analogous to that of anticipating the dawn of a new day (*Confessions* 11,19). Since in Augustine's universe all imagination (as distinct from intellection) is timebound, it may be objected that the phrase "secular imagination" is a tautology. The coinage can perhaps be justified in relation to more modern notions of the imaginative faculty, which are not necessarily determined—for all that they may be conditioned or inflected—by an Augustinian sensitivity to the "interim" quality of the present. The next section attempts such a justification, through arguments derived partly from Augustine's own work and partly from consideration of the longer tradition of historical narrative, biblical exegesis, and literary production in which it is embedded. The introduction is completed by a survey of recent scholarship on the *City of God* (by Karla Pollmann) and a synopsis of the essays to follow.

---

6. For a full explication of Augustine's complex, evolving and never fully systematic thinking on this subject, see now G. [J. P.] O'Daly, *Augustine's Philosophy of Mind* (London: Duckworth, 1987) 106–130. There is a fine concise account by T. Breyfogle, s.v. "Imagination" in *Saint Augustine through the Ages: An Encyclopedia,* ed. A. Fitzgerald (Grand Rapids, Mich.: William Eerdmans, 1999); see also, by the same author, "Memory and Imagination in Augustine's *Confessions*," in *Literary Imagination, Ancient and Modern: Essays in Honor of David Grene,* ed. T. Breyfogle (Chicago: University of Chicago Press, 1999) 139–54, esp. 146: "Augustine—to repeat—does not have a theory of the imagination, but he does appear to have a coherent threefold use of the word *imaginatio* meaning 'fantasy,' 'simple mental image,' or 'a mental image produced by an intentional act or combination of analogical reasoning.'"

7. As R. J. O'Connell writes, "It is more than doubtful that Augustine's theory of imagination could account for the magnificent achievements of his artistic imagination" (*Art and the Christian Intelligence in St. Augustine* [Oxford: Basil Blackwell, 1978] 123). O'Connell's studies of Augustine's imaginary art, including his recent *Soundings in St. Augustine's Imagination* (New York: Fordham University Press, 1994) and *Images of Conversion in St. Augustine's "Confessions"* (New York: Fordham University Press, 1998) are models of a kind of analysis that could usefully be extended to the *City of God*.

The City and the Book

When William Blake pronounced the Old and New Testaments to be "the Great Code of Art," he would have had in mind that they made an impressive book. From its use since Late Antiquity as a unitary container for collections of imperial laws, the spine-hinged book or *codex* (> *code* in French and English) gave its name in due course to other sets of written rules or conventions, including those of literary composition and interpretation. Northrop Frye took Blake's phrase for the title of a study of the Bible and literature, using it as a formula for the narrative integrity of *ta biblia* ("the little books") and arguing, against other forms of criticism, that "what matters is that 'the Bible' has traditionally been read as a unity, and has influenced Western imagination as a unity."[8] Blake and his fellow Romantics—in whose writings our modern, subjective notion of the "truth" of imagination is first set forth[9] —were certainly attentive to the grand design of this biblical history. As M. H. Abrams has shown, with consistent reference to Augustinian paradigms,

> a conspicuous Romantic tendency, after the rationalism and decorum of the Enlightenment was a reversion to the stark drama and suprarational mysteries of the Christian story and doctrines and to the violent conflicts and abrupt reversals of the Christian inner life, turning on the extremes of destruction and creation, hell and heaven, exile and reunion, death and rebirth, dejection and joy, paradise lost and paradise regained. . . . But since they lived, inescapably, after the Enlightenment, Romantic writers revived these ancient matters with a difference: they undertook to save the overview of human history and destiny, the experiential paradigms, and the cardinal values of their religious heritage, by reconstituting them in a way that would make them intellectually acceptable, as well as emotionally pertinent, for the time being.[10]

---

8. N. Frye, *The Great Code: The Bible and Literature* (New York: Harcourt Brace Jovanovich, 1982) xiii; cf. 137, on Revelation: "the Bible deliberately blocks off the sense of the referential from itself: it is not a book pointing to a historical presence, but a book that identifies itself with that presence. At the end the reader, also, is invited to identify himself with the book." Blake's aphorism appears on his engraving of the Laocoön.

9. E.g., John Keats, Letter to Benjamin Bailey (November 22, 1817): "I am certain of nothing but of the holiness of the Heart's affections and the truth of Imagination . . . . The Imagination may be compared to Adam's dream [of the creation of Eve in Milton's *Paradise Lost* 8,452–90]—he awoke and found it truth."

10. M. H. Abrams, *Natural Supernaturalism: Tradition and Revolution in Romantic Literature* (New York: W. W. Norton, 1971) 66; and cf. S. Goldsmith, *Unbuilding Jerusalem: Apocalypse and Romantic Representation* (Ithaca, N.Y.: Cornell University Press, 1993). For a different approach

To take one example: in Wordsworth's *Prelude,* a work profoundly influenced by Augustine's *Confessions,* "the imagination plays a role equivalent to that of the Redeemer in Milton's providential plot"—a plot that could not itself have been imagined without the prior disclosures of the *City of God.*[11] It is not only in works of poetry that the post-Enlightenment imagination can be seen reinterpreting the biblical code. In a study complementary to Abrams's and similarly sure in its citation of Augustine, Frank Kermode makes a strong case for reading much of modern fiction as the work of "sceptical clerks." His *Sense of an Ending* revolves the end-book of Scripture, to reveal the literary structures of a post-Aristotelian, bibliological unity of beginning, middle, and end:

> Revelation, which epitomizes the Bible, puts our fate into a book, and calls it the book of life, which is the holy city. Revelation answers the command, "write the things which thou hast seen, and the things which shall be hereafter" [Rev 1,19] . . . and the command to make these things interdependent. Our novels do likewise. Biology and cultural adaptation require it; the End is a fact of life and a fact of the imagination, working out from the middle, the human crisis. As the theologians say, we "live from the End," even if the world should be endless.[12]

Joseph Brodsky acknowledges the same biological and cultural facts, in a "Homage to Marcus Aurelius" that is incidentally also a homage to Aurelius Augustinus:

> What the past and future have in common [he writes] is our imagination, which conjures them. And our imagination is rooted in our eschatological dread: the dread of thinking that we are without precedence or consequence.[13]

---

to the relations between "modern" kinds of fiction, historiography, and biblical hermeneutics in the Romantic period, see now S. Prickett, *Origins of Narrative: The Romantic Appropriation of the Bible* (Cambridge: Cambridge University Press, 1996).

11. Ibid., 119; C. A. Patrides, *Milton and the Christian Tradition* (Oxford: Clarendon Press, 1966), ch. 8: "The Christian View of History," expanded in his *The Grand Design of God: The Literary Form of the Christian View of History* (London: Routledge & Kegan Paul, 1972). For the apocalyptic strain in English literature to Milton and beyond, see the classic studies of E. L. Tuveson, *Millennium and Utopia: A Study in the Background of the Idea of Progress* (Berkeley & Los Angeles: University of California Press, 1949) and M. Fixler, *Milton and the Kingdoms of God* (Chicago: Northwestern University Press, 1964).

12. F. Kermode, *The Sense of an Ending: Studies in the Theory of Fiction* (New York: Oxford University Press, 1967) 58. On Frye and Kermode as narrative theorists, with particular reference to Kermode's theory of the transformations of Apocalypse, see P. Ricoeur, *Temps et récit*, 3 vols. (Paris: Le Seuil, 1983–86) 3.17–48. Kermode's work has recently borne late fruit in *Classical Closure: Reading the End in Greek and Latin Literature,* ed. D. H. Roberts, F. M. Dunn and D. Fowler (Princeton: Princeton University Press, 1997).

Deeply read in the canons of Western literature, these critics also share Blake's alertness to the hermeneutical pressure of the Bible as a singular book. Indeed, Frye and Kermode were once cited, though not named, by Edward W. Said as representatives of a new class of "religious critics," "cleric[s] in the worst sense of the word," readers whose sense of religiously sanctioned "systems of authority [and] canons of order" blinded them to the social and political conditions and consequences of cultural production.[14] Against their school, Said advocated a responsibly "worldly" or "secular criticism." It is not a very helpful distinction. For if studies like those cited above suggest one thing, it is that the workings of the Western imagination over the last two millennia cannot be understood *without* reference to the literary canon(s) of the Christian religion. And if they hint at another, it is that the unity of the biblical plot—that powerful determinant of the ways in which succeeding generations of men and women have found (or sought) their salvation in and from the present moment— is an artifact of the late antique world of Augustine's *Confessions* and *City of God.* To explore the relations between book and narrative, Bible and history, in the life and works of Augustine of Hippo is to begin deciphering the great code of the Western imagination.

In order to make sense of Augustine's life, his first biographer borrowed the tripartite scheme of the narrative section of the *City of God* (Books 11–22), promising to relate his subject's "origin, career, and appointed end."[15] Augustine had his own devices. After the *Confessions,* his self-narration is mainly contained in a work of his last days, the *Retractationes,* a chronological record of his "progress in writing" (cf. *Retr.* 1, prol. 3) which remained (how else?) unfinished at his death. Yet he did not willingly leave his works unperfected.[16] However fallible they might be on points of doctrine, their form should so far as possible answer the plan he had announced for them. It is at this period (ca. 427) that he completed the *De doctrina christiana,* a work as programmatic as any he ever devised and with a unity dictated by the task that he had conceived—since the mid–390s—as the primary occupation of the Christian

---

13. J. Brodsky, *On Grief and Reason* (New York: Farrar, Strauss and Giroux, 1995) 269. Brodsky's sense of the *City of God*, like his view of history (see "Profile of Clio" in the same collection), owes much to W. H. Auden.

14. E. W. Said, *The World, the Text, and the Critic* (Cambridge, Mass.: Harvard University Press, 1983) 290–92; cf. 1–30: "Secular Criticism."

15. Possidius, *Vita Augustini*, praef.

16. M. Vessey, "*Opus Imperfectum*: Augustine and His Readers, 426–435 A.D.," *Vigiliae Christianae* 52 (1998) 264–85.

teacher: to expound the sense of the Bible, from Genesis to Revelation. The *City of God* also grew to its unity and final length around this date. Its main divisions, though not their dimensions, had been given at the outset of the work (1,35). An apology *contra paganos* would refute the arguments of traditionally minded religious Romans, to be followed by a three-stage narrative of those temporally intermingled but eschatologically separate "cities" or societies of human and angelic beings, respectively of God and the devil. Already from this prospectus it would have been clear that the narrative and constructive part of the projected work would supply the sense and unity of the whole, just as the glorious *civitas dei* would give that whole a name. To adapt Kermode's description of Revelation: Augustine would put the fates of all human beings into a book, and call it the *City of God*.

As he launches at length on his history of the two cities, Augustine makes a profession of authority that is also a disclaimer of authorship:

> Civitatem dei dicimus, cuius ea scriptura testis est, quae non fortuitis motibus animorum, sed plane summae dispositione providentiae super omnes omnium gentium litteras omnia sibi genera ingeniorum humanorum divina excellens auctoritate subiecit. (*Civ.* 11,1)

> What we call the City of God is vouched for by that Scripture which, not by the chance impulses of mortal minds but manifestly by the guiding power of supreme providence, stands above the literature of all peoples and, excelling in divine authority, has subordinated to itself every kind of human ingenuity.[17]

The difference of the two cities is conveyed by grammatical number. The City of God is the realm of unity: one city, chartered by a single and unitary text (*scriptura*) which by the providence of the One God compels the whole human race to recognize its unique authority. Contrastingly, the unnamed other city—which is really no city at all since it consists of many different societies, united only by the misdirection of their loves—is a realm of plurality and dispersion, subject to the random motions of different peoples, issuing in every kind of literature (*litterae*). Located at the structural center of a bipartite work, this is truly a cardinal statement. Having spent ten books in a laborious critique and overwriting of the cultural encyclopaedia of the Greeks and Romans, Augustine now means to gather his own proliferating discourse, so far as he can (that is, so far as God grants), into the supreme unity of Scripture. His announcement

---

17. Translation of the *City of God* by the editors, adapted in places from the version by H. Bettenson (Harmondsworth: Pelican Books, 1972).

at this point needs to be read against the corresponding one at the beginning of Book 1. Before turning there, however, it may be useful to take a step back, in order to see the *City* as a whole.

To a greater extent than is generally recognized, the groundwork for the constructive project of the *City of God* is laid in the *Confessions,* especially in Books 10 and 11. In this respect, as in others, the *Confessions* is the necessary supplement to its author's first essay on the Bible and literature, the incomplete *De doctrina christiana* of ca. 397.[18] In Book 2 of the *Christian Teaching* Augustine is led by his treatment of biblical signs to consider the disciplinary knowledge of things (*res*) afforded by contemporary "pagan" culture. The discussion (2,19,29–42,63) is designed to contribute directly to his larger rhetorical and hermeneutic enterprise of finding (*invenire*) and producing (*proferre*) the one Thing fit for human enjoyment, which is the Trinity. The same undertaking is triply exemplified in the *Confessions*: as autobiographical narrative in Books 1 to 9, as biblical exegesis or *enarratio* in Books 12 and 13, and as something else—call it "theory"—in Books 10 and 11. In a recent analysis of this work, Brian Stock construes the relation of its parts as a set of transactions between three kinds of memory: the natural memory of an individual human mind, the artificial memory of a life humanly "transcribed in writing," and the artificial but divinely programmed memory of Scripture.[19] To complete Stock's analysis and extend it to works such as the *Christian Teaching* and *City of God,* we must add one further source of accumulated knowledge, namely the collective memory encoded in the texts and practices of a given culture. It is this collective memory, in its late Graeco-Roman form, which Augustine inventories in Book 2 of the *Christian Teaching* and to which he returns, with polemical intent, in the first part of the *City of God.* Meanwhile, in the first nine books of the *Confessions,* he tells a story of his own critique of that culture and simultaneous initiation into the providential memory of the Bible.

Books 10 and 11 of the *Confessions* focus the author's concern with discovery and discursive production more narrowly.[20] How can God be (made)

---

18. See now K. Pollmann, *Doctrina Christiana: Untersuchungen zu den Anfängen der christlichen Hermeneutik unter besonderer Berücksichtigung von Augustinus, "De doctrina christiana"* (Freiburg: Universitätsverlag, 1996), with the discussion in *Augustinian Studies* 29 (1998): 99–137.

19. B. Stock, *Augustine the Reader: Meditation, Self-Knowledge, and the Ethics of Interpretation* (Cambridge, Mass.: Harvard University Press, 1996), ch. 8.

20. Translation of the *Confessions*, here and below, by M. Boulding, The Works of Saint Augustine: A Translation for the 21st Century, I/1 (Hyde Park, N.Y.: New City Press, 1997), occasionally modified.

known? Not content to answer "in and by Christ" (though cf. *Conf.* 10,32–33; 11,2,4), Augustine ransacks the treasure-house of his memory and prepares to do the same with Scripture. His first model of knowledge is a narrative one. Ideally, mental images derived from sense perception come to mind in the order in which they are wanted, "the earlier members giving way to those that follow and returning to their storage places, ready to be retrieved next time I need them. All of which happens when I narrate anything from memory" (10,8,12). Images of things already past or yet to come, whether derived from personal experience or from credible authorities, make those things available "as if they were present," *quasi praesentia* (10,8,14). There are other kinds of knowledge—Augustine lists the liberal arts—that are not derived from sense perception, but instead "collected" from scattered sites within the memory (10,9,16: *cogitando quasi colligere*). Along with *narrative*, this *collective* principle structures the Augustinian order of discourse. Both are principles of presence and unity, means of holding together things that are otherwise (and naturally) transitory, multiple, and diffuse. The ultimate model of presence and unity is God, who is beyond narration or collection. Awed by the spreading fields of his own memory, by all the things that it contains and that endlessly distract him (10,17,26: *per haec omnia discurro et volito hac illac . . . et finis nusquam*), Augustine prays for the gift of continence, "for by continence we are collected and brought back into the one from which we have slid away into the many" (10,29,40: *per continentiam quippe colligimur et redigimur in unum, a quo in multa defluximus*). A parallel movement of prayerful self-collection occurs at the beginning of Book 11. There Augustine renounces further biographical narrative, on the grounds that time will run out before he can relate all God's mercies in their order (*ex ordine*), and asks instead to be granted space (*spatium* [sc. *temporis*]) in which to "confess to you whatever I have found in your books . . . from the beginning when you made heaven and earth to that everlasting reign when we shall be with you in your holy city" (11,2,3). Given time, Augustine's confession will be of the City of God.

"Space of time" is an ordinary Latin idiom. Augustine will argue, however, that there is strictly speaking no such thing: the spatiality or extension we attribute to time itself is properly to be considered a tension of the human mind.[21] This mental tension he represents in dynamic terms as a kind of stress;

---

21. There is an extensive modern bibliography on the treatment of time in Book 11. See now R. J. Teske, *Paradoxes of Time in Saint Augustine* (Milwaukee: Marquette University Press, 1996), esp. 28–45, with refs. to earlier studies. Ricoeur (above, n. 12) 1.19–53 is fundamental for any discussion of Augustine's theory of time in relation to his practice of narrative, although Ricoeur

at worst it is an experience of dissolution (*distentio*), at best a purposeful summoning of (an image of) the future into the present (*intentio*).[22] The argument of Book 11, which is almost wholly devoted to the subject of time and its measurement, is quite clear on these points and, for all its aporias, evidently meant to be compelling. But there is more than argument in this book; as throughout the *Confessions,* there is also the poetry of the Psalms. Before pressing on to annul the space of time by a process of dialectic, Augustine stops the clock and lets his text expand for a moment into a vision of peace:

Yours is the day, yours the night,

a sign from you sends minutes speeding by;

spare in their fleeting course a space for us

to ponder the hidden wonders of your law:

shut it not against us as we knock.

Not in vain have you willed so many pages to be written,

pages deep in shadow, obscure in their secrets;

not in vain do harts and hinds seek shelter in those woods,

to hide and venture forth,

roam and browse, lie down and ruminate.

Perfect me too, Lord, and reveal those woods [or pages] to me. (11,2,3)

Scripture is a vast landscape with many hidden recesses, like the human memory. But whereas Augustine's own memory has come to seem a dreadful place to him, the *loci amoeni* of this divinely written text appear as places of Sabbath rest.

---

himself scarcely considers the latter. See also E. Vance, *Mervelous Signals: Poetics and Sign Theory in the Middle Ages* (Lincoln: University of Nebraska Press, 1986), ch. 2: "Saint Augustine: Language as Temporality."

22. Conf. 11,27,36: *praesens intentio futurum in praeteritum traicit*; 29,39: *extentus, non secundum distentionem, sed secundum intentionem sequor ad palmam supernae vocationis, ubi audiam vocem laudis et contempler delectationem tuam nec venientem nec praetereuntem.* See G. J. P. O'Daly, "Time as *Distentio* and St. Augustine's Exegesis of Philippians 3,12–14," *Revue des Études Augustiniennes* 23 (1977): 265–71.

Amid all the incipient or potential analogies of written and oral text, life, and memory in the *Confessions,* the discursive performance which finally captures attention in Book 11 is the recital of a song or psalm:

> Suppose I have to recite a psalm I know by heart. Before I begin, my expectation is directed to the whole psalm (*in totum*), but once I have begun, whatever I have plucked away from the domain of expectation and tossed behind me to the past becomes the business of my memory, and the vital energy of what I am doing is in tension between the two of them (*distenditur vita huius actionis meae*): it strains toward my memory because of the part I have already recited, and to my expectation on account of the part I have still to speak. But my attention is present all the while, for the future is being channeled through it to become the past. As the psalm goes on and on, expectation is curtailed and memory prolonged, until expectation is entirely used up, when the whole completed action has passed into memory. (11,28,38).

The strain (*distentio*) affecting the "life of this action" Augustine takes to be paradigmatic:

> What is true of the psalm as a whole is true equally of its individual parts and syllables. The same is true of the whole long performance, in which this psalm may be a single item. The same thing happens in the entirety of a person's life, of which all his or her actions are parts; and the same in the entire sweep of human history (*in toto saeculo filiorum hominum*), the parts of which are individual human lives. (Ibid.)

Not even a psalm can be held together in the mind as it is progressively found, produced, and returned to the memory. How much more scattering must be the experience of a human life! "My life," Augustine confesses again, "is distraction (*distentio*) . . . . I have flown apart into times whose order I do not know" (11,29,39). God alone can gather him, who alone can encompass the whole history of humanity. Musing on the divine knowledge of all that has been and will be, Augustine rejects the notion that it could be like his own knowledge of a poem (11,30,40). God suffers no distraction, no pull between past and future, memory and expectation. That feeling is particular, and general, to the action of human life in time.

Looking forward to the day when he will escape this "secular" predicament, Augustine envisages an end to the social divisiveness that already appears to him (ca. 400) a basic feature of fallen humanity:

> Then I will stand still and find firm footing in you (*stabor atque solidabor in te*), in your truth which shapes me, and no longer have to put up with the

questions of people who, sickly under sin's punishment, crave more than they are able to take in (*plus sitiunt quam capiunt*). (11,30,40)

Again, the future peace and stability of a mind united with God are set against a present restless incapacity. The restlessness and incapacity, we infer, are as much Augustine's as his interlocutors'. No one raises more questions in the *Confessions* than its author, and rarely can there have been a philosopher who more frequently admitted his inability to grasp what he nonetheless somehow knew to be true.

A little over a decade later, the same disabused and disabusing hope of future rest finds more ambitious expression in the opening sentence of the *City of God*:

Gloriosissimam civitatem dei

The most glorious City of God,

      sive in hoc temporum cursu

     whether in this course of time

         cum inter impios peregrinatur ex fide vivens,

         while it lives by faith as a pilgrim among the impious,

      sive in illa stabilitate sedis aeternae,

     or in that stability of its eternal seat

         quam nunc expectat per patientiam,

         which now it expects with patience

            quoadusque iustitia convertatur in iudicium,

            until justice turns into judgment [Ps 93,15],

         deinceps adeptura per excellentiam victoria ultima et

          pace perfecta,

         and which then it will receive for its excellence, when

           the final victory is won and peace perfected,

hoc opere instituto et mea ad te promissione debito defendere adversus eos,

in this work, as planned and owed by my promise to you, to defend against those

      qui conditori eius deos suos praeferunt,

     who prefer their gods to its founder,

   fili carissime Marcelline,

   my dearest son Marcellinus,

suscepi,

I have undertaken;

> magnum opus et arduum,

> *a great and arduous task—*

sed deus adiutor noster est. (1, praef.)

but God is our helper.

In a revelatory misreading of this sentence, one of the century's greatest Augustinian scholars complained that it only mentioned the subject of the later books, and cited it as an example of the author's artlessness in the design of his works. Correcting himself a few years later, he took the opportunity to point out the subtlety and richness of Augustine's exordium, its "solemn and mysterious grandeur."[23] In fact, the logic of the sentence is consistent with that of the opening statement of Book 11 (discussed above) and with the conception of the work as a whole. The writer's purpose, following the psalmist, is to hymn the One City. Thus there is no mention yet of the "other" city that exists only as a shadow, though its members are already numbered among the "impious" who "prefer their own gods." Likewise, the apologetic project of the earlier books, while fully integrated in the syntax of the sentence (*civitatem dei . . . defendere . . . suscepi*), is rhetorically subordinate to the constructive project of the later ones, which stands at the front of the announcement.

There is more to Augustine's book-opening art than this. If we consider his prose psalmody as he considers the performance of a psalm in the *Confessions,* we shall see how carefully this book of the *City of God* is set to mimic the experience of life in the course of time (*in hoc temporum cursu*). Even by the standards of Augustine's own Ciceronianism, this is an unusually as well as magnificently suspenseful sentence. And that of course is its point or, to speak more appropriately, its "intention." While grammatical, rhetorical, and rhythmic *cursus* pull the reader in different directions, he or she holds fast in expectation to the direct object of the sentence, mentioned at its outset, "the most glorious City of God." The result is at once a readerly *distentio* comparable to that described in the memorial delivery of a psalm and a mental *intentio* or present apprehension of future bliss. The whole of Augustine's "theory" is subsumed in this movement. Like God himself, with whom it is ultimately identical,

---

23. H.-I. Marrou, *Saint Augustin et la fin de la culture antique* (Paris: E. de Boccard, 1938) 66–67, with his *Retractatio* (1949) 668–70.

the City of God is to be found, for the time being, in the individual's natural memory and in the artificial memory of Scripture. Now it is discursively produced in the very first words of a literary work, even as it remains essentially supradiscursive, an object of hope and patient expectation, beyond the present attention and capacity of the mind. This duality of the One City as discursive sign and supradiscursive thing, present image and future reality, is aptly rendered in Augustine's syntax, which comes to rest spiritually in one place and literally in another. For the Christian caught in the action of the present life, the only true resting place lies ahead, *in illa stabilitate sedis aeternae.* Meanwhile, for the reader caught in the action of the present sentence, there is a breathing space just beyond the periodic *suscepi,* in the *magnum opus* itself, named but never to be mistaken for the City of God. Adapting Augustine's analysis in Books 10 and 11 of the *Confessions,* we may say that the City of God, as an object of discourse and imagination, is progressively transferred in the course of this sentence—as it will be, on a larger scale, in the course of the ensuing books—from the artificial memory of Scripture, via the natural memory of Augustine (assisted by whatever notes, handbooks, or other aids he may have used), into the literary memory of the *De civitate dei,* there to be stored in a form that will make it readily collectable by future readers.

At length, this most "arduous" work was completed. Declining to discuss every one of the seven ages of the world in detail (cf. *Conf.* 11,2,2), Augustine fixes his own and the reader's attention on the Great Sabbath: "There we shall be still and see; we shall see and we shall love; we shall love and we shall praise. Behold what will be, in the end, without end! For what is our end but to reach that kingdom which has no end?" (*Civ.* 22,30) The work ends in the same "intention" as it had begun, only now with the City of God proleptically an object of sight. We are at the limit of Augustine's timebound or secular imagination. There was no more to be written or said:

> And now, as I think, I have discharged my debt, with the completion, by God's help, of this huge work. It may be too much for some, too little for others. Of both these groups I ask forgiveness. But of those for whom it is enough I make this request: that they do not thank me, but join with me in rendering thanks to God. Amen. Amen.

Augustine's "too much" and "too little" are his own, especially his "too much." In the *Retractations,* he wrote, "This great work on the *City of God* has finally been finished in twenty-two books" (2,43). In a letter composed around the same time, he made suggestions for binding up the books (which he calls *quaterniones,* quires or booklets) in two or more codices, recognizing that they were too bulky to fit in one: *quaterniones sunt XXII quos in unum corpus redigere multum est.*[24] It is worth observing the convergence of this language of book contents and containers with that of human "continence" in Book 10 of the *Confessions,* cited earlier: *per continentiam . . . colligimur et redigimur in unum, a quo in multa defluximus* (10,29,40).[25] For all its fixity of intention, Augustine's literary *opus* remains as discursive as his "self." And that at least was fitting. The imagination might reach beyond the *saeculum* at times, but only the Great Redactor could make One Book of the many little books of human history. [M.V.]

The *City of God* in Current Research (1991–1999)

Twentieth-century scholarship has devoted considerable attention to the *City of God*, focusing chiefly on its author's political ideas, his use of sources (especially historical and philosophical), the theological implications of the work, and to a lesser degree its influence in later periods. For research up to 1990 the relevant literature can be conveniently located through the **bibliographical guide** by D. Donnelly and E. Scherman,[26] G. J. P. O'Daly's article for the *Augustinus-Lexikon,*[27] and the extensive annual "Bulletin Augustinien" of the periodical *Revue des Études Augustiniennes* (Paris). The following paragraphs seek to provide a concise overview of the main trends in research during the past decade, particularly in relation to the themes of the present collection.

Augustine's conception of human **history** as a place of homelessness and suspense has been analyzed by M. A. Claussen in a study of the motif of *peregrinatio.*[28] In his monograph on the conception and sources of the *City of God* J. van Oort emphasizes the role of archaic Jewish-Christian writings like the *Shepherd of Hermas*, the *Didache,* and the *Pseudo-Clementines* in preparing the way for Augustine's description of history in terms of the *cursus* of two antithetical societies.[28a] A complementary study by C. Müller shows how

---

24. *Ep. ad Firmum (CCSL* 47).

25. See also Stock (n. 12 above), 223–26: "Of Containers and Continence."

26. D. Donnelly and E. Scherman, *Augustine's City of God: An Annotated Bibliography of Modern Criticism* 1960–1990 (New York: Peter Lang, 1991).

27. G. J. P. O'Daly, "Ciuitate dei (De-)," *Augustinus-Lexikon* 1 (Basel: Schwabe & Co., 1994) 969–1010.

28. M. A. Claussen, "*Peregrinatio* and *Peregrini* in Augustine's *City of God* and the Image and Idea of Pilgrimage as a Metaphor for the Christian Life in the Writing of the Early Church Fathers," *Traditio* 46 (1991): 33–75.

far (in the *City of God* and his other writings) Augustine was exploiting a widely held and ancient set of symbols embedded in pagan, Jewish, and Christian traditions of viewing the divine purpose in human history.[29] This complex of ideas and narratives has recently been set in its late antique historiographical and ideological context by H. Inglebert.[30] There is a fresh treatment of Augustine's **philosophy of history** by R. Bittner.[31]

P. J. Burnell brings out Augustine's ambivalent attitude toward **politics**, considered as a necessary evil that cannot create anything morally good but is sometimes helpful in maintaining peace on earth.[32] J. M. Rist dedicates a section of his book on Augustine to "Individuals, Social Institutions and Political Life."[33] As he sees it, Augustine's view of society concedes no positive educational power to the state, and is thus in sharp contrast to the "classical" conception. Augustine considers human beings less as political than as social creatures by nature, characterized by a natural desire to establish a loving relationship with each other and with God. An ideal human society would thus be utterly spiritual, with no secular or political space left; but that condition is not achievable in the present life, in which complete separation from the earthly city is impossible. Consequently, whereas in our private life we may at least approach the City of God, public life often requires us to commit evil deeds for the sake of a higher good and is therefore incompatible with that ideal.[34]

28a. J. van Oort, *Jerusalem and Babylon: A Study into Augustine's "City of God" and the Sources of His Doctrine of the Two Cities* (Leiden: E. J. Brill, 1991).

29. C. Müller, *Geschichtsbewusstsein bei Augustinus: Ontologische, anthropologische und universalgeschichtlich-heilsgeschichtliche Elemente einer augustinischen "Geschichtstheorie"* (Würzburg: Augustinus Verlag, 1993).

30. H. Inglebert, *Les Romains chrétiens face à l'histoire de Rome: Histoire, christianisme et romanités en Occident dans l'Antiquité tardive (IIIe-Ve siècles)* (Paris: Études Augustiniennes, 1996).

31. R. Bittner, "Augustine's Philosophy of History," in *The Augustinian Tradition*, ed. G. B. Matthews (Berkeley & Los Angeles: University of California Press, 1999) 345–60.

32. P. J. Burnell, "The Status of Politics in Augustine's *City of God*," *History of Political Thought* 13 (1992): 13–29.

33. J. M. Rist, *Augustine: Ancient Thought Baptized* (Cambridge: Cambridge University Press, 1994) 203–55.

34. See also P. I. Kaufman, "Augustine, Martyrs, and Misery: An Examination of the Pastoral Effectiveness of the Political Theology of His *City of God* in Conjunction with the 5th-century Donatist and Pelagian Controversies," *Church History* 63 (1994) 1–14, and J. R. Bowlin, "Augustine on Justifying Coercion: The Christianization of the Roman Empire and the Limits of Political Authority and Pluralism in the *City of God*," *Annual of the Society of Christian Ethics* 17 (1997): 49–70.

The treatment of **grace and free will** in the *City of God* continues to engage the attention of scholars of Augustine, as for example in the recent studies by B. Studer[35] and D. R. Creswell.[36]

A number of **collections of articles** dedicated to the *City of God* have been published in recent years. A volume edited by D. Donnelly, in **English**, contains reprints of previously published work, with three new pieces.[37] Among the latter, F. van Fleteren's contribution[38] reconsiders the central tenets of Augustine's thought as represented in the *City of God* and has a philosophical-political focus, while a political-social view is adopted by J. V. Scott.[39] In a close analysis of *City of God* 15,10–14; 16,11 and 18,41–44, P. Pulsiano shows how, through the incarnation of the Word in Jesus Christ, the human word is able to take on divinity, and language comes to mediate between the human and divine. Accordingly, in *City of God* 16 to 18, the narrative of the history of humanity is structured on a theory of linguistic progress as a movement from the tower of Babel, where multiplicity of languages creates confusion and obstacles to mutual understanding, toward the events of the Pentecost, where a similar multiplicity becomes a vehicle for disseminating the message of divine salvation and bringing about understanding between communities that were previously unable to communicate.[40]

In Italy, several collective volumes on the *City of God* have now appeared, containing only previously unpublished papers. The first of these **Italian** volumes— which, however, typically contain articles in other languages as well—has a strongly philosophical and theological focus,[41] and includes a contribution by G. Madec

35. B. Studer, *The Grace of Christ and the Grace of God in Augustine of Hippo: Christocentrism or Theocentrism?* (Collegeville, Minn.: The Liturgical Press, 1997; trans. M. J. O'Connell, from the German edition of 1993) 115–24.

36. D. R. Creswell, *St Augustine's Dilemma: Grace and Eternal Law in the Major Works of Augustine of Hippo* (New York: Peter Lang, 1997) 91–114.

37. *The City of God: A Collection of Critical Essays,* ed. D. Donnelly (New York: Peter Lang, 1995).

38. F. van Fleteren, "*De Civitate Dei*: Miscellaneous Observations" (415–29).

39. J. V. Scott, "Augustine's Razor: Public versus Private Interests in the *City of God*" (151–167). See also M. Ruokanen, *Theology of Social Life in Augustine's De Civitate Dei* (Göttingen: Vandenhoeck & Ruprecht, 1993).

40. P. Pulsiano, "Language Theory and Narrative Patterning in *De Civitate Dei*, Books XV–XVII" (241–252). Also relevant is R. Dodaro, *Language and Justice: Political Anthropology in Augustine's De Civitate Dei* (Unpublished D.Phil. thesis, Oxford University, 1992).

41. *Interiorità e intenzionalità nel "De Civitate Dei" di Sant'Agostino: Atti del III° Seminario internazionale del Centro di Studi Agostiniani di Perugia,* ed. R. Piccolomini (Rome: Institutum Patristicum Augustinianum, 1991).

emphasizing the dual intention of the *City of God*, as on the one hand apologetically directed against pagan polytheism and misguided ideas of the divine, and on the other as a protreptic representation of Christian cult and culture of God as the only true fulfillment of pagan Platonism.[42] A second collection, of major importance for the lines of inquiry pursued in the present volume,[43] opens with studies of Augustine's work in relation to such figures and influences as Sallust, Virgil, Origen, Manichaeism, Pelagianism, and Tyconius. It also contains substantial sections on the later reception and influence of Augustine's work, and on the city in Christian iconography (documenting, *inter alia,* the emblem of the two cities). A third Italian collection contains nine contributions on the topics of freedom, theodicy, moral responsibility, and Abelard and the *City of God*.[44] There now also exists, in Italian, a small collection of articles on Augustine's idea of history as a pilgrimage for the members of the *civitas dei,* and on its moral consequences as expounded in the *City of God*.[45]

The best of modern **French** scholarship on the *City of God* is epitomized in the bilingual edition with notes in the series Bibliothèque Augustinienne.[46] The volume of commentary by P. Piret contains extensive paraphrase and selective discussion of theological subjects.[47]

A **German** collection has also been published, with contributions on various philosophical issues in the *City of God,* such as the question of evil, justice, and free will; the eschatological theory of the state; and natural law.[48]

42. G. Madec, "Le *De civitate Dei* comme *De vera religione*" (7–33), reprinted in Madec, *Petites études Augustiniennes* (Paris: Études Augustiniennes, 1994) 189–213. See also his *Chez Augustin* (Paris: Études Augustiniennes, 1998) 65–69.

43. *Il De Civitate Dei: L'opera, le interpretazioni, l'influsso,* ed. E. Cavalcanti (Rome: Herder, 1996).

44. *Il mistero del male e la libertà possibile (III): Lettura del "De Civitate Dei" di Agostino. Atti del VII Seminario del centro di Studi Agostiniani di Perugia,* ed. L. Alici et al. (Rome: Institutum Patristicum Augustinianum, 1996). On the history of the reception of the *City of God*, note also I. Bejczy, "Thomas More, *Utopia* and a Systematic Investigation into the Influence of Augustine, *City of God* and Other Patristic Writings on His Principles of Social Theodicy: The City of God on Earth," *Speculum* 46 (1995): 17–30.

45. *La Città di Dio nel Tempo: "Homo Viator,"* ed. M. Adriani et al. (Rome: Città Nuova, 1997).

46. I. Bochet, G. Combès and G. Madec, *La Cité de Dieu*, 3 vols. (Paris: Études Augustiniennes, 1993–1995).

47. P. Piret, *La destinée de l'homme: La Cité de Dieu. Un commentaire du De Civitate Dei de Saint Augustin* (Brussels: Éditions de l'Institut d'Études Théologiques, 1991).

48. *Augustinus: De civitate dei*, ed. C. Horn (Berlin: Akademie Verlag, 1997). Note also M. Fleischer, "Der Ursprung des Bösen und wie wir ihn 'wissen' können: Eine systematische Erörterung in engem Anschluss an Augustin, Der Gottesstaat XII 6 und 7," *Philosophisches Jahrbuch* 104 (1997) 80–88.

Philosophical syntheses of Augustine's historical and political thought have been attempted by J. Mader,[49] D. de Courcelle,[50] C. Horn,[51] J. Kreuzer,[52] and D. X. Burt.[53]

There is a new **English translation** of the *City of God* by R. Dyson.[54] Introductory **surveys** of the work are offered by G. Gould[55] and G. J. P. O'Daly.[56] Finally, there is now a printed **concordance**.[57] [K.P.]

History, Apocalypse, and the Secular Imagination: New Essays on the *City of God*

Written in the light of previous scholarship, with an eye to future synthesis, the essays in this volume may be regarded as so many attempts to catch the elusive presence of Augustine's *City of God*. Many of them are themselves part of larger works in progress, not necessarily centered on Augustine. Like all such collections, this one strains in several directions at once. At the same time, it is unified by a number of overriding concerns and shared intentions: to grasp the logic or sense of Augustine's apologetic-constructive work as a whole; to situate it within the horizon of contemporary, late antique discourses of the past, present, and to come; to delineate the complex operations which it performs (or attempts) upon the Roman cultural memory, especially as encoded in "classical" texts; to uncover its designs upon Christian collective consciousness, especially as informed by the imagery, plot, and rhetoric of the biblical

---

49. J. Mader, *Aurelius Augustinus: Philosophie und Christentum* (Vienna: Niederösterreichisches Presshaus, 1991), esp. 225–27; 261–94.

50. D. de Courcelle, *Augustin ou le Génie de l'Europe* (Paris: Éditions Jean-Claude Lattès, 1995) 205–17.

51. *Augustinus* (Munich: C. H. Beck, 1995) 111–27, on Augustine's concept of the state and his philosophy of history.

52. J. Kreuzer, *Augustinus* (New York: Campus, 1995) 120–57, on the perplexity of history.

53. D. X. Burt. *Augustine's World: An Introduction to His Speculative Philosophy* (Lanham, Md.: University Press of America, 1996) in a chapter on "Human Destiny" (167–200).

54. *Augustine: The city of God against the Pagans*, ed. R. Dyson (Cambridge: Cambridge University Press, 1998).

55. G. Gould, *St. Augustine and the Doctrine of the City of God* (Bangor: Headstart History, 1993).

56. G. J. P. O'Daly, *Augustine, City of God: A Reader's Guide* (Oxford: Clarendon Press, 1999).

57. R. H. Cooper, L. C. Ferrari et al., *Concordantia in XXII libros de civitate Dei S. Aurelii Augustini*, 6 vols. (Hildesheim: Olms-Weidmann, 1998), based on the Corpus Christianorum edition, itself derived from the Dombart-Kalb Teubner text of 1928–1929.

revelation (and Revelation); to trace its impact upon subsequent visions of human society in time, down to the present premillennial *fin de siècle.* For the sake of initial clarity, the contributions have been ranged under the three rubrics of "History," "Apocalypse," and "The Secular Imagination," and in an order that runs from the reconstructed place and time of Augustine's Hippo, through the histories and prophecies of his and other writers' texts, to a modern affirmation of the temporality of the Augustinian idea of the *saeculum.* Other trajectories could no doubt be suggested, and will, we hope, appear in the course of a reading.

History

"For Augustine," G. J. P. O'Daly observes, "the object of history is none other than the study of the mind and will of God." Historical narration or "telling" already has a special place in the cultural inventory of his incomplete *Christian Teaching* of ca. 397. There it is assimilated to demonstration or "showing," on the grounds that it represents what is past in time in a manner analogous to that by which the demonstrative arts of "natural history" (not the term he uses) or astronomy represent what is removed in space. In fact, he points out, astronomy has a narrative quality too, since it makes possible predictions of the future positions of heavenly bodies (2,28,42–29,46). Rightly conceived and executed, history, "natural history," and astrology are all discourses of what God has disposed in the universe throughout time—modes of setting forth what human beings have discovered of his eternal will. Thus they approximate the discourse of biblical interpretation, as presented in the *Christian Teaching*; or rather, in Augustine's view, they are ancillary to it. History as related by human annalists is useful only in conjunction with the "authorized" history of the Bible. Yet it does have its use, and nowhere more obviously in Augustine's own writings than in the *City of God,* where his tale of two cities refers continually to a narrative of Roman and other pasts for which the Bible itself offers only the barest hints. The essays in the first section of this volume seek to show how and why Augustine produces *his* Roman history, and to understand its interconnections with his scriptural demonstration of God's purposes for humankind.

In an opening essay on "Augustine's Roman Empire," Neil B. McLynn supplies the indispensable political and prosopographical coordinates for a reading of Augustine's own prologue to Marcellinus in Book 1. Augustine's earthly city, he argues, was first of all a product of his own experience, not least of his social contacts. Only if we have a secure sense of that social reality can we form a correct estimate of the task he faced in coopting a public for the *City of God*. Related considerations of audience and readership underlie the next four papers, all of which treat Augustine's reworking of texts and ideologies from the canon of "classical" historians available in his day.[58] In "Thinking through History: Augustine's Method in the *City of God* and Its Ciceronian Dimension," Gerard O'Daly takes as his starting-point Augustine's recourse to Cicero's *Republic* in his correspondence with the pagan Nectarius, which predates the *City of God* by several years. To the extent that Cicero's methods and assumptions as a historian of the Roman state could be taken for granted in debate with traditionally minded patriots, Augustine was able to use them to recommend his own, more radical theology of empire, itself based on a historical reading of the Bible. Dialogue over Roman history and historiography is the subject as well of Catherine Conybeare's "*Terrarum Orbi Documentum*: Augustine, Camillus, and Learning from History." By a combined analysis of the fifth books, respectively, of Livy's *History of Rome* and the *City of God,* this essay reveals something of the extraordinary richness and subtlety of Augustine's intertextual encounters with the great writers of the Roman past, and of the skillfulness of his engagement of a contemporary readership which, even without this text of Livy to hand or by heart, would quickly have found itself implicated in his version of its ideological plot. Not incidentally, Conybeare also provides a gloss on the kinds of "glory" evoked and contested by the initial superlative of the *City of God.* If that work is in some sense addressed *ad(versus) Livianos,* it is even more clearly targeted on the company of Virgilians to which its author once belonged and from which he would never entirely free himself.[59]

Philippe Bruggisser's "City of the Outcast and City of the Elect: The Romulean Asylum in Augustine's *City of God* and Servius's *Commentaries on Virgil,*" locates the contest of (late) Roman historiographies in its institutional setting, with eloquent examples from the grammatical exegesis on which the politico-historical consciousness of the late Roman elite was founded. By taking us behind the lines of a highly purposive (anti-Christian?) reinterpretation

---

58. These essays may usefully be read alongside those on Augustine's use of Roman history and of Virgil's poetry in the first section of the volume edited by E. Cavalcanti (above, n. 1). See also K. Pollmann, "Augustins Transformation der traditionellen römischen Staats- und Geschichtsauffassung (Buch I–V)," in the volume edited by C. Horn (above, n. 48).

59. See now S. MacCormack, *The Shadows of Poetry: Vergil in the Mind of Augustine* (Berkeley & Los Angeles: University of California Press, 1998), esp. ch. 5: "'The High Walls of Rome': The City on Earth and the Heavenly City."

of the myth of Romulus, this essay helps demarcate the combat zone for which Augustine designed his heavy armor. Against pagan idealization of a Roman past understood as reaching its climax in the present, he asserted the radical discontinuity of the historical present and eternal hereafter. A similar process of argument is uncovered in Paul Burns's essay on "Augustine's Use of Sallust in the *City of God,*" which almost completes the circuit of late Republican and Augustan authorities arrayed against each other in that work (Varro is a conspicuous absentee).

In a coda to the section which must stand for a much wider range of possible comparison between Augustinian and post-Augustinian approaches to Christian historiography, David Lambert studies "The Uses of Decay: History in Salvian's *De gubernatione dei.*" His essay is a vital reminder that, far from taking the Roman world by storm, the completed *City of God* could for some time be largely ignored, even in milieux directly affected by the "barbarian" challenge to triumphalist theodicy and in circles where Augustine's works were otherwise intently studied.

Apocalypse

A historical consciousness nourished by Scipio's dream and Jove's promise of *imperium sine fine* was bound to retain a taste for prophecy and revelation. To appreciate the liveliness of that appetite in Augustine's day, we have only to glance at contemporary imperial panegyric or the history of Ammianus Marcellinus, most down-to-earth of Greeks. By the time he began the *City of God,* Augustine's ideas of prophecy were firmly anchored in the Bible, regarded as a work of "sacred" or "prophetic" history. "Sacred history," writes Robert Markus, is for Augustine "simply what is in the biblical canon."

> It is history written under divine inspiration and endowed with divine authority, presenting, under this inspiration, its historical material within a perspective which transcends that of the secular historian, for it is throughout conceived as part of the pattern of God's redemptive work. All other history, even where it casts its light directly on the economy of salvation, is "secular," since only God-given insight can possess the prophetic quality required by the "sacred history."[60]

From this distinction arises the ambivalence, already remarked upon, of the narrative of the *City of God,* which is both an explication of canonical

---

60. Markus, *Saeculum* (above, n. 5) 16.

prophecy (*scriptura*) and an addition to the stock of uninspired or "secular" literature (*litterae*). Strict in his insistence on the disparity between the *auctoritas* of the Bible and that of his own writings, Augustine also came to be extremely wary of attaching "sacred" or "prophetic" meaning to any event occurring in the interval between the apostolic period (authoritatively covered by the New Testament) and the Second Coming.[61] Of a piece with this reserve is his often-cited resistance to certain kinds of "literal" or "historical" reading of the Book of Revelation. Nonetheless, as we have also seen, by the time he reached the last books of the *Confessions* he had pledged himself to expound human history from beginning to end. How, then, did he interpret the Apocalypse? And in what sense or senses—recognized by him or not—is that interpretation prophetic or apocalyptic? These are the questions addressed and variously reformulated by the first four essays in the second section below.

In "Approaching the Apocalypse: Augustine, Tyconius, and John's Revelation," Paul B. Harvey, Jr. argues, partly on the basis of two newly recovered sermons, that Augustine's ability to expound Revelation in the later books of the *City of God* depended critically on his prior assimilation of the allegorical hermeneutics of the erstwhile Donatist Tyconius. In doing so, he unsettles a number of points of Augustinian chronology. More fundamentally revisionist is Harry O. Maier's "The End of the City and the City without End," which retrojects Kermode's theory of the fictional or poetic "sense of an ending" onto the *City of God* and proposes that the work as a whole should be seen as a species of extra-canonical prophecy, inspired by the closing books of John's Apocalypse. While such a view of Augustine as seer is unconventional it does not necessarily conflict with readings such as Karla Pollmann's ("Moulding the Present: Apocalyptic as Hermeneutics in *City of God* 21–22") which, by showing how he remythologizes the Christian Apocalypse to make its prophetic meanings applicable before the *eschaton,* offers a refinement of the received opinion of his spiritualizing or anti-chiliastic exegesis. That received opinion receives another kind of refinement in Virginia's Burrus's "An Immoderate Feast," which, by a cross-analysis comparable to the one pursued by Conybeare for a non-biblical intertext, brings out (or up) what Augustine himself appears to have found most "gross" in John's Apocalypse and therefore sought hardest to conceal (or keep down), namely our too solid flesh.

Burrus also raises a more general issue, of clear relevance to several pieces in this section. What is it, her essay encourages us to ask, that we most *desire*

---

61. Ibid., chs. 2 and 3.

to see at the end of history, what do we most *fear* to see, and what kind of resolution of those conflicting impulses—assisted or not by a text like Revelation, or a revelation like the *City of God*—are we able to make in the meantime? Thomas A. Smith ("The Pleasure of Hell in *City of God* 21") provides a historical case study in responses to that challenge, from early Jewish apocalyptic texts to the late medieval Christian celebration of hell's pains in sculpture and preaching; here Augustine is seen converting the "abominable fancy" of hell into a new moral aesthetic. In a complementary study ("Adapted Discourse: Heaven in Augustine's *City of God* and in His Contemporary Preaching") J. Kevin Coyle documents the bishop's careful calculation of what his audiences, popular or learned, would be likely to find instructive, alluring, or bearable. He notes, for example, the relative absence of "bodily" matters from the homilies and a general reluctance on his part to speak of immortalized flesh.

Finally, in a contribution which balances Lambert's at the end of the first section, Kevin L. Hughes cautions against mistaking Augustine's (more or less) spiritualized apocalypticism for an early medieval orthodoxy: in this area, as in the theology of history, there were competing views ("Augustine and the Adversary: Strategies of Synthesis in Early Medieval Exegesis").

The Secular Imagination

It will be clear by now that "history," "apocalypse" (or apocalyptic), and "the secular imagination," as used in this volume, are not mutually exclusive categories. It would be truer to say that history and apocalypse are both modes of expression of the secular imagination, the latter being understood, in a general sense, as a faculty of the human mind capable of constructing narratives of all and every human life "from beginning to end" and, more particularly, as that faculty working in the conditions evoked by Augustine's biblically inspired theory of the *saeculum* as locus of human life-in-time and of its (historically prefigured) end-phase. In the latter sense, by definition, the secular imagination—including its historical and apocalyptic functions—is an essentially Augustinian or post-Augustinian phenomenon. Whether such a narrow and originary definition is sustainable may for the time being remain an open question. At the very least, the phrase can serve to focus attention on discursive practices that suggest, or may be taken to reflect, the distinctive dynamics of the *City of God* and related writings of Augustine. The third section of this volume accordingly presents a number of studies in what could otherwise be termed the "reception" of Augustinian texts and doctrines, all of them with a bearing on the issues raised in the previous sections.

The first two studies jointly open a prospect on the rich and diverse fortune of the *City of God* in the culture of early modern England. In *"Civitas* to Congregation: Augustine's Two Cities and John Bale's *Image of Both Churches,"* Gretchen E. Minton plots the presence and modification of Augustinian texts and doctrines in the work of England's first (post-)Reformation expositor of the Apocalypse. Broadly faithful to Augustine in his ecclesiology, historiography, and hermeneutics, Bale appears to have had an acute sense of the need for a Christian community to discern and act out its divinely ordained role in the drama of history; it is in the light of that expectation, Minton argues, that we must understand his willingness to fill the "hermeneutical spaces" left vacant by Augustine's historically cautious reading of Revelation. In a sequel, "The *Citie of God* (1610) and the London Virginia Company," I attempt to explain the anomaly of an English rendering of Augustine's classic of late imperial, post-colonial theory as a sign of the emergence, in early Jacobean England, of a prophetic sense of the nation's imperial-colonial destiny.

A second pair of papers takes as its focus the linked Augustinianisms of two prophets of modernity, Martin Heidegger and Hannah Arendt. Peter J. Burnell would clear Augustine of criticisms that mistake the quality of his reasoning and imagination of the state of restored humanity ("Is the Augustinian Heaven Inhuman?"), while Joanna Vecchiarelli Scott measures the impact on Arendt's evolving view of the human condition of her lifelong meditation of the *City of God* and other works by that author ("Hannah Arendt's Secular Augustinianism"). The "secular" in Scott's title denotes a discourse that is avowedly of "this" world, even when—as in Arendt's adaptation of Augustine's ideal of *caritas*—it occasionally comes trailing clouds of transcendence. At this point, it is fitting to recall Robert Markus's argument (in *Saeculum*) for Augustine's own "secularization" of politics and, to an important degree, also of the church. That thesis has not gone uncontested, and in the last essay in this collection Michael J. Hollerich presents one of the most powerful and influential critiques of it ("John Milbank, Augustine, and the 'Secular'"). The alternative view outlined there renders Augustine's "secular" vision more ecclesiastical, without making it any less a work of human imagination in its traverse of divinely ordered history. [M.V.]

I. HISTORY

AUGUSTINE'S ROMAN EMPIRE

Neil B. McLynn

The View from Hippo Regius

What was the Roman Empire to Augustine, or he to the Empire? Augustine's own answer in the *City of God*, the proclamation of a different citizenship entirely, has given a high philosophical tone to these questions. In this essay I propose to restate them at a more humdrum level, by examining Augustine's political horizons, as bishop of Hippo, and considering how these might have affected his dealings with, and presentation of, the representatives of imperial authority. My eventual aim is to propose a direct connection between the course of these dealings and the genesis of the *City of God*. But to measure the empire of Augustine's imagination against the viewpoint afforded by his provincial city, we can usefully begin with another, much more mundane, representation of the empire from Hippo. About thirty years before Augustine became bishop, the city council had erected a statue to the emperor Valens. And for all its formulaic grandiloquence, the accompanying inscription

> CONQUEROR BY LAND AND SEA; RESTORER OF PUBLIC LIBERTY; TO OUR LORD FLAVIUS VALENS, CONQUEROR AND TRIUMPHANT, FOR-EVER AUGUSTUS[1]

---

1. E. Marec, "Le Forum d'Hippone," *Libyca* (Arch/Ep) 2 (1954) v: 382–83: *Terra marique victori ac publicae libertatis restitutori d.n. Fl. Valenti, victori ac triumfatori semper Augusto.* The subsequent rubric denotes curial responsibility and civic funding.

is essentially a response to a specific event. The councilors were monumental-izing a news bulletin, teaching their readers, as Augustine did his in the *City of God*, how to interpret events on the other side of the Mediterranean.

The inscription allows us to glimpse the physical setting within which Augustine formulated his own vision. For example, Valens is the only Christian emperor known to have been commemorated at Hippo. But the triumphalism of the inscription proved premature when the emperor perished ignominiously at Adrianople (378). This must have made the monument a dubious advertise-ment of the efficacy of the Christian God, and a correspondingly useful exhibit for argumentative skeptics. The forum of Hippo was only a few hundred yards from the church: so when in the *City of God* Augustine argues the impossibil-ity of judging the felicity of emperors by their success in "taming the foes of the republic, or in . . . crushing citizens who rise up as enemies against them" (5,24), and when Orosius vehemently refuses to allow pagans any legitimate consolation in the fate of Valens the "heretic" and "persecutor" (*Historia ad-versus paganos* 7,33,16–18), we might perhaps hear echoed their characteristically different responses to the mute reproach of the statue, or even to debates held in its shadow. It is also significant that the statue, the last impe-rial monument attested at Hippo, was nearly fifty years old when Rome was sacked. The strong likelihood that the "murmurers of 410" were unable to point to any incriminating inscriptions proclaiming the invincibility of the Christian princeling Honorius (only one such statue base has been found in the whole of north Africa)[2] helps bring home a transformation in commemorative fashions which is directly relevant to Augustine's project. Bishops' prayers had become more important than stone and bronze in implanting the emperor's image in the minds of provincial citizens. Although Roman history, from Claudius to Valens, was still very much present in the forum of Hippo, it had also—in a sense—reached an end: the empire could be seen to be ripe for reconceptualization.[3]

But the principal interest of the Valens inscription, for students of the *City of God*, is the eccentricity of its message. Valens ruled the East, not the West; his brother Valentinian, the western emperor with direct authority over Africa, was notoriously jealous of his own prerogatives and fame; and what is more, no combined land and naval victory that restored "public liberty" is recorded

---

2. *Corpus Inscriptionum Latinarum* VIII.12275.

3. See E. Marec, *Hippone le Royale: Antique Hippo Regius* (Algiers: Direction de l'intérieur et des beaux-arts, 1950) 70–79, for the gallery of statues discovered in the Forum.

in our sources for Valens's reign. The suppression of the usurper Procopius in 366, the only possible candidate for the victory, was actually achieved by attrition, contrived defections, and betrayal.[4] On the other hand, in choosing their theme and their phraseology (which does not recur elsewhere) the councilors were not merely parroting misunderstood propaganda. The decision to fund the monument in effect denotes an investment in Valens, an emperor much underrated in the hindsight of the historiographical tradition but whose energy and efficiency in eliminating Procopius might indeed have seemed to well-informed observers to promise a lasting ascendancy over his so far lackluster brother.[5] And if such prospects were at best speculative, the councilors were not the only investors. Hymetius, proconsul of Africa, also celebrated the victory, erecting a statue at Carthage.[6] A connection can be surmised. Hymetius's gesture will have been reported to the emperors, and perhaps cost him dear;[7] the councilors, playing for lesser stakes, would meanwhile have looked for recognition from the proconsul.

The Hippo inscription thus offers a tantalizing glimpse of the complex dynamics of political power in Roman North Africa. The central part of this essay will sketch a similar background for Augustine's much more extensive commentary on contemporary politics, by considering the extent to which representatives of imperial authority will have noticed him, and the extent to which he sought their notice. Like the councilors, moreover, Augustine was presenting a picture of the empire that was ultimately his own, derived from information that was necessarily provisional and incomplete. Although we will never know exactly why the council decided to commemorate Valens, or why they presented him as they did, we can assume that the experience and connections of individual councilors, direct or indirect, at Carthage or at court, will have weighed heavily. In Augustine's case, on the other hand, we can suggest some direct connections between certain idiosyncrasies in his presentation of the

---

4. The identification was proposed by Marec, "Le Forum," 383. The usurpation of Procopius and its suppression is fully described by J. Matthews, *The Roman Empire of Ammianus* (London: Duckworth, 1989) 191–201.

5. J. F. Drinkwater argues in a forthcoming paper that Ammianus Marcellinus has seriously distorted our perceptions of the late 360s by exaggerating Valentinian's exploits in Germany.

6. *Inscriptiones Latinae Selectae,* ed. H. Dessau, 3 vols. (Berlin: Weidmann, 1892–1916), no. 768.

7. Hymetius's subsequent travails—a fine from Valentinian, then exile to an island after he had tried to mollify the emperor by magic—are described by Ammianus Marcellinus, *Res gestae* 28,2,17–23.

political scene and his own recorded experience. The following paragraphs will provide an introductory outline.

One experience in particular will have distinguished Augustine from his fellow citizens of Hippo: he had not merely seen an emperor's statue, but had actually met an emperor in the flesh. He had not seen imperial prowess at its most imposing. Valens's nephew Valentinian II was just thirteen when Augustine arrived in Milan, an awkward age made more awkward for Valentinian by the frailty of his regime. And Augustine's famously glum account of how he was required to tell transparent lies about the emperor's achievements (*Conf.* 6,6,9) invites us to look for traces of this experience in his vision of contemporary politics. An indication might duly be detected in his brief survey of recent history in the *City of God*. Gratian shows his outstanding merit in preferring Theodosius to his more malleable "little brother" (*Civ.* 5,26: *parvulum fratrem*); Valentinian is again a "little brother" when he is ejected by Maximus and taken in by Theodosius, who could so easily have eliminated him; he is still a "boy" (*puerum*) when Theodosius shows even more outstanding generosity and restores him to his throne. No other account makes Valentinian (who died aged twenty) so consistently so small.[8] We might therefore suspect that Augustine continued to see the boy he remembered from his encounter in Milan. This would allow the further suggestion that by downgrading Valentinian, Augustine might have been led to overestimate Theodosius, whom of course he never met; which will have helped sustain the belief, which continued to distort his judgment for over a decade, in the exceptional qualities of the Theodosian dynasty.[9]

But the Roman emperors are not central to the structure or argument of the *City of God*. The work begins instead in the city of Rome, and attacks the *superbi*, the proud men, who complained against the Christian God. Augustine was again unusual among citizens of Hippo in that he had lived in Rome. And although he says nothing about his experiences in the ancient capital in the *City of God*, a famous description in the *Confessions* of an encounter there with another embodiment of the empire is fundamental for an understanding of his complex attitude to the proud men of Rome. The account of how the

---

8. In Rufinus's account of the same events Valentinian grows from being *parvulus* (*Historia ecclesiastica* 11,12–13) to *adulescentulus* (ibid., 15) to *adulescens* (ibid., 31). The difference is sharpened by the probability that Augustine used Rufinus as a source for this passage: Y.-M. Duval, "L'éloge de Théodose dans la *Cité de Dieu* (V, 26,1)," *Recherches Augustiniennes* 4 (1966) 135–79.

9. R. A. Markus, *Saeculum: History and Society in the Theology of St Augustine,* 2nd ed. (Cambridge: Cambridge University Press, 1988) 29–33.

prefect of Rome was instructed to find a rhetor for Milan, and how Augustine arranged matters so that it was he whom the then prefect, Symmachus, tested and sent, is so familiar that we easily miss how awkwardly Augustine twists the structure of the sentence.[10] The prefect is mentioned twice, with the result that Augustine is able to identify him by name, casually but conspicuously. No other character in the Confessions is introduced like this, with a bare name to adorn an office.[11] And here again a small detail gives an important clue to Augustine's outlook, and allows us to relate his outlook to his experience.

The significance of the care Augustine takes to mention Symmachus is that he believed, some fifteen years after meeting him, that his name was worth dropping. It is interesting in this respect that two decurions of Hippo are recorded in 399, exactly the time when the *Confessions* were composed, as clients of Symmachus:[12] Symmachus thus remained a name to conjure with in Augustine's own city. And Augustine's experience will have taught him that real power resided with Symmachus and his fellow nobles of Rome. His whole life had been changed by the prefect's nod of approval, which propelled him from obscurity to glittering prospects—of wealth, office, and enlightenment—at Milan. If anything, it is likely that Augustine's experience gave him an exaggerated respect for the potency of Symmachus and his kind, for his stay in Rome coincided with a period when, for political reasons, these aristocrats exerted unusually strong influence.[13]

Symmachus's son-in-law possibly makes an anonymous appearance in the *City of God,* as an embarrassed pagan suppliant in a Christian church (5,26).[14] But we cannot be sure, for Augustine now dismisses the heirs of Regulus and Scipio, and in doing so no longer cares to name names. His magnificent caricature of a Symmachan cultural milieu, where proud men soaked in Virgil (1,3) cling to their old gods and wallow in their luxury and avarice (30–31), and in

---

10. *Conf.* 5,15,23: *postquam missum est a Mediolanio Romam ad praefectum urbis . . . ambivi . . . ut me probatum praefectus tunc Symmachus mitteret.*

11. J. J. O'Donnell, *Augustine: Confessions* (Oxford: Clarendon Press, 1992) 2.217–218, discusses the (short) register of persons named in the *Confessions,* but is unconvincing in singling Symmachus out as an "agent of conversion": the proudly swollen supplier of Platonic texts at *Conf.* 7,9,13 has at least as strong a claim on this count.

12. Symmachus, *Ep.* 9,51 (of 399).

13. N. B. McLynn *Ambrose of Milan* (Berkeley & Los Angeles: University of California Press, 1994) 159, 165–68.

14. Flavianus is the only known son of Theodosius's enemies known to have been at Rome in 394. But Augustine's language hardly suggests a specific reference to the urban prefect.

their insane obsession—*O mentes amentes!*—with the theater (32–33), raises questions about the social context that are of direct relevance for this study.[15] We face here the same delicate problems posed by Ammianus Marcellinus's (not wholly dissimilar) satirical sketches of senatorial life:[16] the impression made on their contemporary audience by these trenchant attacks will have depended upon the author's perceived standing in relation to his targets. In the *City of God* Augustine indeed discovered "an ideological opponent worthy of himself";[17] not all his initial readers, however, will have readily accepted that this provincial bishop was himself worthy of his eminent antagonists.

Augustine and the Proconsuls

Students of the *City of God* have felt little need to examine the evidence for Augustine's links with the Roman aristocracy. After 410, Africa was awash with displaced senators: "the whole Roman nobility" was at Carthage in 411.[18] From there the illustrious pagan Volusianus sent polite greetings to Augustine, and set in motion the debate that issued in the *City of God*; meanwhile, Volusianus's sister Albina, one of the bishop's many well-born Christian admirers, was camped with her family virtually on his doorstep, at Thagaste. Rome, it would appear, had come to Augustine. But appearances can be deceptive, and Augustine's social access to these eminent refugees should not be taken for granted. The massive confidence with which Augustine demolishes the Roman cultural inheritance in the *City of God* has tended to govern interpretations of his encounters with the principal heirs, yet there is no evidence, for example, that he ever actually met either Volusianus or Albina.[19] A reassessment of the level

---

15. Augustine's adversaries are specified by T. D. Barnes, "Aspects of the Background of the *City of God*," *University of Ottawa Quarterly* 52 (1982): 64–81, as "pagan Roman refugees of noble birth" (73).

16. In his digressions on Rome (14,6; 28,3) Ammianus excoriates senatorial luxury, greed, and interest in actresses, differing with Augustine only over the extent of classical learning (28,4,14). The historian's Roman audience is most recently discussed by J. Matthews, "The Origin of Ammianus," *Classical Quarterly* 88 (1994): 252–69.

17. J. J. O'Donnell, "The Inspiration for Augustine's *De civitate Dei*," *Augustinian Studies* 10 (1979): 75–79, at 78–79.

18. *Gesta collationis Carthaginensis* 1,149: *nobilitatem omnem hic esse Romanam.* The evidence is collected by P. Courcelle, *Histoire littéraire des grands invasions germaniques,* 3rd ed. (Paris: Études Augustiniennes, 1964) 58–67.

19. Conversations between Augustine and Volusianus have been created by mistranslation of *Ep.* 135 (e.g., Fathers of the Church 20.13). Albina appears in a list of Augustine's noble visitors in F. van der Meer, *Augustine the Bishop* (London: Sheed and Ward, 1961) 245.

of his dealings with such people is therefore overdue; and such an investigation will have the additional benefit of bringing our initial question into sharper focus.

For Augustine's best-attested relations with senators are with those who embodied what he himself called "the power," the governors of Roman Africa.[20] Senatorial pride and imperial rule converged in these men, appointed by the emperor but drawn overwhelmingly from the Roman senate. The Hymetius who honored Valens, for example, was married to a sister of Symmachus's close friend Praetextatus; and the term Symmachus himself served at Carthage while Augustine was a student there had perhaps allowed the latter a first impression, from afar, of his future benefactor. And proconsular authority will have continued to impress itself upon Augustine at Hippo. One of the two proconsular legates probably retained his headquarters there, and there was also a powerful symbolic presence, nicely illustrated by another inscription from the Forum. Even the all-conquering Valens was outclassed by a monument the council had erected several decades before, to the proconsul M. Aurelius Consius Quartus, "a man of all illustrious glories, outstanding in his administration, astonishing in his virtue, exceptional in his honesty." [21]

The bishop's perceptions of, and approaches to, the proconsuls are again likely to have been shaped, at least in part, by his own prior experience. A notable mark of recognition during his youth had been when the proconsul Vindicianus, a "sharp old man," crowned him victor of an oratorical contest in the early 380s with his own hand.[22] The physical aspect here is important, for real power resided in Vindicianus's touch. The *Notitia dignitatum* represents the proconsuls with a picture of an ivory inkstand, to symbolize the judicial sentences that they solemnly wrote out.[23] As Augustine will have been well aware, Vindicianus's hand could as easily have marked him down as a Manichee. Later critics would allege that his sudden departure to Rome in 383 had been an escape from just such an eventuality.[24]

After Augustine's return to Africa the decisions fashioned by proconsuls would also concern him closely, as one of his principal instruments in the

---

20. *Sermo* 302,17: *illam potestatem.*
21. Marec, "Le Forum," 388–390. For the *legatus Numidiae*, see A. Chastagnol, "Les Légats du Proconsul d'Afrique au Bas-Empire," *Libyca* (Arch/Ep) 6 (1958): 7–19.
22. *Conf.* 4,3,5: *proconsul manu sua coronam illam agonisticam imposuerat;* 7,6,8: *acuto seni.*
23. *Notitia dignitatum occidentalis* 18.
24. *Contra litteras Petiliani* 3,25,30.

conflict with the Donatists. Yet as far as our evidence shows, during the thirty years after his "friendly conversations" with Vindicianus he never enjoyed any similar intimacy with any other proconsul or comparable figure in Africa—despite his undoubted fame by the early 400s, despite the number of proconsuls from Christian backgrounds, and despite the opportunities provided by all his visits to Carthage. The real power-holding elite remained beyond Augustine's reach. He himself describes being kept waiting in governors' waiting rooms, and suffering humiliation in their presence.[25] The swaggering derision exhibited in the *City of God* toward the governors' pagan peers acquires fresh interest when seen against this background. For as we shall see, the publication of the first installment coincides with the adoption of a newly self-assured manner in addressing a proconsul, which in turn reflects freshly acquired access to elite circles. The *City of God* should be seen as both a result of this new level of engagement, and a bid to exploit it.

First, however, the assertion that Augustine was, until 412, a politically marginal figure in Africa must be substantiated, for the opposite has often been assumed. The evidence, derived overwhelmingly from the bishop's own writings, provides a picture that is incomplete but nevertheless coherent and consistent. During Augustine's first decade at Hippo there is no record of any dealings with the proconsuls;[26] nor does the first attested encounter, in 404, suggest any previous expertise. Augustine himself, much later, reported a summons of a Donatist bishop before an unnamed proconsul on a heresy charge, and an easy conviction.[27] But Possidius, who was directly involved in the affair, tells a different story. The case was not easy at all. "Urgings of every kind" from Augustine were needed to bring it to court, and only after the third session was a verdict forthcoming.[28] Nor was this the end of the matter. Having won his case, Augustine persuaded the proconsul to remit the fine that he had imposed on the guilty Donatist. But the case was then reopened at Ravenna, and the emperor fined the proconsul, and his office staff, ten pounds of gold each for failing to exercise the proper severity.[29]

---

25. *Sermo* 302,17.

26. It is worth noting that five of the eleven proconsuls attested between 395 and 404 feature among the correspondents of Symmachus.

27. *Contra Cresconium* 3,47,51: *facillimme convictus.*

28. Possidius, *Vita Augustini* 12,7.

29. There is a convenient summary in W. H. C. Frend, *The Donatist Church,* 3rd ed., (Oxford: Clarendon Press, 1985) 260–61.

Although the fines were eventually revoked, after the concerted efforts of the African bishops, we can easily imagine that strong views will have been held about Augustine at the proconsular headquarters in the intervening period; nor, perhaps, will the happy outcome fully have redeemed the meddlesome bishop's credit. It is not surprising, then, that the correspondence between Augustine and this proconsul has not been preserved. Nor ought we to be surprised at Augustine's decision, when he again approached the secular authorities soon afterward, to appeal not to the proconsul but to the lesser but partly overlapping authority of the vicar of Africa.

Augustine's Letter 86 is addressed to "His Magnificence" Caecilianus, plausibly to be identified with the man attested as a vicar in 404.[30] Having begun with praise for Caecilianus's administration and admiration for his Christian faith, Augustine deplores the rampages of the Donatists and regrets that Hippo and its environs have not yet felt the effects of Caecilianus's edict on the issue. He finally declares it his duty, as bishop of Hippo, to ensure that Caecilianus is aware of the omission, so that it could be rectified.

This brief letter has caused some notable confusions for modern prosopographers, whose Roman empire is much tidier that that of Augustine's imagination. André Mandouze inferred from the terms of Augustine's greeting—"Your Excellency"—that Caecilianus was a *vir illustris*, and so reassigned our letter to the following decade, when he had returned to Africa with the higher rank.[31] But this later mission was not an *administratio*, a term which Augustine reserves exclusively for regular administrative posts;[32] and the overloaded honorifics are best read as an index of the earnestness with which the bishop was seeking Caecilianus's favor. [33] On the other hand, the *Prosopography of the Later Roman Empire* supposes that Caecilianus had just been promoted to proconsul, to explain how an edict that had originally been applied to Numidia but not to Hippo (which was located in the proconsular province) could now be enforced there.[34] The error here has arisen from Augustine's

---

30. *Codex Iustinianus* 1,51,4, *ad Caecilianum vicarium.* The diocese is left unspecified.

31. *Prosopographie de l'Afrique chrétienne (303-533),* ed. A. Mandouze (Paris: CNRS, 1982) 177–79.

32. The only other occurrences in Augustine refer to a proconsul and a *consularis* (*Epp.* 112; 116).

33. Note that *tua sublimitas,* one of the two terms on which Mandouze bases his argument, recurs in Ep. 154, to the vicar Macedonius; the other, *tua magnificentia,* also appears in laws addressed to a proconsul (*Codex Theodosianus* 12,1,149) and a *consularis* (*Constitutiones Sirmondianae* 5).

34. *Prosopography of the Later Roman Empire,* vol. 2, ed. J. R. Martindale (Cambridge: Cambridge University Press, 1980) 245.

subtle crafting of his request to Caecilianus. For although he seems to imply it he nowhere states that the governor had any authority over Hippo. The careful phrasing of his lament that "the region of Hippo Regius" and the parts in its neighborhood "bordering on Numidia" had not yet merited the aid of Caecilianus's edict instead suggests that he was stirring the delicate issue of administrative demarcation. In encouraging Caecilianus to "see to it" that his own sound policy was introduced also into the proconsular province, he offers him—should he care to use it—a stick with which to belabor the proconsul. Such an initiative would have particular point if, as the chronology allows, the proconsul with whom Augustine had made his intervention was still in office. But whatever Augustine's motives, the letter shows clearly the distance that separated him from the governor. He did not know him personally, having been impelled to write (he says) by reports of his virtues rather than direct acquaintance; nor does the letter press for further contact.

Augustine's next attested exchange with a governor occurred some four years later. Addressing the proconsul Donatus, the bishop omits formalities and proceeds directly to a lament about the present troubles afflicting the church, and to an appeal for help from the secular arm which he bolsters with a scriptural quotation (*Ep.* 100). This is an entirely different kind of letter, and bespeaks a very different relationship. Donatus owned estates at Hippo, and was known personally to Augustine. But the bishop could not presume upon his acquaintance with the proconsul. This letter has been misunderstood because scholars, assuming that he could, have taken it at face value and have focused upon his pleas, which fill the first two-thirds of the letter, that the newly appointed Donatus should not apply the death penalty against Donatists brought before his court.[35] Yet this plea sits awkwardly with the last part of the letter, which invites the governor to issue an edict to show the Donatists that the laws against them are in fact still in force. The apparent redundancy is explained by Augustine's use of the conditional in his discussion of the trials and punishments. These were hypothetical, and contingent upon the publication of the edict requested in the conclusion. This would suggest that Augustine is uncertain whether or not the heresy laws are still to be applied against the Donatists, and that his purpose in writing to Donatus is not to offer fatherly advice but to

---

35. Frend, *Donatist Church*, 271–72, speaks of Donatus's "zeal" and eagerness to apply the death penalty; cf. G. Bonner, *Saint Augustine of Hippo,* 2nd ed. (Norwich: The Canterbury Press, 1986) 267.

pump cautiously for information. The tortuously indirect politeness of his approach will be familiar to any reader of the letters of Symmachus.

This would require us to assign the letter not to the accepted date of winter 408/9 but to the months immediately following August 408, when the sudden fall of Stilicho had raised the question of the future validity of his heresy laws. The change has the significant result that the letter to Donatus will now precede Augustine's first approach, as bishop, to the imperial court. In his correspondence with Stilicho's supplanter, the new powerbroker Olympius, Augustine politely seeks reassurance that the anti-heresy laws remained in force. In other words, we should infer that Donatus had failed to satisfy Augustine, perhaps by protesting ignorance of the current mood at Ravenna and inviting Augustine to find out for himself. And in feeling his way into court politics Augustine is even more indirect than he had been with Donatus. Having devoted his first letter entirely to the business arrangements of one Bishop Boniface, he reserves the crucial question about the heresy laws for the second, which he must have written immediately upon getting an encouraging reply to his first initiative.[36]

Augustine's tentative approach to Olympius shows the reality of dealings between a provincial bishop and the powerful figures who controlled the government. The bishop has often been assumed to have had influence at the highest levels; his intervention with Olympius has been seen as decisive.[37] But he didn't, and it wasn't. There is no reason to suppose that Augustine had had any previous contact with Olympius. When he twice expresses confidence that Olympius would receive his letter in his "customary" manner (*Ep.* 96,1; 3), he means no more than that Olympius was known to be gracious toward all his correspondents.[38] Augustine's fulsome recapitulation, at the start of the second letter, of Olympius's reply to his first shows clearly that letters from the court did not usually feature in the bishop's mail.

---

36. The second letter was sent *media hieme* (*Ep.* 97,2); *Ep.* 96 had responded to reports of Olympius's promotion in September 408. The beginning of Donatus's term is dated from the Codes to between June and November 408.

37. Frend, *Donatist Church,* 270–71, makes Augustine "well-acquainted with members of rival groupings" at court (citing Paulinus of Nola and Anicius Bassus!) and argues that his request to Olympius "found ready acceptance." The anti-Donatist law which Donatus posted at Carthage on November 24 comes too soon to be credited to Augustine.

38. When Augustine says he is raising the matter of Boniface's estate "again" (*Ep.* 96,2: *rursus*) he likewise means merely that it had exercised Olympius's predecessor.

Even Donatus, the one proconsul with whom Augustine was on familiar terms, remained beyond his direct reach. As the bishop ruefully acknowledges in another letter (*Ep.* 112), he never actually met Donatus during his proconsular term. Augustine had no privileged access to the machinery of government. Like nearly everybody else who encountered the imperial administration, he was groping through a fog in the hope of grasping and manipulating the dimly perceived, barely accessible levers of power.

And Augustine was still groping when Alaric's Goths clattered into Rome in 410. There is no record of any communication with Donatus's immediate successors. Nothing prepares us, then, for Augustine's letter to the proconsul Apringius, in 412 (*Ep.* 134). The bishop begins by reminding Apringius that proconsuls too must one day stand to receive judgment before a heavenly tribunal, and proceeds to urge him—speaking as "bishop to a Christian"—to show mercy. The arrogation of authority is remarkable. And the quality of mercy being urged was calculated to set alarm bells ringing among the proconsul's more senior officials. Fresh Donatist outrages had caused the full severity of the laws to be set in motion, but Augustine insisted that the guilty should be given the chance to repent. This was the same plea that had caused so much trouble, and the threat of a crippling fine, eight years previously. Yet now Augustine appears able to make it with serene confidence.

Marcellinus

The reason for Augustine's confidence with Apringius, of course, was that this time he could count on a powerful seconder.[39] The letter to the proconsul was not sent directly but enclosed in another, Letter 133 to the proconsul's brother, who is invited to deliver it and to help plead the bishop's case. The brother, Marcellinus, was at the time in Africa on a special mission from the emperor; and by the time this letter was written he had become Augustine's trusted friend. For the first time, Augustine had established a working relationship with a high-level imperial official.[40]

---

39. Indispensable for the following is M. Moreau, *Le dossier Marcellinus dans la correspondance de saint Augustin* (Paris: Études Augustiniennes, 1973).

40. A further letter to Marcellinus, number 139, shows that the initial appeal to Apringius was unanswered and so warns us not to overstate the bishop's influence. Earlier constraints still perhaps applied: Augustine's request in his renewed appeal for a stay of execution so that he himself might appeal to the imperial court (citing a precedent to show that clemency would be granted "easily": *Ep.* 139,2) suggests that Apringius (or his staff) was concerned that the Crispinus fiasco might be repeated.

Marcellinus, the *tribunus et notarius* who adjudicated the Conference of Carthage, is of especial interest to readers of the *City of God* as the "dearest son" to whom Augustine dedicated the work (*Civ.* 1, praef.; 2,1). But familiarity with Marcellinus has blinded us to the novelty, for Augustine, of this two-year friendship with a senior imperial administrator on active duty. The relationship offered Augustine access to the empire at a new level and gave him, at last, a platform from which to address Marcellinus's peers. The dedication, then, is not incidental. Marcellinus's name gave substance to Augustine's campaign against Roman pride; and Marcellinus could personally ensure that the book found readers among the elite.

The friendship that Augustine developed with Marcellinus must not, by any means, be taken for granted. One reason why he had achieved nothing similar with any of the other pious Christian governors who had passed through Africa was the practical difficulty of getting close to conscientious imperial officials. When Augustine encountered Marcellinus at the opening of the Conference of Carthage in June 411—quite probably the first time the two men met[41]—he will have seen him attended by a staff proportionate to his authority: some two dozen members are carefully itemized in the preamble to the *Gesta collationis* (1,1). The sheer physical presence of this array helps convey the inaccessibility of men like this to Augustine. On the other hand, the *Gesta* also suggest that Marcellinus's staff was a somewhat makeshift collection, seconded from various African bureaus. This might have helped create an opening for Augustine to make his impression. The sudden prominence he enjoys in the third session, and the encouragement Marcellinus there offers him, can plausibly be seen as a crucial stage in this courtship.[42]

Marcellinus, not the pagan aristocrat Volusianus, is at the center of the debates that occasioned the *City of God*. Nagged by his Christian mother, Volusianus had indeed entered into correspondence with Augustine. But we can legitimately suspect some sly teasing in his exquisite graciousness. He artfully distanced himself from his questions by attributing them to others (*Ep.* 135,2), and later made it clear that he placed little weight on the outcome of

---

41. Moreau, *Le dossier*, 105–111, acknowledges the lack of evidence for prior contacts; her arguments that these nevertheless existed are not compelling.

42. The frequency of Augustine's interventions—six in the first session, five in the second, 59 in the third—tells its own story. See the figures in S. Lancel, *Actes de la Conférence de Carthage,* vol. 1 (SC 194, Paris: Cerf, 1972) 253–73. There is also an instructive change in the manner of Augustine's exchanges with Marcellinus: compare, for example, *Gesta* 1,78–83 with 3,19–21.

the philosophical question he had raised over the Incarnation (*Ep.* 136,2). Marcellinus, who was meeting Volusianus on a daily basis (*Ep.* 136,1), forced the central issues into the open, conveying to the bishop Volusianus's more urgent objections—about the validity of pagan sacrifice, the compatibility of Christianity and service to Rome, and the misfortunes suffered by the state under Christian emperors (*Ep.* 136,2). And Augustine's decision to address his response to Marcellinus (*Ep.* 138,1) shows that he appreciated the relative value of his two interlocutors.

Augustine's problem was not in finding an answer to Volusianus but in getting it heard. An incident reported by Marcellinus illustrates the bishop's plight beautifully: a rich landowner from Hippo had entertained his hearers at Carthage with a story about Augustine's inability to give a convincing answer to his questions (*Ep.* 136,3). Augustine lacked the social authority to bring his intellectual weight to bear upon even the gentry of Hippo, who could slip away from his sermons to belittle him at parties to which he was never invited. He therefore needed Marcellinus as the dedicatee of the *City of God* for the same reason that he needed him as a spokesman in the salons of Carthage (*Ep.* 138,1): only thus could he gain purchase on the governing elite of the empire.

The sudden execution of Marcellinus for treason in September 413 was therefore not only a grievous personal loss for Augustine, but also threatened to abort his massive vindication of the city of God almost before he had begun it. The force of the blow has been disguised by the swiftness with which fortunes were reversed. Within a year, the vicissitudes of court politics had compensated Augustine for the loss of his patron. With the formal exoneration of Marcellinus, he had a martyr on his title page.[43] There is a vivid illustration of Marcellinus's posthumous potency in Letter 151 of 414, where the bishop rehearses the circumstances of his friend's execution to his correspondent of ten years previously, the vicar Caecilianus, now back in Africa on a mission from the emperor. Caecilianus hardly needed to hear the details, having spent the previous year in Carthage, and being associated closely with Marcellinus's executioner. Augustine's carefully pointed letter, entirely stripped of the effusions of a decade earlier, is in fact designed to present his conditions for accepting Caecilianus's pleas that he had not been implicated in the affair. The

---

43. Marcellinus's rehabilitation, while probably less immediate than implied by Orosius, *Historia adversus paganus* 7, 42,17, had been accomplished by September 414, when Marcellinus is mentioned honorably in *Codex Theodosianus* 16,5,5.

roles have been reversed. This time, in the aftermath of Marcellinus's reha-bilitation, it is Caecilianus who needs Augustine's endorsement. As the acknowledged custodian of his friend's memory, Augustine was qualified to give a decisive verdict upon anyone suspected of complicity. He pressed home his advantage, requiring from Caecilianus not only a full account of his ac-tions but also a commitment to receive baptism (*Ep.* 151,14). Caecilianus's baptism would mark not only a symbolic submission to Augustine's authority but also a dramatic acknowledgment of the claims he was making for the city of God.

But in the anxious period before Marcellinus's name was cleared, August-ine had been faced with the prospect of having somehow to relaunch his great and arduous work. Traces of his efforts remain. For during this winter of 413/ 4 he broke his customary policy of refusing to intercede for acquaintances in criminal cases, and sent his trusted emissary Boniface to Carthage to deliver an appeal to the vicar of Africa on behalf of a recently condemned criminal.[44] Macedonius, the vicar, questioned the wisdom of indiscriminate intercession and earned in reply a massive, painstaking response (*Ep.* 153); he also received, eventually, a copy of the first three books of the *City of God* (*Ep.* 154,2).[45] Augustine clearly knew Macedonius personally, having had ample opportu-nity to make his acquaintance during his extended visits to Carthage in 412/ 3.[46] His approach to him now, at a time when he had foresworn any further visits to Carthage after the shock of Marcellinus's execution (*Ep.* 151,3), looks much like a cautious attempt at reengagement with the latter's milieu. The care and effort that are evident in his two long letters were rewarded. Ac-knowledging the need to carry the argument of the *City of God* to the "impudently stubborn" who resisted (*Ep.* 154,2), Macedonius offers his own future services after his return to Italy (*Ep.* 154,3). In the vicar Augustine had meanwhile recognized exactly what he needed: "a man who while wearing the

---

44. Augustine's policy is set out by Possidius at *Vita Augustini* 20; it is also clear that the vicar, approaching the end of his term, was surprised by the intercession. Boniface, who had delivered the letter to Olympius (*Ep.* 96) and also one to Marcellinus (*Ep.* 143), seems to have had some expertise in dealings with the secular authorities.

45. Augustine's promise to send some writings, which Marcellinus reminds him of at *Ep.* 152,3, had probably been made in the letter delivered by Boniface (the pluperfect, *promiseras*, denotes merely that the promise had preceded the books' non-arrival, *non accepi*).

46. Augustine mentions an incident when Macedonius had presented a plea to an ecclesiastical tribunal: *Ep.* 153,10.

belt of office of an earthly judge is already thinking of the heavenly republic" (*Ep.* 155,17).

However, in their combination of high political office and pious commitment to Augustine's cause, Macedonius and Marcellinus remain exceptional, and are marked out as such by the way they are incorporated into his correspondence as partners in a dialogue. Augustine's exchange with Macedonius clearly impressed his biographer Possidius, who gives an entirely misleading impression of the admiration the bishop commanded among with the secular "powers" by quoting extensively, and exclusively, from the vicar's reply (*Vita Augustini* 20). Modern scholars have continued to generalize mistakenly from this untypical case.[47] In thus assuming a ready-made secular audience for Augustine, they have underestimated the challenge he faced in creating one, for a work that looked far beyond his customary competence. Although in the long course of its development the *City of God* would achieve a fame that guaranteed it readers, it owed its initial momentum to the aristocratic, politically involved patrons who provided Augustine a credible link with his ostensible targets.

Some fifteen years years later, when Augustine brought the *City of God* to its "astonishing" culmination, he had narrowed his scope to the immediate surroundings of his own city, a place defined no longer by its statuary but by its handfuls of sacred dust.[48] This vast shift of perspective, from the pagan relics of Rome to the *martyria* of Hippo Regius, has gripped the imaginations of the bishop's readers ever since. The contention of this essay is that the book presupposes another shift that represents a hardly less remarkable achievement. Augustine had reached out from his provincial city of Hippo Regius to present a plausible-sounding challenge to the stiff-necked empire of pagan Rome.

---

47. P. Brown, *Augustine of Hippo: A Biography* (Berkeley & Los Angeles: University of California Press, 1967) 336, thus evokes a succession of administrators in Africa who "would return to Italy with presentation-copies of the *City of God*."

48. P. Brown, *The Cult of the Saints* (Chicago: University of Chicago Press, 1981) 27–28.

THINKING THROUGH HISTORY:
AUGUSTINE'S METHOD IN THE *CITY OF GOD* AND ITS CICERONIAN DIMENSION

G. J. P. O'Daly

When, in 412 or thereabouts, Augustine began to write the *City of God*, the Christian religion had enjoyed for a century a privileged position in the Roman Empire.[1] Indeed, if the Romans had shared our passion for celebrating anniversaries, they would, in 412, have been celebrating the centenary of the conversion of Constantine on the eve of the Battle of the Milvian Bridge—the battle in which Roman troops, for the first time, bore upon their standards the symbol of the Christian cross. Constantine's victory in 312 gave him control over the western part of the Empire. His enthusiasm for Christianity, which had been a persecuted religion only eight years previously, may have been boosted by military success: at all events, in the words of Timothy Barnes, "After . . . October 312 the emperor consistently thought of himself as God's servant, entrusted with a divine mission to convert the Roman Empire to Christianity."[2]

This is not the place to retell the story of the advance of Christianity in the fourth century.[3] It became, in effect, a new established religion, massively

---

1. This essay develops some themes in chapters 1 and 6 of my *Augustine's City of God: A Reader's Guide* (Oxford: Clarendon Press, 1999).

2. T. D. Barnes, *Constantine and Eusebius* (Cambridge, Mass.: Harvard University Press, 1981).

3. For the following see especially Averil Cameron, *The Later Roman Empire* (London: Fontana, 1993), chs. 4 and 5.

45

consolidated by imperial patronage, and enjoying financial and legal privileges. But if this amounted to a revolution in religious and cultural terms, the revolution did not extend to political institutions. There was no radical change in the organization of imperial, provincial, and local government. Constantine placed restrictions on the traditional[4] cultic expression of civic religion: sacrifice was prohibited, for example. One could argue that traditional religious belief, as opposed to cult, was tolerated. But edicts are not always indicators of enforcement, and prohibition of sacrifice was not seriously implemented in the western part of the Empire. There is evidence of sporadic action against expressions of traditional religion throughout the century, but the temples remained open for business, and it was not until late in the century that more sustained attempts to undermine and suppress civic traditions were made. In particular, laws of 391 and 392 promulgated by the emperor Theodosius banned private as well as public sacrifice and other cult, and prohibited use of temples (*Codex Theodosianus* 16,10,10–12). Again, these laws are as much symptoms of the gradual christianization of the governing elite and the growth of church influence, as they are evidence for persecution of traditional practices: they may also be indicators of the resilience of tradition.

Roman Tradition

Even in a heavily christianized area like Roman North Africa (where Augustine grew up, and had been a bishop since 395), there was tension between Christians and defenders of tradition. And traditional rites persisted: Augustine witnessed them as a schoolboy and a student in the 360s and 370s (*Ep.* 17,4). Offerings were made at the temple of Saturn in Carthage until the end of the century.[5] Augustine's correspondence informs us about two incidents when tensions erupted into violence. At Sufes, probably in 399, Christians overturned a statue of Hercules, and in the ensuing riot sixty Christians were

---

4. Here and elsewhere in this essay I use the term "traditional/ist" to refer to Roman state religion and its practitioners, not because I have any serious objection to the term "pagan" (by Augustine's day *paganus* was commonly applied to non-Christians: *Retractationes* 2,43,1), but because "traditional/ist" conveys better the pagans' own sense of what they were defending, and Christianity's consciousness, at this time, of its "newness" (see Ambrose, *Ep.* 18[73],23–24). Cf. G. Fowden, *Empire to Commonwealth: Consequences of Monotheism in Late Antiquity* (Princeton: Princeton University Press, 1993) on "polytheist" (37–60) and "pagan" (38).

5. See C. Lepelley, *Les cités de l'Afrique romaine au Bas-Empire,* vol. 1 (Paris: Études Augustiniennes, 1979) 350, and for the whole topic of pagan survivals in christianized North Africa, 350–95, a seminal account.

killed. But the local senate insisted that the church make good the damage to the statue (*Ep.* 50). At Calama in 408 pagans held an illegal religious procession which led to a riot and looting of Christian property (*Ep.* 91). We may suspect that such incidents were not isolated, but it is important to realize that they were played out against a background of relative prosperity and stability in North Africa. This was not a civilization in decay or upheaval: the institutions of municipal government continued unimpaired, and both Christians and traditionalists participated in them, enjoying the resultant prestige, lavishing munificence on their towns and cities.[6] The newly established Christian religion did not create new civic forms of expression, apart, of course, from the increasingly visible and impressive churches where bishops like Augustine preached and conducted their rites.

In the aftermath of the violence involving Christians and pagans at Calama, a cultured traditionalist called Nectarius wrote to Augustine, requesting his intervention on behalf of fellow pagans charged with holding the illegal procession and attacking a Christian church in the town. We have four letters (*Epp.* 90, 91, 103 and 104) from this correspondence, two each from Nectarius and Augustine. Nectarius's appeal is made on behalf of the civic loyalties of those accused. He writes:

> I pass over the importance of love of one's country, since you appreciate it. For it is the only love which, by right, surpasses the affection felt for one's parents. If there is any measure or limit to the care [for one's country] that the good should have, we have on this occasion deserved to be excused from its obligations. But since the love for, and attraction of, one's city grows day by day, the closer one's life is to its end, the more one wants to leave one's native place free from harm and flourishing. (*Ep.* 90)

Nectarius understands this civic ideal to have a transcendental, afterlife dimension, as a further letter to Augustine makes clear. In it, Nectarius writes of

> [This city] which the great god, and those souls who have deserved well of him, inhabit, which all laws strive towards by different roads and ways, which we cannot express in speech, but might perhaps discover by thought . . . of which most learned men say that, for those who deserve it, a dwelling-place is prepared in the heavens, so that a kind of advancement to the celestial world is proffered to those who have deserved well of their native cities, and these live closer to god, who are shown to have brought salvation to their country by their counsel or their deeds. (*Ep.* 103,2)

---

6. See C. Lepelley, "Africa (A)," in *Augustinus-Lexikon* 1, 1/2 (1986) 180–205, here 183–86.

Nectarius is clearly alluding to the celestial afterlife of deserving Roman statesmen described in the so-called *Dream of Scipio*, the finale of Cicero's masterpiece of political theory, the *De re publica*, to which I shall refer in this essay, with some misgivings, as Cicero's *Republic*.[7] Even before receiving this further letter, Augustine had put his finger on the source of Nectarius's idealism, recognizing the source of his quotation of the phrase "any measure or limit to the care [for one's country] that the good should have." It is, Augustine writes, "those very books on the state, from which you have absorbed that affection of the most devoted citizen" (*Ep.* 91,3). This part of Cicero's work is lost, but it becomes clear from what Augustine says that, in it, one of the interlocutors had asserted that there "is no measure or limit to the care that the good should have for their country" (*Ep.* 91,1,3): it is an assertion of which Augustine approves (*Ep.* 91,1). He approves because he believes that it translates easily into Christian terms:

> For which reason we would wish also to have one such as yourself as a citizen of a certain celestial country, for which, in devoted love, to the best of our ability, we run risks and labor among those for whom we take thought, that they may apprehend it: it would be our wish that you might conclude that there is no measure and limit to the care for even a small part of it that a man in exile on this earth should have. (*Ep.* 91,1).

The moral values advocated by Cicero are, Augustine argues, realized in the Christian church, and prepare those who live by them to attain, with divine help, "to a dwelling-place in the eternal and celestial city" (*Ep.* 91,1). In defending official Christian opposition to traditional civic cult Augustine cites Cicero's critique of stories of the immorality of the gods (*Ep.* 91,4–5), in terms that anticipate the polemic of the *City of God*, including its method of retortion (here using the arguments of Cicero, a hero of the traditionalists, against them).[8] Cicero's views on the afterlife are, Augustine argues, consistent with Christian beliefs (*Ep.*104,3). Throughout this exchange, which antedates the writing of the *City of God* by a few years, Augustine defines the Christian

---

7. Cf. esp. *Rep.* 6,13. On the term *res publica* see M. Schofield, "Cicero's Definition of *Res Publica*," in *Cicero the Philosopher*, ed. J. G. F. Powell (Oxford: Clarendon Press, 1995) 63–83, here 66–69. See the new translation of the work by N. Rudd, *Cicero: The Republic and The Laws* (Oxford: Oxford University Press, 1998) xxxv, for the translation of *res publica*.

8. On the practice of retortion in early Christian apologetic see, for Arnobius's use of Porphyry, M. B. Simmons, *Arnobius of Sicca: Religious Conflict and Competition in the Age of Diocletian* (Oxford: Clarendon Press, 1995) 243–63. Augustine cites the same Ciceronian critique of stories about the gods in *Ep.* 91,4 and *Civ.* 2,9 and 11: it is usually assumed to come from Book 4 of the *De re publica*, and printed in Ziegler's Teubner ed. as *Rep.* 4,11–13.

concept of the society of the good in language that foreshadows the later work—"city," "native country," "country of the flesh" (*Epp.* 91,6; 104,17). The importance of the correspondence with Nectarius lies in the way in which Augustine engages in debate on the basis of common assumptions about cities, real and ideal. The tone is civil rather than polemical, and this may be due as much to Augustine's sense of being at ease with Cicero's (and Nectarius's) views as to the delicate nature of the correspondence. The assumptions shared with Nectarius allow Augustine to articulate his own vision of the city.

When Augustine writes the *City of God*, Cicero's *Republic* is one of the key works informing his engagement with the values of the Roman tradition. Because large portions of Cicero's dialogue are lost, Augustine is an important source for its recovery. But I am not primarily concerned here with that aspect of the reception of Cicero by Augustine. Nor do I wish to speculate about the intriguing similarity of situation that led to the writing of the two works. Cicero's *Republic* was written against the background of political chaos and violence and the breakdown of Republican government in the 50s BCE.[9] Augustine's *City of God* took shape in the aftermath of the spectacular, if largely symbolic, demonstration of the vulnerability of the Roman Empire to the Goths, the sack of the city of Rome in 410. Rather, what I want to argue is that Cicero's use of Roman history in his dialogue influences Augustine's understanding of history in general, and that Augustine's use of history as an element in his argument in the *City of God* both develops and reacts against Cicero's method. In the correspondence with Nectarius, we find a positive use by Augustine of Cicero, exploiting an afterlife myth in Cicero's dialogue. That part of the *Republic* plays no role in the *City of God*.[10] Nor is Augustine concerned with Cicero's analysis of constitutions or forms of government in Book 1 of the *Republic*. But there is evidence that he used the account of Roman history in the second book of Cicero's work, although the explicit references to that book in the *City of God* are chiefly to spectacular details about Rome's early kings, such as the account of Romulus's deification (22,6) and the death of Tullus Hostilius by thunderbolt (3,15). More often, Augustine uses Cicero as a critic of his own society and religion, citing his polemic against the theater from

---

9. For the background to Cicero's *Republic* see E. Rawson, *Cicero: A Portrait,* 2nd ed. (Ithaca, N.Y.: Cornell University Press, 1983) 146–63; for the sack of Rome in 410 see P. Heather, *Goths and Romans, 332–489* (Oxford: Clarendon Press, 1991) 213–18.

10. The reference at *Civ.* 22,28 to Cicero's comments on Plato's myth of Er does not necessarily derive from *Rep.* 6, as E. Heck, *Die Bezeugung von Ciceros Schrift De re publica* (Hildesheim: Olms, 1966) 60f. (cf. 142) rightly argues.

Book 4 of the *Republic* (2,8–13) or his critique of the political and moral decline of the late Roman Republic in Book 5 of the dialogue (2,21). All this is familiar to readers of Augustine: but does a more subtle use of Cicero underlie Augustine's argument?

Although Plato's *Republic* is an important and influential model for Cicero, Cicero also stresses the differences between his method in the *Republic* and Plato's. At the beginning of the dialogue Cicero argues that moral excellence (*virtus*) can only be realized in political action: it is not merely an intellectual possession. The early Greek lawgivers, such as Solon and Lycurgus, were also responsible for the inculcation of the social virtues (*Rep*. 1,2). This is not explicit criticism of Plato, although it suggests that an implicit contrast is being drawn between two approaches to the relation between morality and politics. Elsewhere, however, the contrast is made explicit. At the beginning of Book 2 Cicero's protagonist, Scipio, outlines the reason for the account of Roman history which is to follow: it is to show how Roman political institutions developed gradually, reaching their apogee in the early Republic. Scipio is made to refer to the first work of Roman historiography, written in the mid-second century BCE, the *Origines* or *Beginnings*, and its author Cato the Elder. Cato argued that the strength of the Roman constitution lay in the fact that it was not the work of a single legislator, as Greek constitutions were traditionally understood to be, but that it was rather the achievement of many politicians over a long period of time (*Rep*. 2,2). The biological metaphor of growth to strength is invoked here and elsewhere in Cicero's dialogue, just as the historical explanation of the realization of the perfect state is contrasted with Plato's invention of a fictional ideal (*Rep*. 2,1–3). The imputation of invention to Plato is a traditional point, and other elements of Scipio's account here echo the famous account by the Greek historian of Rome's history, Polybius, in Book 6 of his *Histories*, written, like Cato's *Origines*, in the second century BCE. Polybius had also used the biological metaphor of Rome's development (*Hist*. 6,57), and had contrasted Rome's constitution with those of the Greek lawgivers (*Hist*. 6,43–50) and with Plato's, criticizing Plato's republic for not being tested in action and comparing it to a perfectly sculpted but lifeless statue (*Hist*. 6,47).[11] But there are also differences between Polybius and Cicero. For Polybius, the biological model highlights the inevitable decline, as well as the growth, of the state, whereas Cicero allows the possibility of an immortal state

11. The biological metaphor in Polybius: F. W. Walbank, *Polybius* (Berkeley & Los Angeles: University of California Press, 1972) 142–46.

(*Hist.* 6,57; *Rep.* 3,34), even if political violence threatens to undermine the ancestral constitution and leads to the death of the *res publica*. Again, Polybius's metaphor of growth serves his belief that the progress of states and constitutions is a natural one (*Hist.* 6,10), whereas Cicero insists that the rational planning of successive statesmen brings about the gradually perfected Roman Republic. Cicero's approach is non-deterministic, and is based on the activity of reason in controlling natural processes.[12]

The *City of God*

If we turn from Cicero to Augustine's *City of God*, it becomes immediately apparent that Augustine's account of Roman history in Books 2 and 3 of that work is not based, in any broad sense, on Cicero's version in Book 2 of the *Republic*. Augustine's agenda is to demonstrate that Rome's gods never saved Rome from disasters. His polemical aim is to accumulate evidence for evils and misfortunes throughout Roman history. Even Sallust—for Augustine the historian of the decline of the Roman Republic—is not free from Golden Age assumptions about the early Republic. Yet Sallust also stresses the presence of fear and injustice in Roman society (*Civ.* 2,17–18). By contrast, Cicero's account of even potentially lurid episodes plays down their sensational and disturbing aspects. This is the case with his version of the Romulus story (*Rep.* 2,4–20), for example.[13] The differences between Cicero and the account of Romulus in Livy and historians are obvious, and this is because Cicero wishes to stress the institutional and constitutional aspects in his narrative. Within the dialogue, Scipio, the narrator of the narrative of Book 2, is told by another interlocutor that his account is encomiastic (*Rep.* 2,64). Thus, although Augustine, in the course of his historical polemic (*Civ.* 2,21), engages in critical discussion with Cicero's definition of *res publica* in *Rep.* 1,39, this discussion does not emerge from any explicit consideration of Cicero's vision of Roman history.

It may, however, be possible to discern a pervasive, if subtle, Ciceronian influence in the reason given by Augustine for the political achievements of Rome, and especially its Empire. Augustine famously states that it is because of divine providence that Rome became a great power, and he links Roman power with the virtues of self-sacrifice and valor, illustrated by historical examples

---

12. Cf. *Rep.* 2,30; 2,45,2; 2,57,1; and *Cicero: De Re Publica*, ed. J. E. G. Zetzel (Cambridge: Cambridge University Press, 1995) ad loc.

13. Zetzel 160–61; cf. Zetzel 220 on the story of Julius and Sestus in *Rep.* 2,61.

in *City of God* 5,12–19. Augustine's method is to demythologize imperial ideology, to eliminate the argument that it was Rome's gods that made Rome great. Like his Christian contemporaries Ambrose and Prudentius, Augustine emphasizes the part played by human qualities in the Roman achievement. To understand the significance of this view, we must stand back a little from the uses of history in Augustine and Cicero, and consider some theoretical assumptions underlying their political theorizing. Augustine insists that it is the moral standing of individuals that establishes the quality of a society. Good societies are, in essence, multiplications of good individuals:

> [L]et us refuse to be fooled by empty bombast, to let the edge of our critical faculties be blunted by high-sounding words like "peoples," "realms," "provinces." Let us set before our mind's eye two men; for the individual man is, like a letter in a word, an element . . . out of which a community or realm is built up, however vast its territorial possessions. (*Civ.* 4,3, trans. H. Bettenson, modified)

Augustine then goes on to contrast a rich man, under stress and unhappy, with a modest, lovable, kindly poor man:

> It is the same with two families, two peoples, or two realms. The same canon of judgment applies as in the case of the two men. (Ibid.)

Justice in the individual mirrors justice in the state, and vice versa. To some extent, Augustine may appear to be more like Plato than Cicero in this respect. The focus in Cicero's dialogue is more on states, governments, institutions, and their justice as a series of relations that are not reducible to justice as the virtue of an individual. Yet it is perhaps a question of emphasis rather than a radical difference. For both Cicero and Augustine believe that the moral quality of individuals is a more important formative influence on the quality of government than any kind of constitution.[14] Cicero argues that there is interaction, and mutual interdependence, between social traditions and good citizens. Individuals are the product of, and conserve, institutions:

> [O]ur ancestral way of life produced outstanding men, and those excellent men preserved the old way of life and the institutions of their forefathers. (*Rep.* 5,1, trans. N. Rudd)

This part of the *Republic* is known to us only from its approving citation in *City of God* 2,21. In the same chapter, Augustine points out that just government, in Cicero's view, is possible under each of the three kinds of simple and good constitution, monarchy, aristocracy, and democracy (cf. *Rep.* 1,42). Even

---

14. On the preceding see Zetzel 14, 24f.

if Augustine never engages in a discussion of the merits of the various forms of constitution, he will not have found Scipio's preference for monarchy (*Rep.* 1,54–61) surprising, in view of his assumption of the fact of a kind of monarchical rule in the later Empire, an assumption that becomes explicit when he talks about the desired qualities and achievements of Christian emperors (*Civ.* 5,24–26). It is not surprising that Augustine is attracted to the analogies adduced by Scipio in support of monarchy: the analogy with the single divine ruler of the universe (*Rep.* 1,56) and that with musical harmony (*Rep.* 2,69).[15] The analogy with musical harmony comes at the end of the second book of the *Republic*, and we know it from Augustine's citation of it (*Civ.* 2,21). The analogy with the single ruler of the universe resurfaces in an apology for imperialism in Book 3 of the *Republic*, to which Augustine alludes in *City of God* 19,21, in a discussion of what it means to serve God properly.

We seem to have moved some distance away from the core concern of this essay with the role of arguments based on history in Cicero and Augustine. Yet the preceding observations on theoretical assumptions in our two authors are crucial to the rest of my argument. When Augustine, briefly, considers the elements of the definition of a state (*Civ.* 4,4), he starts from a Ciceronian premise, and his definition is presented, in Ciceronian fashion, as a historical development. The Ciceronian premise is that of the reluctant sceptic in the dialogue, Philus, who, in Book 3 of the *Republic*, propounds the argument that a state cannot exist without injustice. Augustine's paradigm state is a state without justice, developed over time from a criminal gang:

> Remove justice, and what are kingdoms but gangs of criminals on a large scale? What are criminal gangs but petty kingdoms? A gang is a group of men under the command of a leader, bound by a compact of association, in which the plunder is divided according to an agreed convention. If this villainy wins so many recruits from the ranks of the demoralized that it acquires territory, establishes a base, captures cities and subdues peoples, it then openly arrogates to itself the title of kingdom, which is conferred on it in the eyes of the world, not by the renouncing of aggression but by the attainment of impunity. (*Civ.* 4,4)

The several elements here—a leader's command, the compact of association, agreed division of plunder, many recruits, acquisition of territory, attainment of impunity—form a sketch of an account of society's structuring that is expressed in negative terms, but is nonetheless comprehensive enough

---

15. See Zetzel 26.

to be a working definition.[16] Its coloring suits Augustine's polemic against the violence of actual societies. It could not have been composed without its Ciceronian antecedents, including the whole question of what constitutes a *res publica*. And there is evidence that, when polemic is not his immediate aim, Augustine subscribes to a gradualist, progressivist version of history. His version of the biological model of history's, especially biblical history's, development through a series of phases or "ages" (*aetates*) is used in a limited way in Books 15 and 16 of the *City of God*, with explicit reference to the analogy with the periods of human life in 16,43. Furthermore, human inventions that are the basis of civilized life are located chronologically in Book 18, where Augustine synchronizes events of biblical and secular history. Thus he notes the establishment of a legal system and a calendar in the Argolid, and the invention of writing in Egypt (18,3), and the importance of astronomy and other sciences in the unfolding of Egyptian civilization (18,39). Chronology, with Varro adduced as an authority, is important for Augustine in his argument against Egyptian claims concerning the antiquity of their sciences (18,39–40). Thus the notion of the articulation of human progress is not peripheral to Augustine's argument. Varro may have been as influential as Cicero in this respect, but what is important is the perception of social structures from a historical perspective.

In the first eleven chapters of Book 5 of the *City of God*, Augustine, using Cicero's *De fato (On Fate)*, argues against determinism and fate in human affairs. We have seen that a non-deterministic approach to history characterizes Cicero's narrative in the *Republic*. But where Cicero insists on the vital role of human reason in the ordering and control of human nature and the natural processes of social life, Augustine wishes to stress the role of divine reason, in the form of the providence that guides human political achievement. This achievement, in the case of Rome, is sketched in the second half of Book 5 of the *City of God*. In other words, Augustine's ideas are developed within the parameters of a characteristic Ciceronian argument, both in their denial of strict determinism and their advocacy of the place of rational order in Rome's acquisition of empire.

For Augustine, the object of history is none other than the study of the mind and will of God. This idea, which is implicit in the *City of God*, is developed in a seminal work of Augustinian hermeneutics, begun several years

---

16. See O. Hoffe, "Positivismus plus Moralismus: Zu Augustinus' eschatologischer Staatstheorie," in *Augustinus: De civitate dei*, ed. C. Horn (Berlin: Akademie Verlag, 1997) 259–87, here 266–74.

earlier, his *De doctrina christiana* or *On Christian Teaching*.[17] There (2,38–44) Augustine, while talking about various human sciences and pseudo-sciences, distinguishes between "human institutions" (giving the examples of astrology, the alphabet, the fine arts, and shorthand) and "divine institutions," by which he means "those elements of human tradition which men did not establish but discovered by investigation." As examples he gives history, medicine, and joinery. Why history? Augustine says that history "describes human institutions of the past." But, as the past cannot be undone, history discovers pre-existing data by investigation (the characteristic of a "divine institution") and these constitute "part of the history of time, whose creator and controller is God." Historical study leads to an understanding of God's part in human affairs. This coheres with what Augustine says in the *City of God* about the role of providence in Roman history.

In Book 18 of the *City of God* the events of non-biblical history are synchronized with biblical events. The chronographical tradition informs Augustine's method, and in particular the *Canons* of Eusebius, which had been translated and continued by Jerome.[18] Augustine's account is impressionistic and often polemical: he believes that earthly kingdoms are under the power of the apostate angels (16,17). But chronography, by its comparative nature, extends the scope of history. As Momigliano pointed out many years ago, Christian historiographers of the fourth century were universal historians.[19] Traces of this universalism are found in Augustine. The scope of history in the *City of God* extends from the creation in Book 11 to the final judgment and the end of history in the final book of the work. Within this panorama, earthly kingdoms have a limited life span. Augustine's schematic account focuses on what he believes to be the two great examples of empire, Assyria (which he confuses with Babylon) and Rome, one eastern and one western power. For him, all other kingdoms are "like appendages" (18,2) of these two, and Rome is a "second Babylon" (16,17; 18,22). The rise of Rome follows immediately upon the fall of the Assyrian empire. Thus, despite the apparently chaotic violence of

---

17. See the translation with notes by R. P. H. Green, *Augustine: On Christian Teaching* (Oxford: Clarendon Press, 1995), from which I have taken some of the phrases cited in the following.

18. See A. A. Mosshammer, *The Chronicle of Eusebius and Greek Chronographic Tradition* (Lewisburg: Bucknell University Press, 1979); J. N. D. Kelly, *Jerome* (London: Duckworth, 1975) 72–75.

19. A. Momigliano, "Pagan and Christian Historiography in the Fourth Century AD," in *The Conflict between Paganism and Christianity in the Fourth Century*, ed. A. Momigliano (Oxford: Clarendon Press, 1963) 79–99.

the succession of empires, there is a pattern to these historical events. The wish to synchronize biblical and secular history underpins, but also articulates and emphasizes, the succession theme. What Augustine says about the reason for Rome's power in Book 18 echoes what he has said in the earlier parts of the work:

> It was God's design to conquer the world through her [Rome], to unite the world into the single community of the Roman commonwealth and the Roman laws, and so to impose peace throughout its length and breadth. (18,22)

But this view of Rome's achievement, which Augustine found in the Augustan poets, and above all in Virgil, and which is prepared in Cicero's attitude to Roman rule, is now seen in the broader context of world history. Augustine never refers explicitly to the conversion of Constantine in the *City of God,* and, unlike Constantine's apologist Eusebius, does not interpret christianization as the fulfillment of Rome's historical destiny. But he nonetheless sees the christianization of emperors, who succeed those who persecuted Christians and who persecute pagans in their turn, as the most recent significant outcome of the historical process (18,50).

There is a stronger Ciceronian element in another aspect of Augustine's sense of history. Augustine's extrapolation of divine providence—the rational element—from Roman history is applied to his interpretation of biblical history itself. Cicero's account of Roman history places emphasis on the role of great individual statesmen, the ones who are immortalized in the finale of the *Republic.* When Cicero describes the true art of politics, he describes, in Book 5, the qualities found in an individual leader, the *rector rei publicae.* Augustine's account of biblical history also focuses on individuals, such as Abraham and Moses. When Moses is introduced as leader and lawgiver of the Jews in 18,11, we may observe that no place was found for this detail in the chronology of the earlier books, which dealt with biblical history and concentrated on Abraham, Isaac, Jacob, and David. Augustine could have found a place for a more detailed consideration of Moses in Books 16 and 17 had he so wished. But the synchronization scheme of Book 18 allows him to allude to Moses in that most traditional of functions of the statesman in Greek and Roman political theory, the lawgiver, and in the context of an account of the development of Greece and Rome in which he is remarkably silent about the role of lawgivers. There is no mention in Book 18 of Lycurgus or Solon, and no mention of Numa's lawgiving in the reference to him in 18,24. Yet Augustine knows of Solon's and Numa's laws and alludes to them in another context (2,16), where a different kind of polemical point is being made. These omissions emphasize the uniqueness of Moses in Augustine's account, but it is a uniqueness constructed in traditional terms that Cicero would have understood.

Conclusion: Cicero and Augustine

Cicero's history of the *res publica* climaxed in the model constitution of the early Republic. In a sense, Augustine's account of institutions climaxes in the establishment of the Christian church (*Civ.* 18,48–53). The church is not presented in Augustine as the equivalent of a political society. Yet it shares some of the undesirable characteristics of secular institutions. It is not free from dissension. Heretics and other dissidents are a source of scandal and dismay. Distress and anguish are thus features of church society even in a christianized empire, though it is some consolation that these test the patience and wisdom of Christians, as well as giving scope for persuasive teaching and the practice of discipline (18,51). Like history itself, the church has a wider scope:

> The church proceeds in this world, an alien, in these evil days, not merely since the time of the bodily presence of Christ and his apostles, but since Abel himself, the first righteous man, whom his impious brother killed, and from then on until the end of time, among the persecutions of the world and the consolations of God. (18,51)

These inevitable differences between Cicero and Augustine serve to remind us that we cannot hope to adapt Augustine's views on the origins and development of societies and on the potential of societies to achieve justice in such a way that they become Ciceronian in some uncomplicated respect. Augustine's view of political life is predominantly bleak, although one must always be sensitive to the rhetoric of the moment in his writings, and remember that, for everything negative that he says about political activity, he recognizes the importance of human institutions in preserving social order. There is a peace of the earthly city (*Civ.* 19). What I wish to argue is, not that there is an identity of views and approaches in Augustine and Cicero, but rather that Cicero is a fertile source for Augustine, in a subtle and sometimes implicit way. Cicero's historically founded approach is fruitful for Augustine, because Augustine's biblically founded approach is, in essence, historical. Cicero's insistence on the role of reason in political development helps Augustine articulate his concept of a rational divine providence in history. Cicero's emphasis on the moral qualities of citizens, and his relative indifference to constitutional forms—despite his gesture of approval for an interpretation of the Roman constitution as a mixed one (*Rep.* 1,45; 1,69)—provide Augustine with a theoretical focus on human morality as the basis of political order. The optimistic appropriation of Cicero by Augustine in the correspondence with Nectarius remains a formative factor in the argument of the *City of God*.

TERRARUM ORBI DOCUMENTUM:
AUGUSTINE, CAMILLUS, AND
LEARNING FROM HISTORY

Catherine Conybeare

The prefect said: From exactly the time when you began to blaspheme against the gods, and move away from worshipping them, the Roman world has been oppressed by multiple disasters.

Tranquillinus responded: That's not true. For if you peruse the ten-book digest in the style of Livy, you will find there that in one day fell twenty-three thousand young men of the Roman army—who placed incense for Jove. And you are not unaware of that occasion when the Gauls actually besieged the Capitol, and subjugated an entire Roman army with their farcical maneuvers. The Roman world suffered multiple famines and unspeakable plagues, multiple captivities and torrents of blood before men worshipped the one God. But since the invisible and true God began to be worshipped by believers, the Roman Empire rejoices in an access of peace.[1]

This pungent exchange comes from the largely mythical martyr-text, the *Vita Sebastiani*, which may be dated to around the sixth or seventh centuries. Even in a "popular" work like this, and even in one which falls so late, the account in Livy's history continues to be associated with the argument into which Augustine launches with such vigor in the *City of God, adversus eos qui*

My warm thanks to Ruth Morello, in conversation with whom I first came to realize the thematic sympathy between Augustine and Livy, and so to develop the thoughts in this essay.

1. *Vita Sebastiani* 12,42 = *Acta Sanctorum*, Ian. 2.265–78.

conditori eius deos suos praeferunt, "against those who prefer their own gods to the founder [of the City of God]" (*Civ.* 1, praef. 6–7),[2] and attribute the sack of Rome to the neglect of those gods.

But Augustine's position is far more subtle than that of the Tranquillinus portrayed by the anonymous author of the *Vita Sebastiani*. While he clearly knows Livy's account—in, I think, an undigested form[3]—he never succumbs to the temptation of putting the simplistic case that the Roman world has "rejoiced in an access of peace" ever since it started to worship God.[4] On the contrary: his reading of Livy, especially in the first pentad of the *City of God*, is risky and passionate. Rather than adopt a purely oppositional stance, he actually integrates a great deal of Livy's technique and themes, of his reading of history and of Rome, into these five books. Augustine and Livy, as I hope to show here, have very similar views of the exemplary value of history to its readers; Augustine is thoroughly aware of this similarity, and consciously plays on it. Especially, the figure of Camillus, who is central to Livy 5,[5] forms a telling example of how the concerns of the two writers intersect. Moreover, an examination of the reciprocities between Augustine and Livy illuminates the apparent *volte-face* of Augustine's *City of God* 5.[6] After his preponderant vilification of Rome in *City of God* 1–4, this is the book in which Augustine poses the vexed question: why did the Roman empire extend so far, and for so long?[7] and supplements his answer with a startling catalogue of exemplary figures from Roman history.

---

2. All references to the *City of God* are to the text corrected from the Teubner edition by B. Dombart and A. Kalb, in CCSL 47. Citations are by book, chapter and line number in that edition; translations are my own.

3. Following H. Hagendahl, *Augustine and the Latin Classics* (Göteborg: Acta Universitatis Gothoburgensis, 1967) 650–66, who argues that Augustine probably had both a text of Livy himself and some sort of digest of *exempla* available to him.

4. On Augustine's resistance to this idea, and his failure to influence the interpretative tradition, see F. Paschoud, *Roma Aeterna: Études sur le patriotisme romain dans l'Occident latin à l'époque des grandes invasions* (Rome: Institut Suisse de Rome, 1967) 234–75, esp. 273: "Augustin ne fut guère compris ni suivi."

5. References to Livy are to the Oxford Classical Text of *Ab Urbe condita libri 1-5*, ed. R. M. Ogilvie (Oxford: Clarendon Press, 1974). Citations are by book, chapter, and paragraph number; once again, translations are my own.

6. I use the text of Livy 5 and the figure of Camillus as diagnostics, to point up certain features of Augustine's account.

7. *Civ.* 1, praef. 5–8: *iam videamus, qua causa deus . . . Romanum imperium tam magnum tamque diuturnum esse voluerit.*

This strategy was particularly risky given Augustine's audience. We know, of course, that his audience included committed Christians: the letter to Firmus shows that, suggesting as disseminators of the completed text a couple of those *in populo christiano*, "among the Christian population," who are desirous of instruction.[8] But there was also another prospective audience: those who might, with the grace of God, be freed from superstition by the work. Barnes gives the example of Volusianus;[9] in the light of Neil McLynn's essay in this volume, we must also take seriously the "publishing coup" of the dedication to Marcellinus, and the prospective audience of his circle. Either way, these would be men who would have known their Livy well, and who, though interested in Christianity, essentially maintained the polytheistic Roman tradition, and saw no reason why they should devote themselves only to Christ. To such men, an apparent concession to a celebratory reading of Roman history would risk being construed as permission to make Christianity merely one religion among many—we may recall Symmachus's observation, "one cannot arrive at so great a mystery by just one route."[10] Yet at the same time, Augustine's enquiry (*Civ.* 5, praef. 5–8; 5,12,13) why God had deigned to help the Romans to enlarge their empire serves almost as a *captatio benevolentiae* to this second audience. Rome's greatness is acknowledged, the reasons for it to be explored: those who continued to feel the greatness of Rome must have been intrigued. And Augustine, in embarking upon the discussion, calls attention to the common ground between himself and these men: both he and they had received—indeed, he had excelled in—a rhetorical education that celebrated and perpetuated the glorious *res Romana*.

Augustine's project is far from simple. For in the first five books of the *City of God* he essays the remarkable task of teaching back to the Romans their own history—in a new version. He challenges his audience in a rare apostrophe at the end of Book 1: *scitote, qui ista nescitis et qui vos scire dissimulatis, advertite*, "be aware, you people who don't know anything and you who are pretending you don't know; pay attention" (1,32,1–2). His recapitulation at the beginning of Book 4 claims that his audience are *imperiti*, "ignorant people"

---

8. The letter *Ad Firmum* is conveniently printed at iii–iv of the CCSL edition (cited above, n. 2); the quoted phrase is at line 30.

9. T. D. Barnes, "Aspects of the Background of the *City of God*," *University of Ottawa Quarterly* 52 (1982): 64–80, esp. 72f (repr. in his *From Eusebius to Augustine* [Aldershot: Variorum, 1994] no. XXIV).

10. *Relatio* 3,10: *uno itinere non potest perveniri ad tam grande secretum*. The context, of course, is the Altar of Victory stand-off with Ambrose.

(4,1,8), who do not know their history and so think that the happenings of their own times are novelties, confirmed in their erroneous opinion by those who know it to be false with "dissimulation of their knowledge" (4,1,11–12). But in fact, Augustine's case has been constructed *non ex nostra coniectura . . . sed partim ex recenti memoria . . . partim ex litteris eorum,* "not from my own guesswork, but partly from recent memory and partly from their own literature" (4,1,22–24);[11] and he goes on to prove his reliance on *litteris eorum* with a hilarious parody of the digressions of annalistic historiography: *si commemorare voluissem et exaggerare illa mala . . . quando finessem?* "if I had wanted to record and pile up those evils" (there follow 17 lines of evils parenthetically "piled up") ". . . when would I finish?" (4,2,16–35).

To be more precise, Augustine creates—conspiratorially, with one eye upon his truly learned audience—a fictional audience within the text of *City of God,* apparently for the rhetorical purpose of toying with them, sometimes allowing them to be included among the erudite, the *periti,* those in the know—and sometimes not. So he can refer to his argument *contra imperitos,* and immediately add the collusive aside, *nam qui eorum studiis liberalibus instituti amant historiam, facillime ista noverunt,* "for those who are educated in liberal learning and have a love for history know that sort of thing very easily" (2,34–35). Elsewhere, Augustine concedes that there are *intellegentiores gravioresque Romani,* "rather more intelligent and serious-minded Romans" (4,2,45–46), but they do not want to rock the boat of religious convention. The rhetorical maneuver is to invite the members of his (actual) learned audience to participate in his argument, and to feel themselves comfortably excepted when Augustine inveighs against those who have no knowledge of history, or who pretend not to, *dissimulatores suae scientiae* (5,22,30).

Extending his complicity with his learned audience, Augustine emphasizes particularly the written historical tradition of Rome. Note that the Romans *hodie . . . LITTERIS ET HISTORIA gloriosi sunt paene in omnibus gentibus,* "are today renowned *in literature and history* among almost all peoples" (5, 15,16–18). Here Augustine is simultaneously evoking and silencing the traditional *fabulae/historia* dichotomy: instead of adverting to both oral and written historical traditions, he replaces *fabulae* with *litteris* to celebrate a purely written heritage.[12] A later phrase, in the context of teaching the *ignari* and

---

11. The peroration to *Civ.* 4 picks up this contrast: Augustine's case may be proved *de codicibus eorum,* not just by reading *in nostris* (4,34,31–33). Notably, the category of *recens memoria* is omitted: see below on Augustine's emphasis on *written* tradition.

dissimulatores their own history, is the more revealing for its throwaway nature: *recolant . . . qui LEGERANT,* says Augustine: "those who have *read* should remember" (5,22,36). And at *Civ.* 5,18,127–30, he points out that the examples *in litteris eorum* [i.e., *Romanorum*] would not be so widely known without the extent of their empire—coming close to the claim that the Romans' empire stretched so far *in order that* their literature should be more fully disseminated!

All is not quite so cosy and conspiratorial as it seems, however. For Augustine uses the cultural expectations and literary training he shares with the classically educated members of his audience to destabilize their perceptions of their own history and environment, and to substitute a Christian interpretation of events. Augustine compares his writing in the *City of God*—both its content and its manner—directly with Roman historiographical tradition: *neque enim gravius vel graviora dicimus auctoribus eorum—ET STILO ET OTIO multum impares,* "for I am saying nothing more serious, or more seriously, than their writers do—even though I am far from their equal in prose style or leisured life" (3,17,23–24); and he displays a distinctive self-consciousness about the burden of recording *in writing* the horror of history (3,20,13). In fact, he simultaneously embraces and eschews Roman historiographical tradition, expressing a fear of becoming *nihil aliud quam scriptores . . . historiae,* "merely a writer of history" (3,18,11–12).

Augustine is consciously in dialogue with Roman historiography for the delectation of a cultivated, complicit audience; but, typically, he is shaping it to his own ends. He achieves the destabilization of his audience's perceptions most obviously in his explicitly signposted rereadings of Cicero and Sallust in his first five books; but still more effectively destabilizing, not least because more surreptitious, is his implicit dialogue in these books with Livy.

Livy is mentioned by name only twice (at 2,24,4 and 3,7,42); but his influence is subtly pervasive. The dialogue with Livy is first signaled at the very beginning of the *City of God: tot bella gesta conscripta sunt vel ante conditam Romam vel ab eius exortu et imperio,* "so many wars have been recorded, whether before the foundation of Rome, or from its origin and rule" (1,2,1–2). The collocation of *ante conditam Romam* and *ab eius exortu,* coupled with the exhortation to Augustine's Roman audience to reread their history (*legant et proferant,* 1,2,2), could only serve to evoke the title of Livy's monumental

---

12. It is beyond doubt that Augustine was familiar with the *fabulae/historia* convention, for he engages with it explicitly at, e.g., *Civ.* 2,8. For the "traditional" nature of the dichotomy, see, e.g., Livy, praef. 6 (*poeticis fabulis* contrasted with *incorruptis rerum gestarum monumentis*).

work, *Ab Urbe condita* (the *urbs* referred to being, of course, Rome).[13] The subsequent reference to *capta civitas* (1,2,3) also recalls *Troia capta* at the beginning of Livy 1—*urbs capta* is the Livian phrase,[14] but Augustine resolutely represses *urbs* in favour of *civitas*.[15] Again, the phrase *tot bella gesta* may well echo the beginning of Livy 2, *res pace belloque gestas*: such resonances between significant prefatory material would not be surprising, as Augustine shares with Livy an acute numerological awareness, and hence a sense of the numbering and pacing of his books. *Quinque superioribus libris satis mihi adversus eos videor disputasse*, "in the five earlier books, I think I have debated sufficiently against those people," claims Augustine at the beginning of the sixth book of the *City of God*; Livy, at the same position in his *immensum opus*, says that the events from the founding of Rome *quinque libris exposui*, "I have expounded in five books."[16] The respective choices of verb are significant: Livy's *exposui* denotes a more spacious and leisured laying out of evidence and traditions; Augustine's *videor disputasse*, a pugnacious and partisan approach marked by insistent authorial interaction with audience (*videor*).[17] Truly, Augustine and Livy are *et stilo et otio multum impares*; but, as we shall see, they have much in common as well.

It will have been no coincidence that the numerologically aware Augustine should have chosen that the closing of the first pentad of his *magnum opus et arduum* should resonate with the *res . . . immensi operis* of Livy's fifth book, in which the story of Camillus's victory at Veii and liberation of Rome from the Gauls is told.[18] Indeed, Augustine clearly has Livy 5 in mind throughout

---

13. A similar association occurs in *Civ.* 3, when Augustine's systematic retelling of Roman history is flagged by further lexical references to Livy: note especially the use of the phrase *ab Urbe condita* at *Civ.* 3,9,27.

14. See, for example, the preface to Livy 6, with the claim to have expounded the events *ab condita URBE Roma ad CAPTAM eandem.*

15. On the *urbs capta* theme in Livy, see, e.g., C. S. Kraus, "'No Second Troy': Topoi and Refoundation in Livy, Book V," *Transactions of the American Philological Association* 124 (1994): 267–89. Augustine restricts his use of *urbs* in *Civ.* 1–5 to specific references to Rome. An apposite question from Tim Cornell prompted me to reflect on this distinction.

16. *Civ.* 6,1,1–2; Livy 6,1,1; *immensum opus* adapted from Livy, praef. 4: *res . . . immensi operis.* For a similar numerical staging-post, see *Civ.* 10,32,175: *in decem istis libris*; for Augustine's awareness of the importance of the grouping of his books, see *Ad Firmum*, lines 6–22. Note that the first pentad is suggested as a self-contained volume.

17. *Thesaurus Linguae Latinae* 5.1, col. 1449, cites Augustine's use of *disputare* here as equivalent to *litigare, disceptare.*

18. Descriptions from the prefaces of the respective works: *Civ.* 1, praef. 8; Livy, praef. 4.

his first pentad, repeatedly introducing Camillus, with a pocket biography, into lists of exemplary Roman figures.[19] In Livy, Marcus Furius Camillus is given a formal introduction in the middle of Book 5 as *fatalis dux ad excidium illius urbis servandaeque patriae*, "the general destined by fate[20] to destroy that city [Veii] and save his home" (Livy 5,19,2). It is surely no coincidence that *City of God* 5 begins with a discussion of the notion of a *causa fortuita* or *fatalis*. The immediate purpose is to show that the greatness of the Roman empire was not bestowed by chance; accordingly, all events are traced back to the plan of God, who bestows *omnes potestates*—though not *omnium voluntates* (*Civ.* 5,8,9–10). But the implicit repercussions for Augustine's reading of Livy are twofold. First, having utterly demolished the concept of *astralia fata*— astrological determinism—Augustine relegitimates *fatum* with the help of a quotation from Seneca: if it simply means *omnium conexio seriesque causarum*, "the connexion and sequence of causes of everything," which may be attributed to God, there is nothing to quarrel about.[21] This is significant for our purposes because the idea of *fatum* or *fortuna*, and how it pertains to both persons and places, is crucial to Livy 5. Second, Augustine is at pains to validate the free will of the individual:[22] the discussion clearly has a bearing on his sense of the place of the individual in history, and the individual's potential effect on the course of history;[23] and it establishes the framework for the individual examples of Roman greatness—including, of course, Camillus— which Augustine employs later in the book.

There is an obvious parallel of historical themes between the fifth book of Livy and the *City of God* generally, for it is in Livy 5 that the tale is told of the Gauls' destruction of Rome—first, in a magnificent *mise-en-scène*, their slaughter of the aged Roman senators as they sit in their courtyards on their ivory thrones; then the looting and burning of the city, as the Roman survivors look down in horror from their fortress on the Capitol. The similarity with the circumstances of

---

19. See *Civ.* 2,17,31–41; 3,17,73–76; and 4,7,16–19, in which Camillus is, memorably, *oblitus iniuriae, memor patriae*.

20. *Fatalis dux* is an extremely unusual collocation in surviving Livy: he uses it elsewhere only of Scipio (Livy 22,53,6; 30,28,11).

21. Quotation from *Civ.* 5,8,2–3 (cases adapted); the passage from Seneca is at *Civ.* 5,8,14–18.

22. See *Civ.* 5,9,95–102: *NON EST AUTEM CONSEQUENS, ut, si deo certus est omnium ordo causarum, ideo nihil sit in nostrae voluntatis arbitrio* and so on.

23. On *voluntas* as a source of individuation, see, e.g., S. MacCormack *The Shadows of Poetry: Vergil in the Mind of Augustine* (Berkeley & Los Angeles: University of California Press, 1998) 125.

composition of the early books of *City of God* does not need laboring: Augustine does not hesitate to compare the Gallic sack of Rome in the time of Camillus directly with the Gothic sack in his own time—very much to the credit of the Goths![24] However, it does speak to the complex slippage between the actual audience and the fictitious one created by Augustine within the text of the *City of God*. Augustine elides his audience with the Romans of old, as inheritors of both good and bad Roman tradition.[25] Like the Romans of Livy 5, the actual audience has looked on helplessly from afar at the destruction of its city—a city that, far more than being simply a physical space, is also a persistent ideal.[26] But slyly, he reminds his audience of their embarrassing situation: *Roma capta*, they are now refugees at Carthage, their enemy of many centuries' standing. The crucial concerns of Livy 5 are the questions: what is Rome, the *patria* which is to be defended? what are the qualities of the old Rome worth hanging on to? Augustine thus implicitly asks his audience: where, and what, is the ideal *patria* now? is there anything of Rome left in it?

Livy 5 relates a complicated, messy, ambivalent saga of class struggle and inglorious warfare (even Veii, the supposedly crowning victory, falls *operibus . . . non vi*, "to stratagems, not might" [Livy 5,22,8]); but it is also a book in which the importance of a right attitude to the gods is repeatedly emphasized, and, above all, in which the very nature of Rome is under constant discussion. After the prosperous rival city of Veii has fallen to Camillus and his troops, the tribunes of the plebs propose a bill for repatriation there: Veii, both in its situation and in the magnificence of its buildings, is far superior to Rome (Livy 5,24,6). Camillus rejects the measure in the strongest possible terms—"it is *nefas*, a religious crime, to think of inhabiting a city deserted and abandoned by the immortal gods" (Livy 5,30,3)—and the senate, *concitati* ("thoroughly upset"), begs its tribe members with tears not to desert the city for which they and their forebears had fought.[27] On this occasion, the senate is successful; but the episode turns out merely to be the dress rehearsal for the real confrontation, the first element in a doublet. At the end of Livy 5, after Rome has been almost

---

24. Direct comparison: *Civ.* 3,29,6–13; a glancing reference to the Gallic sack at 2,22,32–33.

25. Contrast, for example, *Civ.* 1,33,1: *o mentes amentes!* subject to the very corruption which Scipio feared for *you*; and the magnificent peroration addressed to the *indoles Romana laudabilis*, at *Civ.* 2,29.

26. On this phenomenon, see C. Edwards, *Writing Rome: Textual Approaches to the City* (Cambridge: Cambridge University Press, 1996).

27. This is the context of *non vi . . . sed precibus*: perhaps parallelled in *Civ.* 5,26,21–22, when weapons in battle are turned back *magis orando quam feriendo*.

completely destroyed by the Gauls, and then rescued by Camillus, in an incredible *coup de théâtre,* from the ignominy of being sold, the question of repatriation to Veii arises again. Once again, it falls to Camillus to expound the nature of Rome in a climactic speech (Livy 5,51–54)—it would be *nefas* for him to stand back. His first theme is the gods—*invenietis omnia prospera evenisse sequentibus deos, adversa spernentibus,* "you will find that everything has turned out well for those following the gods, and badly for those who spurn them" (Livy 5,51,5). He avers, in a magnificent tricolon, that Rome is the proper, the only, place for its gods:

> *Urbem auspicato inauguratoque conditam habemus; nullus locus in ea non religionum deorumque est plenus; sacrificiis sollemnibus non dies magis stati quam loca sunt in quibus fiant.* (Livy 5,52,2)

> We have[28] a city founded with the proper auspices and auguries; nowhere in it is not replete with religious associations and with gods; the days for ritual offerings are no more firmly established than the places in which they should be performed.

Camillus moves on to the issue of the priests, and their association with particular places and rituals; and after adumbrating a shaming scenario in which the Gauls occupy a hypothetically abandoned Rome, he reaches his peroration. *Caritas nobis patriae* "our attachment to our homeland" (Livy 5,54,2) should reside in the earth, the land, the position of the city itself—not *in superficie tignisque,* in stone (indeed, simply stone cladding—the choice of word marking the insubstantiality of the substantial) and timber. This thought should move the Quirites to stay at Rome, not make them homesick when they are gone (Livy 5,54,3).[29]

All through Livy 5, there runs a covert awareness of the logic of Roman history: that one city must be destroyed for another to be founded. When the motion is proposed to transpose the inhabitants of Rome wholesale to the conquered Veii, the burden of persuasion lies with Camillus to convince the plebs that the situation is not a repetition of this perceived topos.[30] Augustine, however, gleefully exploits the theme: Rome has been destroyed to seal the superiority of the city of God. And yet he also recognizes the quasi-religious devotion to

---

28. Note the double sense of *habemus*: we both possess and inhabit this city.

29. Revealingly, in Sermon 81,9, which Augustine preached in the autumn immediately after the sack of Rome (Perler's dating), he recalls the words of Camillus: the city consists not merely in stone and timber—*non de lapidibus et lignis*—but in its people and their religious practices (PL 38.505).

30. On this topos, see Kraus (cited above, n. 15).

Rome, epitomized in the emotional appeal of *patres* to *plebs*, "pointing out the Capitol, the temple of Vesta, and the other surrounding temples of the gods . . . and amid their pleas, much mention was made of the gods" (Livy 5,30,5, and 7).[31]

This devotion Augustine seeks to turn toward the *civitas dei*, the *patria superna*. More precisely, he wants to keep the notion of religious obligation and participation in the city to which Camillus and the *patres* appeal, but to detach it from physical location. Camillus states quite clearly, in his climactic speech, that divine presence is efficacious *because of* physical location. It is crucial to continue to perform religious rituals in the same place; the *fortuna loci* is irremovable:

> *quae, malum, ratio est expertis <talia> alia experiri, cum iam ut virtus vestra transire alio possit, fortuna certe loci huius transferri non possit? Hic Capitolium est . . . ; hic Vestae ignes, hic ancilia caelo demissa, hic omnes propitii MANENTIBUS VOBIS di.* (Livy 5,54,6–7)

> What the devil is your reason for trying out something new when you already have experience here? when, even if your courage might travel elsewhere, the propitious place certainly could not be moved? Here is the Capitol . . . ; here are the fires of Vesta, here the sacred shields sent down from heaven; *as long as you stay here*, all the gods will favour you.

Augustine completely inverts Camillus's claim—and it is an essential part of his project in the *City of God* to do so. Physical location is only efficacious because of divine presence. This is particularly relevant to the issue of asylum:[32] the Goths, in their recent sack of Rome, gave to their opponents a sanctuary in the basilicas which the pagan gods themselves could neither bestow nor expect in their own temples (1,4,14–26). This irony underpins Augustine's ongoing mockery of the traveling gods of Rome—their removal successively, under incriminating circumstances, from Troy, Lavinium, and Alba Longa. Alba was destroyed—*more suo . . . fortasse migraverant*, "perhaps the gods had moved on, as is their custom." Thus they come to take care of *quarta Roma*, "the *fourth* Rome" (3,14,84–85; 88). And, Augustine enquires, *haec numinum turba ubi erat, cum longe antequam mores corrumperentur antiqui a Gallis Roma capta et incensa est?* "where was this crowd of divinities, when, long before the old ways were corrupted, Rome was captured and burnt by the Gauls?" (2,22,31–33)—an example taken, of course, from Livy 5.

---

31. This recognition seems to me one of personal engagement, as well as a rhetorical *captatio* for his audience: this places me at odds with Paschoud (n. 4 above).

32. On which see also the essay by Philippe Bruggisser in this volume.

Livy, in fact, does not present the speech of Camillus as decisive, but closes his book with a touch of lifelike bathos. A chance omen halts the senatorial debate and decides the senate against the bill; and the rebuilding of Rome ensues, corrupt and chaotic: Livy seems to be implying that some of the old values of Rome have been dislodged, unsettled by the upheavals recounted in the book, even though the Romans have not physically moved away from the city.[33] However, it is from this speech that my title comes, for its whole tenor expresses the sense of the moral dimension of history that Augustine so clearly shared. *Igitur victi captique ac redempti tantum poenarum dis hominibusque dedimus ut terrarum orbi documento essemus*, "And so we have been conquered, captured, bought; we have been so punished by gods and men as to become a lesson to the whole world" (Livy 5,51,8).

There is another echo of Camillus's speech in Augustine that indicates the similarity of the two authors' concerns. Augustine points out that when Rome was overrun (in his own time, that is), it was by those who gave asylum *ad loca sancta*, "at the holy places." The moral is that *vera religio* should never be deserted *propter praesentes necessitates*, "because of immediate need (*Civ.* 5,23,33 and 5,23,42–43). Camillus draws precisely the same moral, when he observes (Livy 5,51,8–9), *adversae res admonuerunt religionum . . . deorum cultum deserti ab dis hominibusque . . . non intermisimus*, "adverse circumstances reminded us of our religious obligations; when we were deserted by gods and men, we did not neglect to worship the gods."[34] Though they arrive at their conclusion by different routes (as shown in the discussion of asylum above), its content, and its moral force, are the same.

This moral dimension is, for both Augustine and Livy, inherent in both the writing and the reading of history. Each feels himself under an obligation both to provide the *documentum* and to lead his readers to interpret it correctly. For Augustine and Livy, the interpretation of history is a moral endeavor, with profound repercussions upon one's present choices, and this binds together writer and reader. Both are obliged, ideally, to translate their reading of the *documenta* into wise moral choice. Moles, in his exposition of Livy's Preface,

---

33. Which, of course, reinforces the notion of Rome as more ideal than place. Kraus (n. 15) comments, "This is a very strange ending indeed" (285); she, however, explains it as "covertly recalling the enemy occupation" (287).

34. Compare also the gesture of L. Albinius, *de plebe homo*, who takes the Vestal virgins onto his cart when fleeing from the Gauls at Rome, acting *salvo ETIAM TUM discrimine divinarum humanarumque rerum* (Livy 5,40,10).

shows how Livy first plays on this identity of interest, blurring the divisions between writer and reader, then disassembles the identification, not trusting that his fickle, shallow audience will bother with the *Ab Urbe condita* history that he is undertaking.[35] The effect is to suggest the depth of moral commitment it will take to read, and to read *with*, his work. Augustine, meanwhile, from the first page of his preface leaves us no doubt as to his moral commitment: he needs God's strength to help him in the immense task of defending the *gloriosissimam civitatem dei*, the "most glorious city of God," against its enemies.[36]

Livy offers a clear directive about the purpose of history in his Preface: *hoc illud est praecipue in cognitione rerum salubre ac frugiferum, omnis te exempli documenta in inlustri posita monumento intueri*, "in enquiring about events, this is especially healthy and fruitful, for you to gaze upon the lessons of every example, which are erected in an illustrious memorial" (Livy, praef. 10). Augustine is more oblique: his primary purpose, after all, is theological refutation, not the writing of history. But there is a revealing passage in Book 5 of *De civitate dei* on how history is to be read. Although the New Testament revealed what was veiled in the Old, the Jews still put Christ to death, and so *rectissime [Romanorum] gloriae donati sunt*, "they were *absolutely rightly* handed over for the glory of the Romans" (5,18,142–43, 146–47). That chilling adverb *rectissime* illustrates, not only the importance of reading history, but the absolute necessity for a conscious effort to integrate history into the present. The Jews are vilified for their failure to read history correctly, and for spurning the heavenly glory that was offered to them; the Romans, without the advantage of revelation, have proved capable of assigning an appropriate value to theirs, and have at least striven for earthly glory.

Camillus—perhaps I should write "Camillus"—as created by Livy is powerfully aware of his status as literary and lived *documentum*. And as Livy's Camillus is aware of the exemplary status in history of himself and the Roman people, so Augustine likewise holds up the Roman Empire as an *exemplum* for the *cives* of the eternal city, to show by comparison how much it should be loved; *si tantum a suis civibus terrena dilecta est propter hominum gloriam*, "if the earthly city is loved so much by its own citizens for human glory" (*Civ.* 5,16,15–16).

---

35. J. Moles, "Livy's Preface," *Proceedings of the Cambridge Philological Society* 39 (1993): 141–68.

36. *Civ.* 1, praef. 8–9: *deus adiutor noster est*; *Civ.* 1, praef. 12: the transcendent power of *divina gratia donata celsitudo*.

Augustine's Camillus is clearly to be counted among the few whose *virtus* is praised by Cato (*Civ.* 5,12,170–71); we may recall the haughty claim of Livy's Camillus to have conquered the Veians *Romanis artibus, virtute opere armis*, "with Roman skills, strength, tactics, weapons" (Livy, 5,27,4). Later in Livy's account, Camillus again appropriates this *ars*: *hac arte in patria steti et invictus bello, in pace ab ingratis civibus pulsus sum*, "with this skill I stood at home unbeaten in war, while in peacetime I was driven out by the ungrateful citizens" (Livy, 5,44,2). The key to Camillus's character for Augustine is his response to the legendary ingratitude of his compatriots: *Romam . . . sensit ingratam, quam tamen postea OBLITUS INIURIAE, MEMOR PATRIAE a Gallis iterum liberavit*, "he felt Rome ungrateful, and yet later freed her once again, now from the Gauls, *forgetting his insult and mindful of his patria*" (*Civ.* 4,7,18–19).[37]

The importance of responsibility toward the patria resonates through the words of Livy's Camillus. At Ardea, Camillus is found *maestior ibi fortuna publica quam sua*, "more sorrowful about the public misfortune than his own" (Livy 5,43,6); at Rome, he argues for public effort to rebuild the city: "shall we refuse, in this public conflagration, to do what each of us would individually do if our own houses burnt down?" (Livy 5,53,9). Both Augustine and Livy consider that the index of *virtus* is the flourishing of the public good— the common wealth in its most literal sense—alongside *tenues res privatae*, "slender private means" (*Civ.* 5,12,171). The notion of participation in a public good is precisely one of the things Augustine wishes to recommend and praise—though his public good is of course the celestial one.[38] Participation in the celestial *patria* is linked inextricably with the obligation to speak out— and to record history:

> *Quod tamen nostra memoria recentissimo tempore Deus mirabiliter et misericorditer fecit . . . ; quod a nobis si tacebitur, similiter erimus ingrati.* (*Civ.* 5,23,1–5)

---

37. In case it seems that I am overemphasizing the role of a figure who does not, after all, play that large a part in the *City of God*, I would suggest that we may guess at Augustine's sympathy for Camillus from what he suppresses. There is no mention of Camillus's triumphal entry to Rome after his victory at Veii, in *curro equis albis iuncto*, "a chariot hitched up to white horses"—a gesture *clarior quam gratior*, "more conspicuous than welcome" (Livy 5,23,5–6). Moreover, there is no mention of the ignominious episode with which Camillus launches the defence of his *patria*, a nocturnal massacre of the Gauls (Livy 5,45).

38. The discussion in *Civ.* 10 shows that participation in God is crucial to Augustine's notion of citizenship in the *City of God*.

What merciful miracles God has performed in the most recent time, within our own memory . . . ; if we are going to be silent about them, we shall be just as ungrateful.

We *are*, says Augustine, the *patria ingrata*—the true inheritors of Camillus's ungrateful Romans—unless we publish our Christian faith.

But once again, all is not quite as it seems. Augustine casts doubt on the Roman notion of *virtus* early in the text;[39] and in *Civ.* 5, he similarly undertakes to interrogate the concept of *gloria*. We should not forget that *gloriosissimam* is the first word of the *City of God,* qualifying, of course, the *civitas* itself: clearly Augustine will wish to retain the word in some senses. And when Augustine introduces the theme of *veteres . . . primique Romani* (in an account deriving explicitly from *historia*[40]), he uses a line from Sallust, *gloriam ingentem, divitias honestas volebant*, "they aimed for immense glory and honourable wealth,"[41] and goes on to gloss:

> *hanc* [this must refer back to the *gloria*] *ardentissime dilexerunt, propter hanc vivere voluerunt, pro hac emori non dubitaverunt . . . . Ipsam denique patriam suam, quoniam servire videbatur inglorium, dominari vero atque imperare gloriosum, prius omni studio liberam, deinde dominam esse concupiverunt.* (*Civ.* 5,12,16–18, 19–21)

> This glory they loved most ardently, they wished to live because of it and did not hesitate to die for it . . . .[42] In fact, since it seemed inglorious for their own *patria* to be enslaved, but glorious to dominate and command, they zealously desired at first that it should be free, then that it should rule.

The use and context of *gloriosus* here again recalls Camillus's climactic speech:[43] migration to Veii with victory as the cause would at least be *gloriosa nobis ac posteris nostris,* "glorious for us and our descendants"; after the destruction of Rome, *haec migratio nobis misera ac turpis, Gallis gloriosa est,* "this removal is wretched and disgraceful for us, and glorious for the Gauls" (Livy 5,53,4). Augustine, as so often, is not systematic in his use of words: much of his

---

39. See *Civ.* 1,15,44–48, where he observes that a notion of *virtus* is needed which may be applied equally to a person and a *civitas* to make them *beatus/a.*

40. *Civ.* 5,12,11–13; *veteres . . . primique Romani, quantum eorum docet et commendat historia.*

41. Sallust, *Catiline* 7,6; *Civ.* 5,12,16.

42. This is strongly reminiscent of Horace, *Odes* 3,9,24: *tecum vivere amem, tecum obeam libens.* If the echo is intentional, it reinforces Augustine's point about the Romans' "ardent love" of glory by transferring a topos from love poetry into historical writing.

43. Though of course Virgil, *Aen.* 6,853 is close behind this passage as well.

argument in Book 5 depends upon a romanized interpretation of *gloria*, a truly glorious *gloria*, as it were.[44]

However, he also provides an exegesis of a far more problematic *gloria*, in which Roman assumptions about the glorious are carefully dismantled using a combination of historical knowledge with a cultural relativism that decentralizes a conventionally Roman viewpoint. What if, Augustine suggests, the Romans' appropriation of other nations had been peaceful? The outcome would in fact have been better; *sed nulla esset gloria triumphantium*, "but there would have been no glory for the conquerors" (*Civ.* 5,17,7–8). And, he goes on to observe—in direct contradiction of Roman convention—*praeter illum gloriae humanae inanissimum fastum*, "beyond that utterly empty arrogance of human glory," what is the difference between conquerors and conquered? *Gloria*, after all, is *au fond* nothing but boasting: *tolle iactantiam, et omnes homines quid sunt nisi homines?* "take away boasting, and what is anyone but just a human?" (*Civ.* 5,17,28). It is this *gloria* that is glossed elsewhere in the book as *ventosa* and *inanis*.[45]

Both Livy and Augustine make it clear from the very prefaces of their works that *gloria* is the stuff of history—but, at the same time, it is dependent upon the interpretation of history. Neither thinks that there is any point in recording the deeds of *gloria* if you do not learn from them. The difference between the two interpretations lies in the context in which *gloria* is presented, and in what you can expect to learn from it. For Augustine takes Livy's earthly *gloria*, the *gloria* bestowed by men—still a resonant notion for Augustine, as for many other educated Romans—and counterposes it with *gloria superna*. *Gloria*, even if earned on earth, should look toward heavenly glory—or should be of the type that would if heavenly glory were available: this is the oblique move with which Augustine appropriates the best of Roman tradition for Christianity. Note the description of Camillus in Book 5 of the *City of God*: he liberated his *patriam ingratam*, his ungrateful home, from the Gauls, *quia non habebat potiorem, ubi posset vivere Gloriosius*, "because he did not have a better one, where he could live *more gloriously*" (*Civ.* 5,18,39–40). And remember the terrible example of the Jews, who rejected the true *gloria* offered to them, and so were handed over for the *gloria* of the Romans (*Civ.* 5,18,146–150).

---

44. So, for example, in *Civ.* 5,19, where he distinguishes between the desire for *humana gloria* and that for *dominatio*: the former may be felt rightly, and to good effect—*qui autem gloriae contemptor dominationis est avidus, bestias superat* (*Civ.* 5,19,31–32).

45. *Civ.* 5,20,31; 5,24,24.

Camillus is, for Augustine, emblematic as a mediator between the material and the ideal Rome—which is, of course, very much the same mediation as Augustine himself is trying to effect. They both, in their different ways, effect this mediation precisely through their response to the history of Rome. And Augustine's concession to his educated pagan readers has turned out to be only cosmetic: their cultural values have indeed been destabilized by insistent interrogation and revision, under cover of an appeal to the lessons of *historia*. Augustine's project has been entirely to change the terms of historical endeavor, or rather, not so much to change as to transcend them: to integrate a celebratory reading of Rome into a vision of triumphant Christianity. As so often, Augustine has the best of all worlds: he manages to catch the traditionalists unawares, to deliver a swift reprimand to any complacent Christians in his audience, and at the same time to legitimate his own lingering admiration for the idealized notion of Rome.

City of the Outcast and City of the Elect: The Romulean Asylum in Augustine's *City of God* and Servius's *Commentaries on Virgil*

Philippe Bruggisser

In memory of Johannes Straub
(18.10.1912 — 29.1.1996)

Having led the Romans to the banks of light, Romulus dwelt on in the conscience of his offspring. Fascination or repulsion, the reactions inspired by the person of the founder are indissociable, in the last days of the Empire, from the intellectual debate surrounding the perception and representation of Rome's past. Indeed, this question may be said to lie at the very heart of the late antique encounter between Christian and "pagan" sensibilities.

Adopting objections already voiced within Roman society or previously raised against Rome by its subject peoples, Christians refused to honor a city built on sacrilegious practices. In their view, the founder was the son of a *lupa*, a prostitute. He was a fratricide, having killed his twin brother Remus. He had offered asylum to depraved persons (i.e., to those who had formed the original population of Rome). He had violated the sacred laws of hospitality by organizing the rape of the Sabine women; the war with the Sabines was an

I wish to express my gratitude to Mme. Anna Bugnon and Dr. Mark Vessey for their help in establishing the English version of this essay, and to Mme. Nicole Papaux for typing the manuscript. My participation in the Vancouver symposium was made possible by the generous support of the Rectorate and the Seminars in Ancient History and Classical Philology of the University of Fribourg.

iniustum bellum, waged against enemies whom the Romans had insulted. As for the divinization of Romulus, it was nothing but a sham. For their part, pagan traditionalists endeavored to legitimate the national past against such attacks. The deeds of the founder of the *Urbs* constituted a point of special sensitivity. In relating the history of the City, pagan intellectuals defended the conditions of its birth and, in the process, rehabilitated the image of the *conditor*. Thus, at the end of Roman history, the debate on Rome's origins was more violent than ever. A whole society, wracked by a profound crisis of identity, was trying to define or redefine its value system, by approving or opposing certain founding myths. Following in the wake of other writers, Augustine duly denounced all that was dishonorable in the deeds of the *conditor*, and did his utmost to destroy the flattering image of Romulus that persisted in the minds of the pagans.

This essay will address the treatment of one of the most significant episodes in the Romulean story: the establishment of an asylum (or "safe haven") in the emergent city. The asylum shapes the destiny of the city, in virtue of the spirit that motivated its creation and the nature of the population that took refuge there. Concerned as he was to demonstrate that the eternal city has its seeds in the temporal one, Augustine could hardly fail to reckon with this aspect of Rome's genesis. Augustine's vision will be contrasted with that of his contemporary, the grammarian Servius, who, as commentator on Virgil and professional interpreter of the past, proceeded from a pagan vision and was subject to other criteria of judgment.

The *Manes* of Romulus in the Late Empire

Romulus and the Rulers of the Late Empire

In the Roman world, from the dawn of the City to the waning of the Empire, rulers and aspirants to power continually associated themselves, or were associated by others, with the person and memory of Rome's founder.[1] It is

---

1. On the association of men of power with the figure of Romulus down to the end of Antiquity, cf. Ph. Bruggisser, *Romulus Seruianus: La légende de Romulus dans les Commentaires à Virgile de Servius. Mythographie et idéologie à l'époque de la dynastie théodosienne* (Bonn: R. Habelt, 1987) 10–20, 259–261, and the articles cited at nn. 2 and 22 below. For other media, see C. Dulière, *Lupa Romana: Recherches d'iconographie et essai d'interprétation*, 2 vols. (Rome: Institut Historique Belge de Rome, 1979).

enough here to observe the application of this principle from the post-Severan period down to the beginning of the fifth century.[2]

In the third century, after the Severans, sovereigns and usurpers struck coins with the she-wolf's image on them.[3] Aurelian's radiance was such that it produced an interregnum that made him comparable to Romulus.[4] Diocletian abstained from these comparisons but on a bronze medallion of Maximian we find the she-wolf motif on the shield held by the emperor's bust.[5] Galerius considered himself to be of the lineage of Mars and claimed to be another Romulus; to honor his mother, Romula, he gave the name of Romulianum to his own birthplace in Dacia.[6]

Maxentius venerated Romulus's memory, as can be seen from coin issues of his reign.[7] At Rome the emperor undertook a huge program of construction in the area of the Forum, culminating in the enormous basilica which bore his name before taking that of his rival and vanquisher Constantine. This architectural intervention also reinforced the memory of Rome's founder. Near the Lapis Niger, believed to mark the position of the tomb of Romulus, the emperor had erected on April 21, anniversary date of the foundation of Rome, a statue of Mars, mythical father of the twins; the marble base was adorned with an inscription in honor of Mars and the founders of the Eternal City.[8] Following

2. On the prophecy of empire delivered in a dream (*Historia Augusta*, Severus 1,8) to Septimius Severus, founder of the dynasty, who dreamt that, like Romulus or Remus, he was being suckled by a she-wolf, see Ph. Bruggisser, "Septime Sévère et le projet de gémination de la statue de la Fortune (HA S 23, 5–7)," *Bonner Historia-Augusta-Colloquium* 1986/89 (1991) 13–20 at 17.

3. For the continuity of this phenomenon, attested for Maximian the Thracian and his son Maximus, Gordian III, Philip the Arab, Herennius Etruscus, Trebonianus Gallus, Hostilianus, Volusianus, Valerian, Gallienus, Aurelian, Probus and Carausius, see Dulière, *Lupa Romana*, 1.169–76, 2.cat. nos. M78–116 with the corresponding figures.

4. Aurelius Victor, *Caesares* 35,12; *Historia Augusta*, Tacitus 1,1; D. den Hengst, "Some Notes on the *Vita Taciti*," *Historiae Augustae Colloquium Genevense* 2 (1994): 101–107.

5. P. Bastien, *Le buste monétaire des empereurs romains*, vol. 2 (Wetteren, Belgique: Editions "Numismatiques Romaines", 1993) 480; vol. 3 (Wetteren, Belgique: Editions "Numismatiques Romaines", 1994) plate 140,1; Dulière, *Lupa Romana*, 1.176, 185; 2.cat. nos. M117–118, with fig. 174 (but without fig. 175, where the silver multiple of Constantine discussed below is erroneously attributed to Maximian).

6. Lactantius, *De mortibus persecutorum* 9,9; Ps.-Aurelius Victor, *Epitome* 40,16.

7. E. Groag, art. "Maxentius," in *Paulys Real-Encyclopädie der classischen Altertumswissenschaft* [hereafter *RE*] 14.2 (1930) 2458, lines 38–40; Dulière, *Lupa Romana*, 1.183–84, 2.cat. nos. M119–25.

8. *Corpus Inscriptionum Latinarum* [CIL] VI.33856 (*Inscriptiones Latinae Selectae* [ILS], ed. H. Dessau, 8935). The base was perhaps designed to support the group commissioned by the Ogulnii.

the fire of 307 Maxentius had in effect refounded the Temple of the City, named for Venus and Rome.[9] Dedicated by Hadrian to Venus Felix and Roma Aeterna, probably in 135, the temple symbolized the idea of the renewal of the City and of the Empire.[10] As a father, Maxentius placed his hopes of renewal on his son Valerius Romulus. A good argument has been made for identifying the building that commonly passes for the Temple of Romulus erected in memory of this prematurely deceased son with the Temple of Jupiter Stator, located at the site where Romulus's soldiers, fleeing before the Sabines, turned again to face their enemies after their leader had called on Jupiter.[11] The simple rampart raised at the period of the foundation of the City was transformed into a veritable temple in 294 BCE by command of the Senate.[12] On rebuilding it, the argument runs, Maxentius would have dedicated it to his son Romulus. Given this emperor's reverence for the mythical origins of Rome, it would not be at all surprising if the Temple of Jupiter Stator, consecrated, according to tradition, by Romulus himself, was replaced by a dynastic sanctuary dedicated to the memory of one whose name was inspired by the model of the founder— that is, until the victorious Constantine restored the temple to its original cult, thereby offering a sign of his own respect for the figure of Romulus.

Predictably, for the panegyrist who pronounced the praises of Constantine at Trier in 313, the usurper whom he had defeated at the Milvian Bridge was a false Romulus, swallowed by the river that had spared the founder.[13] On a silver multiple of Constantine struck at Ticinum (Pavia) in 315 for the emperor's fourth consulate and *decennalia*, he appears in bust, with his armor on, holding in his left hand a shield decorated with the she-wolf and twins; amid the rich symbolism of a magnificent silver +-coin, this particular ensemble commemorates his

---

9. *Origo gentis Romanorum*, chron. I.148,32; Aurelius Victor, *Caesares* 40,26. Between 307 and 309 the mint of Aquileia produced a series of coins which carry what appears to be a schematic representation of the Temple of the City; the facade of the building bears a simplified image of the she-wolf suckling the twins.

10. J. Gagé, "Le *Templum Urbis* et les origines de l'idée de *renovatio*," *Mélanges F. Cumont*, vol. 1 (Brussels: Secrétariat de l'Institut, 1936) 151–87. The foundation of the building was apparently traced to the feast of the Parilia, April 21, anniversary date of the founding of Rome, which thus became the *dies natalis* of the temple.

11. F. Coarelli, *Il Foro Romano*, vol. 1: *Periodo arcaico* (Rome: Quasar, 1983) 29–33; id., "L'*Urbs* e il suburbio," in *Società romana e Impero tardoantico*, vol. 2: *Roma: Politica, economia, paesaggio urbano*, ed. A. Giardina (Rome: Laterza, 1986) 1-58 at 1–35, esp. 9–20.

12. Livy 10,37,15.

13. *Panegyrici Latini* 12 (ed. E. Galletier, 9) 18,1.

capture of Rome after the battle at the Milvian Bridge. Only, however, from 330 onward, date of the solemn dedication of Constantinople, does the motif become common on coin issues of the founder of New Rome.[14] In a poem composed by Optatianus Porfyrius for the emperor's *vicennalia* (325), Constantine is called *Romuleum sidus*;[15] in verses referring to the same occasion the emperor is given the name of *Romula lux*.[16] A little earlier, the exiled poet had rejoiced in the fact that Romulus had found in Constantine a secure guide for his descendants.[17] In the speech pronounced by Themistius when Gratian associated himself with Theodosius as colleague (379), Constantine is declared the equal of Romulus because he is the founder of one of the two metropolises in the world.[18] His son, Constantius II, triumphally visiting the Eternal City, eclipsed Romulus's prestige—according to the same Themistius,[19] despatched to Rome by the Senate of Constantinople for the *vicennalia* of the emperor in 357. Julian too, in praising the sovereign, compared Constantius with Romulus.[20]

Julian the Apostate considered himself closely connected with Helios and took that god to be Romulus's father: if the founder of Rome owed his physical existence to Ares, from Helios proceeded Quirinus, the soul of the divinized Romulus.[21] On August 24, 376 (on the likeliest dating), Themistius was in Rome again, this time as a guest of the Roman Senate to celebrate the *decennalia* of Gratian's reign. While the emperor was still awaited in the City, he made a speech explicitly declaring the young prince to be a new Romulus.[22]

---

14. Bastien, *Le buste monétaire*, 2.428–29, 3.plates 169 and 170,9. Abundant as it is in Roman iconography, the motif of the she-wolf and twins in fact appears relatively rarely on the shields of monetary busts; apart from the cases of Maximian and Constantine discussed above, there are just two other instances to note, one for Constantius Chlorus (Constantine's father), the other for Crispus (his son): ibid., 2.481, 3.plates 145,4 and 181,6.

15. Optatianus Porfyrius, *Carm.* 9,32. For the dates of this and other poems see vol. 2 of the edn. by G. Polara (Turin: G.B. Paravia, 1973) ad loc. These passages are also discussed in Bruggisser, "Gratien" (below, n. 22) 202–203.

16. Optatianus Porfyrius, *Carm.* 19,12. The poet also gives the emperor the title of *lux pia Romulidum* in *Carm.* 15,10.

17. *Carm.* 7,34–35.

18. Themistius, *Or.* 14,182a.

19. *Or.* 3,43c. On another view, it was only a copy of the speech, delivered at Constantinople, that was sent to Rome: cf. W. Stegemann, art. "Themistios (2)," *RE* 5A.2 (1934) 1658, lines 51–58.

20. Julian, *Or.* 1,10b.

21. Julian, *Or.* 11(4),154c.

79

The reign of Theodosius's sons and their protector, Stilicho, is pervaded with the image of Romulus. The ascendancy of Stilicho signals a return to Romulus's laws.[23] Stilicho is the avenger whom Mars, shocked by the depravity of Eutropius, has chosen to reestablish past splendors. The god has put all his confidence in the general and is now asking his son Romulus to excuse his delays.[24] Stilicho's avenging hand produces a Romulean renaissance.[25] When the poet Claudian welcomes his sovereign to Rome, he reminds Honorius of his first visit inside Romulus's walls in 389 when he had accompanied his father Theodosius on the occasion of the triumph over Maximus.[26] The Tiber exults on seeing Quirinus's sceptre again.[27] The Romans rejoice over the beneficence of a reign that conciliates martial Quirinus and peaceable Numa.[28] Claudian even relates a tale of two wolves killed while attacking the emperor's escort at Milan.[29] From their sides appeared two hands. Alarmists discerned in this prodigy an intervention by the animal associated with Romulus and interpreted it as the sign of a threat against the empire; the omen of the twelve vultures appearing to Romulus is therefore brought into play.

Romulus and Late Latin Literature

The deeds of the hero are deep-rooted in the Latin literature of the fourth and fifth centuries. They are present in both pagan and Christian works. With respect to the former, they appear in diverse genres: in oratory, with the Latin Panegyrics; in historiography, with Eutropius, the *Origo gentis Romanae* and the *De viris illustribus* of Pseudo-Aurelius Victor, the *Calendar of 354*, the

---

22. Themistius, *Or.* 13,179c. On the parallel, cf. Ph. Bruggisser, "Gratien, nouveau Romulus," in *Historia testis: Mélanges d'épigraphie, d'histoire ancienne et de philologie offerts à Tadeusz Zawadzki*, ed. M. Piérart et O. Curty (Fribourg: Editions Universitaires, 1989) 189–205, esp. 202, and, despite the omission of Themistius's explicit parallel between Romulus and Gratian, J. Doignon, "Le titre de *nobilissimus puer* porté par Gratien et la mystique littéraire des origines de Rome à l'avènement des Valentiniens," in *Mélanges d'archéologie et d'histoire offerts à A. Piganiol*, vol. 3 (Paris: Ecole Pratique des Hautes Etudes, 1966) 1693–709, for a rich analysis of Romulean connotations in the publicity of the Valentinian dynasty.
23. Claudian, *Carm.* 21 (Stil. 1), 331.
24. Claudian, *Carm.* 20 (Eutr. 2), 141–43.
25. Claudian, *Carm.* 24 (Stil. 3), 123–24.
26. Claudian, *Carm.* 28 (VI Hon.), 57.
27. Claudian, *Carm.* 28 (VI Hon.), 642.
28. Claudian, *Carm.* 8 (IV Hon.), 491–93.
29. Claudian, *Carm.* 26 (Goth.), 249–66.

Liber genealogus and the *Historia Augusta*; in literary exegesis with Servius and Claudius Donatus; in poetry, with Ausonius and, above all, Claudian. Christian authors—Arnobius, Lactantius, Prudentius, Jerome, Augustine—also deal abundantly with Romulus.

Romulus's Asylum in the Tradition before Augustine

When Augustine comes to the point of considering Romulus's asylum, he stands at the confluence of two literary traditions, respectively favorable and unfavorable to the founder's initiative. At the same time, he is reacting to the shock of a recent historical event—the capture of Rome by Alaric, during which the institution of asylum had been put to a severe test. Our author, searching for the seeds of the heavenly city in the earthly one, predictably joins past and present in his eschatological projection. Let us start, however, by retracing the history of Roman ideas about the institution of the asylum by Romulus, in order to set clear boundaries to the double perception generated by that event.

The oldest mention of Romulus's asylum now extant in Latin literature is to be found in a fragment of the annalist Calpurnius Piso.[30] (It is possible that Fabius Pictor may have referred to it at an earlier date; since that author relates the rape of the Sabine women,[31] one can reasonably suppose that he described the asylum as well.) Among the reasons offered to justify the asylum is the urgency of peopling the City.[32] This is the position taken by Livy, who thereby explains the recourse to a typical process of foundation, one which gathered slaves and free men under the cover of a fictitious autochthony.[33] Defence of the asylum can also take the form of a refutation of charges of immorality brought against those who populated the site. This is the position taken by Dionysius of Halicarnassus. The author of the *Roman Antiquities* denies that Rome could have been the "refuge of barbarians, fugitives and homeless individuals."[34]

---

30. Calpurnius, *Hist.* 4 (ed. H. Peter [2nd edn.]). The annalist's interpretation is transmitted to us by Servius Danielis in a scholion to *Aen.* 2,761: *quem locum deus †Lucoris, sicut Piso ait, curare dicitur.* On the form "Lycoris," regarded as a Latin transcription from Greek, see R. Ganszyiniec, art. "Lykoreus," *RE* 13.2 (1927) 2384–85.

31. Fabius Pictor, *Hist.* 7 (ed. Peter).

32. This point of view appears in Velleius Paterculus 1,8,5.

33. Livy 1,8,5–6.

34. Dion. Hal., *Ant.* 1,89,1. At 1,4,2 Dionysius criticizes the majority of Greeks of his time and the prejudices of those who believed that Rome's power was founded on chance and unjust Fortune rather than on piety and a sense of justice.

By means of the asylum, Romulus sought to procure a refuge for those banished by the intolerant, tyrannical, and oligarchic regimes of some Italian cities—provided, that is, the poor wretches were free men.[35] We shall return to this principle of compassion for the unfortunate, in which Dionysius of Halicarnassus perceives the dominant feature of the asylum. According to the rules of rhetorical *synkrisis*, Ovid, in his diptych of Romulus and Augustus glorifying the sovereign, opposes the toleration of crime in the Romulean asylum to his own banishment by Augustus.[36] However, by situating the temple of Veiovis at the site of the asylum instituted by Romulus, the poet insists on the security that could be enjoyed at the time of the founder by anybody taking refuge within the sacred space.[37] Plutarch evokes the reasons that induced Romulus and Remus to found Rome rather than share the throne of Alba with their grandfather, one of which is that the twin brothers were accompanied by a troop of slaves and outlaws, who were scorned by the Albans who refused to receive them.[38] He goes on to say that, before taking the auspices to found the city, the two brothers feigned allegiance to the Pythian oracle and increased the population by means of a sanctuary founded in honor of the god Asylum, where immunity was granted to slaves, debtors, and murderers.

Opinions transmitted to us from antiquity concerning the asylum are by no means unanimously positive. The founder's detractors denounce the protection granted to criminals and its disastrous consequences for the history of a city whose future was shaped by a corrupt people. The following three passages, in which the word *convenae* is used in a pejorative sense,[39] may all be taken with more or less certainty to refer to Romulus's asylum:

Cato, *Origines* 20 (ed. H. Peter [2nd edn.]), as quoted by Aulus Gellius, *Noctes Atticae* 18,12,7: *Eodem* convenae *conplures ex agro accessitavere. Eo res eorum auxit.* [40]

---

35. Dion. Hal., *Ant.* 2,15,3.

36. Ovid, *Fasti* 2,140.

37. Ibid. 3,429–32.

38. Plutarch, *Romulus* 9,2–3.

39. The *Thesaurus Linguae Latinae,* s.v., insists on the element of chance attaching to the sense of *convenae,* to the exclusion of notions of law or right: *speciatim de peregrinis, adventiciis casu, non per ius et leges, congregatis.* Wherever possible, English translations of Latin texts cited below have been taken from the Loeb Classical Library, adapted where necessary. For the *City of God,* translations are those of H. Bettenson (Harmondsworth: Pelican Classics, 1972), modified in places.

40. On this fragment, see W. A. Schröder *M. Porcius Cato, Das erste Buch der Origines: Ausgabe und Erklärung der Fragmente* (Meisenheim am Glan: A. Hain, 1971) 178–81.

("Many vagabonds came to that same place from the country. Therefore their wealth waxed.")

Cicero, *De Oratore* 1,37: *An vero tibi Romulus ille aut pastores et convenas congregasse aut Sabinorum conubia coniunxisse aut finitimorum vim repressisse eloquentia videtur, non consilio et sapientia singulari?*[41]

("Or does it perhaps appear to you that Romulus, when he gathered together herdsmen and vagabonds, or contracted marriages with the Sabines, or repulsed the attacks of neighbouring peoples, did so by his eloquence and not by his exceptional policy and wisdom?")

Sallust, *Epistula Mithridatis* 17: *An ignoras Romanos . . . convenas olim sine patria, parentibus, peste conditos orbis terrarum?*[42]

("Do you not know that the Romans . . . once vagabonds without fatherland, without parents, [were] created to be the scourge of the whole world?")

The third extract expresses the virulent reaction of Rome's enemies. Seeking an alliance against the Romans, Mithridates in his letter to king Arsaces belabors the doubtful origins of this criminal nation.[43] The term *convenae* (vagabonds) likewise designates the first inhabitants of Rome in Livy, who affirms that royal authority had had a salutary effect on them.[44]

Christian authors prior to Augustine do not spare their criticisms of Romulus's institution:

Minucius Felix, *Octavius* 25, 2: *Nonne in ortu suo et scelere collecti et muniti immanitatis suae terrore creverunt? Nam asylo prima plebs congregata est: confluxerant perditi, facinerosi, incesti, sicarii, proditores.*

("Was it not crime that brought them together at their origin, and did they not flourish under the protection of the terror inspired by their savagery? For the first people was gathered in asylum: wasters, criminals, profligates, assassins and traitors all merged in one.")

---

41. For the bearing of this passage on the subject of the asylum, see A. D. Leeman and H. Pinkster, eds., *M. Tullius Cicero, De oratore libri III*, vol. 1 (Heidelberg: C. Winter, 1981) 117.

42. For the discussion provoked by the context to which this passage alludes, viz. Romans taking refuge in the Romulean asylum rather than Trojans fleeing their city, see V. Paladini, ed., *C. Sallusti Crispi orationes et epistulae de historiarum libris excerptae* (Bologna: R. Pàtron, 1965) 167.

43. One finds a similar note of antipathy to Rome in Justin's abridgment of the *Historiae Philippicae* of Trogus Pompeius (28,2,8–10): *quos autem homines Romanos esse? Nempe pastores, qui latrocinio iustis dominis ademptum solum teneant, qui uxores cum* propter originis dehonestamenta *non invenirent vi publica rapuerint, qui denique urbem ipsam parricidio condiderint murorumque fundamenta fraterno sanguine adsperserint.*

44. Livy 2,1,4; cf. 5,53,9.

Cyprian, *Quod idola dii non sint* 5: *Ceterum si ad originem redeas, erubescas. Populus de sceleratis et nocentibus congregatur et asylo constituto facit numerum inpunitas criminum.*

("On the other hand, were you to go back to the origin, you would be embarrassed. A people is assembled from criminals and delinquents, and, once an asylum has been established, impunity gives rise to numerous offences.")

Romulus's Asylum in Augustine's *City of God*

There can be no doubt, then, that the non-Christian tradition prepared the way for Augustine's interpretation of the asylum, as much by the positive arguments he would have to oppose as by the negative hints that he would be able to exploit. The Christian tradition, meanwhile, could only confirm him in his unfavorable perception of the Romulean institution.

Asylum and Church

At the very beginning of the *City of God*, the experience of recent events leads Augustine to evoke the principle of the asylum in order to point out that the Christian invader, in taking Rome, had respected inhabitants of the City who sought refuge in churches, even though some of these were implacable enemies of Christianity.

Civ. 1, 1 (ed. B. Dombart and A. Kalb): *Testantur hoc martyrum loca et basilicae apostolorum, quae in illa vastatione urbis ad se confugientes suos alienosque receperunt.*

("The sacred places of the martyrs and the basilicas of the apostles bear witness to this, for in the sack of Rome they afforded shelter to fugitives, their own people and strangers too.")

For Augustine the *alieni* are obviously strangers in the faith, i.e., pagans. According to Orosius, Alaric personally ordered his troops to spare the refugees, especially those in the two basilicas, St.Peter's and St.Paul's.[45]

Asylum at the Birth and at the Fall of Rome

Pursuing the same idea in chapter 34 of Book 1, Augustine endeavors to lessen the impact of the fall of Rome by proving to survivors that divine mercy, in saving their lives, had offered them an opportunity for conversion.

---

45. Orosius, *Historiae adversum paganos* 7,39,1.

*Civ.*1,34: *Et tamen quod vivitis dei est, qui vobis parcendo admonet, ut corrigamini paenitendo; qui vobis etiam ingratis praestitit, ut vel sub nomine servorum eius vel in locis martyrum eius hostiles manus evaderetis.*

("And yet it is thanks to God's grace that you are still alive. In sparing you he warns you to amend your ways by penitence. Despite your ingratitude he gave you the means of escape from the enemy's hands either by passing as his servants or by taking refuge in the shrines of his martyrs.")

The fact that Christian sanctuaries remained inviolate during the taking of Rome leads our author quite naturally to consider the phenomenon of inviolability proper to the sacred space established at the City's foundation:

Ibid.: *Romulus et Remus asylum constituisse perhibentur, quo quisquis confugeret ab omni noxa liber esset, augere quaerentes creandae multitudinem civitatis.*

("We are told that Romulus and Remus established a refuge, their aim being to increase the population of their city, and anyone who sought refuge there was exempt from all ill.")

The city of the first Romans and the city of Christians become analogous, in virtue of the asylum. It was thanks to the asylum that the original city acquired its population. In the same way, the Christian city was ready to assure its own increase by granting the asylum of its churches. Progress is the common denominator for both phenomena: moral improvement in the case of the pagan asylum at Rome's beginnings under Romulus; spiritual conversion in the case of the Christian asylum during Rome's capture by Alaric. The eternal city, in its genesis, finds a counterpart in the nascent temporal city.

There is, however, a nuance to be considered. The term *noxa* is highly complex, since it denotes not only an offense or crime (or the resultant damage, or the perpetrator) but also the punishment of the offence, and because its derivative *noxia* intrudes on the semantic field.[46] Christians used the word to denote sin, especially original sin.[47] In the whole of Augustine's works, there are just

---

46. Festus 180,25–32 (ed. W. M. Lindsay). For a thorough study, see Z. Lisowski, "*Noxa* und *noxia*," *RE* Supplementband 7 (1940) 587–604.

47. See A. Blaise, *Dictionnaire latin-français des auteurs chrétiens* (2nd edn., Turnhout: Editions Brepols, 1962) s.v., with esp. Prudentius, *Cathemerinon* 2,104. The word also appears with sense of "crime" in non-Christian literature of the later period (e.g., several times in Ammianus and Symmachus, *Relatio* 34,4: *gravium noxarum poena*).

48. Augustine, *De anima et eius origine* 2,13,18: *animas . . . ab omni noxa propaginis liberas*; *Contra duas epistulas Pelagianorum* 4,4,4: *eum tamquam ab omni noxa liberum*; 4,5,9: *ab omni noxa liberi . . . infantes.*

three other instances of the expression *ab omni noxa liber*.[48] They are embedded in a theological discussion of the soul of an infant, presented as free of all offence. In these three cases, the notion of offense is clearly more salient than that of punishment. By analogy, we may postulate that in this passage of the *City of God*, even if the idea of punishment is not absent, that of offense is intimately associated with it. It is possible, in fact, that Augustine's formula conceals an element of provocation. Augustine remains true to the idea of inviolability proper to the asylum, but in his usage the impunity accorded to those who gather there is contaminated by a sense of the protection guaranteed to offenders. Thus the polysemy of the term *noxa*, which covers both the offence and the corresponding sanction, allows Augustine to construct a statement *in utramque partem*, as if, in his mind, the first Romans had only to take refuge in the asylum in order to escape their offenses by escaping their due punishment. (For this reason, unlike other translators who emphasize either the idea of offense[49] or that of punishment,[50] I have preferred a translation which, so far as possible, restores the double sense of the original: "anyone who sought refuge there was exempt from all ill," that is, from all ill committed [in the sense of crime] and from all ill suffered [in the sense of repression of crime]. The passage from Book 4 analyzed below would seem to bear out this interpretation.) Already in this passage, the ambivalence of Augustine's statement is a covert sign of the frontal attack he is about to make on the founder's initiative.

At first, Augustine feigns approval of the pagan precedent whose model has found a Christian application:

Ibid.: *Mirandum in honorem Christi processit exemplum. Hoc constituerunt eversores urbis quod constituerant antea conditores.*

("This formed a precedent for a remarkable honor done to Christ; the destroyers of Rome followed the example of its founders.")

Then, in one of those rhetorical pirouettes at which he is so expert, Augustine unveils the antiphrastic turn of his admiration:

---

49. G. E. McCracken (Loeb Classical Library): "an asylum where any man might seek refuge and be free from guilt."

50. D. B. Zema and G. G. Walsh (Fathers of the Church, 8): "an asylum where refugees were to be immune from every molestation"; H. Bettenson (Pelican Classics): "and anyone who fled there was secure from any harm"; G. Combès (*Bibliothèque Augustinienne,* 33): "un asyle où quiconque se réfugierait, serait à couvert de tout châtiment"; C. J. Perl (*Aurelius Augustinus" Werke* [Paderborn: Schöningh, 1979]): "wo jeder, der sich dahin flüchtete, straffrei bleiben sollte."

Ibid.: *Quid autem magnum, si hoc fecerunt illi, ut civium suorum numerus suppleretur, quod fecerunt isti, ut suorum hostium numerositas servaretur?*

("Now is it surprising that the founders should have taken this course to increase the numbers of their citizens, when the destroyers acted in the same way to preserve large numbers of their enemies?")

By concealing the train of his thought, or rather by the progressive disclosure of what he really thinks, Augustine discredits the object under discussion. It is a trick based on irony, according to a definition attributed in a scholion to Dionysius Thrax: "What is irony ? It is a kind of mockery where instead of showing openly one's reprobation, one seems to use flattering words."[51] This form of causticity, disguised as sham approval, belongs to the category of irony classified in rhetoric as *diasyrmos*.[52]

At first glance, the comparison between present destroyers and former founders could lead one to believe that Augustine concedes the superiority of the pagan past. But the parallel ends to the disadvantage of the creators of the City and of its inhabitants. To achieve this result, Augustine sets a negative interpretation on one of the facts traditionally construed as favourable to the *conditor*: the will to populate the town. The Romulean asylum is thus already relativized and diminished in the perspective of the temporal city.

The Asylum of Romulus and the First Romans

In his first three books Augustine strives to demonstrate the importance of the divine consolations granted during the conflict to good and bad alike (*Civ.* 4,2). In Book 4, he lays the blame on pagans who attribute to their gods the propagation of the Roman Empire in space and time (4,3). Then he develops ethical considerations to show that the Empire of the good alone justifies itself and that its desired end is eternal life. The essential criterion of a kingdom is justice, without which it is no better than brigandage. Here Augustine mentions the gladiators' revolts that had shaken the Roman empire, threatening it with enslavement to another empire founded on brigandage. And he wonders aloud about the role of the gods in such events.

---

51. Scholia on Dionysius Thrax, *Ars grammatica*, ed. A. Hilgard, *Grammatici Graeci*, vol. 1.3 (Leipzig, 1901) 14, 3–4.

52. Julius Rufinianus, *Rhet.* 5, in C. Halm, ed., *Rhetores Latini Minores*, vol. 5 (Leipzig: B.G. Teubner, 1863) 39,24–25: *haec figura fit, cum rem aliquam aut personam elevamus.*

Before evoking this crucial phase in the history of Rome, Augustine makes a preterition, feigning not to linger over the quality of those who populated the city at its origin:

> *Civ.* 4,5: *Proinde omitto quaerere quales Romulus congregaverit, quoniam multum eis consultum est, ut ex illa vita dato sibi consortio civitatis poenas debitas cogitare desisterent, quarum metus eos in maiora facinora propellebat, ut deinceps pacatiores essent rebus humanis.*

> ("I shall not discuss the question of what kind of people Romulus collected; it is known that he took measures to ensure that when they were granted a share in the community after abandoning their former way of life, they should no longer have to think about the punishment to which they were liable, the fear of which had impelled them to greater crimes, so that in the future they should be more peaceable in their attitude to society.")

Augustine recognizes the beneficial role of the Romulean asylum in motivating those who took refuge there to mend their ways. Even so, his preterition loses none of its rhetorical effect: the asylum had sheltered guilty persons and restrained them from committing further offenses in their attempts to escape justice.

The Romulean Asylum and the Heavenly City

In Chapter 17 of Book 5 Augustine argues that the goods done or ills endured by those seeking to enter the heavenly city should be no cause of pride. If, moreover, they are compared to what the Romans had accepted for the sake of their earthly city, Christians are bound to abstain from self-congratulation,

> *Civ.* 5,17: *praesertim quia remissio peccatorum, quae cives ad aeternam colligit patriam, habet aliquid, cui per umbram quandam simile fuit asylum illud Romuleum, quo multitudinem, qua illa civitas conderetur, quorumlibet delictorum congregavit inpunitas.*

> ("especially because the remission of sins, the promise which recruits the citizens for the Eternal Country, finds a kind of shadowy resemblance in that refuge of Romulus, where the offer of impunity for crimes of every kind collected a multitude which was to result in the foundation of the city of Rome.")

Once again Augustine avails himself of the asylum of Romulus for the sake of an argument. The Christian is invited to pass a test of humility, by considering that he or she is scarcely different from one of the criminals who, at the origins of Rome, had benefited from the immunity of the Romulean asylum. However, because Augustine's purpose is to exalt the heavenly country over the earthly, the amnesty granted to the first Romans in the Romulean asylum is merely a pale reflection of that full remission of sins accorded by divine grace in the eternal fatherland.

For all that, the asylum is merely a kind of *umbra*, a reflection. Whereas in Book 1 the Romulean asylum had been made to appear inferior to the Christian asylum observed by the invaders and was thus relativized as a precedent, here, by contrast, it is raised to the rank of a prefiguration. A quality inherent in the temporal city at its genesis provides an *a fortiori* argument for its culmination in the heavenly city. For the sake of this new thesis, Augustine reverses his opinion of the crimes inseparably associated with the Romulean asylum, substituting admiration of the amends made for indignation against the immunity granted.

Already depreciated in Book 1 in the context of the historical wayfaring of the temporal city, suspended between pagan precedent and Christian fulfillment, the Romulean asylum is now relativized anew in a comparison between the history of the temporal city and that of the eternal one.

In Augustine's view, the advent of Christianity transformed the course of Rome's history. He inveighs against pagan beliefs and practices, and warmly invites their adepts to return to the heavenly mother-country. Once again the model of the Romulean asylum comes to his mind to justify the new mother-country and he addresses an apostrophe to a personification of the Roman national character:

> *Civ.* 2,29: *Ad quam patriam te invitamus et exhortamur, ut eius adiciaris numero civium, cuius quodam modo asylum est vera remissio peccatorum.*
>
> ("It is to this country that we invite you, and exhort you to add yourself to the number of our citizens. The kind of refuge we offer is the true remission of sins.")

The Asylum of Romulus in the Perception of a Scholiast

The Commentator Servius

The grammarian Servius composed his *Commentaries on Virgil* during the reigns of the Theodosian emperors. His commentary has come to us in a shorter, authentic version—the object of our study—and in a longer, apocryphal version (the *Servius Danielis*, named after its first editor, Pierre Daniel [1600]) that dates back to Aelius Donatus. Servius was particularly appreciated among pagan scholars, as is attested by Macrobius's *Saturnalia*.

At the end of antiquity, the poetry of Virgil was implicated in a tense intellectual debate between pagans and Christians who used Rome's past for propaganda purposes. Required by his profession as grammarian to explain the *historiae* contained or suggested in the commented work, Servius is heavily engaged in this ideological contest.

I have discussed the dating of Servius elsewhere.[53] To summarize: in the dialogue of the *Saturnalia*, whose fictional date is 384 (the death of Praetextatus) and whose real date seems most probably to be later than 430,[54] Macrobius apologizes (1,1,5) for having introduced one or another person whose *matura aetas* fell after the time of Praetextatus. Two guests, Servius (7,11,2) and Avienus (6,7,1; 7,3,23), are described as *adulescentes*, and doubtless it is they who are meant. Contrary to other opinions, I have argued (citing an analogous passage from Jerome) that *matura aetas* is here opposed to *adulescentia*.[55] Like Avienus, Servius was in fact an *adulescens* at the dramatic date of the conversation (384), reaching maturity closer to the time in which Macrobius composed his work. If it is granted that Servius was an *adulescens* in 384 and if we apply Varro's scheme (transmitted by Censorinus 14, 2) in which the human life span is divided into periods of 15 years, with *adulescentia* falling between 16 and 30 years of age, then it is clear that Servius was born between (384 − 30=) 354 and (384 − 16=) 368. Thus the apogee of our commentator can be placed some 40 years later, between the last decade of the fourth century and the first decade of the fifth.

Servius and the Asylum of Romulus, a Replica of the Altar of Pity in Athens

In his treatment of the legend of Romulus, which modern readers can reconstitute on the basis of fifty scholia, Servius variously conforms to the prior tradition, adapts it, and innovates upon it.[56] It is particularly interesting to follow him in his approach to the asylum, since there his commentary on the founder's deeds proceeds by innovation.

In presenting the asylum, the grammarian refutes the accusations brought against the Romulean institution. He takes up one of the positive arguments

---

53. Ph. Bruggisser, "Précaution de Macrobe et datation de Servius," *Museum Helveticum* 41 (1984): 162–73.

54. A. Cameron, "The Date and Identity of Macrobius," *Journal of Roman Studies* 56 (1966): 25–38.

55. Jerome, *In Ezech.* 8,25,12–14: *erroresque adolescentiae aetas matura condemnat.*

56. For each aspect of this technique, see Bruggisser, *Romulus Seruianus* (above, n.1) passim.

and considers that the founder's disposition aimed at providing the city with a population. In this perspective, Romulus reproduced a Greek model.

Let us consider the scholia. The first engrafts itself on the mention of Juno's asylum in the Trojan citadel, now fallen into Greek hands:

> Servius, on *Aen.* 2,761: *IVNONIS ASYLO templo; unde nullus possit extrahi. Dictum "asylum" quasi "asyrum."*[57] *Hoc autem non est in omnibus templis nisi quibus consecrationis lege concessum est. Primo autem apud Athenienses statutum est ab Herculis filiis, quos insequebantur hi qui erant a patre oppressi, sicut docet in duodecimo Statius. Hoc asylum etiam Romulus imitatus est; unde est "quem Romulus acer asylum / rettulit,"*[58] *non "statuit."*

("IN THE ASYLUM OF JUNO in the temple; whence no one can be forcibly removed. "Asylum" is said for "asyrum." This privilege does not apply in all temples but only in those to which it has been granted by the law of consecration. It was first instituted among the Athenians by the sons of Hercules, who were being pursued by those who had suffered at the hands of their father, as Statius informs us in Book 12. It was this asylum that Romulus also imitated; hence "which the valiant Romulus reestablished as an asylum," not "instituted.")

It should be noted that there is no necessary connection between the lemma and the scholiast's explanation. Servius takes advantage of an association to graft into the exegesis of the passage a notice relating to the legend of Rome's founder.

The second scholion is inserted into the narrative of Evander receiving Aeneas in his palace. He relates the ancient history of Latium, then talks to his guests about the future Rome and notably the asylum of Romulus:

> Servius, on *Aen.* 8,342: *ASYLVM RETVLIT Postquam Hercules migravit e terris, nepotes eius timentes insidias eorum quos avus adflixerat, Athenis sibi primi asylum, hoc est templum misericordiae, collocarunt unde nullus posset abduci, quod etiam Statius dicit, ut "Herculeos fama est . . . / . . . fundasse nepotes."*[59] *Ideo ergo ait "quod*[60] *Romulus acer asylum / retulit," hoc est fecit ad imitationem Atheniensis asyli: quod ideo Romulus fecit ut*

---

57. Whereas the Greek term *asylon* is in fact derived from *sylan* ("strip [a warrior] of his arms, carry off, take possession of," occasionally "exercise a right of capture"), and thus designates a place where one cannot be seized, Servius seems to connect the Latin calque *asylum* to Gk. *syrein* ("pull, draw by force") and to explain its derivation by a phonetic substitution of liquids.

58. Virgil, *Aen.* 8,342–43.

59. Statius, *Thebaid* 12,497-98: *fama est . . . / . . . Herculeos . . . fundasse nepotes*.

60. The reading *quod* here is Servius's; our manuscripts of Virgil have *quem*.

haberet advenas plures cum quibus conderet Romam. Iuvenalis "et tamen ut longe repetas longeque revolvas / nomen, ab infami gentem deducis asylo. "[61]

("REESTABLISHED AS AN ASYLUM After Hercules left the earth, his descendants, fearing the ambushes of those who had been ill-treated by their ancestor, were the first to set up an asylum—that is, a temple of pity— for themselves, at Athens, whence no-one could be taken away, as Statius also says: "fame has it that the descendants of Hercules founded [the asylum]." Thus he says "which the valiant Romulus reestablished as an asylum," that is, created on the model of the Athenian asylum. And this Romulus did in order to have more foreigners with whom to found Rome. Juvenal: "and yet, however far back you seek your name, however far you search, you derive your line from a base asylum.")

Eurystheus, king of Mycenae and Tiryns, who assigned Hercules his twelve labours, swore an everlasting enmity toward the latter's descendants in order to prevent them coming to power. Before reconquering the Peloponnesus, which they considered their homeland, the Heraclides received succor from the Athenians against their enemy, whom they managed to kill. According to the oracle, their victory over the king was obtained at the cost of a human victim, the spontaneous sacrifice of Macaria, Hercules's daughter. Athens and Attica offered refuge to the sons of the divinized hero,[62] while they awaited the day when they could return to their country.

The innovation that appears in Servius's text is the relation established between Romulus's asylum and the altar of Pity. Servius finds himself obliged to explain an institution whose character is perceived by the Romans as specifically Greek.[63] Therefore, convinced of the Hellenic origins of the Romans,[64] he proposes an interpretation conferring a Greek—more precisely, an Athenian—model upon the asylum of Romulus. Like Diodorus Siculus (13,22,7), our commentator rightly ascribes priority in this cult to the Athenians,[65] while Pausanias (1,17,1) wrongly credits them with an exclusive claim to it.[66]

---

61. Juvenal, *Sat.* 8,272–73.

62. On the altar of Pity where the Heraclides sought refuge, see Apollodorus, *Bibl.* 2,8,1; Philostratus, *Ep.* 39; Zenobius 2,61; Scholia on Aristophanes's *Knights* 1151.

63. Livy 35,51,2: *templa quae asyla Graeci appellant.*

64. Servius, on *Aen.* 1,292: *constat autem Graecos fuisse Romanos.*

65. Servius, on *Aen.* 2,761 *primo*; 8,342: *primi.*

66. See O. Waser in *RE* 5.2 (1905) 2320, lines 38–48.

Servius dignifies the refuge created by the founder by making the asylum of Romulus at Rome into a replica of the altar of Pity in Athens, the civilizing city par excellence. He backs up his demonstration with the authority of Statius who places the altar under the protectorship of *Clementia*.[67] At the same time, he recalls the lowliness of the original institution with a quotation from Juvenal. In so doing, he touches upon a recurrent theme of Roman ideology: the pride of the Romans in having raised their city from poor beginnings to the height of power—a proof that the nation had forged its destiny by its own valor and did not owe it merely to Fortune's generosity.

The recourse to Statius and Juvenal testifies to a renewed interest in poets of the Early Empire on the part of late Roman men of letters. Servius, indeed, is one of the architects of this late fourth-century literary renaissance.[68]

Statius and the Altar of Clemency

Statius's *Thebaid*, referred to by Servius, contains the most famous Latin evidence of the altar of Pity. The poet shows how *Clementia*, too, follows her vocation and becomes the protectress of the afflicted in the refuge created by the Heraclides.

In the analysis made by J. F. Burgess, six categories of individual stand out in the author's presentation:[69] (1) victims of tyrannical regimes (assuming a hendiadys at lines 504–505 *iraeque minaeque / regnaque*), (2) those who have suffered changes of Fortune, (3) those defeated in battle, (4) exiles, (5) rulers expelled from their thrones, (6) those who have committed crimes in a moment of frenzy:

Statius, *Thebaid* 12,481–85; 497–509:

Urbe fuit media nulli concessa potentum

ara deum; mitis posuit Clementia sedem

et miseri fecere sacram; sine supplice nunquam

illa novo, nulla damnavit vota repulsa.

Auditi quicumque rogant . . .

. . .

---

67. The equivalence is confirmed by the scholiast on Statius, *Thebaid* 12,481.

68. Bruggisser, *Romulus Seruianus*, 165.

69. J. F. Burgess, "Statius' Altar of Mercy," *Classical Quarterly* 22 (1972): 339–49, esp. 343.

Fama est defensos acie post busta paterni

numinis Herculeos sedem fundasse nepotes.

Fama minor factis: ipsos nam credere dignum

caelicolas, tellus quibus hospita semper Athenae,

ceu leges hominemque novum ritusque sacrorum

seminaque in vacuas hinc descendentia terras,

sic sacrasse loco commune animantibus aegris

confugium, unde procul starent iraeque minaeque   (1)

regnaque, et a iustis Fortuna recederet aris.   (1)(2)

Iam tunc innumerae norant altaria gentes.

Huc victi bellis patriaque a sede fugati,   (3)(4)

regnorumque inopes scelerumque errore nocentes   (5)(6)

conveniunt pacemque rogant . . . .

("... there was in the midst of the city an altar belonging to no god of power; gentle Clemency had there her seat, and the wretched made it sacred; never lacked she a new suppliant, none did she condemn or refuse their prayers. All that ask are heard . . . . Fame says that the sons of Hercules, protected by an army[70] after the disappearance in fire of their divine father, set up this altar; but Fame comes short of truth: it is right to believe that the heavenly ones themselves, to whom Athens was ever a welcoming land, as once they gave laws and a new man[71] and sacred ceremonies and the seeds that here descended upon the empty earth, so now sanctified in this spot a common refuge for travailing souls, whence the wrath and threatenings of monarchs might be far removed, and Fortune depart from a shrine of righteousness. Already to countless races were those altars known; hither came flocking those defeated in war and exiled from their country, kings who had lost their realms and those guilty of grievous crime, and sought for peace.")

The importance of this enumeration resides, for us, in the common denominator uniting all these classes of individual: they do not bear responsibility for what happens to them. This crowd of unfortunates is the sport of adversity.

---

70. My translation; cf. Sallust, *Hist.* 3,106 (as quoted by Nonnus 538,34): *duplici acie locum editum multo sanguine suorum defensum* , "an elevated position which he had defended with a double battle-line and at the cost of many of his men" (trans. P. McGushin [Oxford: Oxford University Press, 1992]).

71. On the identity of this man, see the edition of the *Thebaid* by R. Lesueur (Paris: Les Belles Lettres, 1994) 182, n. 43.

The description of the altar of *Clementia* in the work of Statius, whose authority Servius borrows, undoubtedly exerted a humanitarian influence on Latin culture. The influence is detectable in the writings of other Latin authors, in Servius's time and earlier. Rhetorical precept presented the altar of Pity as a gripping example of compassion.[72] Arguing for the restoration of the schools of Autun in the closing years of the third century, Eumenius invokes historical antecedents for the realization of an ideal, among which figures the altar of Pity at Athens.[73] The same motif appears later in the work of Claudian. In the war against Gildo, Stilicho dissuades Honorius from taking the head of his army against the enemy, urging him instead to place there the son of the tyrant, Mascezel, whose sons Gildo had eliminated, not even permitting their proper burial. In his exhortations, Stilicho refers to the altar of Pity erected at Athens to protect the unfortunate.[74]

The Asylum of Romulus and Assistance to the Distressed: An Antecedent in Dionysius of Halicarnassus

According to Dionysius of Halicarnassus,[75] whose testimony has already been quoted, Romulus, planning to augment the population of the city, heard that a considerable number of inhabitants of Italian cities were fleeing tyrannies and oligarchies. He decided to welcome these refugees, provided they were freeborn, without discrimination either of their misfortunes (*symphoras*) or their social condition (*tychas*). Honor of a god supplied the pretext for this action. He therefore consecrated an area between the Capitol and the citadel, known at the time of our author as "between-the-two-groves," and designated this as an asylum for supplicants (*hiketais*). There he erected a temple to a divinity whose precise name the writer does not know, a temple for miserable refugees, with the guarantee that they will not suffer from their enemies in any way. To this place stream those escaping calamities at home. They are touched so much by the founder's daily presence and kind attentions that they decide to stay for good. It is clear that, for Dionysius of Halicarnassus, Romulus was moved by feelings of humanity and pity toward those who had been laid low by misfortune and subjected to an abusive power, toward uprooted persons

---

72. Seneca, *Controversiae* 10,5,10; Quintilian, *Institutio oratoria* 5,11,38; cf. the metaphorical use in Apuleius, *Metamorphoses* 11,15.

73. *Panegyrici Latini* 9 (ed. Galletier, 5) 7,1.

74. Claudian, *Carm.* 15 (Gild.) 404–405.

75. Dion. Hal., *Ant.* 2,15,3–4.

reduced to the condition of suppliants. The founder adopts the attitude of protector and benefactor, granting citizenship and land to those who remain with him.

In spite of the attempts of antiquaries,[76] tradition had not put the asylum of Romulus explicitly under the protection of any divinity, a fact which Dionysius confirms (2,15,4). To ground the association he wished to make, Servius therefore took advantage of the latitude allowed by prior exegesis. Dionysius certifies (1,89,1) that he has borrowed from numerous Greek and Roman written works on the origins of the Romans. Thus he confirms that a humanitarian and philanthropic perception of the asylum of Romulus had long been firmly established in the Roman tradition by the time Servius connected it with an Athenian institution representing the same ideal. Indeed, according to Pausanias (1,17,1), the altar of Pity was an initiative that manifested the *philanthropia* of the Athenians. Thus, if Servius really is the inventor rather than the relayer of this version of events, his linking, under the sign of assistance to the afflicted, of the asylum of Romulus with the altar of Pity acquires the guarantee of opportunity. That guarantee is reinforced by the fact that, in his search for a Greek antecedent, he is not alone within the world of exegesis: one of his peers, commenting on the very passage of Juvenal adduced by Servius in the scholion on *Aeneid* 8,342, also insists on the Athenian character of the institution.[77] But unlike him, Servius does not retain the ignominious character of the asylum. Moreover, in order to stress that Rome has not been built on a criminal basis, he is careful to distinguish the occupants of the asylum by the term *advenae* (foreigners), while a great number of authors use the pejorative term *convenae* (adventurers or, as I have translated it, vagabonds).

The Asylum of Romulus between Model and Prefiguration

Our inquiry has so far concentrated on the asylum of Romulus. It could include other facets of the hero that stir the passions of Christians, and particularly of Augustine: the fratricide, the rape of the Sabine women and the war that followed it, Tarpeia's treason, the sharing of hegemony with Titus Tatius, the apotheosis.[78] Although the motif of the asylum is not, among

---

76. See above, nn. 30 and 37.

77. On the Athenian character of the asylum, Scholiast on Juvenal, *Sat.* 8, 273: *Romulus ut augeret populum Romanum secutus Atheniensium morem asylum in luco constituit.* On its ignominious character, id. on *Sat.* 8,275: *Fertur [sc. Romulus] nam latronum aut perditorum collegisse populum.*

78. For contemporary evidence relating to the apotheosis, see the Appendix.

Romulean episodes, the subject most extensively treated in the *City of God*, it nevertheless provides a guiding thread for a type of analysis that promises to be productive. Comparison of the points of view adopted in the debate by Augustine and Servius throws a particularly revealing light on the conception each author has of the City as a human institution.

Servius: The Necessity of a Perfect Antecedent

As a commentator on Virgil, Servius indirectly rejects the charges that would make the place of refuge no more than an assembly point for assorted riffraff. Transforming the asylum into a replica of the Athenian model, the altar of Pity founded by the Heraclides, he imparts a Hellenic legitimacy to one factor in the genesis of the City, and credits Rome with a mission of philanthropy derived from the precedent that inspired the new foundation. Furthermore, by referring to the mention of the altar of Pity in the *Thebaid* of Statius, Servius covers himself with the authority of a poet who made *Clementia* the protecting deity of afflicted persons whose common grief was to suffer reversals of fortune for which they were not themselves answerable. In this perspective, Rome becomes the inheritor of the city of civilization par excellence. Servius's vision of the asylum is entirely positive.

In his overall interpretation of the Romulean legend, Servius appears as a defender of the *conditor*. His attitude is that of a pagan traditionalist, for whom the destiny of Rome is determined at its birth. Purity of origins is an indispensable postulate. Rome must be born in legitimacy, precisely because it is destined to be a legitimate power, endowed with universality and eternity. That is why the deeds of its founder cannot be stained with crime. Within this system of thought, Servius looks for a valorizing paradigm for the asylum.

Augustine: Wayfaring Toward a Perfect Model

Augustine is not mistaken about this fundamental mechanism of pagan perception when he exclaims that, in the minds of his adversaries, laying the blame on Rome means laying the blame on its founder:

Augustine, *Sermo* 81,8 (PL 38.505): *Iniuria fit Romae, quia dicitur: cadit? Non Romae, sed forte artifici eius. Conditori eius facimus iniuriam, quia dicimus: Roma ruit, quam condidit Romulus.*

("Is it an injury to Rome to say it falls? Not to Rome, but perhaps to its creator. To its founder we do injury, because we say: Rome is ruined, which Romulus founded.")

97

For his part, Augustine needs an imperfect antecedent, in order to make the asylum evolve toward something more perfect. In his eyes, the Romulean asylum remained a suspect place, the sole merit of which was to have saved its occupants from plunging themselves deeper into crime. He draws a circle of scepticism round the institution that had presided at the creation of the City, and that would not achieve its full human realization until the City's capture by Christian invaders who respected the rights of the besieged pagans—notwithstanding that, in the event, the invaders were Arians. For Augustine, in any case, the true asylum was located beyond the city of men, in the realm of divine mercy; the Roman asylum, from Romulus to Alaric, was inscribed in the wayfaring of a temporal city that had yet to attain its spiritual perfection.

This treatment of the asylum motif as something anchored in the human order and summoned to a higher realization in the divine provides a significant illustration of Augustine's thought concerning the intermingling of the two cities, *perplexae . . . invicemque permixtae*, as he himself says.[79] By means of the asylum, the eternal city makes its progress in the temporal city, according to a process described in the preface to his work:

> *Civ.* 1, praef.: *Gloriosissimam civitatem dei siue in hoc temporum cursu, cum inter impios peregrinatur ex fide vivens, sive in illa stabilitate sedis aeternae, quam nunc expectat per patientiam, "quoadusque iustitia convertatur in iudicium," deinceps adeptura per excellentiam victoria ultima et pace perfecta, hoc opere instituto et mea ad te promissione debito defendere adversus eos, qui conditori eius deos suos praeferunt, fili carissime Marcelline, suscepi.*

> ("Here, my dearest son Marcellinus, is the fulfilment of my promise, a book in which I have taken upon myself the task of defending the most glorious City of God against those who prefer their own gods to the Founder of that City. I treat of it both as it exists in this world of time, a stranger among the ungodly, living by faith, and as it stands in the security of its everlasting seat. This security it now awaits in steadfast patience, until "justice returns to judgement"; but it is to attain it hereafter in virtue of its ascendancy over its enemies, when the final victory is won and peace established.")

---

79. *Civ.* 1,35: *Perplexae quippe sunt istae duae civitates in hoc saeculo invicemque permixtae, donec ultimo iudicio dirimantur* ("In truth those two cities are interwoven and intermixed in this era, and await separation at the last judgement").

Modalities of an Antagonism

The *City of God* is—though it is more than that—a refutation of the charges brought by pagans who considered the downfall of Rome to be the gods' punishment for its inhabitants' desertion of ancestral cults. Through the intrusion of Christianity, the Romans had broken the covenant that bound them to their gods. Consequently, the gods were released from the duty of protection granted to the city of their votaries:

Augustine, *Retractationes* 2,43,1: *Cuius eversionem deorum falsorum multorumque cultores, quos usitato nomine paganos vocamus, in christianam religionem referre conantes, solito acerbius et amarius deum verum blasphemare coeperunt. Unde ego exardescens "zelo domus dei" adversus eorum blasphemias vel errores libros de ciuitate dei scribere institui.*

("The worshippers of the many false gods, to whom we commonly give the name of pagans, attempting to attribute this disaster to the Christian religion, began more sharply and more bitterly than usual to blaspheme the true God. Burning with the zeal of God's house, I decided to write against their blasphemies and errors the books on the *City of God*.")

This refutation stretched over several years. The writing and publishing of the *City of God* took places by stages, from 412 to 426.[80] In 413, Augustine published the first three books of his work. This first edition, he remarks, had been widely diffused and provoked a written answer from the pagan side, whose instigators awaited a favorable moment for publication (*Civ.* 5,26). Puzzling over the identity of these pagan adversaries, scholars have proposed Rutilius Namatianus and his *De reditu suo* of 417.[81] Despite strong arguments in its favor, this position has not won unanimous assent.[82] But even if the identity of the pagan or pagans involved in this response cannot be precisely discerned, specialists agree in locating its provenance in the aristocratic milieu of the

---

80. See the introduction by G. Bardy to the edition in *Bibliothèque Augustinienne,* 33 (Paris: Desclée De Brouwer, 1959) 22–35.

81. A. Dufourcq, "Rutilius Namatianus contre saint Augustin," *Revue d'Histoire et de Littérature Religieuses* 10 (1905): 488–92; J. Lamotte, "Buts et adversaires de saint Augustin dans la *Cité de Dieu,*" *Augustiniana* 11 (1961): 434–69; P. Courcelle, *Histoire littéraire des grandes invasions germaniques,* 3rd edn. (Paris: Études Augustiniennes, 1964) 104–107; A. Cameron, "Rutilius Namatianus, St. Augustine, and the Date of the *De Reditu,*" *Journal of Roman Studies* 57 (1967): 31–39.

82. F. Paschoud, *Roma Aeterna: Études sur le patriotisme romain dans l'Occident latin à l'époque des grandes invasions* (Rome: Institut Suisse de Rome, 1967) 159 n. 21. See now G. J. P. O'Daly, "Ciuitate dei (De-)," *Augustinus-Lexikon* 1 (Basel: Schwabe & Co., 1994) 969–1010, at 974.

City of Rome.[83] Now, according to Macrobius's *Saturnalia*, Servius was close to the intellectual elite of the Urban pagan aristocracy. I do not mean to suggest that the anonymity of Augustine's opponent conceals the name of Servius. The first purpose of a scholiast is literary exegesis and Servius's commentary on Virgil cannot be mistaken for an anti-Christian apology. Nevertheless, in his approach of the legend of Romulus, Servius appears either neutral or favorable to the founder. His vision of the original Rome is the opposite of that which predominates among Christians. In his interpretation of Romulus's deeds, he is in sympathy with members of the Roman upper class who remained passionately attached to the religious and literary patrimony.

It can hardly be said too often how problematic a phenomenon is the so-called "pagan reaction." It is so, in the first place, because—as a modern scholarly construct—it has been defined against or as the reflex of a Christian concept: the mechanism of "reaction" is imagined from the opposed point of view of Christianity, whereas a pagan in the last days of the Empire would have been far more conscious of belonging to a continuity than to a reaction. The pagan resistance (to speak more carefully) is a problem calling for delicate methodology. The documentary situation is complex: the constitution, or restitution, of our dossier of evidence depends in large part on persons—the Christians—who, in a fragmentary or tendentious way, preserved particular items for the purpose of refutation. Furthermore, the phenomenon in its evolution is never entirely religious without being literary, or entirely literary without being religious. This indissociability of attributes is well expressed in the credo of Julian, defender and restorer of paganism par excellence, for whom religion and literature are sisters, as Libanius reports in his funeral speech for the emperor.[84] To repeat the point: Servius's interpretation is essentially literary, but it converges with the aspirations and impulses of aristocratic circles attached to ancestral beliefs.

An attentive analysis of the motif of the asylum in Servius's commentary shows, as if by reflection, that the combat of Augustine against Romulus in the *City of God* is not at all chimerical. His objections to the asylum are the more pertinent, because, at the time he voiced them, profane literary scholarship—as represented by Servius—was endeavoring by means of a revived exegesis to give credit to a positive and philanthropic vision of the Romulean

---

83. Bardy (above, n. 80) 25.
84. Libanius, *Or.* 18,157 (ed. R. Foerster); cf. *Oratio* 62, 8.

institution. We should not forget that, as a teacher of Virgil at Rome,[85] Servius enjoyed a certain ascendancy over the educated youth of that city. As a result, the interpretation of the works of the poet that he proposes, especially of the deeds of the City's founder, would have had an immediate intellectual impact on the society of his time.

Conclusion: The Value of a Comparison

Servius joins the current of interpretation that presents the asylum of Romulus as a refuge given to persons broken by misfortunes. Rome's first inhabitants are not responsible for the adversity that crushes them. They form the city of the excluded or outcast, under the protection of a founder whose magnanimity is thereby thrown into relief. At a time when literary exegesis at Rome was tending, through Servius, to reverse arguments against the Romulean asylum and to make its occupants the *victims* rather than the *agents* of injustice, it was more important than ever for Augustine[86] to defend a relative—or indeed negative—vision of the founder's initiative, and to subordinate it to an eschatological perspective on the history of the City. For the bishop of Hippo, the asylum of Romulus is only a preliminary phase in the emergence of the heavenly city, the shadow of an institution that will attain its perfection in the city of the elect.

---

85. His activity at Rome is corroborated in several ways: (1) the *subscriptiones* of two manuscripts of Juvenal, viz. the Laurentianus 34.42 (*legi ego Niceus apud M. Serbium Romae et emendavi*) and the Leidensis 82 (*legi ego Niceus Rome apud Servium magistrum et emendavi*), (2) a passage of Macrobius, *Saturnalia* 6,6,1 (*cotidie enim Romanae indoli enarrando eundem vatem),* and (3) a note of Ps.-Acro on Horace, *Sat.* 1,9,76 (*sic Servius magister urbis exposuit*). Regarding (3) there is no reason to follow O. Keller in his Teubner edn. (Leipzig: G.B. Teubner, 1902–1904) in bracketing *urbis*; see now L. Holtz, *Donat et la tradition de l'enseignement grammatical: Étude sur l'Ars Donati et sa diffusion (IVe-IXe siècle) et édition critique* (Paris: CNRS, 1981), 223 n. 1.

86. Other Christian authors of Augustine's time do not ignore the legend of the asylum. Jerome's tone is variable: neutral in the *Chronicle* (ed. R. Helm, 88a: *ob asyli inpunitatem magna Romulo multitudo coniungitur*), he turns polemical at *In Amos* 1,1,1 (*congregata pastorum et latronum manu, Romulus sui nominis condidit civitatem*). Prudentius, in an invective against the ancestral gods of the Romans, denounces the terror behind such superstitions, from which the Romulean asylum had benefited (*Contra Symmachum* 1,196: *talis et antiquum servavit terror asylum*). Among pagan abbreviators Eutropius relates the matter without disdain (1,2,1: *multitudinem finitimorum in civitatem recepit*), while the *De viris illustribus* of Ps.-Aurelius Victor is more incisive (2,1: *Romulus asylum convenis patefecit*).

101

In the pagan approach, as in the Christian one, the genesis of the City conditions the subsequent course of its history. Whereas the commentator Servius refers to a perfect precedent that perpetuates itself throughout the civilized world and of which Rome is custodian, Augustine envisages the development of a human reality that is perfectible and perfected by God's providence. In one case, the human institution is the model; in the other, it is a prefiguration. For Augustine, history appears as evolution; for Servius, as continuity. Both lay claim to an Eternal City. But Augustine's eternity dispenses with the city of Servius.

Appendix:
The Apotheosis of Romulus in the Light of Recent Research

The resistance Augustine had to confront was not confined to literature, as may be demonstrated with reference to another Romulean motif, the apotheosis—target of violent attacks in the *City of God*. The proof consists of a new interpretation by Gianfranco Paci of previously neglected epigraphic data.[87] The point of departure for Paci's argument is the redating to a later period, on palaeographic grounds, of two inscriptions *deo Romulo*, one from Fulginiae (modern Foligno), the other from Sestinum (Sestino, likewise in Umbria), respectively numbers 5206 and 5997 in Volume XI of the *Corpus Inscriptionum Latinarum*. The dedication of Sestinum was found in 1856, at the same time as other inscriptions of a public nature. The provenance, which corresponds exactly to the location of the city's forum, dispels any doubt about the public character of the inscription. Its exact similarity with the Fulginiae dedications suggests an identical context for the latter. Along with these and other points of convergence, the two inscriptions present two interesting singularities in the formulation of the text: the absence of the name of the dedicator, and a surprising attribution of divinity. The anonymity of the dedicator may be plausibly explained by the fear of Christian censure. As for the terms of the dedication, instead of giving the name of Romulus once he had become divine, which was Quirinus, they assert that *Romulus* is a god. Paci's arguments are designed to show that these inscriptions, by proposing—as late as the fourth or early fifth century[88]—in a public and official form, the name and image of the founder of the *Urbs*, constitute an instrument of propaganda; their purpose is to

---

87. G. Paci, "Due dediche al dio Romolo d'età tardo-antica," *Cahiers du Centre G. Glotz* 7 (1996) 135–44.

88. Paci 143.

exalt the divine nature of Romulus in opposition to Christian opinion, which held him to be merely a human creation, a misleading fiction.

I would add a number of considerations, which corroborate Paci's thesis—in my opinion, a convincing one. First, by way of counterexample, we may confront the text of our two inscriptions with that of the Augustan tribute to Romulus in the forum at Pompeii:

CIL I (2nd edn.) 189 n. 4 (= X.809); ILS 64: . . . *receptusque in deoru[m] / numerum Quirinu[s] appellatu[s est]*. (". . . and having been received into the number of the gods, he was called Quirinus.")

The intention of this inscription seems to be quite different. The formula is meant to stand surety for Romulus's transformation into a god and for the change of name resulting from the apotheosis. In this connection, we would do well to set our two Umbrian inscriptions in the context of a denunciation by Lactantius: [89]

Lactantius, *Institutiones divinae* 1,21,22-23: *Solent enim mortuis consecratis nomina immutari, credo ne quis eos putet homines fuisse. Nam et Romulus post mortem Quirinus factus est . . . .*

("For the custom is to change the names of the dead who have been deified, in my opinion so as ensure that no-one supposes that they were once human beings. For Romulus too became Quirinus after his death . . . .")

Lactantius's argument has considerable force because it takes place against a background of pagan authority, that of euhemerism, according to which the gods are nothing other than famous persons deified by their own contemporaries in recognition of their great deeds. By contrast, we can see how the Umbrian inscriptions accredit, in a public place, a "decoding" of Romulus's divinized name that runs counter to the current Christian interpretation. The inscriptions thus present a manifesto of opposition, from which there emanates a profession of pagan faith: the founder of Rome is revealed, not as a human being falsely divinized, but in his true divinity. The belief in Romulus's divine nature kept its hold on pagan imaginations. In the contest between pagans and Christians over the vision of Rome's past, Romulus, founder of the earthly city, was set against Christ, founder of the eternal one.

Augustine combats this attachment with passion. Among other passages that could be cited, we may retain the following one from the final book of the *City of God*, which refers to the antagonism between Romulus's divinity and Christ's:

---

89. Also cited by Paci 137, n. 8.

Civ. 22, 6: Roma conditorem suum iam constructa et dedicata tamquam deum coluit in templo; haec autem Hierusalem conditorem suum deum Christum, ut construi posset et dedicari, posuit in fidei fundamento. Illa illum amando esse deum credidit, ista istum deum esse credendo amavit.

("Rome worshipped her founder as a god in a temple after she had been built and dedicated; but this Jerusalem made her founder, the God Christ, the basis of her faith, so that she might be built and dedicated. The one city believed Romulus to be a god because she loved him; the other loved Christ because she believed him to be God.")

Rome and Bethlehem both boasted of having sheltered a miraculous birth—the twins with the she-wolf and the infant Jesus—and Jerome opposes Romulus's hut to the birthplace of the Messiah.[90] Similarly, in a sermon for the feast of the apostles Peter and Paul on June 29, 441, Pope Leo the Great draws a parallel between the two founders of Christian Rome and Romulus and Remus, founders of the pagan city.[91] Read in this context, the two dedications from Umbria are rich in significance. Against Christian attempts to obliterate the Romulean apotheosis, the inscriptions from Fulginiae and Sestinum militate for a pagan fundamentalism: Romans should remember that *their* god is Romulus, not Christ. In the landscape of ideological struggle that these monuments help us to reconstruct, Augustine is far from being a Don Quixote tilting at windmills.

---

90. Jerome, pref. to Didymus, *De spiritu sancto* (PL 23.103).
91. Leo, *Sermo* 82,1.

AUGUSTINE'S USE OF SALLUST IN THE *CITY OF GOD*: THE ROLE OF THE GRAMMATICAL TRADITION

Paul C. Burns

Augustine's connection with the more learned members of his audience was built on a shared experience of the late antique training in Latin language and literature and the particular resources employed therein. The impact of that experience will influence his choice of terms and his use of evidence and arguments based on established authors.[1] Many scholars have contributed to our understanding of the surviving textual evidence of the grammatical traditions of the late fourth and early fifth centuries. An important source for the work of the grammarians is the *Commentary on Virgil* by Servius, published in a critical edition a century ago.[2] Seminars and publications at Harvard over the intervening years have illuminated the complex relationships between the text of that commentary and collections of scholia. They have also yielded a number of studies on the methods of this grammatical tradition and, in particular,

---

1. For the role of Republican authors as authorities in grammatical writings of the imperial period, see H. D. Jocelyn, "Ancient Scholarship and Virgil's Use of Republican Latin Poetry," *Classical Quarterly* 14 (1964): 280–95, 15 (1965): 126–44; R. A. Kaster, "Servius and *Idonei Auctores*," *American Journal of Philology* 99 (1978): 189-209; R. B. Lloyd, "Republican Authors in Servius and the Scholia Danielis," *Harvard Studies in Classical Philology* 65 (1961): 291–341. On Sallust in other scholia: E. Rawson, "Sallust in the Eighties," *Classical Quarterly* 37 (1987): 163–80.

2. G. Thilo and H. Hagen, *Servii grammatici qui feruntur in Virgilii Carmina Commentarii*, 3 vols. (Leipzig: Teubner, 1881–1889).

its focus on the *quadriga* of Terence, Virgil, Sallust, and Cicero and its appeals to other Republican authors as arbiters of language and meaning.[3] More recent studies, notably those of R. A. Kaster,[4] have explored the social function of the grammarian in the Latin culture of this period. This scholarship helps account for the pivotal role of Sallust in Augustine's treatment of Roman history, especially in 411–413 as he began the *City of God* in the aftermath of Alaric's sack of Rome.

That event was interpreted in diverse ways, not only within the Christian community but also among the surviving "pagan" members of the Roman senatorial class who blamed Christians for the crisis.[5] The attitudes of pagans at Rome and in the Greek East during this period are well attested.[6] Over several decades, Christian emperors had reduced support for pagan cult while leaving the religious practices themselves largely intact. In due course, Gratian eliminated imperial funding for pagan priests, left positions in priestly colleges unfilled and dropped the title of *Pontifex Maximus*.[7] In 391 Theodosius moved more aggressively in edicts to the prefects of Rome and Egypt prohibiting pagan sacrifice;[8] then on 8 November 392 he prohibited all pagan sacrifice in any cult practice or divination, and all veneration of household deities (*lares* and *penates*).[9] This legislative agenda against the pagans was continued by his son Honorius. In addition, there were many episodes of destruction of pagan

---

3. *Servianorum in Virgilii Carmina Commentariorum*, vol. 2, ed. E. K. Rand et al., (Lancaster, Pa.: American Society of Philology, 1946) and vol. 3, ed. A. F. Stocker et al., (Oxford: Oxford University Press, 1965). G. P. Goold, "Servius and the Helen Episode," *Harvard Studies in Classical Philology* 74 (1970): 101–68, provides an authoritative discussion of the relationship between the text of Servius and collections of additional scholia.

4. R. A. Kaster, *Guardians of Language: The Grammarian and Society in Late Antiquity* (Berkeley and Los Angeles: University of California Press, 1988), and n. 1 above.

5. F. Paschoud, *Roma aeterna: Études sur le patriotisme romain dans l'Occident latin à l'époque des grandes invasions* (Rome: Institut Suisse de Rome, 1967); H. Inglebert, *Les Romains chrétiens face a l'histoire de Rome: Histoire, christianisme et romanités en Occident dans l'Antiquité tardive (IIIe-Ve siècles)* (Paris: Études Augustiniennes, 1996). My use of "pagan" follows the caution and example of J. J. O'Donnell, "Paganus," *Classical Folia* 31 (1977): 163–69, and "The Demise of Paganism," *Traditio* 35 (1979): 45–88.

6. For an appeal for tolerance towards pagan religion, cf. Libanius's treatise *On the Temples*, composed probably in the early 390s.

7. On the status of pagans under Christian Emperors, see N. Q. King, *The Emperor Theodosius and the Establishment of Christianity* (London: SCM Press, 1961).

8. *Codex Theodosianus* 16,10,10 (from Milan) and 11 (from Aquileia).

9. *Codex Theodosianus* 16,10,12 (from Constantinople).

temples or expropriation of them for Christian use.[10] Early in the *City of God* Augustine shows his awareness of the specifically religious element in the pagan reaction to recent events.[11]

Augustine was concerned not simply to dismiss pagan claims but to prove his case against them, both to pagans and to Christians who looked to him for assistance. In the course of the *City of God* he appeals to Roman authors on the history of Roman religious practice. He frequently cites Marcus Terentius Varro, who catalogued a wide range of ancient Roman religious customs.[12] However, the religious debate is not so much about the history of pagan Roman cult itself as it is about certain shared assumptions and their application. Both communities believed in the presence and activity of the divine in human affairs. The issue is over the ways of providence in history, specifically Roman history. But which *period* of Roman history?

Pagans were dismayed by the initiatives of fourth-century emperors who were sympathetic to Christians or who championed Christian orthodoxy against heretics—and now, it would appear, against pagans too. They had scathingly designated this period under Christian emperors *tempora christiana*. To some influential Christians, the same developments had seemed to announce a new order of religious and social relationships.[13] Augustine, for his part, discusses the period of the Christian emperors only briefly and in muted tones in Letter

---

10. For a hostile pagan reaction, see Book 6 of Zosimus's *New History*, concluding with the disasters of 410.

11. This issue lies behind his treatment of the episode of Regulus in Book 1 of the *City of God*, written in 412. "Why," asks Augustine, "do our antagonists bring false accusations against the established Christian order [*tempora christiana*], alleging that catastrophe has come upon the city just because it has left off the worship of its gods?" (1,15). He returns to the same point in his summaries at 2,2 and 4,2. The issue of changes in religious sacrifice is also hinted at in Letter 138.

12. "Pagans" of this period such as Macrobius and Martianus Capella do likewise. On the shared interest of these three writers, all probably African, in Varro, see the note by J. J. O'Donnell, *Augustine: Confessions* (Oxford: Clarendon Press, 1992) 2.278. Both Augustine and Macrobius also make use of the more analytical interpretations of Roman religion by Cornelius Labeo.

13. Eusebius of Caesarea and later Ambrose of Milan saw Constantine and Theodosius respectively as harbingers of a new polity linking Christianity and Empire. Damasus associated this prospect more directly with the city of Rome itself. But Jerome's apocalyptic interpretation of the sack of Rome seems to have marked the end of the *Reichstheologie* of the fourth century. See Inglebert, *Les Romains chrétiens*, 286–95, and J. Doignon, "Oracles et prophéties sur la chute de Rome (395–410): Les réactions de Jérôme et d'Augustin," *Revue des Études Augustiniennes* 36 (1990): 120–46.

138 and later in the *City of God*.[14] In *City of God* 5, 24–25 he ascribes the temporal felicity under Constantine and Theodosius to three factors: the success of their policies, their peaceful deaths, and the relative ease of their succession. He acknowledges, however, that those conditions existed for some of the pagan emperors. He also points out that evils had befallen Christian emperors, selecting Jovian and Gratian as reminders that true happiness is not to be looked for in the present life. Letter 138 offers a similarly restrained evaluation of the Christian emperors.[15] By such means, Augustine diverts attention from the fourth century as a period in which to demonstrate the workings of providence.

He chooses to focus instead on a phase of Roman history that had ended in all but name about 440 years earlier: the Republic. Modern scholarship suggests three reasons for this choice. Many have recognized the rhetorical strategy of appealing to times of Roman history rife with disasters and culminating in the devastations of civil war. Further, Goulven Madec has demonstrated Augustine's development toward a more formally theological understanding of the *tempora christiana*; rather than emphasizing the political accession of Constantine as Eusebius and others had, Augustine began to invoke the incarnation of Christ as a decisive moment in God's action in human history. Finally, it was the (late) Republican period of Roman history and culture that informed the curricula of the grammarian and the rhetorician through the fourth century and beyond. For the grammatical tradition, it is the period privileged in the *Commentary* composed by Servius close to the time when Augustine began to compose the *City of God*.[16]

---

14. For his caution on this subject, see the classic study of R. A. Markus, *Saeculum: History and Society in the Theology of St. Augustine*, 2nd ed. (Cambridge: Cambridge University Press, 1988), ch. 2, with G. Madec, *"Tempora christiana*: Expression du triomphalisme chrétien ou récrimination païenne?"* in *Scientia Augustiniana: Studien über Augustinus, den Augustinismus und den Augustinerorden: Festschrift A. Zumkeller OSA zum 60. Geburtstag*, ed. C. P. Mayer and W. Eckermann (Würzburg: Augustinus Verlag, 1975) 112–36, and Markus, *"Tempora Christiana* Revisited,"* in *Augustine and His Critics*, ed. R. Dodaro and G. Lawless (London: Routledge, forthcoming).

15. Note especially *Ep.* 138, 16: *ut intellegerent vel hominum haec esse vitia non doctrinae vel non imperatorum sed aliorum, sine quibus imperatores agere nihil possunt.* The addressee of the letter, Marcellinus, had hitherto been a very successful member of the imperial administration; see below, n. 24.

16. For a probable dating of Servius's *Commentary* in the years after 410, see A. Cameron, "The Date and Identity of Macrobius," *Journal of Roman Studies* 56 (1966): 25–38 at 30, 32; cf. the discussion by Philippe Bruggisser at n. 53 in his essay in this volume.

In Servius's *Commentary on Virgil*, there are frequent citations from the work of Sallust. By my own rough calculation there are 32 from *Catiline* and 26 from *Jugurtha*. A 1992 study of the fragments of the *Histories* has identified 119 passages quoted in Servius.[17] Moreover, Servius cites 20 times the grammarian Asper's lost commentaries on both Sallust and Virgil.

In the main, Servius cites relatively short passages from Sallust[18] to illustrate the issue under discussion.[19] His primary concerns are textual readings, orthography, morphology, meaning, and the usage of Latin words. There are also brief comments on history, mythology, and geography. Near the beginning of his commentary at *Aen.* 1,96, Servius introduces Sallust as *Sallustius Romani generis disertissimus,* which succinctly identifies his role throughout the commentary. Three examples will suffice. At *Aen.* 1,13 Servius illustrates the word *longe* in Virgil's text with a passage from the beginning of Cato's response to Caesar in Sallust's *Catiline*. At *Aen.* 1,253 Servius says the form *labos* (for *labor*) is characteristic of Sallust. At *Aen.* 10,411 *sed* in the text of Virgil is explained as merely an inceptive particle, not a rational alternative, and this is said to be common usage in Sallust.

In passages with a potential for controversial interpretation which Augustine will explore, Servius remains interested only in the function of words. At *Aen.* 7,48 and again at 7,678 he says he accepts Sallust's position on the foundation of Rome. At *Aen.* 1,488 he cites Sallust's description of the courageous circumstances of Catiline's death without any evaluation of the complexities of the historian's portrayal of the corruption of virtue in his villains. At *Aen.* 6,540 Servius raises the Carthaginian Wars in order to cite Sallust's use of *ultimum* rather than *tertium*. Sallust's view, very important for Augustine, that this war was a turning point in the moral decline of Rome, is passed over by the grammarian. Early in his commentary on Book 1 of the *Aeneid*, Servius mentions the foundation of Carthage, the Roman fear of Carthage, its destruction

---

17. P. McGushin, *Sallust: The Histories*, vol. 1 (Oxford: Oxford University Press, 1992) 8–9.

18. Servius takes care to name the author and sometimes the actual text. He names the treatise on Catiline at *Aen.* 1,6 (*in bello Catilinae*) and at *Georg.* 2,499 (*in Catilinae bello*). Two of the scholia, at *Aen.* 4,283 and *Aen.* 8,8, name Sallust's second treatise as *in Jugurtha*. The DS scholia identify the third work as *Historiae* at *Aen.* 8,278 or elsewhere indicate a book number which helps to reconstruct the shape of this lost text (*Aen.* 2,502; 4,283; 10,45; 12,694) while the basic Servian text gives the title at *Georg.* 3,383 and a book number at *Aen.* 9,486.

19. For discussion of Servius's understanding of linguistic usage, to be distinguished from the archaizing taste of the character "Servius" in Macrobius's *Saturnalia*, see Kaster, *Guardians of Language*, ch. 5.

and its restoration (at lines 12, 18, 20 and 23). These facts are simply recorded, without any of the extended pessimistic evaluation of Sallust.

Augustine's recourse to the writings of Sallust is amply demonstrated in the 1967 work of H. Hagendahl who collected all the relevant quotations and commented upon them.[20] His study shows that Augustine's use of Sallust increased dramatically in 411. Prior to that time he had cited him only seven times; in his letters from 411 there are nine references, in the *City of God* the total jumps to 64, and from other writings during this period there are twelve passages. Thus, at the very period we are considering, Augustine seems to have turned deliberately to texts of Sallust.

Years earlier Augustine had illustrated his familiarity with the traditions and authors of the grammatical curriculum. He had demonstrated the method of the grammarian in an episode recounted in the education of Licentius in *De beata vita,* written in 386. The discussion is over the appropriate word to use as the opposite of "want" (*egestas*). Licentius supplies *plenitudo* but Augustine, citing the authority of Sallust—described *as lectissimus pensator verborum*—prefers *opulentia.* He concludes with a playful reference to the authority of grammarians and a pun on the generosity of their host Verecundus, a grammarian himself.[21]

Acknowledgment of the grammarian as the traditional commentator on standard authors appears in the *De utilitate credendi* of 391:

> Without being imbued with some poetic training [Augustine writes], you would not venture to take up Terentianus Maurus without a teacher. Asper, Cornutus, Donatus and countless others are required so that any writer can be understood.[22]

---

20. H. Hagendahl, *Augustine and the Latin Classics,* 2 vols. (Göteborg: Acta Universitatis Gothoburgensis, 1967): 1.225–44, 2.631–49. See also J. J. O'Donnell, "Augustine's Classical Readings," *Recherches Augustiniennes* 15 (1980): 144–75 at 163–4.

21. *De beata vita* 4.31: *Postea, inquam, de verbo quaeremus fortasse diligentius; non enim hoc curandum est in conquisitione veritatis. Quamvis enim Sallustius, lectissimus pensator verborum, egestati opposuerit opulentiam, tamen accipio istam plenitudinem. Non enim nec hic grammaticorum formidine liberabimur aut metuendum est, ne ab eis castigemur, quod incuriose utimur verbis, qui res suas nobis ad utendum dederunt. Ubi cum adrissent . . . .* For the grammatical careers of Verecundus and of Nebridius, another companion of this period, see Kaster, *Guardians of Language,* 356–59, 314–15.

22. *De utilitate credendi* 17: *nulla inbutus poetica disciplina Terentianum Maurum sine magistro adtingere non auderes, Asper, Cornutus, Donatus et alii innumerabiles requiruntur, ut quilibet poeta possit intellegi.*

These commentaries are all sources for Servius. He refers to Asper twenty times, frequently with approval; Donatus he mentions less frequently and often simply to disagree with him.[23]

Augustine's first extensive use of Sallust in a new context occurs in Letter 138, written in 412 to Marcellinus, to whom the first two books of the *City of God* are also dedicated.[24] In the letter he discusses four questions posed by the pagan senator Volusianus,[25] and in addressing two of them he refers to Sallust. He summons the Republican author when dealing with the alleged incompatibility between Christian teaching on "turning the other cheek" and the welfare of the Roman state, and in connection with the evils that occurred under Christian emperors. There are clear hints of his reason for choosing Sallust as an authority for this audience. At the outset Augustine says that he has chosen the letter form rather than the stricter form of a treatise. If the present attempt is not successful, he will have to resort to more subtle reasoning or to established authorities that his readers would be embarrassed to resist.[26] I suggest that the authority being invoked is the curriculum and standard authors of the grammarian. For now Augustine appeals to the familiar voice of Sallust not simply to establish patterns of speech but to invoke standards of historical judgment.[27] He even frames a contrast between the authority of Roman school-texts and the divine authority proclaimed by Christian preachers, as if in universal schools, to persons of all ages and classes and of both sexes.[28]

---

23. For example, at *Aen.* 8,383 Servius's note concludes with a reference to both Sallust and Asper: *Item in Sallustio ad bellum Persi Macedonicum. Sic Asper.* At *Aen.* 10,539 he defends the reading *insignibus armis* with a judgment of Asper that relies on Sallust: INSIGNIS ARMIS *Asper sic legit et utitur Sallustii exemplo, qui ait, "equo atque armis insignibus"* (see J. E. G. Zetzel, *Latin Textual Criticism in Antiquity* [New York: Arno Press, 1981] 69–70). At *Aen.* 11,801 he cites Asper against Sallust: *nec "huius custodias" secundum Sallustium qui ait, "castella custodias thesaurorum" pro "custodiae": ita enim Asper intellegit.* At *Georg.* 2,324 he cites Asper in support of a textual reading, this time against Donatus but without any reference to Sallust.

24. On Augustine and Marcellinus, see the essay by N. B. McLynn in this volume, with M. Moreau, "Le dossier Marcellinus dans la correspondence de saint Augustin," *Recherches Augustiniennes* 9 (1973): 3–181, and the commentary of J. J. O'Donnell, http://ccat.sas.upenn.edu/jod/augustine/151intro.html. (January 1996).

25. On Volusianus and his milieu, see A. Chastagnol, "Le sénateur Volusien et la conversion d'une famille de l'aristocratie romaine au Bas-Empire," *Revue des Études Anciennes* 58 (1956): 240–53; P. Brown, "Aspects of the Christianisation of the Roman Aristocracy," *Journal of Roman Studies* 51 (1961): 1–11; J. J. O'Donnell, http://ccat.sas.upenn.edu/jod/augustine/volusian.html. (January 1996).

26. *Ep.* 138, 1: *vel uberiore vel subtiliore ratione vel certe auctoritate, cui resistere indignum putent.*

Referring to the charge of incompatibility between Christian teaching and the security of the Roman state, Augustine paraphrases a passage from *Catiline* 52,19: "How could they have brought the state from a small and poor one into a rich and wealthy one?"[29] He answers this question by quoting a passage from a different section of the *Catiline* on the policy of mercy toward defeated enemies: "They preferred to pardon injuries received rather than to seek revenge."[30] In neither passage does he identify the author or the text, perhaps considering that he had excused himself with the earlier observation that this was a letter and not a treatise. Or perhaps the very familiarity of this voice from the Roman classroom made formal identification superfluous.

In answer to Volusianus's question about evils befalling the state under Christian emperors, Augustine cites Sallust to illustrate the moral degeneration of Rome in the Republic and the even worse evils which afflicted the state at that time. He quotes a passage from the *Jugurthan War* on the venality of Romans, once again without naming his source: "O mercenary city and ripe for plucking, if it could find a buyer."[31] Augustine names the text but not the author, presuming no doubt that the latter would need no further identification. "That same person," he continues, "the most noble historian in the book on the *Catiline War* well before the coming of Christ, does not omit to mention . . ."[32] and he offers a detailed list from Sallust of the greed of Romans in piling up things taken from private and public, religious and secular sources.[33]

---

27. The use of historical *exempla* in making ethical judgments is standard practice in the Roman rhetorical tradition. As I hope to demonstrate elsewhere, Augustine engages in a critical reappraisal of those *exempla*. For his treatment of *exempla* from Livy, see Catherine Conybeare's essay in this volume.

28. *Ep.* 138, 10: *Cum vero legitur praecipiente auctoritate divina non reddendum malum pro malo, cum haec tam salubris admonitio congregationibus populorum tamquam publicis utriusque sexus atque omnium aetatum et dignitatum scholis de superiore loco personat, accusatur religio tamquam inimica rei publicae.*

29. *Ep.* 138, 9: *unde quid opus est, ut diutius laboremus ac non ipsos potius percontemur, quo modo poterant gubernare atque augere rem publicam, quam ex parva et inopi magnam opulentamque fecerunt.* Cf. Sallust, *Cat.* 52,19: *Nolite existumare maiores nostros armis rem publicam ex parva magnam fecisse.*

30. *Ep.* 138, 9: *qui "accepta iniuria ignoscere quam persequi malebant"*? Sallust, *Cat.* 9,5: *et accepta iniuria ignoscere quam persequi malebant.*

31. *Ep.* 138, 16: *"O urbem venalem et mature perituram, si emptorem invenerit!"* Sallust, *Iug.* 35,10: *Sed postquam Roma [Iugurtha] egressus est, fertur saepe eo tacitus respiciens postremo dixisse: "urbem venalem et mature perituram, si emptorem invenerit."*

32. *Ep.* 138, 16: *In libro etiam belli Catilinum ante adventum utique Christi idem nobilissimus historicus eorum non tacet.*

He concludes his indictment of the moral corruption of Rome with his longest quotation in this letter, from Juvenal's *Sixth Satire*.[34]

The early books of the *City of God* were composed around the same time as Letter 138. In Book 1 Augustine cites Sallust only occasionally, but the latter's influence can be felt in his choice of operative terms such as *libido dominandi* at 1,1 and in his emphasis on greed and ambition as characteristically Roman vices. He quotes Sallust explicitly at 1,5, introducing him as *Sallustius nobilitatae veritatis historicus,* and then wrongly attributes a passage on the ravages of war to the speech by Cato in the *Catiline* rather than to one by Caesar. Book 2 is marked by many more quotations from Sallust and by a more analytical, as opposed to rhetorical, presentation of his historical case. Augustine makes extensive use of Sallust's presentation of the history of the Republic as a fall from an original condition of natural justice. He prefers texts, such as the *Histories*, which place that fall early in the history of Rome, even as early as the period of its foundation, rather than dating it from the destruction of Carthage in 146 (the pivotal date in the *Jugurthan War*). Book 2 also provides a good illustration of Augustine's resort to the grammatical tradition.

At 2,3 he points to the ground shared by educated members of his audience: "For those instructed in liberal studies love history and know these things."[35] In fact, Augustine seems to organize Book 2 around the standard authors of the grammatical curriculum: Sallust, Cicero, Terence, and Virgil. But he selects examples and themes suitable to his interpretation of Roman history as a decline from an ideal condition. The first section is an extended critique of the practices of the Roman theater, concluding with a brief acknowledgment of *Terentius vester* at 2,12. Then comes a key section with a number of passages from Sallust followed by an extended treatment of Cicero's views of the ideal state. Virgil is cited heavily throughout.

At 2,17 and 2,18 Augustine cites a number of passages from Sallust, using *Catiline* 9,1 three times as an ironic refrain: "Justice and morality prevailed

---

33. *Ep.* 138, 16: *quando "primum insueverit exercitus populi Romani amare, potare, signa, tabulas pictas, vasa caelata mirari, ea privatim et publice rapere, delubra spoliare, sacra profanaque omnia polluere"* (= Sallust, *Cat.* 11,6).

34. Juvenal was introduced into the commentaries of the grammarians in the late fourth or early fifth century: A. Cameron, *Journal of Roman Studies* 56 (1966): 30, n. 43.

35. *Civ.* 2,3: *Nam qui eorum studiis liberalibus instituti amant historiam, facillime ista noverunt.* Cf. *Ep.* 138, 9: *cum viris liberaliter instituti.*

among them by nature as much as by law."[36] Then he mentions three events from the early history of the Roman Republic: the deceitful trick with the Sabines, the expulsion of Lucretia's husband from the consulship, and the mean-spirited treatment of their hero Camillus. He lets these familiar episodes of injustice speak for themselves. At 2,18 he repeats the refrain and appeals to passages from the *Histories* that describe the conflict of the *patres* and *plebs* from the very beginning of the Republic. He moves quickly through the period of the wars with Carthage, to the destructive experience of the Civil Wars under Marius and Sulla. He next quotes two passages of judgment from Sallust, and claims that other Roman historians agree but do not express themselves so effectively. A passage from *Catiline* 5,9, right at the end of Sallust's prologue, has a ring of Jonathan Swift: "From the most beautiful and best condition Rome has become the worse and most flagrant."[37] The second passage, from the *Histories,* is an impassioned description of Roman moral degradation as a devastating flood.[38] Augustine asserts that this view is shared by all Roman authorities on the course of Roman history. These authorities are from a time before the coming of Christ, before the *tempora christiana* on any reckoning.

In conclusion: Augustine in Letter 138 and in the early books of *City of God* invokes a familiar and authoritative author from the Roman school curriculum in order to engage the educated part of his audience. In subsequent books he continues his review of the calamities that have befallen Rome throughout its history. At 3,17, he uses Sallust's *Histories* to recount those misfortunes in some detail.[39] And he reminds his audience once again that he is using authorities whom they have taken great pains to master and to have their children read.[40]

---

36. Ibid. 2,17 (and 2,18): *sicut Sallustius ait, "ius bonumque apud eos non legibus magis quam natura valebat?"*

37. *Civ.* 2,18: *"ex pulcherrima atque optima pessima ac flagitiosissima facta est."* Sallust, *Cat* 5,9: *ut paulatim inmutata ex pulcherruma [atque optuma] pessuma ac flagitiosissuma facta sit.*

38. *Civ.* 2,18: *"Ex quo tempore, ut ait, maiorum mores non paulatim ut antea, sed torrentis modo praecipitati, adeo iuventus luxu atque avaritia corrupta, ut merito dicatur genitos esse, qui neque ipsi habere possent res familiares neque alios pati."* This and other fragments of the *Historiae* are now best consulted in L. D. Reynolds, *C. Sallustii Crispi Catilina, Iugurtha, Historiarum fragmenta selecta, Appendix Sallustiana* (Oxford: Clarendon Press, 1991), here 158, trans. with commentary by McGushin (n. 17 above) 1.13.

39. Augustine repeats much of the quotation from Sallust's *Historiae* which he had used back at 2,18. He adds a passage from the same source which is also preserved by Aulus Gellius, *Noctes Atticae* 9,12,13–15.

40. *Civ.* 3,17: *Neque enim gravius vel graviora dicimus auctoribus eorum et stilo et otio multum impares; quibus tamen ediscendis et ipsi elaboraverunt et filios suos elaborare compellunt.*

THE USES OF DECAY: HISTORY IN SALVIAN'S *DE GUBERNATIONE DEI*

David Lambert

About twenty years after Augustine wrote the later books of the *City of God*, a work of similar ambition and scope was composed by Salvian, a priest at Marseille.[1] This work, *De gubernatione dei*, is addressed to those for whom the prosperity of the wicked and, in particular, the victories of the barbarians over the Romans called into question the providence and justice of God.[2] In the *City of God* Augustine came to use a work that had been occasioned by a specific event to express profound and long-meditated ideas about human society and its relationship to God. Salvian expresses ideas of considerable depth on the same theme, but, unlike Augustine, he does not give them systematic exposition in their own right. *De gubernatione dei* remains a work primarily

I would like to thank Matthew Kempshall and Simon Loseby for reading drafts of this essay, and also Tracey Rosenberg.

1. There is no direct evidence for the date of *De gubernatione dei*, but it can be securely placed in the first half of the 440s from internal references to historical events. Salvian's other extant work, *Ad ecclesiam*, is slightly earlier.

2. I cite Salvian's works from the edition of G. Lagarrigue, *Salvien: Oeuvres*, vol. 1, *Ad ecclesiam* (hereafter *Eccl.*) and *Epistulae* (SC 176; Paris: Cerf, 1971); vol. 2, *De gubernatione dei* (SC 220; Paris: Cerf, 1975). The most important general study of Salvian is J. Badewien, *Geschichtstheologie und Sozialkritik im Werk Salvians von Marseilles* (Göttingen: Vandenhoeck & Ruprecht, 1980); see also R. A. Markus, *The End of Ancient Christianity* (Cambridge: Cambridge University Press, 1990) 168–77, and J. J. O'Donnell, "Salvian and Augustine," *Augustinian Studies* 14 (1983): 25–34.

of apologetic directed toward the time and place in which its author lived. Immediate concerns are dominant: Salvian's desire to explain the historical situation in which his audience found themselves, and to inspire them to repentance and reform. His more fundamental ideas are rarely expressed directly, but must be inferred from the arguments he puts forward to achieve these goals. Not unnaturally, therefore, there has been considerable disagreement about Salvian's beliefs. Merely as regards his attitude to Augustine, claims have been made ranging from discipleship to polemical hostility. In this essay I will not attempt to give a full account of Salvian's thought, but to examine key themes that *De gubernatione dei* shares with *De civitate dei*. I will discuss Salvian's interpretation of historical events as judgments of God, his understanding of the historical development of the church and of the Roman empire, and, finally, his attitude toward Augustine.

Judgment and Justice

In the thirty or so years that elapsed between the sack of Rome and the composition of *De gubernatione dei*, the political and military position of the western empire steadily deteriorated. Gaul, Spain, Italy, and Africa all experienced invasion and warfare. Barbarian peoples established kingdoms within the frontiers of the empire, the most important being the Visigoths in southwestern Gaul and the Vandals in Africa. The sources give a picture of great devastation, and though not every region was affected, and some were affected only briefly, it is clear that, if not violence itself, the fear of violence from these armed outsiders was something that affected everybody.[3] It is therefore not surprising that people in Gaul in the 440s should have felt doubts and worries similar to those that Augustine had once addressed.

While Augustine directed the *City of God* (or at least the first ten books) mostly against pagan arguments, while hoping to influence both Christians and pagans,[4] Salvian's work is directed against Christians who doubted God's justice, and not against pagans (1,1; 3,5). There is no reason to doubt his claims about the audience he envisaged. The content of *De gubernatione dei*, which portrays most Christians as morally corrupt, and suggests that they are indeed

---

3. Graphically described in the final chapters of Possidius's *Life* of Augustine: *V. Aug.* 28–30, ed. A. Bastiaensen (Milan: A. Mondadori, 1975).

4. On Augustine's audience, see O'Donnell, "Salvian," 29; G. J. P. O'Daly, *Ciuitate dei (De)*, in *Augustinus-Lexikon*, ed. C. Mayer (Basel: Schwabe & Co., 1994) 1.969–1010, at 978.

responsible, at least indirectly, for the empire's misfortunes, would have made it worse than useless as a piece of apologetic directed at pagans. The belief Salvian sets out to refute is that God is not interested in the world; that he has abandoned it, or perhaps never governed it at all.[5] People believe this because of the general inconsistency between the moral character of individuals and their enjoyment of good or bad fortune, and, more specifically, because the Romans are Christian and orthodox, but are defeated by enemies who are not (1,1,6, 13; 2,1; 3,2; 4,54, 57). Salvian responds with two arguments. The first is that the political and military decay of the Roman empire is the result, not of God's neglect, but of his deliberate judgment. The second is that this judgment has been provoked by the failure of most Christians to live according to the standards of morality to which they are committed by their membership in the church.

In the first two books of *De gubernatione dei*, Salvian uses abstract reasoning and incidents from the Bible to demonstrate that God punishes sinners within the world; what he calls *praesens iudicium*, "present judgment."[6] In succeeding books, he develops his arguments in relation to contemporary events. In Book 3 he begins his argument about morality by confronting Christians who believe that they should enjoy security in this life as a "payment for faith," *stipendia fidei* (3,6). He portrays a church whose members indulge in every kind of sin and disdain the commandments of Jesus, yet still complacently regard themselves as good Christians. Books 4 and 5 attack the brutal and exploitative behavior of Roman aristocrats and officials. Book 6 condemns the games and the theater. Books 7 and 8 are an indictment of those who had been the most obvious victims of punishment by events. The Aquitanian landowners dispossessed by the Visigoths are portrayed as merciless sexual exploiters of their female slaves (7,8–25), while the Romans of Africa, conquered by the Vandals, are accused of homosexuality, transvestism, participation by Christians in pagan rites, and disrespect to monks (7,76–84; 8,9–25).

While Salvian uses these varied forms of immorality to build up an indictment of Christian Roman society, he also develops an argument about the nature of God's judgment. He begins from the principle that God judges and punishes sinners within the world as well as after death; using examples from the Old Testament, he argues that such punishments are not merely judgments on the

---

5. See Badewien, *Geschichtstheologie*, 31–50.

6. "Immediate judgment" perhaps conveys the expression better in English.

individuals concerned, but signs indicating to the whole community that God is angry and that it must renounce the sins which have been punished in such a manner. In Books 3 to 5 Salvian is mainly concerned with undermining his audience's belief in the adequacy of their Christianity; only toward the end of Book 5 (5,46–50) does he argue explicitly that Rome's contemporary defeats are judgments of the kind outlined in Book 1. The exposition of the claims about God's judgment made briefly in this passage becomes the main theme of his argument in the later books. After attacking the immorality of games and spectacles, he describes how they have died out in Gaul and Spain because the destruction caused by the barbarian invasions no longer permits wealth to be squandered on such activities (6,39–45). The remainder of the book portrays recent history as a contest between the sins of the Romans and God's inclination to mercy. God is reluctant to punish, but in the end is compelled to by the sheer scale of the Romans' wickedness. He therefore punishes them mercifully, by permitting parts of the empire to be chastened by the barbarians, but sparing the rest, so that their inhabitants have a chance to recognize that the invasions are a sign of God's anger and respond by changing their way of life. But so great is the obstinate corruption of the Romans that they fail to respond to these signs, even though their meaning is obvious (6,52, 66–71, 75) and therefore compel God to punish them more and more severely, though never as much as they deserve (6,90). Even so, they have not been reformed (6,76, 82, 91–99; 7,4). In Books 7 and 8, Salvian claims that God has awarded victory to the Goths and the Vandals because of their greater chastity and humility. It is the Vandals, after their conquest of Africa, who have finally succeeded in reforming the Romans (7,107).

That Salvian's view of the relationship between human action and divine judgment is very different from Augustine's will be obvious from this summary and has often been remarked upon.[7] The differences center on two issues: the extent to which the severity of the punishment inflicted through events corresponds to the sinfulness of the victims of such punishment, and the extent to which God's purpose in causing events to take the course they do is intelligible to human beings. In Augustine's first response to the sack of Rome, when he interpreted the event to congregations in Hippo and Carthage, he sought to minimize the extent to which it surpassed the trials that Christians could expect to suffer in temporal life.[8] He argued that earthly affliction had

---

7. Most recently by Markus, *End*, 171.

always befallen the good as well as the evil, illustrating this claim with examples like Job, Daniel, and the apostles.[9] He employs the same argument in his consideration of the sack in the *City of God* (*Civ.* 1,10, 14, 26). Augustine claims that temporal suffering may be a punishment, but stresses that those who experience such a punishment may be reformed by their experience (*Civ.* 1,1, 24, 28). He argues that temporal suffering, like that caused by the sack of Rome, is an act of mercy if it corrects those who experience it. Therefore such punishment does not signify that God was particularly angry either with the people of Rome in general, or with the individual victims of the sack.[10] Salvian, conversely, argues that God inflicts present judgment only when people's obstinate sins have exhausted his patience, with the implication that, while it may be a sign to others, its direct victims are destined for eternal as well as temporal punishment.

In the *City of God*, Augustine develops a general interpretation of the significance of temporal suffering or prosperity.[11] He maintains that some people are rewarded or punished by God within the world, but others are not. God does not do this capriciously; he is acting on his infinite knowledge and wisdom, but the reasons why he makes some people but not others experience the consequences of their actions in this world will frequently be inscrutable to humans, with their severely limited knowledge and understanding. The very lack of a consistent relationship between actions and consequences has a purpose, because it teaches people neither to value temporal goods nor to be too anxious to avoid temporal evils, since each may be experienced by good or evil people. Moreover, if sin were always punished within the world, there would appear to be no need for a final judgment, while if it were never punished, people would doubt whether God's providence existed at all (*Civ.* 1,8). Augustine accepts that the meaning of temporal success or affliction is sometimes apparent, as when he claims that God granted a long and prosperous reign to Constantine in order to demonstrate that it was not necessary to be a

---

8. *Sermons* 81, 105 (PL 38.499–506, 618–25), 296 (*Miscellanea Agostiniana* 1.401–12) and *De excidio urbis* (CCSL 46,243–62). On these see T. S. de Bruyn, "Ambivalence within a Totalizing Discourse: Augustine's Sermons on the Sack of Rome," *Journal of Early Christian Studies* 1 (1993): 405–21.

9. *Sermons* 81,2, 7; 105,11; 296,6, 8, 10; *De excidio* 9.

10. *De excidio,* passim.

11. For Augustine's theodicy, see G. W. Trompf, "Augustine's Historical Theodicy: The Logic of Retribution in *De civitate Dei*," in *Reading the Past in Late Antiquity,* ed. G. Clarke et al. (Potts Point, NSW: Australian National University Press, 1990) 291–322.

pagan in order to obtain power, but allowed the reigns of Jovian and Gratian to be prematurely terminated in order to show that Christianity should not be seen as a way of securing power (*Civ.* 5,25). Generally, temporal suffering has a corrective role, because even the most virtuous human beings have sins that require chastisement, and tend to be too attached to worldly things. God may inflict punishments of varying severity to correct them. However, why God determines that particular individuals should suffer and others prosper is usually opaque to human understanding (*Civ.* 1,9; 19,15; 20,1–3).

Salvian, by contrast, claims that God's present judgment has an unambiguous meaning. It is a sign that he is angry because most Christians have betrayed their faith. Salvian sometimes uses arguments that resemble Augustine's, but they are subordinated to this claim. Like Augustine, he uses the prophets and apostles as examples to refute the idea that the suffering of the good is evidence against God's government (*Civ.* 1,7–17, 30; 3,6). Like Augustine, he insists that the loss of temporal goods should be a matter of indifference. But Salvian uses these claims merely as an *ad hoc* argument to explain why some of the minority of true Christians are caught up in the punishment God inflicts on the majority. For Augustine, everyone possesses some degree of guilt, and temporal punishments may be the means by which people are saved from damnation. Salvian portrays a church divided into two groups, a minority of sincere Christians, and a majority that is guilty of sustained, willful disobedience to God.[12] The meaning of God's temporal punishments, which should be apparent to all, is that God wishes to display his anger and warn people to reject the guilty majority and join the relatively innocent minority.

To interpret events as manifestations of God's judgment was the almost universal practice of ancient Christians; it is Augustine who is unusual in partially rejecting the practice.[13] By comparison with Augustine's treatment, Salvian's may seem simplistic. Compared with most other authors, however, the quality in his writing that is most striking is the discipline with which he exploits the theme. As commonly used, God's judgment provided an indiscriminately edifying explanation for events. Those who anger God are visibly punished; those who please him are visibly rewarded. In its latter aspect, this

---

12. For the distance between this view of the church and Augustine's, see R. A. Markus, *Saeculum: History and Society in the Theology of St Augustine* (Cambridge: Cambridge University Press, 1970) 105–32, 166–86.

13. His attitude was shared by Cassian (*Collatio* 6), showing that this issue was not one on which there was a simple division between Augustinians and non-Augustinians.

often approaches the *do ut des* ethic of paganism.[14] In its former, God's anger can be used as an explanation for virtually any destructive event—plague, famine, natural disaster—whether or not the victims are the same as those whose actions caused the event.[15] In *De gubernatione dei*, Salvian takes great care to demonstrate that Christians deserve punishment as a community. He portrays a reciprocal relationship between Christians' collective betrayal of their duty to God and the punishment of invasion and conquest that God inflicts on them. Salvian never portrays people receiving temporal punishments from God because of their actions as individuals.[16] He never implies that individual experiences like illness, or oppression of the kind he denounces in his social criticism, are examples of God's judgment. He never claims that obedience to God will bring temporal benefits, even to the community. His work implies that renunciation of sin would cause cessation of punishment, but this is never explicitly stated. He does not offer God's help in defeating the barbarians as an incentive to his audience to reform.[17] As he implies that there is no possibility of such reform occurring, perhaps he saw no need.

The portrayal of God's judgment in *De gubernatione dei* is thus based as much on Salvian's ideas about the church as those about the nature of God. To understand it, one must examine Salvian's beliefs about the nature of the Christian community, and the historical development that had brought it to a state where it deserved the punishment he depicts.

The Decay of the Church

For Salvian, the church is defined by its morality.[18] His definition of a "true" Christian diminishes, or even dismisses, doctrine.[19] To give his definition at

---

14. For example, Sidonius, *Ep.* 3,1,2–3, in which a man who has given an estate to the church is rewarded by God with a legacy.

15. For example, Orosius, *Historia adversus paganos* 2,1,1; 7,15,5, 21,5, 22,2, 22,6–9.

16. An apparent exception, the defeated Roman general Litorius (7,39–44), can be attributed to his position as a representative of the Roman state.

17. Unlike, for example, Maximus of Turin, *Sermons* 81–83.

18. See Badewien, *Geschichtstheologie*, 51–83, 150–51; G. W. Olsen, "Reform after the Pattern of the Primitive Church in the Thought of Salvian of Marseilles," *Catholic Historical Review* 68 (1982): 1–12; R. Nouailhat, *Saints et patrons: Les premiers moines de Lérins* (Paris: Les Belles Lettres, 1988) 272–80; R. Nürnberg, *Askese als sozialer Impuls: Monastisch-asketische Spiritualität als Wurzel und Triebfeder sozialer Ideen und Aktivitäten der Kirche in Südgallien im 5. Jahrundert* (Bonn: Borengasser, 1988) 169–72.

19. Salvian saw orthodoxy as a necessary condition for salvation, at least for Romans, but also as valueless unless one obeyed God's moral commandments.

its briefest, "Faithfully to believe in Christ, that is to be faithful to God, is to carry out God's commandments" (3,7). These commandments are the precepts for living given by Jesus in the Gospels, all of which, in Salvian's view, are as binding on Christians as a master's orders are on his slaves (3,27–30). The words that he normally uses to refer to them are *lex* and *mandata* (orders). For Salvian, being subject to these *mandata* is the very essence of what it is to be a Christian. He portrays baptism as an act of admission to a community dedicated to obedience, within which those who persist to the end will achieve the ultimate reward (3,8).

If one recognizes the implications of Salvian's claim that the church is an entity whose very nature is constituted by obedience to God's commandments, one can understand why the actual behavior of Christians should constitute for him an almost indescribable scandal. In Book 3 of *De gubernatione dei*, when he describes how Christians constantly indulge in lying, swearing, litigation, and so on, he is concerned less with the acts themselves than with the perversion in the nature of the Christian community that they embody: a veritable *trahison des Chrétiens*, as one writer has described it.[20] Salvian's view of sin in the Christian community is very different from Augustine's.[21] Salvian does not claim that it is possible to live without sin. To have done so would have been to court the accusation of heresy, but there is no reason to believe that his denials of the idea are merely politic. He is really concerned with complacency; with the fact that most Christians hardly attempt to avoid sin, yet still think their faith should be rewarded by God. The minority of true Christians are not sinless; they are simply sincere in their attempts to obey God's commandments. However, Salvian has far more confidence than Augustine in people's capacity to avoid sin simply on the basis of their knowledge of God's commandments, and of the rewards of obedience and punishments for disobedience. He regards failure to act on this knowledge as the result not of weakness, but of sheer perversity. In this respect, his view of moral duty bears an undeniable resemblance to that of Pelagius.[22] Salvian's ideas about grace are obscure,

---

20. Nouailhat, *Saints*, 275; cf. Badewien, *Geschichtstheologie*, 193.

21. *Civ.* 19,27 is a typical expression of Augustine's view. See Markus, *End*, 45–62, 174–76.

22. On Salvian's relation to Pelagianism, see Badewien, *Geschichtstheologie*, 177–99; O'Donnell, "Salvian," 29–30; Nürnberg, *Askese*, 199–204. That Salvian's thought ran along the same lines as that of the Pelagians in certain respects is undeniable, but one should be cautious before concluding, as Badewien does, that he would have been aware of this, or that, even if he was, he would have felt that such shared attitudes implied agreement about doctrine. Salvian almost certainly regarded Pelagianism as being constituted by those doctrines which had been formally condemned, and which he rigorously avoids.

and there is nothing in his works comparable to Augustine's analysis of the constraints of habit and the weakness of the fallen will, which can give assent to God's commands, but still not have the power to act on that assent. A classic study of Augustine once characterized Pelagianism as "an excessive confidence not so much in man's natural goodness as in the natural supremacy of his reason over his appetite,"[23] and it is hard not to be reminded of this when reading, for example, Salvian's expressions of frustration and bafflement that Christians should still try to acquire wealth even though God has stated that avarice will be punished by damnation (*Eccl.* 2,47–59; 3,61–64).

It would have been meaningless for Salvian to express such views about the nature of the church, and to claim that Christians had begun to be punished in a manner that had not occurred before, unless he believed that Christians had once lived in the way God had commanded. He does so emphatically. Once, he claims, a single sinner would have been expelled from the church; now a Christian community would think itself fortunate if even half its members were not corrupt (6,2–5). Complaining that God does not govern the world is something "never seen before in the church" (4,53). Salvian's moral rigor, founded on the commandments of the Gospels, is supported by his perception that in the past the church had been a community united in a sincere attempt to fulfill these commandments. He does not limit this idealized church to the apostolic period. He claims that at one time every single Christian had equaled Paul in his or her willingness to suffer for Christ, and cites as evidence "books about religion" written later than the time of Paul (3,22). He is therefore basing his idealization of the early church not only on the New Testament, but on the portrayal of Christian communities by authors like Tertullian.[24]

A key image for Salvian, as for many rigorists of late-antique Christianity, is the apostolic community portrayed in Acts 4:32–37. Salvian's older contemporary, Cassian, had used this passage to produce a striking historical myth about the origin of monasticism, which he portrayed as a reaction to the dilution of the Acts community by less committed converts.[25] In one of his own references to the Acts community (*Eccl.* 1,2–5), Salvian echoes Cassian, claiming that the early church, in which all Christians gave up earthly wealth and were united in heart and soul, has decayed because of an influx of merely

---

23. J. Burnaby, *Amor Dei: A Study of the Religion of St. Augustine* (London: Hodder and Stoughton, 1938) 59.

24. For example, *Apologeticum* 39, a work which Salvian knew.

25. *Collatio* 18,5, on which see now Markus, *End*, 165–68.

nominal Christians. Salvian does not use this to argue for withdrawal from the world, however, and elsewhere (*Eccl.* 3,41–44) he draws a completely different moral. In the latter passage the significance of the Acts community is held to be precisely that it did *not* constitute an elite but the entire church. It was not a very few who lived a truly Christian life, but whole peoples. Salvian goes so far as to try and quantify the numbers involved.[26] Their scale shows that it is possible for a whole society to live according to Christian precepts.

Salvian's use of the Acts passage displays the way in which his thought about the church differed from that of Cassian, and certain other ascetic writers. In spite of his own monastic background, Salvian never suggests that the solution to the unsatisfactory nature of ordinary society is to withdraw from it. There is a gulf between his attitude and that of Cassian, who comes close to dismissing the possibility of living a Christian life in secular society.[27] Salvian approves unreservedly of marriage, procreation, and involvement in all activities of ordinary life that do not conflict with Christianity. He also resolutely argues that all Christians must live according to the true nature of the church, as was achieved in Jerusalem, and, he implies, throughout the early history of the church. However, there is an unresolved tension around this issue, signaled by the way in which, in the earlier of the two passages discussed (*Eccl.* 1,2–5), he attributes the moral decay of the church to the increase in the number of its members. Salvian bases his critique of society on the fact that it is Christian and must live by Christian standards, but appears unable to visualize a church true to its own nature except as a minority within a hostile society. The contrasts he draws between past and present often give the impression that he sees the adherence of most of the population to Christianity as having led to the subversion of the church by sinners. There is therefore an element of ambivalence in Salvian's thought about the church; a desire for it to be the vehicle for universal salvation, combined with nostalgia for a church of the pure, closely bound to each other and separate from the corrupt world. This tension, however, gives much of the force to Salvian's critique of society. He would not be so intolerant of social injustice were it not for his ideal of the church as a close, fraternal community.

---

26. Salvian argues that merely on two days which happen to be mentioned (Acts 2:41, 4:4), eight thousand men joined the Jerusalem community, without counting women and children (*Eccl.* 3,42).

27. See especially *Collatio* 21.

The Decay of the State

Augustine's attitude to the Roman past is complex, partly because he was contending against the pagan belief that Christianity was the cause of the empire's decline.[28] Admiration for a glorious past was probably as strong among Christians as pagans, but it could not easily be freed from anti-Christian connotations. Augustine tried to close the gap between present and past by demonstrating that Rome's history contained disasters equal to, or worse than, the sack by Alaric (*Civ.* 1,2–7; 2,13, 18; 3 passim). He does not dispute the idea that the early Romans were particularly courageous and austere. But he argues that these qualities were based not on true virtue, which cannot exist in someone who does not worship God, but on love of glory, which is a vice, but brings about the renunciation of other, worse vices (*Civ.* 5,12–20).

For Salvian there are no such complexities.[29] The early Romans were unambiguously good, just as the Romans of his own time are unambiguously bad. That he uses Roman republican austerity as a model for Christians without attempting to qualify its nature (*Gub.* 1,10–11) is merely the most superficial manifestation of this attitude. *De gubernatione dei* is full of nostalgia for a past in which Romans had been virtuous and the empire had been strong. Contemporary Romans, however, are utterly corrupt.[30] The Romans of former times had conquered justly (7,1–2); their state had been prosperous (6,50–51); they were powerful and feared. Now they pay tribute to the barbarians (6,98–9). Moral decay has caused decay of military and political power.[31]

Salvian's portrayal of Roman history is the product of several factors. It was rhetorically advantageous for someone who wished to denounce the immorality

---

28. On Augustine and Rome, see Markus, *Saeculum*, 45–71; A. Schindler, "Augustine and the History of the Roman Empire," *Studia Patristica* 22 (1989): 326–36; H. Inglebert, *Les Romains chrétiens face à l'histoire de Rome: Histoire, christianisme et romanités en Occident dans l'Antiquité tardive (IIIe-Ve siècles)* (Paris: Études Augustiniennes, 1996) 414–84.

29. On Salvian and Rome, see Badewien, *Geschichtstheologie*, 116–21; F. Paschoud, *Roma aeterna: Études sur le patriotisme romain dans l'Occident latin à l'époque des grandes invasions germaniques* (Rome: Institut Suisse de Rome, 1967) 293–310; S. Teillet, *Des Goths à la nation gothique: Les origines de l'idée de nation en Occident du Ve au VIIe siècle* (Paris: Les Belles Lettres, 1984) 169–83; Inglebert, *Romains*, 657–69.

30. A dichotomy rightly noted by Inglebert, *Romains*, 661, 668. Some other studies, like those of Paschoud and Teillet, are flawed by stressing one side of Salvian's attitude and minimizing the other.

31. This is the message of all the later books of *De gubernatione dei*, summed up in the conclusion to Book 7: *Sola nos morum nostrorum vitia vicerunt* (7,108).

of his own time. However, there is no reason to doubt that it reflected his own views, which were those of an educated Roman who, unlike Augustine, did not feel constrained by his religion to reexamine the ideas his education had inculcated. The most interesting feature of Salvian's attitude toward the Roman past is the way in which he reconciles this conventional historical idealization with the radical ideals about community derived from his religious outlook. In Book 5, the most obviously political part of *De gubernatione dei*, Salvian denounces various forms of oppression by the rich and by officials, especially those involved in levying taxes (5,17–45), and describes the response of their victims: flight to the barbarians, and the rebellion of the Bacaudae. He defends the resistance of the lower classes on the grounds that they have no choice given the intolerable pressure under which they live. He also implies that this situation is new and scandalous. In the past, Roman citizenship was a dignity and an honor to be sought out (5,22–3). This *ought* still to be the case, but is not, due to the oppression of the upper classes. The Bacaudae "lost the right of Roman liberty, the honor of the Roman name" (5,24); they "began to be like barbarians because they were not permitted to be Roman" (5,26). The accusation against Roman society is that it no longer includes all those who are legally its citizens within a community of true citizenship, because those who hold power in the state exploit it so ruthlessly in their own interests. Salvian obviously believes that in the past the empire did embrace all its citizens, and that everybody had an interest in being a member of it. The failure of the Roman state that he condemns is a failure to achieve standards of behavior toward its citizens, or rather to control the behavior of the powerful toward their fellow citizens, that it had achieved in the past and that are still incumbent on it.

It is in this context that Salvian's ideal of a Christian society becomes particularly relevant. He sees earlier Roman society as having approached this; if not in community then in the restraint and self-discipline of the powerful. Great differences in power are acceptable to Salvian; what matters is that those who exercise it are *paternal* to those in their power. This was indeed the image that the Romans had of their own early society, and Salvian has appropriated it. The predatory lack of community in contemporary society is portrayed as the result of a process of decay analogous to that which had occurred in the church. For Salvian, as is demonstrated by the language he uses about it, it is a similar case of a community betraying its own nature, and being punished accordingly. As he concludes, "Are we surprised that the barbarians capture us, when we make captives of our own brothers?" (5,46).

Rome and Israel

By judging the Roman Empire according to the same criteria as the church, Salvian might appear to be inappropriately confounding two entities that have utterly different natures. The logic behind his approach becomes clearer if one examines Book 1 of *De gubernatione dei*. In this book, Salvian narrates the Exodus and the passage of the Hebrews through the desert (1,40–60). He describes how God enabled the Israelites to escape, showed them their route in the desert, fed them, and provided water. Yet even amid such care, the bond between God and those he protected disintegrated and turned into rebellion. The Hebrews longed for the rich foods of Egypt, worshipped the golden calf, and rebelled against God and the leadership of Moses. They did this in spite of unambiguous demonstrations of God's anger. Everyone was involved in the guilt of the golden calf, but not everyone was punished. This was because God's mercy outweighed strict justice, and though a minority was struck down, the guilty majority was not destroyed but given a sign, by which it might be corrected (1,48). Instance after instance followed where rebellions were punished with miraculous violence, which was inflicted on a few but observed by all, without, however, changing people's ways. In the end God lost patience, and all those who had left Egypt were condemned to die without setting foot in the promised land (1,55–9).

The story narrated in the Pentateuch has thus given Salvian a model of the relationship between a sinful people and God, and he applies it to the Romans of his own time. The cycle of crime and punishment is identical among the Israelites and the Christian Romans. Perhaps because Salvian's account of the Exodus story is embedded in the preliminary arguments of Books 1 and 2, its relevance to his thought about his own society has received little attention.[32] This is surprising since the parallels he draws between ancient Jews and contemporary Romans are quite explicit: "We, when we are punished repeatedly, are not reformed; so also they, though they were struck down constantly, were not corrected" (1,57). The stress on God's reluctance to punish is as strong in this narrative as in Salvian's account of his own time. But eventually God's mercy was exhausted: *all* of those who had repeatedly sinned were destroyed. Again, the warning to the Romans is explicit: "This should encourage both

---

32. Even the best study of Salvian ignores its importance for the main argument of *De gubernatione dei* (Badewien, *Geschichtstheologie*, 150–51). It receives more recognition from Inglebert, *Romains*, 667.

our fear and our reformation, in case we, who are not corrected by their example, may be punished with their death" (1,59). Although Salvian has not discussed the sins of the Romans or the ways in which they are being punished at this stage in *De gubernatione dei*, he implies already that they are on a path to destruction, unless they heed the message from God that is conveyed by their punishments. Salvian ends his narrative at this point. There were plenty of subsequent instances of lapsing and punishment he could have related from the Old Testament, but is easy to see why he should not have done so. The fatal conclusion to the Exodus story provided the strongest possible warning, and it would only have been weakened by listing examples from subsequent books of the Bible. Salvian does use such examples later in *De gubernatione dei*; the defeats by external enemies that were inflicted on the Jews provided too exact a parallel with contemporary events for him to ignore. But the narrative in Book 1 has established the possibility not merely of defeat, but of total destruction, a threat Salvian eventually repeats in relation to his own time (6,96–8).

The belief that Christians were the successors to the Jews as the people of God was shared by Christian writers of all shades of opinion. The simple use of the events narrated by Salvian as examples to be avoided was widespread in Christian literature.[33] But for Salvian, the implication of his appropriation of the history of the Jews as a model for the Romans is that, through its conversion to Christianity, the Roman empire had become a politico-religious entity of the same kind as Israel under Moses. This is why Salvian does not distinguish between the political status of the Romans and their religious allegiance. The Jews in the time of their independence provided a model for such blurring of distinctions. If the religious and political identity of the Romans is indissoluble, there is no possibility of inappropriateness in the infliction on them of defeat and conquest as a punishment for their failure to fulfill their duty as Christians.

For all his anger at contemporary Romans, Salvian's attitude to the Roman empire emerges as a version of the Theodosian concept of the empire as the political vehicle of the church, enjoying God's special care. Christians in the fifth century were faced with the problem of reconciling this idea with the disasters the empire had suffered. Augustine's response was to reject the idea that the fate of the empire had any religious significance. Salvian responds in the way that the prophets had to similar situations. He continues to regard the empire as the special object of God's concern, but believes that God is expressing

---

33. It went back to 1 Cor 10,1–11.

not favor toward it but anger. God's concern for his people remains, but it is no longer that of a patron but of a judge.

De civitate dei *and* De gubernatione dei

The *City of God* had long been available when Salvian wrote, but his extant works contain no reference to Augustine, and no evidence of familiarity with his works. Attempts to discover debts to the *City of God* in *De gubernatione dei* have been tenuous in the extreme.[34] When Salvian deals with issues that appear in the *City of God*, he fails to engage with Augustine's ideas, even when there were strong arguments he could have used against them.[35] He sometimes uses arguments that resemble ones used by Augustine, but never closely enough to establish a debt. In the absence of textual evidence, it is impossible to be certain whether he had read the *City of God*; however, as a Christian intellectual in the mid-fifth century, one singled out for his learning in contemporary sources,[36] it is inconceivable that he could have been unaware of Augustine, and at least of the existence of the *City of God*.

It will be apparent from this essay that Salvian's ideas on a number of issues differed radically from Augustine's. His attitude to Augustine was certainly not one of discipleship.[37] His work has been claimed as a direct attack on Augustine, but, once again, the supposed evidence in the text is flimsy.[38] I would suggest that *De gubernatione dei* should be seen not as anti-Augustinian, in the sense of being a piece of overt polemic, but simply as independent of Augustine.[39] The predominant view of Augustine in

---

34. P. Lebeau, "Hérésie et providence selon Salvien," *Nouvelle Revue Théologique* 85 (1963): 160–75, 167; W. Blum, "Das Wesen Gottes und das Wesen des Menschen nach Salvian von Massilia," *Münchener Theologische Zeitschrift* 21 (1970): 327–41, 335. Both are unconvincing.

35. Note the complete failure of his discussion of post-mortem judgment (1,22–6) to engage with anything in the later books of the *City of God*.

36. Eucherius, *Instructiones*, pref.; Gennadius, *De viris illustribus* 68.

37. As claimed by J. A. Fischer, *Die Völkerwanderung im Urteil der zeitgenössischen kirchlichen Schriftsteller Galliens* (Heidelberg: Kemper, 1948) 103, 172–3, followed by Teillet, *Goths*, 176.

38. P. Badot, "L'utilisation de Salvien et de la *Vita patrum iurensium* comme sources historiques," *Revue Belge de Philologie et d'Histoire* 54 (1976): 391–405. Badot claims (400) that the invective against Africans in Books 7 and 8 is directed at Augustine. This suggestion is undermined by the fact that Salvian exempts the African clergy from his attack (7,74). Badot also claims that an unnamed churchman denounced by Salvian is Augustine, but the details of Salvian's attack (5,52–61) make this impossible.

39. O'Donnell, "Salvian," comes to a similar conclusion, though he gives more emphasis than I do to the attitudes shared by the two men.

Gaul in the mid-fifth century was one of respect for the bulk of his work, but rejection of his later teachings on predestination, an attitude conventionally (though somewhat misleadingly) termed "semi-Pelagian."[40] The belief that Augustine had gone awry in his last years caused some Gallic authors to treat him with a detachment, sometimes sharpness, not seen elsewhere.[41] In such a milieu, if Salvian found Augustine's ideas uncongenial, there was no reason why he should feel obliged to acknowledge them. That he never criticizes Augustine may be due to caution, but it is more likely that he simply wanted to put forward his own positive message.

Augustine's stature can easily conceal the extent to which, in his own time, his ideas were unusual. Augustine transformed or rejected many ideas that were generally accepted, as with his denial of the Theodosian view of the Roman Empire, or of a simple relationship between wrongdoing and temporal suffering. Salvian's conclusions are usually based on the acceptance of such received ideas (which, of course, he could support by reference to the Bible and other authoritative texts). Idealization of the early church, or belief in something approximating to Salvian's "present judgment," were ideas that a Christian audience would hardly have questioned. What makes Salvian unusual is his willingness to connect beliefs most people were able to keep isolated, to pursue their implications, and to force his audience to consider the relevance of such beliefs to their own lives. Doing so, he was able to produce an interpretation of contemporary events that was both coherent and challenging.

---

40. On the issues see R. A. Markus, "The Legacy of Pelagius: Orthodoxy, Heresy and Conciliation," in *The Making of Orthodoxy,* ed. R. Williams (Cambridge: Cambridge University Press, 1989) 214–34; M. Vessey, "*Opus Imperfectum*: Augustine and his Readers, 426–435 A.D.," *Vigiliae Christianae* 52 (1998): 264–85; R. H. Weaver, *Divine Grace and Human Agency: A Study of the Semi-Pelagian Controversy* (Macon, Ga.: Mercer University Press, 1996).

41. See *Gallic Chronicle of 452,* 81 (Monumenta Germaniae Historica, Auctores Antiquissimi 9.646–62) and the striking comments by Gennadius or an early copyist, printed by Richardson in the apparatus criticus to *De viris illustribus* 39 (Texte und Untersuchungen 14.1) and translated in R. W. Mathisen, *Ecclesiastical Factionalism and Religious Controversy in Fifth-Century Gaul* (Washington: The Catholic University Press of America, 1989) 245.

II. APOCALYPSE

APPROACHING THE APOCALYPSE: AUGUSTINE, TYCONIUS, AND JOHN'S REVELATION

Paul B. Harvey, Jr.

We study no static discipline: we cannot predict when and where new texts may emerge to challenge our assumptions and conclusions. Thus, about two decades ago, Johannes Divjak startled several scholarly communities by his discovery and swift critical publication of a new dossier of letters from, to, and about Augustine.[1] We now have, courtesy of François Dolbeau's acumen and industry, a series of newly identified, complete *sermones* by the bishop of Hippo, preserved in the Stadtbibliothek at Mainz. That collection comprises 62 sermons, of which 26 are either completely new or complete texts of sermons previous known only in précis. These texts were "preliminarily" (in fact, all but definitively) published and annotated by Dolbeau from 1991 on, primarily in the two French Augustinian journals—*Revue des Études Augustiniennes* and *Recherches Augustiniennes*—as well as in *Revue Bénédictine, Analecta Bollandiana*, and assorted *Festschriften*. Dolbeau's editions of these sermons have now been conveniently published in one volume.[2] Meanwhile, the texts

---

1. J. Divjak, ed., *S. Augustini sermones nuper in lucem prolatae*, CSEL 88 (1981); English trans. by R. B. Eno, *St. Augustine: Letters 1*–19** (Washington, D.C.: The Catholic University of America Press, 1989).

2. Fr. Dolbeau, *Augustin d'Hippone: Vingt-six sermons au peuple d'Afrique* (Paris: Études Augustiniennes, 1996); English translation (with introduction and survey of Dolbeau's work) by Edmund Hill, *Sermons* III/11. *Newly Discovered Sermons:* The Works of Saint Augustine. A Translation for the 21st Century (Hyde Park, N.Y.: New City Press, 1997).

were the subject of a magisterial survey by Henry Chadwick and catalogued, in distinctive fashion, by Dolbeau himself.[3] Students of Augustine have not been slow to respond: these new texts have begun to be discussed and cited as evidence for Augustine's pastoral practice and concerns.[4]

The new sermons do not offer the high drama we encounter in some of Divjak's letters: Augustine's memorandum, for example, concerning a priest who somehow found himself in bed with a nun (*Ep.* 13*); or the sober report on slave raids on North Africa and a congregation's violent and effective response (*Ep.* 10*). Nonetheless, carefully examined in context, they may speak eloquently to us of the late antique intellectual and social contexts in which Augustine lived and wrote.

The new sermons range over a ca. 25-year period (from ca. 385 to 410); the lack of recognizable contextual comment in many of them, however, makes their secure dating impossible. Taken as a whole, they illustrate themes known from Augustine's sermons as previously dissected (notably) by F. van der Meer, A. Olivar, and G. Bonner. These sermons amplify, rather than modify, our understanding of Augustine and our appreciation of his presbyterial and episcopal concerns. Familiar pastoral issues are addressed: the family life of parishioners (M12 and 41);[5] a congregation coming to church a little too inebriated (M7,7) or simply inattentive (M55); the application of doctrinal issues to daily life (on what *confessio* means, for example: M21) and so on. The cultural landscape of late antique North Africa looms in the background: the condescension of learned non-Christians, those who sneered at belief in a savior born of low status, for example (M54,12; cf. M13; 61 and 62). We also read of the lack of Latinity among some parishioners and the survival of Punic culture (M7);[6] the continuing vitality of Roman civic life in the form of

---

3. H. Chadwick, "New Sermons of St. Augustine," *Journal of Theological Studies* 47 (1996): 69–91; Dolbeau, "Le sermonaire augustinien de Mayence (Mainz, Stadtbibliothek I 9): Analyse et histoire," *Revue Bénédictine* 106 (1996) 5–52.

4. E.g., C. B. Tkacz, "The Seven Maccabees and the three Hebrews," *Revue des Études Augustiniennes* 41 (1995): 59–78, on Mainz Sermon 50 (= *Analecta Bollandiana* 110 [1992] 296–304); R. MacMullen, *Christianity and Paganism in the Fourth to Eighth Centuries* (New Haven; Yale University Press, 1997) 6, 163, 188; G. P. Lawless, "Augustine of Hippo as Preacher," *Saint Augustine the Bishop*, ed. F. Le Moine and C. Kleinhenz (New York: Garland Publishing, 1994) 13–37.

5. I follow Dolbeau's designation of the sermons, wherein M12 = "Mainz Sermon 12," etc.

6. M7 thus informs our understanding of the continuity of Semitic culture in north Africa: cf. J. Lecerf, "Notule sur saint Augustin et les survivances puniques," in *Augustinus Magister*, ed. F. Cayré (Paris, 1954) 1.31–33.

spectacula and festive days (M61,9; 12,14f.—themes familiar from Tertullian's *De idolatria* and *De spectaculis*[7]); the stubborn adherence of some Christians to astrology (M44 and 61). The new collection also includes two elegant homilies on St. Quadratus of Utica and the Martyrs of Maxula (M45 and 50). Those who have read Augustine's comments in *De anima et eius origine* 1,10,12 and G. Bonner's concise discussion in the *Cambridge History of the Bible*[8] will not be surprised to learn that Augustine used Quadratus and the Maxula martyrs as inspiring exemplars rather than as sources for instruction and doctrine[9] —an appropriate approach, for the council of Hippo in 393 had affirmed that it was fitting to preach the *passiones martyrum*.[10] Several of the new sermons offer (as we would expect) comment on Donatism (M7; 9; 45; 61–63). One sermon is richly textured in terms of secular life: M62, preached on the Kalends of January and deliberately extended to keep the congregation out of pagan harm's way.

I focus here, however, on one of the shorter new sermons (M12), which, when considered in the light of other texts old and new, may assist us in appreciating the development of Augustine's understanding of apocalyptic thought, especially as we see that understanding reflected in his *De doctrina christiana* and the later books of the *De civitate dei*.

Sermo Mainz 12 and Augustine's Apocalyptic Repertoire

This sermon (M12) was published by Dolbeau in *Revue des Études Augustiniennes* 39 (1993), along with another short sermon, on Psalm 81 (M13). Internal references indicate that M12 was delivered on a Sunday, perhaps at Carthage, perhaps in December, and probably before 399 (so Dolbeau). On a first reading, M12 seems not to offer much content for comment. Augustine's

---

7. *Tertullianus: De idolatria*, J. H. Waszink and J. C. M. Van Winden, eds. (Leiden: E. J. Brill, 1987) nos. 13–23, and 222; for *De spectaculis*: see now the edition by M. Turcan (Paris: Cerf, 1986), supplementing that of E. Castorina (Florence: "La Nuova Italia" Editrice, 1961), and esp. Castorina lxxvi–xci.

8. *Cambridge History of the Bible*, vol. 1, ed. P. R. Ackroyd and C. F. Evans (Cambridge: Cambridge University Press, 1970) 544.

9. Cf. M50,1 and 62,47; Tkacz, *Revue des Études Augustiniennes* 41 (1995): 59–78, on M50; see also F. van der Meer, *Augustine the Bishop: The Life and Work of a Father of the Church*, trans. B. Battershaw and G. R. Lamb (New York: Sheed and Ward, 1961; repr. 1978) 487–92; van der Meer notes Augustine's comparatively late enthusiasm for saintly relics, notably *Civ.* 22,8 on St. Stephen.

10. *Concilia Africae 345-525*, C. Munier, ed., CCSL 49 (Turnhout: Brepols, 1974) 21, can. 5.

opening remarks are somewhat amusing and thoroughly typical: the preacher states unambiguously that the divine reading was not his choice; nonetheless, he will speak to the text at hand (M12,1). M. Pontet, A. Olivar, F. van der Meer, and H. Chadwick have noted that Augustine preferred to sermonize on the Psalms, not least because the Hebraic songs offered ample scope for original comment.[11] Augustine's frequent allusions in this sermon to Psalm 66 (67 in the King James Version)—"God be merciful unto us and bless us"—and Psalm 147 (one of the several "Praise ye the Lord" hymns that conclude the book of Psalms) suggest that one or both of those texts were what he had planned to discuss.

The congregation heard instead the preacher's *ex tempore* response to the reading from the gospel. That *evangelica lectio* was Luke 17:20–27, where Pharisees attempt to pin down the man of Nazareth: and just when *will* the kingdom of God arrive? Jesus responded with vague statements and a homily on days of suffering to come, illustrated by reference to the days of Noah: flood; Sodom and Gomorrah.

Augustine therefore chose to focus on the apocalyptic aspect of Jesus's response to the Pharisees. Dolbeau remarks that Sermon M12 reads as though it is a popular version of the end of Book 2 of the *City of God,* that florilegium of Ciceronian and Virgilian exempla expressed in quasi-Lucretrian rhetoric (see esp. *Civ.* 2,29). The message of M12, then, is to turn away from secular affairs and live righteously; be certain that dark days will come, but the heavenly kingdom awaits those who create a heavenly kingdom within their lives here and now; times will be difficult but the Christian may be secure. Augustine's historical specificity in this sermon is spare: we may therefore presume that M12 was preached before the disaster of 410 and subsequent horrors.

Our first response to this sermon may be that here there is little of interest, certainly nothing as dramatic as the peroration of the other sermon published with M12: castigation of those who assert that rape and assault have increased in *tempora christiana*: "you say that adulterers and fornicators flourish . . . but do not remark the multitude of sacred virgins, the increasing number of couples living in chaste marriage, the rise in charity to the poor (M13,253ff.)."[12]

---

11. *Enarrationes in Psalmos* 138,1 offers a classic example: the lector read a different Psalm than expected; Augustine preached on the text as read because the "error" was clearly owed to the *voluntas dei*. M. Pontet, *L'exégèse de S. Augustin prédicateur* (Paris: Aubier, 1944) 2–4; van der Meer (above, n. 9) 414–15; A. Olivar, *La predicación cristiana antigua* (Barcelona: Herder, 1991) 606.

M12 contains nothing as rhetorically potent and historically specific as to *tempora et mores*, but among the topical texts we expect to find employed in this sermon for comment on the coming apocalypse and final judgment is a remarkable omission.

Connoisseurs of Christian sermons on last days know the appropriate texts to employ: Matthew 19:22–24, Jesus's parable on the kingdom of heaven; 1 Timothy 6:14–16, on the (eventual) reappearance of Jesus; 1 Thessalonians 5:2–5, on the day of the Lord that will come as a thief in the night; 1 Peter 1:3–5, on the salvation to be revealed in the last time; 1 Corinthians 15, on Jesus's resurrection and the sounding of the last trumpet; select passages from the prophetic books of Isaiah, Daniel, Ezekiel, and Malachi, and so forth. In this sermon, Augustine cites or alludes to almost all of these familiar texts. Historically and in our contemporary religious life, however, the preeminent text for preaching on last things has been the Apocalypse of John, because the book of Revelation (especially chapters 3 and 19) offers eschatological imagery of seemingly infinite scope for sermons and diatribes of hope, judgment, damnation, salvation, and comment on the contemporary political scene.[13] But not for Augustine: among the range of typical eschatological texts cited, quoted, and alluded to in sermon M12, Revelation does not appear.[14] That omission is not confined solely to this particular sermon on last things. For what has been

---

12. See G. Madec, "'Tempora Christiana': Expression de triomphalisme chrétien ou récrimination païenne?" in *Scientia Augustiniana: Festschrift A. Zumkeller* (Würzburg: Augustinus Verlag, 1975) 112, with C. Ligota, "La foi historienne: Histoire et connaissance de l'histoire chez S. Augustin," *Revue des Études Augustiniennes* 43 (1997): 111–71, at 115–16. Compare M54,16 for Augustine's similar, but differently phrased, distinction between pagan and Christian eras and generations.

13. Some recent, representative works: D. Jeremiah with C. C. Carlson, *The Handwriting on the Wall: Secrets from the Prophecies of Daniel* (Dallas: Word Publishing, 1992); R. Van Kampen, *The Sign: Biblical Prophecy Concerning the End Times*, expanded edn. (Wheaton, IL: Crossway Books, 1993); H. Lindsey, *Apocalypse Code* (Palos Verde, CA: Western Front Ltd., 1997). In each of these texts, we observe the citation and (allegorical) interpretation of Revelation and Old Testament prophetic passages, as well as a consistent tendency to use that English version of the biblical text (KJV, Revised KJV, RSV, etc.) most dramatically demonstrating an asserted interpretation. For critical discussion, see P. Boyer, *When Time Shall Be No More: Prophecy Belief in Modern American Culture* (Cambridge, Mass.: Belknap Press, 1992) 115–290; M. A. Noll, *The Scandal of the Evangelical Mind* (Grand Rapids, Mich.: W. B. Eerdmans, 1994) 109–45.

14. In M12, a range of the "minor" prophets are appositely quoted or clearly alluded to: Hos 14,3; Zech 1,13; Joel 2,13 (M12,2–3); Augustine also cited in M12 standard New Testament texts for apocalyptic preaching: Mt 19,21–22 (M12,8,9,12); 1 Cor 15,50 (M12,12); 1 Tim 6,17–19 (M12,12–13); Heb 11,9 (M12,6).

said about M12 also applies to another new sermon concerned with final things: M44, on the text of Mark 1:15: "the time is fulfilled; the kingdom of God is at hand; repent and believe." In this short (because incomplete in the Mainz MS) sermon, delivered (it appears) in the summer of 397, a range of New Testament texts and Old Testament prophetic utterances (Ezekiel and Isaiah, in particular) are employed to comment on coming judgment, difficult times, and ultimate eternal salvation, but Revelation is not exploited in this sermon, either.[15]

The absence of Revelation in M12 and M44 is all the more remarkable when we recall Augustine's use of this apocalyptic text in the *City of God*: there we find that he cites Revelation from time to time, as apposite, in Books 1–17. But when he comes to treat of "the day of the last judgment of God" in Book 20, the full panoply of biblical texts is displayed: those New Testament texts noted previously and at least seventeen references and quotations from John's Apocalypse. Indeed, the texts cited in Book 20 of the *City of God* are worthy of a modern evangelical doomsayer.[16]

To understand why Augustine does not cite Revelation in these new sermons (M12 and M44), we should read them in the light of Augustine's magisterial work, *De doctrina christiana*. At *De doctrina christiana* 2,8,13, Augustine offered an often-cited canon of Old Testament and New Testament books. The *De doctrina christiana* was in the process of composition in the 390s (Book 2 may have been completed by the death of Ambrose in April of 397), but Augustine broke off work at 3,25,35, to return to its completion and revision in his latter days, completing the work by 426/7.[17]

A.-M. La Bonnardière, G. Bonner, and other students of Augustine have observed that Augustine's canon of biblical works in *De doctrina christiana* 2 reflects the canon of Scripture specified at the several conclaves constituting the Council at Carthage in the summer of 397.[18] More precisely (for this point

---

15. In M44, the biblical texts cited for apocalyptic exegesis include: Ezek 33,12 (M44, 5, 7–8); Isa 46,8 (M44,7); 1 Cor 15,9 and 1 Tim 1,16 (M44, 8). Bede, incidentally, employed this sermon for his exposition of Mark: Dolbeau, *Revue Bénédictine* 103 (1993): 313; 106 (1996): 34.

16. See the useful notes and citation indices in *La Cité de Dieu*, ed. G. Bardy, trans. G. Combès, Bibliothèque Augustinienne (Paris: Études Augustiniennes, 1959–60), esp. vol. 37 (1960), containing *Civ.* 19–22.

17. *De doctrina christiana*, R. P. H. Green, ed. (Oxford: Clarendon Press, 1995) xi; see Appendix 1, below.

18. G. Bonner (above, n. 8) 544; A.-M. La Bonnardière, "Le canon des divines Écritures," in *Saint Augustin et la Bible*, ed. A.-M. La Bonnardière (Paris: Beauchesne, 1986) 287–301; R. Hennings, *Der Briefwechsel zwischen Augustinus und Hieronymus und ihr Streit um den Kanon des Alten Testaments und die Auslegung von Gal. 2,11–14* (Leiden: E. J. Brill, 1994) 203–17.

is sometimes overlooked), the *acta* of that council included the *acta* (with adoption of the canon) of the council held at Hippo in 393, a council that Augustine attended as presbyter, as he did the council at Carthage in 397 as bishop: this we learn from Augustine (*Retr.* 1,17[16],1), as well as from Possidius's *Life of Augustine* (8 fin. and 21).[19]

In both *De doctrina christiana* 2,8,13 and the conciliar *acta* of 397 (again, reporting the *acta* of 393), the last canonical book listed is John's Revelation—and Augustine, we know, took the canon of Scripture as established by councils of the church seriously (*Ep.* 64,3; cf. 29,2).

Augustine therefore had warrant by (at the earliest) 393 for citing Revelation appositely in his writing and preaching. But he does not explicitly cite or even allude to Revelation in the two new sermons on last things and fulfillment of human existence (M12 and 44). Why not? The question is not methodologically irrelevant. For those who would preach on the Christian vision of the end of time—including the Augustine who wrote Book 20 of the *City of God*—have consistently exploited precisely the same texts Augustine did in M12, but with the distinction of frequently citing and quoting from the Apocalypse of John.

The answer may reside in the textual and canonical history of Revelation, considered in the context of Augustine's response to a fellow North African scholar.

John's Apocalypse in North Africa

The Apocalypse of John has a curious history. The famous Muratorian Canon of (I believe) the end of the second century includes Revelation at the end of the list,[20] but the textual and citation histories of the book indicate that ancient Christians had ambiguous responses to this eschatological vision. A reading of Eusebius's *Ecclesiastical History* permits us a view of the controversies as to authority and exegesis Revelation stimulated among ancient Christian scholars: Origen affirmed authenticity and canonical status (but he may have changed

---

19. K. J. von Hefele, *A History of the Councils of the Church*, English edn., vol. 2 (London: T & T Clark, 1896) 394; see also the French edition: C. K. J. von Hefele and H. Leclercq, *Histoire des Conciles*, 7 vols. (Paris: Letouzey, 1907–52) 2.82–100. For the texts and a summation of the *acta*: Munier, CCSL 49.xx–xxii, 21, 43.

20. J. Stevenson and W. H. C. Frend, *A New Eusebius*, rev. edn. (London: SPCK, 1987) nos. 103, 123–25; see also K. and B. Aland, *Text of the New Testament* (Leiden: E. J. Brill, 1987) 48; R. M. Grant, "The New Testament Canon," *CHB* 1 (above, n. 8) 300–301; L. M. McDonald, *The Formation of the Christian Biblical Canon* (Peabody, Mass.: Hendrikson, 1995) 209–20.

his mind); Alexandrine scholars after Origen debated whether the book should be interpreted literally or allegorically; Methodius found in *Revelation* divine inspiration for ascetic doctrines; and Eusebius himself seems to have vacillated as to the book's author and value as a function of which author he had most recently read.[21] The great heresiologist Epiphanius exploited Revelation's format and imagery, but would not cite it, while his younger contemporary Jerome accepted the book as canonical.[22] In brief, Christian scholars down through the fourth century had no uniform opinion as to how or even whether this eschatological vision should be presented to the Christian community.

The textual studies of J. Schmid, as advanced by K. and B. Aland, and B. Metzger,[23] have shown that Revelation has a textual tradition different from the rest of the New Testament—an indication of the book's distinct status and reception. Another index of Revelation's place in early Christian societies is what we know of the pre-Vulgate text of Revelation. There is only one complete Old Latin MS of Revelation extant (codex "Gigas," of a Benedictine Bohemian origin), along with assorted paraphrases and fragments (in the Fleury palimpsest, for example, of the sixth century). North African witnesses to the *Vetus Latina* text of Revelation are minimal.[24]

H. von Soden famously argued for an African and a "European" (that is, southern Gallic and Roman) recension of the New Testament.[25] More focused research has emphasized that each collection of New Testament books (e.g., the synoptic gospels; Pauline letters) must be studied separately in terms of

---

21. Origen affirms: Eusebius *Historia ecclesiastica* 6,25; exegetical controversies: ibid. 7,24–25 (Dionysius of Alexandria, one of Origen's pupils); Methodius, *Symposium* 1,5 and 6,5, citing Rev 14,3f. Eusebius's opinions (and their sources, from Irenaeus through Apollonius to Dionysius): cf. Jerome *Chronicle*, ed. Helm, 192, with *HE* 3,18, 25, 39; 4,18, 24; 5,8, 18; 6,14; 7,24f. See esp. R. M. Grant, *Eusebius as Church Historian* (Oxford: Clarendon Press, 1980) 126–41, with R. L. Wilken, "Eusebius and the Christian Holy Land," in *Eusebius, Christianity, and Judaism*, ed. H. W. Attridge and G. Hata (Detroit: Wayne State University Press, 1992) 736–60.

22. Cf. Epiphanius, *Panarion* 1,4, with Hegesippus *apud* Eusebius, *HE* 4,22 and, e.g., Rev 1,20f. on the significance of the number seven. Jerome: *Ep.* 53,5 and 9, to be dated before 397: M. Vessey, *Journal of Early Christian Studies* 1 (1993): 189–90.

23. J. Schmid, *Studien zur Geschichte der griechischen Apokalypse-Textes* (Munich: Zink, 1955–56); Aland and Aland (above, n. 20) 4-51, 242; B. Metzger, *Text of the New Testament*, 3rd ed. (New York: Oxford University Press, 1992) 73, 245.

24. Codex Gigas and the Fleury palimpsest: H. J. Vogels, *Untersuchungen zur Geschichte der lateinischen Apokalypse-Übersetzung* (Düsseldorf: L. Schwann, 1920) 37f., 165f., 209–11. See also Metzger (above, n. 23) 72–74; Birdsall, *CHB* 1 (above, n. 8) 373.

translation, reception, canonical status, and circulation. Furthermore, the history of the text of Revelation in North Africa—in contrast to what we may deduce of its ambiguous status in eastern Mediterranean, Greek-speaking circles—is not easy to trace. Nonetheless, a few certain points can be charted for the trajectory of the Apocalypse through North African time and space.

Tertullian, for example, knew Revelation, but his knowledge of a North African Latin text of the New Testament is not certain. He often appears to have translated from the Greek for his own polemical purposes.[26] Cyprian, on the other hand, used in his treatises and letters thirty different quotations of John's Apocalypse in 53 contexts.[27] Of those citations, we may observe, first, that Cyprian accepted Revelation as canonical, to judge from his introductory formulae of statement and those Old Testament and New Testament books he does not cite.[28] Second, Cyprian used John's Apocalypse primarily to discuss Christology and martyrdom, not eschatology; only rarely does he cite Revelation in the context of the prophetic texts.[29] Third, at least one citation strongly suggests that the student Cyprian used the same text as his master Tertullian (Tertullian, *De cultu feminarum* 2,12; cf. Cyprian, *De opere et eleemosynis* 14, on Rev 3,17–18).[30] Schäfer thus argued that Cyprian offers the first unambiguous indication of a North African Latin New Testament text—and what that text owes to Tertullian's study has yet to be determined. The important point for our argument is that, by the mid-third century, Revelation was accepted as authoritative and canonical, but not widely exploited for eschatological exegesis.

---

25. The basic thesis of H. von Soden's *Das lateinische N.T. in Afrika zur Zeit Cyprians* (Leipzig: J. C. Hinrichs'sche Buchhandlung, 1909); see also Vogels (above, n. 24) 144; K. T. Schäfer, "Bibelübersetzungen II. Lateinische," *Lexikon für Theologie und Kirche* 2 (1958) cols. 380–84, at 380–81.

26. T. P. O'Malley, *Tertullian and the Bible: Language-Imagery-Exegesis* (Nijmegen: Dekker and Van de Vogt, 1967) 4–8, reviewing the basic studies of Th. Zahn, *Geschichte des neutestamentlichen Kanons* (Erlangen: A. Deichert, 1885) 50f., and G. J. D. Alders, *Tertullianus' citaten vit de Evangelie* (Amsterdam: H. J. Paris, 1932) 196.

27. For example: Cyprian, *Ep.* 12,1; 14,2; 19,1; 55,22, citing Rev 2,5, 10, 20–22; 3,21; 14,9–11.

28. M. A. Fahey, *Cyprian and the Bible: A Study in Third-Century Exegesis* (Tübingen: J. C. B. Mohr, 1971) 29, 40.

29. Fahey (above, n. 28) 535–54; cf. 43. Cyprian, *Ep.* 65 (cf. *Ep.* 58,7) on last things, citing Rev 14,9–15, along with Isa 2,8f.; 57,6 and Ezek 22,19.

30. Fahey 536, 542–43; Schäfer (above, n. 25) cols. 380–81.

The theological and literary landscape had changed by the fifth century, as we can see at distant Tipasa—on the African coast, east of Caesarea (modern Cherchell)—where, some time in the fifth century, bishop Alexander was buried with elegant, metrical epitaphs reflecting the author's knowledge of Virgil and the specific eschatology of Revelation.[31] But that text is exceptional. For otherwise, whereas churchmen in North Africa from the eras of Tertullian and Cyprian knew of and occasionally cited Revelation, we have no compelling reason to assume that Revelation circulated widely and was commonly read in North African communities in Augustine's day, or at least not in the earlier stages of his career.

Augustine, of course, knew Revelation. We need look no further than one of these new sermons (M62,51) to remark his awareness of the significance of the number seven as (repeatedly) employed in John's vision. But the use to which Augustine puts Revelation in *De doctrina christiana* is notable. In the earlier section (up to 3,25), drafted by, it seems, ca. 397, Augustine alludes to once, but does not quote, Revelation; this allusion occurs in the context of Christian behavior, not last things (1,33,36). Augustine at this point in his career was therefore using Revelation as had Cyprian: the text was canonical and hence suitable for instruction. He could employ Revelation for illustrative quotation, but not as a standard New Testament reference for specific discussion of doctrine or eschatology. The situation in the latter part of the *De doctrina christiana* is strikingly different: we find Revelation quoted and discussed five times after Augustine took up the work anew.[32]

---

31. Corpus Inscriptionum Latinarum [CIL] viii.20905, line 8 (= H. Diehls, *Inscriptiones Latinae Christianae Veteres*, 1103); cf. Rev 20,5; CIL 8.20903: altar dedication honoring the reburied(?) Alexander, paraphrasing Virgil, *Aen.* 2,63–64, 239. On the site and the church: St. Gsell, "Tipasa, ville de la Maurétanie Césarienne," *Mélanges d'Archéologie et d'Histoire de l'Ecole Française de Rome* 14 (1894) 291–450 at 391; F. Windberg, "Tipasa 1," *Real-Encylopädie der classischen Altertumswissenschaft*, Reihe 2.6 (1937) cols. 1414–23 at 1421; S. Lancel, "Tipasa de Maurétanie," *Aufstieg und Niedergang der römischen Welt*, II.10.2 (Berlin: de Gruyter, 1982) 739–86; see also C. Pietri, "La Bible dans l'épigraphie de l'Occident latin," in *Le monde latin antique et la Bible*, ed. J. Fontaine and C. Pietri (Paris: Beauchesne, 1985) 189–205 at 200. These texts are not easy to date: probably early-fifth century, perhaps later: cf. the Arian bishop at Tipasa in Victor of Vita, *Historia persecutionis Vandalorum* 3,29. An Arian foundation would explain an extra-mural, third, major church at the modest town of Tipasa: cf. CIL viii.20913-927.

32. The relevant sections are 3,25,36 (on Rev 5,5; 17,15); 3,30,42 (on Rev 1,20); 3,34,49 (on Rev 21,1); 3,35,51 (on Rev 7,4). For the last passage, see M. Dulaey, "La sixième règle de Tyconius et son résumé dans le *De doctrina christiana*," *Revue des Études Augustiniennes* 35 (1989): 83–103; K.B. Steinhauser, "*Recapitulatio* in Tyconius and Augustine," *Augustinian Studies* 15 (1984): 1–5.

Apocalypse Revised: Augustine and Tyconius

We can ascertain why Augustine now found Revelation significant: every comment on and quotation of Revelation in *De doctrina christiana* in 3,25ff. appears in the context of Augustine's study of and grappling with the exegetical methodology of the sometime Donatist scholar Tyconius,[33] who, in the early 390s (perhaps by 393), promulgated his *Regulae* ("Rules of Exegesis"), a prescriptive treatise on how to interpret in an allegorical mode passages in biblical texts that were difficult to comprehend. That hermeneutical handbook was complemented by a commentary, also largely allegorical, on John's Apocalypse, which has partially survived because it became a standard work of biblical reference in Spain and had, through Bede, influence on the Anglo-Saxon eschatological tradition.[34]

Tyconius appears not to have been widely known, in his time, outside North Africa. He wrote too late to be included in Jerome's *De viris illustribus*, although by the time Jerome came to revise Victorinus's commentary on the Apocalypse, he had learned how to exploit Tyconius.[35] Gennadius's continuation of Jerome's *De viris illustribus*, however, includes an entry (chapter 18) on

---

33. Tyconius: see Appendix 2 (below) for a translation of Gennadius's entry. See also A. Mandouze, *Prosopographie chrétienne du Bas-Empire*, vol. 1: *Afrique: 303–533* (Paris: CNRS, 1982) 1122–27; note esp. H. Chadwick, "Tyconius and Augustine," Study VI in his *Heresy and Orthodoxy in the Early Christian Church* (Aldershot: Variorum, 1991) 49–55. As Chadwick notes, Gennadius's mention of Tyconius's work *De bello intestino* implies no little activism (at least on the literary front) concerning Donatist and Catholic issues. The latter work by Tyconius, along with Augustine's exploitation of Tyconius's name in the *Contra epistolam Parmeniani* 1–3 (see below, n. 47), suggests the independent viewpoint of Tyconius.

34. A basic discussion, especially for the *Nachleben* of Tyconius's *opera*, is Vogels (above, n. 24) 55–57, 178f.; see also K. B. Steinhauser, *The Apocalypse Commentary of Tyconius* (Frankfurt am Main: Peter Lang, 1987) 141. M. A. Tilley, *The Bible in Christian North Africa: The Donatist World* (Minneapolis: Fortress Press, 1997) 112–28, within the context of a traditional discussion of Tyconius, offers a lucid and detailed explication of the *Regulae* and their application. For the specific texts: F. C. Burkitt, *The Book of Rules of Tyconius* (Cambridge: Cambridge University Press, 1894; Nendeln, Liechtenstein; Kraus reprint, 1967); F. Lo Bue, *The Turin Fragments of Tyconius' Commentary on Revelation*, ed. G. G. Willis (Cambridge: Cambridge University Press, 1963), the fundamental critical edition of the Turin codex. These fragments from a Bobbio manuscript are also available (without comment) in PLS 1 (2) (Paris, 1959) cols. 621–52. For Bede and his use of Tyconius, see especially R. A. Markus, "Bede and the Tradition of Ecclesiastical Historiography," Study III in his *From Augustine to Gregory the Great* (Aldershot: Variorum, 1997) 3–19, esp. 19 n. 23.

35. Victorinus (d.304?): see Jerome, *De viris illustribus* 74; *Ep.* 61,2; Vogels (above, n. 24) 49, 176–78; Steinhauser (above, n. 34) 30–44; see now esp. M. Dulaey, *Victorin de Poetovio: Sur l'Apocalypse* (Paris: Études Augustiniennes, 1997) 15–41.

Tyconius, where we read that the Donatist scholar explained the entire Apocalypse and interpreted all of the imagery in Revelation not in a carnal, but in a spiritual, sense (see below, Appendix 2). The fragments of Tyconius's *Regulae* suggest that we should take this comment by Gennadius seriously; for the typological or allegorical approach to Revelation is what made that New Testament book accessible for one, such as Augustine, who would preach to a diverse congregation on this difficult text. Scholars from (at least) Monceaux forward have drawn attention to the impact on Augustine of Tyconius's exegetical rules.[36] Brown and Babcock, for example, noted the influence of Tyconius on Augustine's exegesis of Pauline letters.[37] The new Mainz sermons offer little corroboration: M54, for example, preached, it seems, in the winter of 403–404, discusses at some length Romans 11:33 ("O the depth of riches both of the wisdom and knowledge of God!"), but without recourse to allegorical/typological method. We do meet in this sermon allusion to Mark 1:15, *impleta sunt tempora* (cf. above, on M44) and reference to things to come (M54,16–17), but no specific discussion of apocalyptic matters and no reference to Revelation.[38]

Pincherle and Dulaey were surely correct, however, in seeing Tyconius's greatest impact on Augustine in the latter's response to Revelation.[39] For what survives of Tyconius's literary *opera* indicates that, in *De doctrina christiana*, Augustine's report and comment on these works is accurate: Tyconius offered a method for making allegorical, and therefore "common" sense (that is, a sense comprehensible to a given contemporary audience) of difficult texts, above all Revelation. We can thus appreciate the suggestion that Augustine completed the *De doctrina christiana* precisely because, after reading Tyconius, he now knew how to interpret difficult biblical texts.[40]

---

36. P. Monceaux, *Histoire littéraire de l'Afrique chrétienne*, vol. 5 (Paris: E. Leroux, 1920) 178–95; van der Meer (above, n. 9), 443; Chadwick (above, n. 33) 49–55.

37. P. Brown, *Augustine of Hippo* (Berkeley & Los Angeles: University of California Press, 1967) 151–53, 271–72; W. Babcock, "Augustine and Tyconius: A Study in the Latin Appropriation of Paul," *Studia Patristica* 17.3 (1982): 1209–15.

38. M54 on Rom 11,33: Dolbeau, *Revue des Études Augustiniennes* 37 (1991): 261–88; *Revue Bénédictine* 106 (1996): 36–37.

39. A. Pincherle, *La formazione teologica di S. Agostino* (Rome: Edizioni Italiane, 1947) 185; M. Dulaey, "L'Apocalypse: Augustin et Tyconius," *Saint Augustin et la Bible* (above, n. 18) 369–86.

40. M. Simonetti, *Sant'Agostino: L'istruzione cristiana* (Milan: A. Mondadori, 1994) x–xii, xvi–xvii, 513–17; A. Pincherle, "Sulla composizione del 'de doctrina Christiana' di S. Agostino," in *Storiagrafia e storia: Studi in onore di E. D. Theseider* (Rome: Bulzoni, 1974) 541–59; Ch. Kannengiesser, "Local Setting and Motivation of *De doctrina Christiana*," in *Augustine: Presbyter factus sum*, Collectanea Augustiniana 2, ed. J. Lienhard et. al. (New York: Peter Lang, 1993) 333–39.

Tyconius's *Commentarius in Apocalypsin* has largely been known through later summaries and extracts.[41] Our understanding of Tyconius's method in that commentary now has dramatic confirmation in R. Gryson's publication of a 73-line fragment (from Budapest) of the *Commentary*. This fragment offers fresh evidence for the Old Latin text of Revelation and enables us to see precisely how Tyconius explained in allegorical fashion the seven-sealed book described in chapters 5 through 8 of Revelation. The disorder in cosmic and human affairs unleashed by the sixth seal, for example, Tyconius understood as "the most recent persecution" and the attendant tribulations of the church.[42]

This style of exegesis, I emphasize, is the reason why Augustine was receptive to Tyconius's mode of interpretation. For Augustine was neither ignorant of, nor antagonistic to, a typological or allegorical hermeneutic of scripture: much of the first two books of the *De doctrina christiana* (see esp. 1,2,2; 2,1,1–4,5) were concerned with distinguishing between literal historical circumstances (*res*) and possible allegorical significance (*signa*).[43] Furthermore, the Platonist in Augustine preferred the ideal, elevated truth to be found in an enlightened understanding of mundane matters and seemingly absurd old Hebraic texs. Hence the well-known instance in the *Confessions* (6,4,6) where Augustine recorded his delight at hearing Ambrose reveal spiritual truth in Old Testament texts previously assumed to be perverse.[44] Indeed, Augustine's enthusiasm—or,

---

41. For which Steinhauser (above, n. 34) is a detailed guide.

42. R. Gryson, "Fragments inédits du commentaire de Tyconius sur l'Apocalypse," *Revue Bénédictine* 107 (1997): 189–226. For example: lines 69–72 (Gryson 226) on Rev 6,12–17. Tyconius's allegorical/typological exegesis in this new fragment frequently focuses on perceived historical context, not prophetic possibility. The fragment thus illustrates how Tyconius applied his famous sixth *regula de recapitulatione*: cf. Tilley (above, n. 34) 123–28; Dulaey, *Revue des Études Augustiniennes* 35 (1989): 83. The seven-sealed book of Rev 5–8 has, in Tyconius's hermeneutic, reference to the Christian community's recent (and perhaps contemporary) history. Note, thus, Budapest fragment, lines 35–39 (Gryson 225), commenting on Rev 6,6 (the "third seal") and citing Dan 9,27, etc. and Mt 24,15 (the "abomination of desolation"); Tyconius refers these passages to the *ecclesia in Africa*. This historicist aspect of Tyconius's commentary is not prominent in the Turin fragments, although there also we read of Tyconius's attempt to relate the imagery of Rev to the history of the persecutions: Tyconius on Rev 11,13 = Lo Bue, nos. 406–407, PLS 1.647.

43. Simonetti (above, n. 40) xx–xxxii, 377.

44. The context suggests that Ambrose was explicating the Pentateuch and Prophets; see also van der Meer (above, n. 9) 442–49; cf. 298–301 on Augustine and symbolism; J. J. O'Donnell, *Augustine: Confessions* (Oxford: Clarendon Press, 1992) 2.349–54. For Augustine and Neo-Platonism, see J. O'Meara, "Augustine and Neo-Platonism," *Recherches Augustiniennes* 1 (1958): 91–111; H. Chadwick, "Christian Platonism in Origen and Augustine," Study XII in his *Heresy and Orthodoxy* (above, n. 33) 217–30; R. T. Wallis, *Neoplatonism*, 2nd ed. (London: Duckworth,

at least, developed predilection—for allegorical flights of fancy applied to the Psalms would attract the harsh criticism of his distant contemporary Jerome.[45]

We can see in those works of Augustine definitely composed after he had written the first part of the *De doctrina christiana* (to 3,25) several indications of the influence of Tyconius. The *Regulae* are prominent in the concluding part of the *De doctrina christiana*—hence, as I suggested above, the relative prominence of Revelation in the latter sections of that work. At *De doctrina christiana* 3,30,43, furthermore, Augustine recommends to *studiosi* of the Bible a careful reading of Tyconius, as he does in a stern letter to Restitutus, written before the end of the year 411 (*Ep.* 249).[46] Earlier (by 403), Augustine had adduced Tyconius in anti-Donatist polemic: "certainly a man endowed with sharp intellect and copious eloquence, even though a Donatist" (*Contra epistulam Parmeniani* 1,1).[47] Tyconius's *acre ingenium* had formulated exegetical rules Augustine could employ in *De doctrina christiana* 3,25ff. to explain Revelation and in the *Quaestiones in Heptateuchum* (2,47,3) to make sense of the chronology of the book of Exodus.[48]

Book 3 of *De doctrina christiana* and these other texts thus offer illustration of the impact of Tyconius's works on Augustine's hermeneutic of difficult biblical texts. Sermon M12 offers another (but negative) illustration. In an early letter in our epistolary collection, Augustine (and Alypius) assure Bishop Aurelius that they are not unmindful of his suggestion: they are prepared to study Tyconius's *septem regulae vel claves*, but seek the bishop's guidance (*Ep.* 41,2). This letter appears to have been written at (approximately) the time of Augustine's elevation to the bishopric (he and Alypius address "Papa Aurelius"). Augustine also appears not to know (or, at least, does not note) Tyconius's commentary on John's Apocalypse.[49] I suggest that it is within the

---

1995) 61–90, 100; see now esp. J. M. Rist, *Augustine: Ancient Thought Baptized* (Cambridge: Cambridge University Press, 1994) 3–9, 23–147.

45. Jerome *Ep.* 105,5 (ca. 403?), perhaps commenting on an early version of the *Enarrationes in Psalmos*; cf. van der Meer (above, n. 9) 106.

46. For the date, see Mandouze (above, n. 33) 1125 n. 47.

47. The qualification (*sed tamen donatistam*) indicates that we should not accept *Contra epistulam Parmeniani* as enthusiastic acceptance of Tyconius. Augustine cited Tyconius as ammunition for the polemic against Parmenianus. For the date of this work (perhaps not begun until 403): Dolbeau, *Recherches Augustiniennes* 26 (1992): 81, and *Revue des Études Augustiniennes* 39 (1993): 68 n. 66.

48. The *Quaestiones in Heptateuchum* were written between 418 and 422; cf. Augustine *Retractationes* 2,44,4; Mandouze (above, n. 33) 1125.

context of precisely that letter that we should view M12. To be explicit: M12 reflects Augustine's profound knowledge of New Testament eschatological texts *and* (by its omission) his discomfort with Revelation, *because* M12 was delivered before Augustine had come to terms with Tyconius. M12 may thus be dated to ca. 397 or earlier and will be among Augustine's earliest datable sermons.[50]

Augustine chose in Sermon M12 not to adduce the dramatic images and potent eschatological language of John's Apocalypse. He employed instead the familiar language of a tradition he could not escape. In these trying times, we must look to higher things: *inter haec mala,* etc.—a quotation from the Latin translation of Plotinus (*Enneads* 1,4,7), a tradition (and author) with which (and whom) Augustine remained comfortable,[51] as another of these new sermons vividly demonstrates (M61).

Augustine, then, felt comfortable with listing the Revelation of John as canonical in *De doctrina christiana.* But M12 and other sermons datable to before ca. 400 strongly suggest that he was leery of discussing that bizarre text with his congregation. Augustine elsewhere in these new sermons tells his congregation that they need not rely on either the lector's reading or his (Augustine's) explication of holy writ. Go to the booksellers, he exhorted, buy a copy yourself and read: *codices venales*—Bibles are available for sale (M12,14; 62,20).[52] Considering Augustine's apparent reluctance to cite Revelation, we may wonder how many of those Bibles for sale in Carthage or Hippo contained a text of *Revelation* that was often read or consulted before Tyconius's works were widely known.

Conclusions

In 1900, Hahn suggested that Augustine's vision of two *civitates* emerged from the Catholic bishop's reading of the Donatist scholar; more recently, Rist

---

49. Vogels (above, n. 24) 56, assumed that Tyconius's *Commentary on the Apocalypse* dated to 380 or before. We do not know. Augustine and Alypius's letter (*Ep.* 41,2) is the first unambiguous evidence as to the circulation of the *Liber regularum.* The commentary *In Apocalypsin* may, as many have thought (cf. Mandouze [above, n. 33] 1126), have been written after the *Regulae,* but we do not know that with any certainty.

50. For a recent discussion, with appropriate bibliography, of dating the earlier sermons, see Tkacz (above, n. 4) 61 n. 8.

51. Cf. *De doctrina christiana* 2,40,60. The quotation from Plotinus was also employed by Augustine's diligent biographer, but Possidius (*Vita Augustini* 28,11) used this text for what he saw as a truly apocalyptic event, the Vandal ravaging of north Africa.

52. *Recherches Augustiniennes* 26 (1992): 105.

has noted anew Augustine's use of Tyconius's first and third *regulae* in the conception of the Christian community set out in the *City of God*.[53] We offer a more precise suggestion: Augustine's sermon M12, when read in the light of later Augustinian works, offers evidence for the simple hypothesis that Tyconius's writings taught Augustine how to approach John's Apocalypse. We need read only *City of God* 20 to appreciate how far Augustine was prepared to follow Tyconius. Revelation is cited sparingly in previous books of the *City of God*, while Book 20, "On the day of God's last judgment," cites a generous range of Old Testament and New Testament texts suitable for apocalyptic exegesis, including no less than seventeen references to Revelation. At *City of God* 20,14, Augustine discusses Revelation 20:12, alludes to other "sacred books" mentioned in John's Apocalypse (Rev 3,5; 13,5; 17,8; 20,12; 21,27), and refers clearly, but without specification, to Tyconius's "sixth rule," the hermeneutical principle he prominently brought to his readers' attention in *De doctrina christiana* 3,36,52.

But Augustine's prominent use of Revelation in *City of God* 20 does not imply that he followed Tyconius blindly. For while Tyconius offered—as we can see in the Budapest fragment of his *Commentary*—a method for comprehending Revelation within a recent historical framework, Augustine preferred less historical specificity in his reading of difficult *libri sancti*. Thus would Revelation be of greater utility to any Christian community, present or future, because it was, in modern critical parlance, an open text, suitable for any age.

Finally, the significance of Tyconius's *Rules* and his *Commentary on Revelation* for our understanding of the late antique reception and use of Revelation is reflected in Cassiodorus's discussion of the New Testament canon, where John's Apocalypse is treated last and with notation of Tyconius's works. Cassiodorus sternly cautions the reader to use the works of this heretic with due care and then notes Augustine's use of Revelation in the *City of God* (*Institutiones* 1,9,3–4). Those remarks reflect, I think, precisely the correct relationship: Augustine could use the Apocalypse in the *City of God*—as he did, especially in the latter books and notably in Book 20—because he had read Tyconius and accepted, but not uncritically, that sometime Donatist's allegorical hermeneutic of Revelation.[54]

---

53. T. Hahn, "Tyconius-Studien," *Studien zu der Theologie und der Kirche* 6.2 (Leipzig: Dieterich, 1900) 1–116 at 29; for an evaluation of this suggestion, see Brown (above, n. 37) 314, and Rist (above, n. 44) 284–85. An informed review of Augustine's debt in the *City of God* to Tyconius is offered by J. van Oort, *Jerusalem and Babylon: A Study into Augustine's City of God and the Sources of His Doctrine of the Two Cities* (Leiden: E. J. Brill, 1991) 254–74.

Appendix 1: Dating the *De doctrina christiana*

R. P. H. Green's discussion in his Oxford Early Christian Text edition and translation of *De doctrina christiana* (Oxford, 1995) xi–xiv, is, I think, accurate, but Green's necessarily succinct treatment does not indicate fully the bases for our dating of that text and other relevant Augustinian works.

1. The *De doctrina christiana* was completed by 426/27. That date is established by Augustine's reference at 4,24: eight years previously, he had visited, on episcopal business, Mauretanian Caesarea. That visit has occasioned considerable modern discussion.[55] The visit was noted several times by Augustine (*Ep.* 190,1 and 193,1; *Retractationes* 2,51,77) and by his biographer (Possidius,*Vita Augustini,* 14,3). While in Caesarea, Augustine met with the Donatist bishop Emeritus; a transcript of that discussion has survived, dated *Honorio XII et Theodosio VIII consulibus XII Kalendas Octobres Caesareae in ecclesia maiore* = 20 September 418.[56]

2. At *Retractationes* 2,30, Augustine notes that he finished an incomplete *De doctrina christiana* which went up to "the Gospel parallel about the woman . . . who hid leaven in three measures of grain"(= Luke 13:21). That notice refers to *De doctrina christiana* 3,25. Augustine then states (ibid.) that he later completed Book 3 and added Book 4. Completion is dated by *De doctrina christiana* 4,24 (above, 1).

3. Augustine does not indicate when he began the *De doctrina christiana* nor does he offer unambiguous evidence for when he stopped work at 3,25.

---

54. *Civ.* 20,14, with Bardy's notes in BA 37 (above, n. 16) 259 and 781. See now especially E. Romero-Pose, in *Il De Civitate Dei: L'opera, le interpretazioni, l'influsso*, ed. E. Cavalcanti (Rome: Herder, 1996) 325–54, advancing M. Dulaey's discussions; Romero-Pose is no doubt correct in seeing Augustine's use of Revelation in *Civ.* as not solely a function of Tyconius, but Dulaey, in turn, is also correct in viewing the citation of Revelation in *Civ.* 20f. as at least prompted by Augustine's study of Tyconius: Dulaey (above, n. 39) 369. For Augustine's modifications of Tyconius, see especially Ch. Kannengeiser, "The Interrupted *De doctrina christiana*," in *De Doctrina Christiana: A Classic of Western Culture*, ed. D. W. H. Arnold and P. Bright (Notre Dame, Ind.: University of Notre Dame Press, 1995) 3–13.

55. G. Bonner, "Augustine's Visit to Caesarea in 418," *Studies in Church History*, vol. 1, ed. C. W. Dugmore and C. Duggan (London: Nelson, 1964) 104–13; S. Lancel, "Saint Augustin et la Maurétanie Césarienne (2): L'affaire de l'évêque Honorius . . . ," *Recherches Augustiniennes* 30 (1984): 251–62, esp. 259; J. E. Merdinger, *Rome and the African Church in the Time of Augustine* (New Haven: Yale University Press, 1997) 136–53.

56. CSEL 53.181; cf. R. Bagnall et. al., *Consuls of the Later Roman Empire* (Atlanta: Scholars Press, 1987) 370–71.

The considerations which suggest (but do not prove) that Augustine was working on *De doctrina christiana* 1–3,25 in the mid–390s are these:

At 2,61 Ambrose is not listed among those Christian authors who have mentioned the Egyptians but are no longer alive. Ambrose died in April, 397.[57] Augustine is assumed to have composed Book 2 before the death of Ambrose in April of 397, for *noster Ambrosius* is spoken of, seemingly (but not unambiguously), as alive and well, in 2,28. But this assumption has less cogency when we observe that Ambrose is referred to in the present tense at 4,21,48 — unless *sanctus Ambrosius* at 4,21,46 (also in the present tense) means "the blessed, dead Ambrose."

Augustine refers in the *Contra Faustum* (22,91), written by 398 (cf. *Retr.* 2,7 [33]), to what he had written at *De doctrina christiana* 2,40. That remark implies circulation of some part of the latter work by 398. Manuscript evidence in fact suggests circulation of an edition of Books 1 and 2.[58]

There is therefore no firm evidence to deny the *communis opinio* that *De doctrina christiana* 1–3,25 was composed in the mid–390s, but I stress that any presumption that Augustine broke off ca. 397 is probable, not certain, and rests upon the assumptions listed here.

Precisely why Augustine broke off work on the *De doctrina christiana* at that point we may never know. Diverse hypotheses have been advanced, ranging from a species of "writer's block," through a felt need to respond to the literary *opera* of others, to an explicit perceived necessity to assimilate and reply to Tyconius. These are not mutually exclusive hypotheses.[59]

---

57. Paulinus, *Vita Ambrosii* 47, with A. A. R. Bastiansen, ed., *Vite dei santi*, vol. 2 (Milan: A. Mondadori, 1975) 330.

58. W. M. Green, "A Fourth-Century Manuscript of Saint Augustine?," *Revue Bénédictine* 69 (1959): 191–97; Simonetti (above, n. 40) x, xl; see also K. B. Steinhauser, "Codex Leningradensis Q.v.I.3: Some Unsolved Problems," in *De Doctrina Christiana: A Classic of Western Culture* (above, n. 54) 33–43.

59. J. J. O'Donnell (above, n. 44) 1.xli–li; Simonetti (above, n. 40) x–xii, summarizing cautiously the arguments of Pincherle (above, n. 40) 541, whose argument has been restated by Kannengeiser (above, n. 40); M. Vessey, "Conference and Confession: Literary Pragmatics in Augustine's 'Apologia contra Hieronymum,'" *Journal of Early Christian Studies* 1 (1993): 175–213, offers a sophisticated argument stressing Augustine's grappling with the works of Paulinus and Jerome, and suggesting that we read the *Confessions* as a continuation of *De doctrina christiana* by other means: see esp. 191–95.

Appendix 2: Gennadius, *De viris illustribus* 18

Because most of our understanding of Tyconius's life, apart from Augustine's scant references, derives from Gennadius's brief biographical sketch, I offer here a translation.[60]

Tichonius the African was learned in Scripture and, according to the historical tradition, not at all ignorant of worldly business, and in addition diligent in ecclesiastical affairs. He wrote books entitled "On the Civil War" and "Explanations of Various Legal Cases," in which he recalled ancient synods, thus to defend his own folk. From these works the reader recognizes that he was a Donatist. He formulated eight "Rules" for the study and understanding of the meaning of Scripture. He also set out a comprehensive explanation of the Revelation of John, understanding nothing in that book as referring to the flesh, but everything as spiritual. In that explanation, he said that the body is an angelic way-station.[61] He also advanced the opinion that, after the resurrection, the just would reign on earth for a millennium. He taught that there would not be two resurrections in the flesh of the dead—one of the just, another of the unjust—but only one resurrection of all mankind, when even the aborted and deformed would rise up, so that no human being deformed or imbued with a soul would perish. He thus made a clear distinction between the two resurrections: the first, which Revelation says is of the just, we should believe concerns only the growth of the church, wherein those justified by faith are awakened through baptism from the deadly state of their sins to the reward of eternal life; the second resurrection in fact is of all mankind. This man was active in the same era as Rufinus, whom I have mentioned (*De viris illustribus* 17); that is, during the reign of Theodosius and his sons (ca. 379–ca. 408).

---

60. Ed. E. C. Richardson, in Texte und Untersuchungen 14.1 (Leipzig: Hinrichs, 1896); cf. W. Herding's Teubner text (Leipzig: Teubner, 1879).

61. I read with Richardson *angelicam stationem corpus esse*; Herding reads *angelicam rationem corpus esse*. Neither editor offers any relevant manuscript evidence.

I acknowledge with pleasure and gratitude critical commentary and discussion on drafts of this essay by Karen J. Harvey, *socia laborum mea*, and by Gretchen E. Minton of the University of British Columbia.

THE END OF THE CITY AND THE CITY WITHOUT END: THE *CITY OF GOD* AS REVELATION

Harry O. Maier

"Behold what will be in the end, without end!" (*Civ.* 20,30).[1] "Behold!" Augustine's *City of God* is a revelation. His final triumphant "behold!" is the last in a series, for throughout the work Augustine appeals to God to reveal to him the true meaning of biblical texts or historical events or even how to structure the complex tale of two cities he sets out to tell. "The task is long and arduous; but God is our helper" (1, praef.); "as far as God gives me power" (20,1; 1,36); "as far as the Lord deigns to help us see" (22,29); "with God's help" (11,28; 17,24); "God helping me" (12,28); "with the assistance of our Lord and King" (11,1); "with the help of God's spirit" (17,1): this is the constant refrain of the *City of God*. By invoking God's assistance, Augustine shows that it is not just another chronicle he is writing but an unveiling of how truly to read the signs of the times encoded in the dizzying rise and fall of empires and the chaotic events of his own day. "If I were to attempt to recall and relate those calamities [of pagan Rome], I should turn into just another chronicler," he remarks when telling of the task before him (3,18). Augustine's is not a chronicle but a revelation. Only the slow of mind, he insists, would be satisfied with the superficial, literal meaning of texts and the events they signify (20,21, exegeting Isaiah 65).

---

1. Quotations from the *City of God* follow the translation of H. Bettenson, (Harmondsworth: Penguin Classics, 1972).

Elsewhere, in sermons and in catechesis (e.g., *De catechizandis rudibus* 19,31; 21,37; *Enarrationes in Psalmos* 61,6–7; 64,2–3), Augustine had already indicated that his theme of two cities was the means to interpret the totality of human existence and the place of the Christian within the world. Now, in the *City of God,* he tells by showing, stretching the point out in time to reveal the plot of history by allegorically recoding it as the progress and ends of the two cities and the desires they dramatize.Thus does Augustine, with divinely illumined eyes, claim to lift the mysterious veil of human history to peer through its bewildering opacity, to detect within the ambivalence of time the divine arrangement of things, and to expose humankind's perverse loves.

Augustine is aware of his limits. Much of the explanation for God's ordering of history remains a mystery to him (11,22; 4,33; 5,19.21–25). He never claims to know the whole truth. But his is more than an educated guess. With its appeals to divine assistance the work expressly practises Augustine's theory—outlined in Book 12 of *De Genesi ad litteram,* as well as in the first three books of *De doctrina christiana* and his *De magistro* 11,36–14,46—of the necessity of divine guidance for full understanding, whether of the words of the biblical text or of historical events. For Augustine, history is a web of signification awaiting unveiling as the one with illumined eyes teases out its true meaning in all its spiritual richness (16,1–2; 17,3; 20,21). Most of the *City of God* is the record of Augustine's patient unveiling of the deeper significance of the course of historical events and their actors and the cosmic powers warring through them. Were he describing what he was doing in the *City of God* in the categories outlined in his *De Genesi ad litteram* (especially in 12,7,16–18; 10,21; 14,28–30; 24,50–51; 25,52–26,54; 36,69), he would say he was offering an intellectual vision of history, that is, the true way of reading the corporeal signs of history, and the right means of emplotting their meaning in a divinely ordered narrative. Intellectual vision is employed "to seek out the meaning that [corporeal] things have or the useful lessons that they teach. And with God's help the intellect prudently judges the nature of importance of those matters" (ibid. 12,14,29–30). "I am cooperating, in my small measure, with the grace of the true God, relying on the help of him who alone can accomplish this design," Augustine states, describing his ambitious work (*Civ.* 7, praef.). In the course of the lengthy narrative Augustine the seer gives his audience eyes to behold and reveals to it the fruit of his cooperative venture with God concerning the right interpretation of history, the Apocalypse and the *saeculum.*

Back to the Future: Bringing Sense to History

As Robert Markus has suggested, Augustine finds in the biblical narrative the contrapuntal themes to discover the divine melody in the seemingly discordant strains of pagan and sacred history (16,2).[2] It is here that Augustine finds his hermeneutical key of the two cities to make sense out of the chaos of time and history. But the *City of God* also tells a sacred narrative that is teleological. When Augustine portrays the city of God it is with the heavenly Jerusalem descended to earth of Revelation 21,1–2 in mind that he writes. For example, when he interprets the holy city of the Old Testament as a prefigurement of the heavenly city in 15,2, using as his proof text Galatians 4,22–5,1, he is not merely contrasting type and anti-type, as though one were a platonic shadow of the other,[3] or solely a prophetic promise anticipating fulfillment.[4] Rather he is emplotting the former in a narrative whose ending is revealed in the descent of the city in Revelation 21,1–2. To speak with Paul of Jerusalem our mother is of course to speak of the New Covenant, but a New Covenant that points ahead of itself: speaking of Jerusalem our free mother, Augustine writes in 20,21: "There, after the hardships of our anxieties and worries in this mortal state we shall be comforted like little children carried on their mother's shoulders and nursed in her lap" (also 17,3). This is what Paul's reference to Jerusalem our free mother finally refers to for Augustine. The story of Jerusalem the city of God and of Babel the city of man is one told from its ending.

The end of his book is an apocalypse of the imagination, an imaginary unveiling of what will be in the end without end. Again, Augustine is aware of his limits, and because of this his is a paradoxical revelation.

> Now let us see, as far as the Lord deigns to help us see, what the saints will be doing in their immortal and spiritual bodies . . . . And yet, to tell the truth, I do not know what will be the nature of that activity . . . . I have never seen it with my physical sight; and if I were to say that I had seen it with my mind—with my intellect—what is the human understanding, in capacity or quality to comprehend such unique perfection? (22,29)

---

2. R. A. Markus, *Saeculum: History and Society in the Theology of St Augustine* (Cambridge: Cambridge University Press, 1970) 43–44.

3. Thus H. Leisegang, "Der Ursprung der Lehre Augustins von der Civitas Dei," *Archiv für Kulturgeschichte* 16 (1925): 127–58.

4. Thus Markus, *Saeculum*, 18.

What will be Augustine can only imagine. "Who is capable of imagining [the grades of honour and glory to come], not to speak of describing them?" (20,21). But imagine Augustine must, for it is from the vantage point of this unimaginable imagined end point that he tells his tale of two cities; it is to this point that his stories of the cities point. His is a narrative dominated by the future tense. Wherever he tries to find the sense in things past or present it is to the future he looks where all will finally be revealed. The narrative, like life which, according to Augustine, "is nothing but a race toward death," (13,10), stumbles impatiently ahead of itself to its ending (how often Augustine complains that he is taking too long to tell his story, e.g., 16,37; 17,11), only there to have its ending deferred in his vision of the kingdom which will have no end (22,30). Thus when one comes to the end of the *City of God*, to the limit of Augustine's ability to narrate the future of the city and to imagine the unimaginable, one not only encounters Augustine's finitude, but also catches a glimpse in Augustine's paradoxical telling of what cannot be told ("the end, without end" of 22,30). Here is the vanishing point of Augustine's historical canvas, the single point by which he has brought all else into perspective and which has given both him and his reader eyes to see afresh our too easily imagined world. Without this the story Augustine tells could not have been told. By the end of Book 22, where Augustine unveils the nature of the beatific vision of the saints in eternal felicity, properly trained readers have been disciplined by their faithful and steady guide not only to trust that the true meaning of history has, with divine help, been revealed to them, but also to believe that they behold between the covers of his book the whole of history in their hands. They stand with Augustine outside of history to look back upon it. It is from the unimaginable vista of the concluding chapters of his final book that all falls into place. Augustine's faithful readers sit and rest with their guide and from there find the point to survey and take in the "long and arduous" pilgrimage along which he has led them. It is from this end-point that the whole journey takes its meaning and all the sites along the way find their true significance. Without Augustine's end without end, the effort expended to complete his narrative journey would be meaningless, or at least without direction.

But Augustine is not left to his own devices to imagine the unimaginable. If Augustine the revealer interprets the course of history with illumined eyes, it is with stolen light that he does so. Where Augustine looks to fire his imagination is to the end of the biblical story itself, the Book of Revelation, especially chapters 20 to 22,1–5.

Borrowed Light from the Book of Revelation

To speak of the importance of the Book of Revelation to the *City of God* is to mark a departure from the consensus of Augustinian scholarship. The place of the Book of Revelation in Augustine's thought generally and in the *City of God* more particularly continues to be a largely neglected topic in Augustinian studies.[5] This is especially puzzling since the final books of the *City of God* are, as I shall show, structured mimetically after the final chapters of John's Apocalypse. At least the final three books (20–22), and arguably Books 18–22, reflect topically the narrative sequence of Revelation from chapters 18 to 22 (the identification of the two Babylons; the millennium; judgment and resurrection of the body; descent of the heavenly Jerusalem; life in the city and the beatific vision). Where scholarship has focused on the relation of the *City of God* to the Apocalypse attention has been on Book 20 and Augustine's resistance to a literal interpretation of the millennium.[6] It has even been suggested that outside of Book 20,7, where Augustine rejects a chiliastic interpretation of the millennium, he shows little or no interest in the Book of Revelation.[7] However, not only is the Apocalypse central to the narrative structure of the final books of the *City of God*, it is to the themes of the closing two chapters of Revelation, especially 20,1–21,2 (from the millennium to the judgment to the descent of the heavenly Jerusalem) and 22,1–5 (the description of the idyllic life of the descended Jerusalem resting in the vision of God) that Augustine repeatedly points not only throughout the course of his epic narrative of Books 11–22, but also in the more static philosophical and polemical arguments of Books 1–10.[8] Augustine's eschatology is best described as apocalyptic. To be

---

5. For a survey of studies see E. Romero-Pose "La utilización del Apocalipsis en el *De civitate Dei,*" in *Il De civitate Dei: L'opera, le interpretazione, l'influsso,* ed. E. Cavalcanti (Rome: Herder, 1996) 325–54. Romero-Pose limits his own investigation to direct citations of the Apocalypse.

6. Most notably, J. K. Coyle, "Augustine and Apocalyptic: Thoughts on the Fall of Rome, the Book of Revelation, and the End of the World," *Florilegium* 9 (1987): 1–33; P. Frederiksen, "Apocalypse and Redemption in Early Christianity: From John of Patmos to Augustine of Hippo," *Vigiliae Christianae* 45 (1991): 151–83, and G. Bonner, "Augustine and Millenarianism," in *The Making of Orthodoxy: Essays in Honour of Henry Chadwick*, ed. R. Williams (Cambridge: Cambridge University Press, 1989), 235–54.

7. Thus Coyle, "Augustine and Apocalyptic," 14.

8. Of course, the biblical influences on *City of God* are diverse and have been thoroughly discussed elsewhere, notably by A. Lauras and H. Rondet, "Le thème des deux cités dans l'oeuvre de saint Augustin," in H. Rondet et al., *Études augustiniennes* (Paris: Études Augustiniennes, 1953) 99–162, and by G. Bardy, "La formation du concept de 'Cité de Dieu' dans l'oeuvre de saint Augustin," *L'Année Théologique Augustinienne* 12 (1951): 5–19.

sure, Augustine is not an "apocalypticist," his eschatology is not evidence of a social millennialist movement bred of discouragement and suffering.[9] But the phrase "apocalyptic eschatology" is apt because it signals the importance, literarily, of John's Apocalypse in shaping Augustine's narrative consideration of last things in the *City of God*. In its concluding books Augustine's commentary reperforms the final chapters of Revelation.

In the course of Book 20 Augustine offers his exegesis of the events that will unfold at the end of the age. At the conclusion of Book 20 he gives a thumbnail sketch of the events that have guided the order of his own reflections:

> And so in that judgment, or in connection with that judgment, we have learnt that these events are to come about: Elijah the Tishbite will come; Jews will accept the faith; Antichrist will persecute; Christ will judge; the dead will rise again; the good and the evil will be separated; the earth will be destroyed in the flames and then will be renewed. All those events, we must believe, will come about; but in what way, and in what order they will come, actual experience will then teach us with a finality surpassing anything our human understanding is now capable of attaining. However, I consider that these events are destined to come about in the order I have given. (20,30)

From the reference to the judgment of Christ onward, this is the sequence of the final chapters of Revelation from 20,11–21,2. Augustine's summary at 20,30, coming as it does at the end of Book 20, functions as a kind of resting place to consider the general structure of his narrative retelling of the future of the pilgrim city of God. From the start of Book 20 his narration has been guided by the sequence presented in Revelation 20,4–21,4. Beginning with a discussion of the proper interpretation of the millennium (Rev 20,4–6; *Civ.* 20,7), he discusses in turn the loosing of Satan (Rev 20,7; *Civ.* 20,8); the first resurrection (Rev 20,6; *Civ.* 20,10); Gog and Magog (Rev 20,8; *Civ.* 20,11); the condemnation of the devil, the judgment from the throne, and the meaning of the book of life (Rev 20,9, 11–12; *Civ.*20,14); the meaning of the sea giving up the dead and death and Hades (Rev 20,13–14; *Civ.* 20,15); the new heaven and new earth (Rev 21,1; *Civ.* 20.16); and the descent of the heavenly Jerusalem (Rev 21,2; *Civ.* 20,17). In the remainder of Book 20 (18–29) he harmonizes

---

9. I follow here the conventions of biblical scholars who distinguish between "apocalypse" as the name of a literary genre, "apocalyptic eschatology" as the designation of a body of tradition appearing in, though not confined to, "apocalypses," and "apocalypticism" as a title of a social phenomenon most usually arising from social discontent and explaining present realities by reference to literally interpreted apocalypses. Augustine was opposed to "apocalypticism," but readily made use of apocalyptic eschatology in his telling of the warfare of the two cities.

other biblical apocalyptic passages (from the four Gospels, Paul's letters, the Petrine epistles, and from the Old Testament—from Isaiah, Zechariah, the Psalms, and Daniel) with this narrative as he has exegeted it, thus offering a complex intertextual commentary on the final chapters of Revelation. At 20,30 Augustine pauses to summarize the narrative and catch his breath before going on in Books 21 and 22 to provide a more detailed exegesis of the concluding chapters of Revelation.

The *City of God* as Apocalypse

In the final two books Revelation continues to function as the master narrative organizing Augustine's reflections, but now implicitly and more subtly. Nowhere in these books does Augustine directly cite the Apocalypse, as he does in Book 20, but the focus of his discussion and his ordering of it reveals that he is being guided by it. In Books 21 and 22 Augustine picks up the narrative to consider in turn the punishment of the condemned (whether it is reasonable to conceive of eternally burning bodies and punishment: again, Revelation 20,14–15, but now with particular reference to 20,10—the beast and the false prophet thrown into the lake of fire and tormented forever) and the bliss of the saints. The sequence continues to be guided by the narrative of the Apocalypse, but now Augustine focuses in far more detail, as indeed does Revelation itself from 21,1 to 22,5. Again, he works intertextually, exegeting the narrative of Revelation by reference to other passages. In Book 21 his focus is on all passages treating testing or judgment by fire. In Book 22 he continues the detailed narrative by moving from judgment to resurrection life. The description of the general resurrection of Revelation 20,12 gives rise to a lengthy account of the resurrection body, and this in turn leads to an extended exegesis in chapters 29–30 of the life, light, and vision of the *City of God* described in Revelation 21,2–22,5, especially 21,23 ("And the city has no need of sun or moon to shine upon it, for the glory of God is its light") and 22,4–5 ("they shall see his face and night shall be no more; they need no light or lamp or sun, for the Lord God will be their light, and they shall reign for ever and ever"). Here Augustine's focus coincides with that of the Apocalypse: the light of the city and the vision of its citizens.

What Augustine offers in his final three books is a lengthy and detailed intertextual exegesis of the concluding three chapters of Revelation. The concluding books mimetically reperform the final three chapters of the Apocalypse. Augustine in no way ignores the Book of Revelation or only cites it with reluctance in the *City of God*. Rather, the Apocalypse's final chapters furnish Augustine with the core narrative to bind together the concluding books of his work.

In the Meantime: Life "in the Middest"

Frank Kermode reflects an idiosyncratically Augustinian sentiment when he writes, "Men in the middest make considerable imaginative investments in coherent patterns which, by the provision of an end, make possible a satisfying consonance with the origins and the middle."[10] Augustine's end, the ceaseless contemplation of God's face in the descended heavenly Jerusalem of Revelation 20:1–5, provides the ending to bring about a consonance with the origins and middle of historically lived life. Books 20–22 draw out in explicit detail what is repeatedly foreshadowed or implicit in the earlier books. Augustine, of course, remains consciously ignorant of how present-day events are conspiring to usher in the end of the time, a point that has been thoroughly discussed by Robert Markus, Paula Frederiksen, and Gerald Bonner in works cited above, to name only representative studies. But not investigated enough is the way in which Augustine's consideration of the future leads him retrospectively to treat past and present. Though his account of the cities begins with creation, it is from the end of the story that their tale is told. Whenever he refers to history to tell the story of the cities, it is back to the future that he looks. (One sees this clearly, for example, in his interpretation of the seven days of creation and the unending Sabbath of the seventh day in both the *City of God* 22,30 and *Confessions* 13,36). The preceding narrative of Books 11–18, which recounts the origin and progress of the cities, continually points ahead of itself to this ending. From the very outset of his discussion of the origin of the cities, where Augustine treats the prelapsarian happiness of Adam and Eve and their subsequent fall, in Books 13 and 14, he turns the historical retelling into an unveiled forecast of things to come. As he recounts the fall of Adam and Eve in 13,14–24 he finds himself unable to resist the temptation to jump ahead to the end of the book to steal a glimpse of how it will all turn out in the end and there find the sense of the present. The first death of Adam sets off a calamitous sequence of corruptions ending in the second death to come

---

10. F. Kermode, *The Sense of an Ending: Studies in the Theory of Fiction* (Oxford: Oxford University Press, 1967) 17. The phrase "in the middest" is borrowed from the *Apology for Poetry* (ca. 1580) of Sir Philip Sidney: "a Poet thrusteth into the middest, even where it most concerneth him, and there recoursing to the thinges forepaste, and divining of thinges to come, maketh a pleasing analysis of all."

(13,11, 14; 14,1); the subjection of mind to body in the fall points ahead of itself to its reversal in the resurrection life to come (13,19); the hungry fallen body of Adam, with its hair, fingernails, and fat, is interpreted in the light of the rebeautified resurrection body of Revelation 20,8 (22,19; 13,20): eating as possibility but not necessity reveals the tragic bondage to food of a fallen world (13,22). Even the prelapsarian story of Edenic bliss offers clues for imagining the future:

> And so the first man was more blessed in paradise than any righteous person in this state of mortal frailty, as far as concerns the enjoyment of present good. But as for the hope of the future, anyone in the extreme of bodily suffering is happier than the first-created. For it has been revealed to humankind with the certainty of truth . . . that, free from all distresses, it will share with the angels the endless enjoyment of God most high, whereas that first man, in all that bliss of paradise, had no certainty about his future. (11,12)

"For the first immortality, which Adam lost by sinning, was the ability to avoid death; the final immortality will be the inability to die and in the same way, the first free will is the ability to avoid sin. For as humankind cannot lose the will to happiness, so it will not be able to lose the will to piety and justice," Augustine writes in the final paragraphs of his epic tale (22,30), making the life of Paradise incomprehensible without reference to the apocalyptic vision of deathless beatitude in Revelation 21,4. For Augustine the happiness of Adam and Eve always points forward: had they not sinned, Augustine argues, they would have become what Christians will be "when our bodies are restored to incorruptibility at the resurrection of the dead" (14,10).

As life in its origin, so life "in the middest" is oriented by Augustine to its ending. Wherever Augustine speaks of felicity, which is virtually on every page of the work, he points ahead to his conclusion. In the *City of God* happiness is always a question of endings, an orientation toward final goods whether they be of the self or of God (8,3; 10,1; 19,1). But they are not timeless endings; rather they are oriented toward the end. For Augustine a cyclic history is not worth living because it holds no promise of happiness: only one that ends, as Revelation unveils, at the end, in the ceaseless contemplation of God's face, holds any promise of felicity (12,11–14, 21). The happiness we discover in the contemplation of God here "in a mirror darkly" either blurredly in ourselves or scattered in nature around us always points ahead of itself to the unfettered vision of the city where we shall see God's face (e.g., 11,24–28; 20,21). Augustine rarely considers happiness without referring to the end of the narrative.

From the perspective provided by the end, felicities, the many false ones and Augustine's true and holy one, are revealed for what they are. Thus does one with the help of Augustine's imagined ending of the descended heavenly Jerusalem of Revelation 21,1–2 and its felicity described in 21,3–5, 22–27, and 22,1–5 find one's present shaped and revealed. It is from the end of the story, both Augustine's and the Bible's, that the reader is to take his or her cue regarding how to be a pilgrim living in its middle:

> [T]he life of felicity, which is also a life of eternity, will show a love and a gladness that are not only right but also assured . . . . Hence it is clear what must be the quality of the citizens of God's City during their earthly pilgrimage. They must live a life according to the spirit and not according to the flesh . . . . And it is also apparent what will be their quality in that immortality towards which they are making their way. (14,9)

In the meantime, "in the middest," Christians live Apocalypse. Augustine finds in Revelation a mythological figuration of time to make sense of the present. He unveils the present as the time of the millennium, the first resurrection of Revelation 20:5, the time Christians live from the birth of the church to the second coming of Christ. Augustine's has been called a realized eschatology. But it is not a wholly realized one. As Catherine Keller has argued, if Augustine is anti-apocalyptic in his resistance to chronologically and bodily literalising interpretation of the thousand-year reign of Revelation 20,4, he nevertheless offers as a replacement his own apocalypse, his own catalogue of end-events structured by the final chapters of Revelation, amplified with the help of apocalyptic texts culled from the two testaments and harmonized with his interpretation of the Apocalypse's timetable. He emplots his readers in his own signification of the end.[11] Inscribed by his narrative in the thousand-year reign of Christ, Augustine's readers discover themselves to be living the Apocalypse now in anticipation of the great apocalyptic advent to come. Meanwhile, the conversion of the nations and daily miracles of healing are signs of the growing age of the world and the interruption of the present with intimations of future restorations (18,40)—a perspective that demands some qualification of the prevalent scholarly view that Augustine's eschatology is spiritualized or interiorized.[12] It is in the light of that future, indeed stolen from it, that the present is unveiled. Augustine remains apocalyptic, literarily, in this his allegedly most spiritual millennialism. The subjugated body is an outpost of

---

11. C. Keller, *Apocalypse Now and Then: A Feminist Guide to the End of the World* (Boston: Beacon Press, 1996) 96–103.

12. Thus, Frederikson, "Apocalypse and Redemption," 160–68.

millennium for Augustine, in its continued warfare with sin, anticipating the final conflict when Satan fully unleashed will attack. Similarly it foreshadows the life to come in its nurturing of virtue and conduct becoming of the Heavenly City. Apocalypse is realized in the warfare against vices, by which the Beast attacks the saints. Augustine does not use the Apocalypse to interpret the events of his day as literal fulfillment of prophecy. He resists any attempt to forecast the end of the world based on the events of his day. Nevertheless, his story of the human condition is "apocalyptic" in the sense that the Apocalypse's narratives reveal the deeper truth of present life and its struggles as the site of a cosmic apocalyptic battle (20,9).

Augustine's Vision

It is at the end that Augustine discovers himself able to see the most clearly. The total war of the end of the age described in Revelation 13 and inserted by Augustine in his explication of Revelation 20,7–10 (*Civ.* 20,13, 19, 23) reveals the substance of the warfare of the two cities from its beginning. For Augustine the final chapters of Revelation provide the hermeneutical key for exposing the true ends and forces behind each of the two cities and the nature of their relationship, and it is this end that provides him with the orientation to interpret the course of historical events. It is not just the biblical narrative, but that narrative oriented toward its conclusion in the Book of Revelation, that offers Augustine the right way to interpret the saeculum. It is from the end of the story, where Augustine reads that the age will end with the persecution by Antichrist of the pilgrim city of God, that the truth is most clearly revealed of the inimical relation of the two cities from their origin. Already foreshadowed in the murder by Cain of Abel (18,51), the beast and the Antichrist of Revelation are the fullest revelation of the pretense of the earthly city, governed by demons and the desire for the destruction of the saints (20,9,14), whose hallmark in history has been the persecution of the earthly citizens of the heavenly city. The final conflict of the two cities is the end-point of the antithesis of contrary phenomena through which God speaks so eloquently in history (11,18). To extend this metaphor: Revelation 20 and 13 provide Augustine with the grammar for understanding God's language in events. Here we find unveiled the true character of the city of man governed by demonic forces.

It is with these grammatical elements that Augustine finds the speech to expose the truth of the city of man and its perverse loves. Revelation, with its ending of a complete unveiling, a total *apokalypsis* of the Beast in history, furnishes Augustine with the hermeneutic of suspicion to unmask the pretense and false worship of the earthly city. It is his interpretation of the beast as the pretentious, hybristic city of man (20,9) that brings Books 1 to 10 and 11 to 22 into a narrative unity. When chronicling the role of pagan deities in bringing happiness to the Roman state Augustine becomes the privileged seer, revealing to otherwise blind pagans the marks of the beast they are unable to perceive:

> [T]he intelligent are infected by a gross mental disorder which makes them defend the irrational workings of their minds as if they were logic and truth itself, even when the evidence has been put before them as plainly as is humanly possible. Either they are too blind to see what is put before their face, or they are too perversely obstinate to admit what they see. The result is that we are forced very often to give an extended exposition of the obvious, as if we were not presenting it for people to look at, but for them to touch and handle with their eyes shut. (2,1)

What follows is Augustine's uncensored history of Rome's hubris, exposed in part by Sallust and others, but now fully unveiled as demonic as he retells the story of Roman corruption and immorality. "Can anyone fail to see and understand what efforts these malignant spirits use, to give by their example a presumed divine authority to criminal acts?" (2,25). "Let us strip of the veils, remove the whitewash of illusion and subject the facts to a strict supervision," Augustine insists (3,14); "let us refuse to be fooled by empty bombast, to let our critical faculties be blunted by high-sounding words like 'peoples,' 'realms,' 'provinces'" (4,3). He seeks to expose what he considers to be a too often suppressed history, a past whose course, with only a few notable exceptions, has been guided by demons. Augustine offers his reader eyes to see the truth masked by empty pagan slogans about commonwealths and religion. Books 1 to 10 are an exposé of the pagan past. Standing over that past at the conclusion of the first part of his work (10,32) is again a narrative description of the end of the age—Augustine's assurance of the end of the story, of the unending vision of the city of God, whence he finds the eyes to pierce through the lies and deception of pretentious pagan self-love and religion.[13]

The *City of God* is a Revelation. It is an unveiling offered by a seer confident of the end of the story where all, if unimaginable, is nonetheless paradoxically made clear. It is a narrative meaningless without its final three books, themselves unimaginable without the final chapters of the Apocalypse.

---

13. As observed by R. J. Deferrari and Sr. M. J. Keeler, "St. Augustine's *City of God*: Its Plan and Development," *American Journal of Philology* 50 (1959): 109–37, the work was conceived as a whole from the start—or, better, from its beginning it was told from its anticipated ending.

MOULDING THE PRESENT: APOCALYPTIC AS HERMENEUTICS IN *CITY OF GOD* 21–22

Karla Pollmann

Qui prend le ton apocalyptique vient vous signifier, sinon vous dire, quelque chose. Quoi? mais la vérité, bien sûr, et vous signifier qu'il vous la révèle, le ton est révélateur de quelque dévoilement en cours. Dévoilement ou vérité, apophantique de l'imminence de la fin, de quoi que ce soit qui revient, finalement, à la fin du monde. Non pas seulement la vérité comme vérité révélée d'un secret sur la fin ou du secret de la fin. La vérité elle-même est la fin, la destination, et que la vérité se dévoile est l'avènement de la fin. La vérité est la fin et l'instance du jugement dernier. La structure de la vérité serait ici apocalyptique. Et c'est pourquoi il n'y aurait pas de vérité de l'apocalypse qui ne soit vérité de la vérité.

J. Derrida[1]

Definitions

As there does not exist final clarity about the often vaguely used terms "apocalyptic" and "eschatology" I wish to define here briefly in advance how I am going to use these terms for the purposes of the following essay. *Eschatology* means "the doctrine of the last things," a theological reflection about the last things that are going to happen to humanity, which normally

---

1. J. Derrida, *D'un ton apocalyptique adopté naguère en philosophie* (Paris: Galilée, 1983) 69.

includes death; the end of the world, time, and history; resurrection of the body; final judgment, hell, and heaven. This view implies the abolition of a belief in the regularly recurring repetition of primordial happenings, but a faith in final solutions, which applies a conviction about the ultimate character of reality to that unknown which lies ahead. Apocalyptic is the wider term, meaning "the revelation of divine secrets." The term is applied (1) to a literary genre, namely Jewish or Christian writings that claim to expound these secrets of the world and its history which concentrate on the last events, and of which John's Apocalypse (=Revelation) is a paramount specimen;[2] (2) to historical movements showing a characteristically extreme and world-denying behavior that is the consequence of their expectation that this final revelation is about to happen (e.g., the Essenes, but also other sects up to the very present); (3) to theology, especially eschatology, as far as it tries to systematize these ideas and to link them to other aspects of the Jewish or Christian faith.[3]

Two Possible Interpretations of Revelation

"Such things [wars, earthquakes, or epidemics] have often happened and do still happen, and how can these be signs of the end of the world?"

(*Julian, Contra Galilaeos,* frg. 92, ed. Masaracchia [=frg.3, ed. Neumann])

This is the critical question of the pagan emperor Julian (who reigned 361–363) in his polemical work *Against the Christians*, whom he prefers to call "Galilaeans." With this question he wishes to undermine the Jewish-Christian apocalyptic belief that certain conventional signs like wars, eclipses, and earthquakes will indicate the imminent end of the world and the final judgment. Indeed, from early Christianity until the twentieth century it has been popular to identify certain external events or persons with the signs mentioned in John's Revelation to announce the end of time and history.[4] Many early ecclesiastical

---

2. The roots of an apocalyptic view of world history and the developments beyond antedate the Jewish culture: see A. Gall, *BASILEIA TOU THEOU: Eine religionsgeschichtliche Studie zur vorkirchlichen Eschatologie* (Heidelberg: C. Winter, 1926); E. Salin, *Civitas Dei* (Tübingen: J. C. B. Mohr, 1926) 142–45; and N. Cohn, *Cosmos, Chaos and the World to Come: The Ancient Roots of Apocalyptic Faith* (New Haven: Yale University Press, 1993), who also deals with the Book of Revelation (212–19).

3. See R. K. Emmerson, *Antichrist in the Middle Ages: A Study of Medieval Apocalypticism, Art, and Literature* (Seattle: University of Washington Press, 1981) 13–14.

4. See R. C. Fuller, *Naming the Antichrist: The History of an American Obsession* (New York: Oxford University Press, 1995) and *Apocalypse Theory and the End of the World*, ed. M. Bull (Oxford: Blackwell, 1995).

writers in east and west, like Justin, Irenaeus, Hippolytus, Tertullian, and Lactantius, combined this practice with the expectation that thereafter a 1000-year reign of the chosen would take place in a sort of earthly paradise before the final coming of Christ, as could be understood from Revelation 20 (so-called millenarianism or chiliasm).[5] Moreover, it was tempting to use the numbers given in Revelation to calculate when this event would take place in the historical future. In the early church, these calculations were generally made in a way that proved the end not to be imminent.[6]

However, besides this "literal" interpretation of Revelation that concentrated on the predictable sequence of external, singular events, there existed a second, more "spiritual" interpretation of the apocalyptic prophecies and images, from Origen onward, who in his *Commentary on Matthew* 35 (on Mt 24,6; GCS 11.65–68) pleaded for an allegorical interpretation (*moralis intellectus et spiritalis*) of eschatological statements in the Bible.[7] The apocalyptic symbolism was then to be understood in terms of the continuing struggle between good and evil, in the present, either in the heart of every Christian—thus Origen[8]—or within the church as a whole, as asserted by Tyconius, a North African quasi-Donatist at the end of the fourth century.[9] This mode of interpretation emphasized the present, immanent, and continuous struggle rather than a final opposition or cosmic fight between good and evil, without denying the reality of such a future final event. Hence, the original revolutionary, anti-imperial intention of Revelation with its concrete, material hopes for political change taking place in history[10] was transformed into a more spiritual, interiorized aim for each faithful individual to strive for moral improvement.

---

5. Helpful surveys by B. E. Daley, *The Hope of the Early Church: A Handbook of Patristic Eschatology* (Cambridge, 1991) 20–104; G. Maier, *Die Johannesoffenbarung und die Kirche* (Tübingen: J. C. B. Mohr, 1981) 106; 130f.; G. Kretschmar, *Die Offenbarung des Johannes: Die Geschichte ihrer Auslegung im 1. Jahrtausend* (Stuttgart: Calwer, 1985) 71–76.

6. See B. Kötting, "Endzeitprognosen zwischen Lactantius und Augustinus," *Historisches Jahrbuch* 77 (1958) 125–39, and H. Inglebert, *Les Romains chrétiens face à l'histoire de Rome: Histoire, christianisme et romanités en Occident dans l'Antiquité tardive (IIIe-Ve siècles)* (Paris: Études Augustiniennes, 1996).

7. Origen is therefore scornful of those millenarians who, in his opinion, interpret the eschatological Jerusalem as an extended period of idealized earthly beatitude (*De principiis* 2,11,2); cf. B. McGinn, *Antichrist: 2000 Years of the Human Fascination with Evil* (San Francisco: Harper, 1994) 64f.

8. Best survey in Daley 47–60.

9. See K. Pollmann, *Doctrina Christiana* (Fribourg: Universitätsverlag, 1996) 38–51, and Maier 134.

10. Cf. P. A. Souza Nogeira, *Der Widerstand gegen Rom in der Apokalypse des Johannes: Eine Untersuchung zur Tradition des Falls von Babylon in Apokalypse 18* (Diss., Heidelberg, 1991); A. Y. Collins, *Cosmology and Eschatology in Jewish and Christian Apocalypticism* (Leiden: E. J. Brill, 1996) 20; 198–217; C. Keller, *Apocalypse Now and Then* (Boston: Beacon Press, 1996) 99; 102 ("sublimation" of Revelation).

It has long been observed that Augustine follows the latter line of interpretation.[11] As is characteristic of his rich, multi-dimensional personality, he has various reasons for doing so. First, he follows a pragmatic line of argument that seems to be a direct answer to Julian's polemical question quoted at the beginning of this section: signs traditionally thought to indicate the end of the world were unreliable guides because of their omnipresence throughout history. The earth had always been scourged by wars, floods, or earthquakes at different periods and places; there had never been a lack of morally decadent, ungodly individuals or even nations, as Augustine argues in *Ep.* 199,34f. to a fellow bishop, Hesychius of Salonae (presumably written in AD 418/419). So it would simply be embarrassing to attempt to predict the end of the world based on any such indication (even if one thinks this is endorsed by Scripture itself), as one can be proven wrong too easily.

Augustine, however, also employs a second, more profound line of argument, which is closely linked to his theology in general, with consequences that to my knowledge have not yet been outlined by scholarship in great detail.

In the *City of God*, the ongoing struggle between good and evil forms the fundamental dynamic mechanism of human history, though the dividing lines between good and bad cannot always be drawn with safety; the final resolution, understanding, and abolition of this struggle will only be made in the final judgment at the end of time and history. God's plans cannot be understood by humanity in its earthly state in history, as Augustine keeps emphasizing.[12] When he comes to the discussion of the last things Augustine splits the apocalyptic prophecies in a peculiar way: on the one hand, we will have a New Jerusalem, as announced in Revelation, but it is a purely ahistorical heaven that will become reality only after the end of time and history.[13] On the other hand, the millennial prophecy of Revelation 20, the 1000-year reign of the saints, is an allegorical representation of the historical church in its present state. Following Tyconius, after 394 Augustine ceased to use the millenarian tradition[14] and claimed that the number 1000 had to be understood symbolically: the precise length of this reign cannot be determined and the events

---

11. See, e.g., Daley 131–50; McGinn, *Antichrist*, 76–8; Fuller 32f.; B. McGinn, "The End of the World and the Beginning of Christendom," in *Apocalypse Theory and the End of the World*, ed. M. Bull (Oxford: Blackwell, 1995) 58–89, here 62; Keller 92, 98.

12. Cf., e.g., *Civ.* 18,50, 53; 20,9; 22,30. For further references cf. Daley 134f.

13. Cf. most recently J. B. Russell, *A History of Heaven: The Singing Silence* (Princeton: Princeton University Press, 1997) 84–90.

14. Cf. Daley 249 n. 18, who is also instructive on Tyconius (127–31).

announced in Revelation are happening right now, in a kind of "realized eschatology."[15] This approach makes it easier in general to apply apocalyptic ideas to the present itself, including the historical church, which before the end of time is fallible, a body composed of good and evil members. Here and now the dividing line cannot always be drawn with certainty; in a kind of eschatological suspense the final separation of good and bad has to wait till the end of time.[16]

One can say therefore that Augustine's (as Tyconius's) apocalyptic thinking comprises two approaches to eschatology, (1) a pragmatic one that outlines its present realization, both in the soul of the individual and in the social institution of the historical church, and (2) an ahistorical and transcendent one, by positing it as an indescribable future event, which nevertheless gives meaning to the temporal historical process as its *telos*.[17] This ineffable future horizon also has consequences for our understanding of the present as the aspect of uncertainty is extended to our limited ability to make ultimately correct statements about the present itself.[18]

Furthermore, in Augustine's view the sacred narrative of scripture has a gap in it between the apostolic age of the church and the second coming (parousia) of Christ at the end of the world.[19] For the intervening period of human history there exists no divinely authorized account; hence no "meaning" can be securely attributed to it from a Christian point of view. On the other hand, there is the post-historical (or eschatological) reality of eternal hell and eternal bliss for which there exists a divinely authorized prophecy in several biblical books including Revelation, but about whose precise outline

---

15. See Daley 133f.

16. Already quite sharply put by Augustine in his work *De Baptismo contra Donatistas* (written around 400) 5,38f., where he points out that neither will everybody inside the church be automatically saved (as they may be false members) nor will everybody outside the church be condemned (as they can be converted before their end).

17. Cf. McGinn, "The End of the World," 62.

18. This complicates the view that Augustine's apocalyptic thinking is purely ahistorical, as in Keller 92. As he insists on a final literal fulfillment of all apocalyptic prophecies, his approach cannot even be called only spiritual, as in S. D. O'Leary, *Arguing the Apocalypse: A Theory of Millennial Rhetoric* (New York: Oxford University Press, 1994) 73–76. Though the latter correctly sees that apocalyptic imagery is used to exhort to a saintly life (75), he is wrong to suggest that this is its only use.

19. See Keller 95 and especially R. Herzog, "Vom Aufhören: Darstellungsformen menschlicher Dauer im Ende," in *Das Ende: Figuren einer Denkform*, ed. K. Stierle and R. Warning, Poetik und Hermeneutik 19 (Munich: Fink, 1996) 283–329, here 301.

and nature the human mind cannot have a clear perception in its present historical limitedness. Outside the boundaries of the rule of faith as the norm of belief there exists a broad field for free speculation, and Augustine, like other ecclesiastical writers, is aware of the responsibility of the intelligent believer to struggle for clearer understanding. In the case of the *City of God*, Augustine is faced both with the apologetic and the protreptic challenge[20] to draw a convincing and coherent picture of the Christian view of history, which includes for him the post- and ahistorical "last things." Thus, in order to create the narrative of the *City of God* in his own limited, secular imagination Augustine applies the transcendent truths[21] of divine revelation about the end of the world to the historical present of uncertain meaning.

According to Augustine, the ability to understand the doctrine of the last things in this way is a gift of God himself, as is all human understanding (*Civ.* 22,25: *crediturum [sc. mundum] ipse [sc. deus] laudavit, ipse promisit, ipse complevit*; "God himself approved the belief that the world would come to hold; he promised this belief, and he has fulfilled that promise"). He turns the apocalyptic focus from predicting an unknowable future back to bear on the present time—more precisely, on its ethics. Instead of being a historical forecast, apocalyptic imagery thus becomes a kind of Christian myth, a Christian interpretation or hermeneutical frame of reference for the historical situation of humanity, both as a community and as individuals.[22] This explains why Augustine, by "turning Revelation on its feet," is able to insert into the final books of his *City of God*, which deal first and foremost with the hereafter,[23]

---

20. On the twofold purpose of the *City of God*, cf. G. J. P. O'Daly, "Ciuitate dei (De-)," in *Augustinus-Lexikon* (Basel: Schwabe & Co., 1994) 1.969–1010, here 977f.

21. Augustine gave these transcendent truths a special emphasis; cf. Russell 85: "Augustine moved beyond the idea of eternity as perpetuity or endless time (*aiôn; saeculum*) to the idea of a transcendent eternity, ever present, ever here, ever open to those who yearn for it."

22. See also Herzog 304: "der klassische Fall einer Remythisierung." Here one can observe both an amazing affinity and the precise difference between Augustine and Bultmann. R. Bultmann, *The New Testament and Mythology* (Philadelphia: Fortress, 1984; original German ed. 1941) claimed that the whole of the New Testament had a mythological world-view, which had to be "de-mythologized." This meant for Bultmann that the historically untrue, i.e., mythical, statements of the New Testament had not to be eliminated but to be interpreted in a proper way, by using the contemporary, modern world-view (as shaped by existential philosophy) as the hermeneutical horizon. Augustine, on the other hand, would have been happy to acknowledge a certain mythical dimension for Revelation, without denying its historical validity. However, for him the hermeneutical horizon for interpreting Scripture correctly always had to be the Bible itself; cf. Pollmann 143–46. Moreover, the events told in Revelation can themselves be taken as the referential framework for understanding the human condition, as we shall see further below.

elements of his theological thinking that are more concerned with the earthly conditions of humanity.

A few examples, taken from the last two[24] books of the *City of God*, will illustrate this process, partly by comparison with other writings of Augustine where he deals with the same topics in other contexts.

Turning Revelation on Its Feet

Predestination and Grace

In *City of God* 21, which deals with the eternal punishment of sinners, Augustine reacts to a theological position which suggests that punishment after death is merely for purification and that finally everybody will enjoy salvation (which was Origen's view). Secondly, he intends to argue against a position which claims that salvation is confined to Catholic Christians (i.e., that it excluded "heretical" Christians) who will be pardoned in spite of their crimes and errors because they adhere to the "right" faith. Such concepts show a concern to integrate apocalyptic ideas of final judgment, punishment, and salvation into a managable scheme of Christian life, in order to remove the otherwise irritating and virtually unbearable incalculability of the apocalyptic threat. On those lines, the consequence for an individual's thinking could be *either* that salvation will finally be universal and one therefore does not have to worry too much about a punishment that will be limited in time,[25] *or* that one does not have to bother as a Christian at all, because by joining the (Catholic) Christian church one has already acquired a first-class ticket for the life to come. Augustine vehemently opposes such complacent attitudes, which in his eyes weaken and even destroy the radical biblical message of eternal salvation *and* eternal condemnation (especially in Mt 25,31–46, but also, e.g., Rev 20–22; cf. *Civ.* 21,23). By emphasizing over and over again that no human mind can know which individuals will be saved and which will not, regardless of whether they are momentarily and visibly inside or outside the church, he aims first at

---

23. *Civ.* 20 (final judgment and definite separation of good and bad); *Civ.* 21 (eternal hell and condemnation); *Civ.* 22 (eternal bliss and happiness).

24. For *Civ.* 20 (especially ch. 9), which I will not take into consideration in this study, see the essays by Coyle and Maier in this volume.

25. Cf. T. Matsuda, *Death and Purgatory in Middle English Didactic Poetry* (Woodbridge, Suffolk: D. S. Brewer, 1997) 5–13.

removing any Christian complacency or self-righteousness in this respect. Secondly, he wishes to maintain and even reinforce the urgency and importance of the biblical message, concerning both the moral improvement of members within the church and the improvement of the world by missionary activity.

As a further line of argument against any moral indolence on the part of Christians he introduces his doctrine of grace (*Civ.* 21,15f., 26–8; 22,2f., 25) and predestination (*Civ.* 21,24–7; very briefly 22,24).[26] The doctrine of grace permeates many of the major writings of Augustine from 396 onward.[27] In the last books of the *City of God*, where he wishes to expound the final things as seen by the Christians, this is only possible for him through faith and divine grace in the first place. This grace will also, eventually, bring about the final salvation of some chosen people, who are all stained by original sin. But the universal impact of grace starts already in the present of every believer. It enables people to have the right understanding about the process of salvation and to try to get out of human misery (*Civ.* 21,15f., 26; cf. *De gratia et libero arbitrio* 17,33); to recognize their own state of sin; to ask for God's forgiveness, compassion, and love for their neighbours; to get themselves baptized and thus become and remain true members of the true faith (*Civ.* 21,27f.; cf. Ep. 215,5–7; *De gratia et libero arbitrio* 5,10–7,18; *De correptione et gratia* 2,3f.; 12,38). Through Christ's grace God enables human beings to wish and think the good (*Civ.* 22,2f.; cf. Ep. 214,4; *De praedestinatione sanctorum* 2,6). The field of operation for divine grace is the present in a crucial way, as Augustine thinks that the only chance for penitence and thus possibility for final salvation is given in this life, and not in the next anymore (see below). As a whole, the concept of grace is as bipolar as Augustine's approach toward eschatology and apocalyptic: besides its soteriological function at the end of time, it already operates with concrete practical and eschatological consequences in this life. This had been made clear by Augustine in several of his earlier and later works on grace and predestination, and features again in the final books of the *City of God*.

---

26. G. Bardy and G. Combès, *Oeuvres de Saint Augustin: La Cité de Dieu livres XIX–XXII* (Paris, 1960) 851 n. 65 are right to caution us that sometimes Augustine uses terms like praedestinare and its derivatives without their full theological implication, but in the cases investigated above the terminology is certainly indicative of Augustine's theological thinking at that time.

27. For en extensive investigation see J. Lössl, *Intellectus Gratiae: Die erkenntnistheoretische und hermeneutische Dimension der Gnadenlehre Augustins von Hippo* (Leiden: E.J. Brill, 1997).

The doctrine of predestination is developed in other treatises written at about the same time as the last two books of the *City of God* (between about 424 and 427 AD), namely his writings addressed to the monks of Hadrumetum and Provence (*De gratia et libero arbitrio, De correptione et gratia, De praedestinatione sanctorum, De dono perseverantiae*), and against the Pelagians and Julian, bishop of Eclanum (especially *De nuptiis et concupiscentia, Contra duas epistulas Pelagianorum, Contra Iulianum, Contra Iulianum opus imperfectum*), written from about 420 till his death in 430 AD. Building on a thorough reflection on 1 Corinthians 4:7 ("What have you that you did not receive? Now, if you did receive it, why do you glory as if you had not received it?"), Augustine comes to the conclusion that nothing humans do is owed to their own independent merit (*De praedestinatione sanctorum* 3,7; *De dono perseverantiae* 21,55). Those who are chosen by God's predestination are enabled by his grace to act in a saintly way that will eventually lead to final salvation (if they persevere until the very end, which is again only possible through divine grave; see below): *inter gratiam porro et praedestinationem hoc tantum interest, quod praedestinatio est gratiae praeparatio, gratia vero iam ipsa donatio*; "then, between grace and predestination there is only one difference, namely that predestination is the preparation of grace, but grace is already the concrete gift" (De praedestinatione sanctorum 10,19). God will show his merciful grace toward the elect, which is prepared by predestination:[28] *haec est praedestinatio sanctorum, nihil aliud: praescientia scilicet, et praeparatio beneficiorum dei, quibus certissime liberantur, quicumque liberantur*; "this and nothing else is meant by predestination of the saints: namely, foreknowledge and the preparation of God's benefits, by which whosoever are to be liberated, most certainly are liberated" (*De dono perseverantiae* 14,35). But God will also act as a punishing judge against those who by their own free will have chosen evil and behaved as sinners. This doctrine, however, does not imply that every striving for moral improvement is futile, because it is unknown to us who will be condemned and who will be saved in the end. During their whole lives, in time and history, there has to be constant struggle for all people— either because they have the constant chance to repent and change their way of living, or because they have already made the right decision, but then have

---

28. This line of thinking, which could be called the "Augustinian revolution," had been first developed by Augustine in A.D. 396, in his writings addressed to Simplicianus, but in his later years it became more dominant and extreme.

to work hard to continue to the end. The abilities to succeed in both of these respects are gifts of God. The doctrine of grace and predestination (and perseverance; see below) is therefore meant by Augustine as a tool for the education and exhortation of all believers (*De dono perseverantiae* 17,41), which is especially supported by the fact that the number and identity of the chosen are unknown to us in time and history (see, e.g., *De correptione et gratia* 9,20) and will only be revealed at the end of time. By inserting here the apocalyptic element of eschatological suspense Augustine both counteracts the complacent hubris of those who deem themselves chosen, and intends to give the doctrine and teaching of Christianity actual relevance and intensity for all people, whether they are already believers or still need to be converted.[29]

This is made clear even as late as *City of God* 22,1 where Augustine, before he dedicates himself to the exposition of the heavenly city in its eschatological dimensions, again returns briefly to the fact that God made a good creation, but left to human beings the free choice to desert him. The free human will chooses this, which is not arranged by God's predestination, and the consequence of divine punishment for this bad choice is just. So the doctrine of grace and predestination is concerned with the eschatological datum of the salvation of the good and the condemnation of the bad, which is also familiar from other roughly contemporary writings of Augustine.[30] He repeatedly displays the double face of God as, on the one hand, the merciful God of predestination and grace, bringing about salvation through Jesus Christ and, on the other, the just judge, who allows human beings to have free will and choice and full responsibility, and to undergo God's just punishment. The reader is made aware of this basic human condition, which is valid from the very beginning of the creation of humanity (*De Genesi ad litteram* 11,9,12) till the end of the world (*Civ.* 22,1). As we have to understand the *City of God* both as a protreptic and as an apologetic work,[31] these statements serve the somewhat paradoxical purpose of exhorting Augustine's readers to work on their next lives already in their present lives. This requirement is expressed appropriately in a paradox at the very end of the *City of God*: *nam quis alius noster est finis nisi pervenire ad regnum, cuius nullus est finis?* "For what other end do we have than to reach the realm which has got no end?"(22,30). By inserting

---

29. This is again owed by Augustine to Tyconius; see Daley 128f., 133.

30. Cf. J. Bouman, *Augustinus: Lebensweg und Theologie* (Giessen: Brunnen, 1987) 324–27, and Bardy and Combès 528 n. 1.

31. See above, n. 19.

reflexions on grace and predestination at this late point within his narrative Augustine reminds his readers once more that these are not noncommital images of a world far beyond, but closely linked with the moral and religious choices of every individual. Insertions like this save the narrative from assuming a fictitious character where "suspension of disbelief" would be the appropriate and indeed comfortable attitude for the reader, who would then not be part of the story. This effect Augustine clearly wants to avoid: every reader is made part of the narrative and implicitly urged to be actively engaged.

Concerning the doctrine of grace and predestination, we have noted a shift from the eschatological future to the contemporary present. This is the case in other works of Augustine, too. While expounding his concept of predestination, Augustine on the one hand emphasizes the eschatological suspense and the unknown number of the chosen, which is useful to prevent complacency among the faithful (*De correptione et gratia* 13,39-41), while on the other hand he insists on the practical, kerygmatic, and homiletic relevance of predestination for present ethical issues (*De dono perseverantiae* 14,34–17,41; 22,57–23,63). The focus on the present is preserved even in the clearly eschatological context of the last part of the *City of God*. Grace enables us to understand more about the "final things," which in turn have to be described as having the same bipolar structure as grace itself. The eschatological perspective proves able to have a guiding and premonitory function for the present itself. Thus, for Augustine, apocalyptic thought has a direct impact on our daily life via his doctrine of grace and predestination, and likewise the other way round—the apocalyptic dimension has a direct impact on Augustine's theological thinking. In this context, Käsemann's famous dictum is certainly illuminating and valid: that Apocalyptic is the mother of all Christian theology.[32] Augustine's hermeneutical starting point is the decision to take the apocalyptic statements of the New Testament both literally (against Origen) and spiritually. He is fundamentally convinced that there will be eternal salvation and condemnation. As a further step, by means of spiritual or allegorical exegesis, this belief is projected "backward" into history, where the battle between good and evil becomes the dominant factor in history's dynamic. Besides time (and history) as opposed to eternity, the other complementary set of opposite

---

32. E. Käsemann, "The Beginnings of Christian Theology," in *Apocalypticism*, ed. R. W. Funk (New York: Herder & Herder, 1969) 17–46, here 40; similarly G. Florovsky, "Eschatology in the Patristic Age: An Introduction," *Studia Patristica* 2 (1957): 235–50, here 235, and McGinn, "The End of the World," 61; much more cautious is Daley 2.

qualities is God's grace contrasted with the free human will that is also a gift of God.[33] Analogous to the world to come, God's acts of grace and judgment will be revealed only at the end of time. Thus eschatological suspense serves as a tool against a deterministic or fatalistic concept of history, and even reinforces ethical and pastoral endeavors. Moreover, the doctrine of grace and predestination (and others, as we shall see) is shaped by the apocalyptic perspective about an end that is certain, even though its hour and details are uncertain. The effort to cope with this suspense leads to theological "by-products" or *Ersatz*-constructions in many strands of Augustine's theology.[34]

Repentance and Perseverance

It is now that each individual has the opportunity for repentance (*Civ.* 21,24: "And this is simply because anyone who has not been transferred to the side of Christ while living in the body is thereafter reckoned as belonging to the Devil's party").[35] In the life to come every change of mind or behavior will be too late, as only our earthly life will determine our situation in the hereafter. This is a thought already found in Tyconius as quoted by Beatus of Liebana, *Commentary on Revelation* 7,2,15: "Those who are not tortured now by penance, will undoubtedly be tortured then in gehenna" (cf. ibid. 1,5,91; 11,5,3). Therefore neither the saints nor the church pray for Satan, the angels of hell and all who are already condemned (*Civ.* 21,24). Here again a close link is made between the earthly church and its habits, and the saints of the hereafter who are said to mirror the practice of that earthly church.

Penitence is possible only for personal sins, not for original sin, which can be remitted only by baptism (*Contra duas epistulas Pelagianorum* 1,14,28; *De natura et gratia* 8,9–9,10). But even this mechanism is not entirely under human control and does not automatically guarantee success. Here we again encounter the suspense brought about by the ultimate necessity of the grace of God that cannot be earned and is not the consequence of good deeds. God chooses the elected saints in a manner that is impenetrable for mortals, even without the elected showing penitence: *sic praedestinatio praedicanda est, quemadmodum eam sancta scriptura evidenter eloquitur, ut in praedestinatis*

---

33. See Bouman 307.

34. Cf., e.g., Matsuda 9: "For Augustine purgation is primarily significant in terms of one's spiritual journey towards God."

35. Daley 137, who also emphasizes the deferral of eschatology in Augustine until the end of time itself and its partial "prejudgment" before that.

sine paenitentia sint dona et vocatio dei; "predestination is to be proclaimed in such a way, as it is evidently announced by the Holy Scripture, so that God's gifts and vocation are in those who are predestined without penitence" (*De dono perseverantiae* 16,41).[36]

But also those who think themselves believers have to be constantly on their guard: their faith has to be proven by good action, and by perseverance in it (*Civ.* 21,25; cf., e.g., *De gratia et libero arbitrio* 7,16–8,19; *De gestis Pelagii* 14,34). This is based on Matthew 10:22: *qui perseveraverit usque in finem, hic salvus erit*; "who endures to the end shall be saved," which is quoted in *City of God* 21,25 and in other instances. In the concept of perseverance we can again observe the already familiar bipolar structure, its innerworldly and its eschatological dimensions. Perseverance is a gift of God given to his elect now as a privilege (*De correptione et gratia* 8,19–9,20; *De dono perseverantiae* 9,21) and it leads them to eternal salvation. Nevertheless, it is worthwhile to pray for this gift as the number and identitiy of the chosen is not known (*De dono perseverantiae* 2,3; 7,15).[37]

This is why for a Christian it is a "normal paradox" that on the one hand Christians set little store by this world, and on the other hand have warm affection for each other.[38] Apocalyptic imagery can even serve to illustrate various concrete stages of more or less salutary ethical behavior in this life. This occurs, for example, in Augustine's treatment of carnal lust (and more generally of love for relatives) in *City of God* 21,26, a topic that is also dealt with in great detail in his writings against Julian of Eclanum, and in *De bono coniugali* 4,4 and *Enchiridion* 21,78.[39] If you indulge in carnal lust with a harlot this means burning eternally in hell; if you love your wife (we may add, or your husband) carnally, this entails purgatory with a view to final salvation. If you

---

36. See Bouman 336, who paraphrases predestination as the preparation of God's grace which has to come before any human action, as otherwise one could construct a Pelagian mechanism of human merit and divine reward.

37. See Lössl 308f., who emphasizes that true faith accepts the unexplainability of God's decisions as a paradox.

38. This is first formulated in the Epistle to Diognetus 5,4 (2nd cent.), and culminates in Augustine's *City of God*; cf. R. Greer, "Alien Citizens: A Marvelous Paradox," in *Civitas: Religious Interpretations of the City*, ed. P. S. Hawkins (Atlanta: Scholars Press, 1986) 39–56. For a broader investigation see R. C. Petry, *Christian Eschatology and Social Thought: A Historical Essay on the Social Implications of Some Selected Aspects in Christian Eschatology to A.D. 1500* (New York: Abingdon Press, 1956).

39. Cf. Bardy and Combès 493 n. 5.

love your spouse spiritually and put Christ first, this means salvation. Augustine is careful, however, to emphasize that these things can change for better and for worse, and that other things besides will be taken into account. Thus, no secure predictions for one's life after death can be made.

Moreover, it is not the outwardly good deed that concerns God but its motive (*Civ.* 21,24; cf. also 21,27): "Anyone who loves Christ . . . gives help [sc. to other human beings] with the intention of coming closer to Christ, not of escaping from Christ unpunished . . . . When we say in the Lord's Prayer "Forgive us our debts," . . . this clause is said because sins are committed, not in order that we should commit sins because it is said." The logic employed in the latter sentence is the same as when Augustine uses the apocalyptic dimension to underpin his doctrines: the future of the request made in the prayer and the seeming future of the apocalyptic visions reflect a reality that has already taken place and perfuses us. In *De nuptiis et concupiscentia* 1,33,38 Augustine emphasizes that without baptism the forgiveness of sins is not possible and penitence would not be effective. But though human beings sin repeatedly, baptism is necessary only once, as the sequence of time is here (as in apocalyptic events) of no impact, because baptism has a universal effect: *Quid enim prodesset vel ante baptismum paenitentia, nisi baptismus sequeretur, vel postea, nisi praecederet?* "For of what use would penitence be, either before baptism, unless baptism followed, or after baptism, had baptism not preceded?" Similarly, the prayer for forgiveness is valid only if spoken by one who is baptized (or who would be baptized) who will also inherit the kingdom of God (ibid.).

Theodicy and Original Sin

In the face of human uncertainty about what precisely is going to happen in the final judgment and the life to come Augustine uses apocalyptic imagery to explain and illuminate the present situation of humanity, but without the cheap threats of "hellfire preaching."[40] In *City of God* 21 he uses this imagery mainly to elaborate rules for the appropriate ethical attitude and behavior of a true Christian. Even as late as the last part of the *City of God* 22, which talks about the eternal bliss of heaven, Augustine comes back to apocalyptic imagery (*Civ.* 22,22–24, in a kind of "everyday-apocalypse"). He states that spoilt human nature is in need of instruction and prohibition throughout. Though he does not say so explicitly, for him this also means that apocalyptic ideas of the end

---

40. On this topic see also the essay by Coyle in this volume.

of the world are meant for a didactic and morally instructing purpose. At least, this is precisely how he uses them on the following pages where he gives a justification for suffering under a good God (theodicy) and for the working of divine grace, by exploiting apocalyptic topics as a means of interpreting and coming to grips with the present: many calamities brought about by human or non-human causes, as outlined in Revelation and other apocalyptic texts, happen repeatedly in order to remind us of the next life and to deter us from loving this life too much. Continuous "hell on earth" shows us the depth of divine grace which will liberate us from that hell in the life to come, so the motivation for becoming a Christian should not be this life but the next. Here divine grace and original sin are the mechanisms by which the issue of theodicy is annihilated. In *City of God* 21,26 Augustine briefly points out that the death of the body came into being through the perpetration of the first sin. The "fault" lies with humanity, and divine grace will finally free us from self-inflicted (and sometimes God-sent) misery. Present miseries can be understood as a test for our faith and/or as the necessary part of our life under condemnation in the postlapsarian state of humanity. These calamities and human struggles will go on until the final day, and they can serve to remind us of the greater importance and quality of the life to come, but they are no indications or signs that this final day is about to come shortly.

Conclusions

This brief survey has perhaps succeded in illustrating Augustine's treatment of apocalyptic thought in the final two books of the *City of God*. He intends to deemphasize the claim that Revelation announces events which will happen once and in the near historical future. Instead, he *remythologizes* Revelation, both by emphasizing that its events are happening repeatedly throughout human history, in a more or less metaphorical way (as had already been done by Tyconius), in order to *interpret* the human individual's situation in the present, and by employing apocalyptic (eschatological) structures like the unknowability of God's judgment and eschatological suspense in order to *exhort* ethical engagement in the present.

In this way, Augustine can use apocalyptic imagery in combination with various theological concepts like predestination, theodicy and the doctrine of grace that may even be partly influenced by an apocalyptic understanding of reality and of the history of salvation. On the other hand, he insists (*Civ.* 20,30; 21,26) that all the prophecies made in Revelation will eventually become true in the sense that there will be a final Antichrist, a final judgment, and an eternal New Jerusalem beyond time and history, about which we know nothing. In order to avoid both an arrogant complacency about the unknowable and a resigned negligence of the apocalyptic visions, Augustine exploits them as a tool of interpretation and a hermeneutical frame to analyse and understand the present. This strategy is justified by the various levels of meaning in Scripture,[41] and the gradual implementation of biblical prophecies (*Civ.* 20,30) in general.

One expects Augustine to talk in these last two books of the *City of God* entirely about the world to come, but this is not the case. I have tried to outline the reasons for and consequences of this proceeding, which avoids a concrete visualisation of the "last things." An interesting exception is *City of God* 22,13–20, where Augustine speculates about the shape and consistency of the bodies of the resurrected. But even here his interests are more innerworldly than orientated toward predicting in an eschatological fantasy certainties about the life to come. First there is an underlying moral quality to his secular imagination: "The late Augustine's heavenly body, in which the flesh is completely at the will of the spirit, paralleled the bishop's understanding of life in this world."[42] Secondly, the statements of this section of the *City of God* form a pragmatic contribution by Augustine to the ecclesiastical discussion about the cults of saints and their relics, in which he was engaged at that time, especially with Paulinus of Nola.[43] Apart from this passage, Augustine's secular imagination tends to be less mimetic than speculative; thus, instead of visualizing a graphic scenario of the final judgment, he rather reflects on the conclusions that can be extrapolated from such a scenario for the human condition and the relationship between God and humanity.

One could argue that Augustine wants to have his apocalyptic cake and eat it too, that is, he does not want to give up the historical validity and the final fulfillment of all apocalyptic prophecies made in Scripture, even though they cannot be grasped by the insufficient human mind at present. In order to maintain a more concrete and secure relevance of Revelation for the present, he transforms it into a myth by spiritualizing it with moral consequences and

---

41. This against Keller 99f., who claims that Augustine is contradicting himself by criticising those who interpret Revelation literally and later on does it himself.

42. C. McDannell and B. Lang, *Heaven: A History* (New Haven and London: Yale University Press, 1988) 67.

43. For this see the forthcoming study by D. Trout, *Paulinus of Nola: Life, Letters, and Poems* (Berkeley & Los Angeles: University of California Press, 1999), ch. 8.

theological implications. For Augustine, the apocalyptic prophecy of the end of the world as we know it helps us less to understand the future than to explain the present.

An Immoderate Feast:
Augustine Reads John's Apocalypse

Virginia Burrus

Shaking out clean sheets
that crisp lightly scented caress,
I make my bed ready for you.

I wash my hair, trim
nails lest they scratch you —
unintentionally.

A new paisley cloth on it,
I sit at the table
studying recipes.

Each recipe is a dance
of seduction, beckoning.
Soon the door will swing wide

to where I wait in my body
crowned and glittering
for the feast to start.

Marge Piercy, "Little Acts of Love"

Now what reply am I to make about hair and nails?

Augustine, *City of God* 22,19

Seductive beckonings, opening doors, anticipated feasts, crowned women—these are motifs fermented in the explosive brew of an apocalyptic imaginary and deposited under seal in the closing book of the Christian canon, to be broken open and served up again and again, and not only by "religious fanatics." Marge Piercy's recent poem—entitled "Little Acts of Love"—is an intriguing instance of the intersection of the apocalyptic with the secular imagination, its secularity manifested not least in its gentle subversions of the futuristic and cataclysmic dualisms that structure the canonical Apocalypse.[1] Piercy's kitchen-table verses refuse to yield up shocking disclosures: however much tinged with longing, or decked in the borrowed finery of heavenly queens, trimming nails and planning menus are the careful acts that get us through one more day, not the risky heroics that make and break worlds. Indeed, in its very self-proclaimed modesty, "Little Acts of Love" performs what theologian Catherine Keller calls a "counter-apocalypse" by enacting an "ironic mimesis of the portentous tones of the original—with which it dances as it wrestles," as Keller puts it; echoing and parodying the apocalyptic script, Piercy's poem "disarm[s] its polarities" and thereby interrupts the violently world-destroying tendencies of what Keller dubs the "apocalyptic habit."[2]

Augustine of Hippo—author of a distinctive doctrine of the "secular"[3]—is also frequently positioned as the anti-apocalyptic theologian *par excellence*: in his magisterial *City of God*, he did not merely counter the effects of John's Apocalypse in textual play but brought the apocalyptic tradition sternly to an end, it would seem.[4] However, as Keller suggests, *anti-apocalypse*, in contrast

---

1. Thanks are due to Harry Maier and Catherine Keller, whose conversation generously nourished this essay. M. Piercy, *What Are Big Girls Made Of?* (New York: Random House, 1997).

2. C. Keller, *Apocalypse Now and Then: A Feminist Guide to the End of the World* (Boston: Beacon Press, 1996) 19–20.

3. R. A. Markus, *Saeculum: History and Society in the Theology of St Augustine* (Cambridge: Cambridge University Press, 1970).

4. A nuanced articulation of this position is J. K. Coyle, "Augustine and Apocalyptic: Thoughts on the Fall of Rome, and the Book of Revelation, and the End of the World," *Florilegium* 9 (1987): 1–34; see also the careful treatment of Augustine as a reader of John's Apocalyse in Paula Fredriksen, "Apocalypse and Redemption in Early Christianity: From John of Patmos to Augustine of Hippo," *Vigiliae Christianae* 45 (1991): 151–83. Note that Gerald Bonner, "Augustine and Millenarianism," in *The Making of Orthodoxy: Essays in Honor of Henry Chadwick*, ed. R. Williams (Cambridge: Cambridge University Press, 1989) 235–54, argues that the historical effects of Augustine's personal rejection of millenarianism have been greatly exaggerated.

to *counter-apocalypse*, frequently "turns out to be an oxymoron."[5] If Augustine tells a story that would put an end to the worlds woven by stories of world-ending, his own text thereby proves unexpectedly continuous with John's Apocalypse, as his *City of God* unveils what he intends to be the final twist on John's spiralling revelation of final times. To shift metaphors: Augustine, I am suggesting, was a greedy consumer of the Apocalypse, despite his notorious grumping on the topic of millenarian feasts. Gobbling the text, he fueled the narrative engines of his *City of God*.[6] However, like the author of the first Apocalypse (or the wolf in "Little Red Riding Hood"), Augustine seems to have discovered that the book which tasted sweet as honey sometimes sat heavily in his belly afterward (Apoc 10,9–10). My topic here is Augustine's digestion of the "master script" of Apocalypse,[7] a text that indeed knows "no bounds of moderation" and "exceeds even the limits of incredibility," to borrow language from the *City of God* (20,7). To be more precise: I am particularly interested in Augustine's *in*digestion, in what sat most heavily in his belly following the immoderate feast.

Those interpreters who have somewhat misleadingly positioned Augustine as the great resister of apocalyptic thought have picked up on his own hint, as if falling into a carefully laid trap. In Book 20 of the *City of God*, as he introduces his reading of Apocalypse 20—the *locus classicus* of millenarianism—Augustine swiftly lays out three basic interpretive options (20,7). The first, which he rejects vigorously, takes literally the notion of a thousand-year "Sabbath" reign of the saints who "spend their rest in the most unrestrained material feasts (*inmoderatissimis carnalibus epulis vacaturos*), in which there will be so much to eat and drink that not only will those supplies keep within no bounds of moderation but will also exceed the limits even of incredibility (*ut non solum nullam modestiam teneant, sed modum quoque ipsius incredulitatis excedant*)."[8] The second view replaces the repulsive fantasy of material feasting with the vaguely imagined enjoyment of "some delights of a spiritual character [which] were to be available for the saints because of the presence of the Lord." Of this view Augustine remarks: "I also entertained

---

5. Keller, *Apocalypse Now and Then*, 15.

6. Cf. M. R. Miles, *Desire and Delight: A New Reading of Augustine's Confessions* (New York: Crossroad, 1992) 43: "To read, for Augustine, was to swallow, to assimilate, to digest, to incorporate, *to eat* the text."

7. Keller, *Apocalypse Now and Then*, 10.

8. All translations of the *City of God* are those of H. Bettenson (Harmondsworth: Penguin Classics, 1972).

this notion at one time." The third interpretive option, and the one evidently endorsed by the author of Book 20 at the time of its writing, abandons both the literalizing chronology and the concept of a first bodily resurrection: on this reading, the thousand years signifies the totality of time between the first and last comings of Christ—thus the "millennium" is already under way—and the first resurrection is understood to be not bodily but psychic. Commentators have eagerly seized on the concise autobiographical line—"I also entertained this notion at one time"—in order to mark a turning point in Augustine's thought, the hinge between the lightly spiritualizing apocalypticism "once entertained" and the thoroughgoing transcendentalizing eschatology that seems to have the final word. If, however, it may be argued that the author of both the *Confessions* and the *Retractations* is always in motion but never really leaves anything behind, should we not suspect that when Augustine professes to have once entertained a millenarian notion he still entertains it in some form, subsumed perhaps but by no means discarded?[9] I think a case can be made that Augustine's position in Book 20 is most helpfully read not as a rejection of, but as an elaborate set of adjustments to, the millenarianism "once entertained."[10] Even a cursory glance suggests that, as "symbolic" exegeses go, Augustine's reading of Apocalypse 20 still cleaves extremely close to the flesh of the text: his millennium loosens its grip on the precision of a thousand-year span but hangs more tightly than ever to the real time and space of history, coming not just soon but now; everyone will get his or her just desserts, and if the logic of rewards and punishments remains fuzzy during the time of the first resurrection, things will be clear enough in the second; a literal bodily resurrection is not denied but merely deferred, and there will be not only food but perhaps also sex for the citizens of Augustine's New Jerusalem, who (unlike the "materialists" with the bad table manners) will know how to enjoy these delights in the right "spirit" with the help of their retuned resurrection bodies; and finally, most "apocalyptically" of all, the periods of the first and second resurrections—into which Augustine (improvising but still following John's lead) has neatly redivided and redistributed his "millennialism"—will

---

9. Bonner, "Augustine and Millenarianism," 235 raises a similar question: "Was Augustine's rejection of millenarianism as uncompromising as is generally assumed?" While going on to demonstrate that Augustine's anti-millenarianism was less absolute and also later and more gradual in its emergence than is commonly asserted, Bonner nevertheless continues to read *City of God* 20,7 as evidence of a shift from literalism to symbolism in Augustine's exegetical practice and eschatological theory.

10. Cf. the comment of Fredriksen, "Apocalypse and Redemption," 166: "Augustine plays stunningly creative variations on the great themes of Christian millenarianism."

be separated by a "short time" in which the Devil, partially restrained in the "millennial" present, will be unloosed and rage with all his strength against the saints.

I want to focus briefly on Augustine's fascination with this cataclysmic wedge of time between the "millennium"—in which (according to his account) the saints already ambiguously reign—and the deferred clarities of the last judgment from which the New Jerusalem will emerge serenely re-embodied. Why does he retain a narrative episode that leaves so *completely* intact the violently homogenizing, materialized dualisms of the Apocalypse? Why does he indeed go out of his way to do so? For he literally goes out of his way. In chapter 8 of Book 20, Augustine writes: "we are told that [the Devil] is going to rage with all his strength, and with the strength of his supporters *for three years and six months*" (emphasis added). Here he shifts—somewhat anomalously—to an explicitly intertextual reading of John: "three years and six months," a temporal specification not found in Apocalypse 20, is the cue for the entry of the characters from Apocalypse 12 onto the scene of Apocalypse 20's millennialism, along the path of a brief slice of time referred to in both chapters. "And he laid hold on the dragon, that old serpent, which is the Devil, and Satan, and bound him a thousand years . . . and after that he must be loosed a little season" (Apoc 20, 2–3, KJV). "Woe to the inhibitors of the earth and of the sea! for the devil is come down unto you, having a great wrath, because he knoweth that he hath but a short time" (Apoc 12,12). The short time that links the two chapters is glossed within chapter 12 by the references to 1,260 days (12,6) and (more cryptically) to "a time and times and half a time" (12,14), references in turn swept into Augustine's reading of Apocalypse 20 with the mention of "three years and six months."

Let us start with Augustine's own account of the hermeneutical significance of this three and a half years that he has retrieved from chapter 12 for his interpretation of chapter 20 of John's Apocalypse. "What have we, to be sure," he asks, "in comparison with the saints and believers of the future, seeing that so mighty an adversary will be let loose against them, whereas we have the greatest peril in our struggle with him although he is bound? And yet there is no doubt," he continues, answering his own question, "that even during this period of time there have been, and there are today, some soldiers of Christ so wise and brave that even if they were living in this mortal condition at the time when the Devil is to be unloosed, they would take the most prudent precautions against his stratagems, and withstand his assaults with the utmost steadfastness" (20,8). The "short time" of the future struggle thus has a revelatory function in relation to the indefinitely extended stretch of the quasi-millennial present: the imagined heroics of the battle to come may be overlaid on the muted majesty of present-day saints in such a way as to sharpen perception of their true valor. If Augustine has seemingly gone to great lengths in the *City of God* to drain present history of melodramatic excesses and exaggerated polarizations (and indeed to drain them into the span of three and a half years!), his argument so often seems primarily epistemological: it is our own clarity of vision, rather than the battle itself, that is deferred. However, even as he insists on this deferral of insight, Augustine cannot resisting taking—and giving us, his readers—a sneak preview, so that epistemological postponements merely intensify the revelatory structure of his text. And what exactly is on view in that potent future historical "short time" of three and a half years that puts such a distinct interpretive spin on the present?

Here are John's verses in fuller citation. "And the woman fled into the wilderness, where she hath a place prepared of God, that they should feed her there a thousand two hundred and threescore days" (Apoc 12,6). "And to the woman were given two wings of a great eagle, that she might fly into the wilderness, into her place, where she is nourished for a time, and times, and half a time, from the face of the serpent" (Apoc 12,14). If Augustine's reading of the "short time" of Apocalypse 12 reveals cataclysmic violence on earth, unleashed in the form of a gape-mouthed dragon in pursuit of a mysterious woman—as we learn from John's text—it thereby "contains" (in both senses of the word) the continuing possibility for the heroics of martyrdom in the here and now. This is important, I think, but I want to press these verses a bit further still, in my own pursuit of the fleeing female who is almost completely reveiled in Augustine's treatment of the text—glimpsed only once in 20,8 in the guise of the Holy City herself, and so further obscured through her conflation with the contrasting figure of the virginal New Jerusalem of Apocalypse 21. The well-fed winged woman whose period of wilderness residence unequivocally marks the span of the three and a half years that draws Augustine out of his way and into chapter 12 in the first place is, of course, the same alluring lady who appears resplendently pregnant earlier in Apocalypse 12 (and also peeks out at us from Marge Piercy's poem) "clothed with the sun, and the moon under her feet, and upon her head a crown of twelve stars." This woman occupies not only a precise *time* in the text of Apocalyse 12 (three and a half years) but also a precise *place*, a place of nourishment, a place that spans (in the stretch of two wings) both heaven and earth, a place that is *not a city*. Chased by the disoriented, orally fixated dragon who is trying to get a mouthy grip on her own strong fix on temporality and locale, *she* is not the one with the food problem, in this text. While the sky jealously protects her newborn son from the dragon's drooling jaws, the desert cradles her body, both feeding her and swallowing what she cannot when the dragon floods her with his vomit. Neither starved out nor drowned by excess, the heavenly woman is nourished in an earthly place and time, from the very face of the serpent itself.

Now what am I getting at if I want to suggest (rhetorically) that part of what Augustine has swallowed but found not quite digestible in John's Apocalypse, part of what he is trying to keep down, is this woman, a woman who waits in her body, crowned and glittering, for the feast to start? Perhaps what is revealed in my own unveiling of Augustine's purported cover-up is simply the limit to the heroic narratives that Augustine's text (and eschatology) can accommodate. In the interval of the spiritual "first resurrection," as Augustine understands it, glory must always be postponed, all congratulations come too soon, and the observed theatrics of this life may yet prove illusory when measured up against the hard facts of history as viewed retrospectively through the sharp eyes of the final judge. The problem with the woman pursued by the dragon is that she is potentially too attractive a martyr. Augustine does not wish to foreclose on martyrdom—far from it—yet he may need to delay too lively a telling of the heroic tales of which the conclusions remain, after all, hidden.

This argument, which I believe to be largely correct, still seems somewhat strained as I twist it through the text of Book 20. At the very least, it does not yet say enough, for the figure of the martyr is well accommodated precisely by the three and a half years at the future edge of time into which Augustine has drained all unveiled heroics. Returning to Augustine's *only* explicit objection in *this* text to *any form* of millenarian interpretation of Apocalypse 20, I cannot help thinking we should take him at his word, in what is after all an oddly literalizing exegesis of a highly poetic work. What is the matter with the well-nourished mother harassed ineffectually by the dragon on the borders of temporality? The problem is not just martyrdom but *matter itself*, the witness of a carnality that lingers ambiguously into what "should" be a clarifying, purifying interval of strife. Indeed, the immensity of the problem posed by the ambiguity of matter or flesh (*caro*) has rendered Augustine speechless: "it would take too long to refute them in detail," he protests feebly when discussing the "materialists" (*carnales*) who imagine the millennium as a time of feasts both "material" (*carnales*) and "immoderate," "keeping within no bounds," "exceeding measure" (20,7). His initial attempt to spiritualize—and thereby moderate—the pleasures of the millennium falters in the face of a first resurrection in which human bodies, still caught up in the web of time and space, remain more or less continuous with their present state, a state marked for Augustine above all by a desire that is both driven by fleshly need and finally excessive in relation to need—sucky, gobbly, greedy.[11] In Book 13, Augustine is already quite clear that "the bodies of the righteous, after the [final] resurrection, will not need any . . . material nourishment to prevent any kind of distress from hunger or thirst . . . . They will eat only if they wish to eat; eating will be for them a possibility, not a necessity" (13,22; see also 22,19 on Christ's resurrection body and food). Like the angels, he notes, they might eat to be polite, to fit in. But food, in itself, will not really matter. In heaven, *matter will not matter.* The problem is that Wilderness Woman is still three and a half years short of attaining her resurrection body. Like the girl in red who strays through the forest, her healthy appetite addresses dangerous questions to the already anticipated resurrection body of the devourer himself: *What is the body for?*[12]

In order to defer the possibly inevitable conclusion ("the better to eat you with")—and also to approach the matter of matter, and its relation to the *mother* as well as to the *martyr,* from a slightly different angle—let me make a short detour back to Book 1 of the *City of God,* where Augustine responds to the report that Christian women have committed suicide so as to avoid rape at the hands of barbarian invaders (1,16–17). Here we observe Augustine encountering human struggles in the real time and space of the ongoing millennium, where (according to him) what is really significant is precisely what does not meet the eye. Coolly withholding the expected praise of the women's chastity,[13] Augustine instead assures his readers that stories of the sexual violation

---

11. Cf. Miles, *Desire and Delight,* 28–9, in reference to the *Confessions:* "Augustine uses metaphors of food and nourishment to express the ungratifying nature of compulsive sexual activity . . . . The quality of relationships with other human beings in this mode of operation is dramatically presented in Augustine's image of 'eating one another up, as people do with their food' (IX.2). The behavior of the infant at the mother's breast is disguised, but structurally unaltered, in adult relationships."

12. This line is borrowed from H. Cixous, "Coming to Writing," in *Coming to Writing and Other Essays,* ed. D. Jenson (Cambridge, MA: Harvard University Press, 1991) 14–15: "So for the sons of the Book: research, the desert, inexhaustible space, encouraging, discouraging, the march straight ahead. For the daughters of the housewife: the straying into the forest. Deceived, disappointed, but brimming with curiosity. Instead of the great enigmatic duel with the Sphinx, the dangerous questioning addressed to the body of the Wolf: What is the body for? Myths end up having our hides. Logos opens its great maw, and swallows us whole."

13. Cf. Ambrose's enthusiastic endorsement of virginal suicide in *De virginibus* 3,7,32–7, as I have discussed it in "Reading Agnes: The Rhetoric of Gender in Ambrose and Prudentius," *Journal of Early Christian Studies* 3 (1995): 30–33.

of Christian women would scarcely dishonor the church—so long as there were no moral assent on the part of the women involved (1,16). Virginity is not a physical but a mental state, so that there can be no true rape of a woman if her mind remains pure. Thus, Augustine concludes, even a raped woman "has no reason to punish herself by a voluntary death. Still less should she do so before the act" (1,18). A woman who kills herself to escape rape has thus become, in Augustine's text, a woman who punishes herself for a crime not yet committed (but whose effects are nonetheless already seemingly proleptically inscribed); furthermore, the crime being punished in advance can only be the potential victim's "moral assent." At this juncture, Augustine cuts to the narrative of the much-celebrated Roman heroine and protomartyr Lucretia in order to sharpen the point, audaciously questioning whether Lucretia's post-rape suicide is justifiable in the light of her purported moral purity (1,19).[14] Here he makes his own suspicions explicit: "What if (a thing which only she herself could know), although the young man attacked her violently, she was so enticed by her own desire that she consented, and that when she came to punish herself she was so grieved that she thought death the only expiation?" (1,19). Augustine has now put himself in the position of straining for a peek at "a thing which only [Lucretia] herself could know."[15] There is something familiar about this pattern, viewed retrospectively from the perspective of Book 20. The "something familiar," I suggest, has to do with the revelatory tweaking of the veil shrouding a supposedly unknowable future from whose vantage point alone the present may be clearly viewed. It has to do also with Augustine's encoding of the present as a desirous, hungry body—as female flesh.

Whereas in Book 20 he plays the devouring dragon in relation to the eating woman of the Apocalypse by attempting to swallow her up in his spiritual feast, in Book 1 Augustine has played the seducer in relation to Lucretia's supposedly lusty Christian counterparts by coercively translating virtuous virgins

---

14. D. Trout, "Re-Textualizing Lucretia: Cultural Subversion in the City of God," *Journal of Early Christian Studies* 2 (1994): 53–70, stresses the strength of the Christian and pagan consensus regarding Lucretia's innocence and heroism, labeling Augustine's "re-textualizing" effort an "act of radical discourse."

15. E. Clark, "Sex, Shame and Rhetoric: En-Gendering Early Christian Ethics," *Journal of the American Academy of Religion* 59 (1991): 240, points to the link in Augustine's rhetoric between the internalized eye of God and the shaming gaze of the bishop who likewise "oversees" all. Clark's suggestion that Augustine's rhetoric reconfigures rather than eradicates the textual dynamics of honor and shame complicates the closing claim of Trout, "Re-Textualizing Lucretia," 70, that Augustine's treatment of Lucretia "struck . . . at . . . the prickly goads of honor and shame."

into willfully wanton women. In each case he has not only displaced and abjected what he nevertheless slyly performs textually; he has also, by bestowing on himself the privilege of the sneak preview, overlaid the invisible future upon the visible present in order to shut down longing and its entanglement in the material stuff of preresurrection bodies, all the while seeming (perhaps indeed trying) to hold the door to the flesh partly open through what remains a strikingly literal reading of John. Distracting attention from actual deaths that might have been narrated as martyrdoms, Augustine dismisses the significance of anticipated bodily rapes, only so as to reinscribe retrospectively the shame of a foreseen rape at the sublime site not of a woman's physical violation (which had not yet taken place anyway, and now never would) but of a woman's imagined desire (which always existed because he says it might have). Similarly, ignoring the terrestrial feeding of the woman of Apocalypse 12 by pushing her into the unearthly future of a holy city whose inhabitants have no need of food, he sustains the power of his horror of carnal feasts. Like the fed-up women of Augustine's day who proclaim with their bodies that "no means no," the well-nourished mother of Apocalypse 12—glimpsed at the future edge of history—materializes clairities about human hopes, fears, strengths, and needs that this Father finds palatable only when misrecognized in the sublimely well-starved figure of the future New Jerusalem.

At its worst, Augustine's "apocalypse of the mind" spiritualizes in such a way as to intensify the particular dualistic habit of apocalyptic thought: even if we cannot precisely predict or immediately bring about the material end of the world, we can perhaps accomplish much the same thing mentally by deciding that this world does not much matter. As Keller notes, "the Augustinian reduction of all things creaturely to means to the timeless End" contributes to the construction of a *sublimated apocalypse,* in a transcendentalization bought at the expense of "something more gross being pushed downward."[16] But, of course, it is a lot to keep down—time, space, death, birth, the pain of starvation or rape, the pleasure of good food or lovemaking. We recall what happened to the dragon! And the earth easily reabsorbed the excess he spewed, taking back its own, moderating the flow. That is how it helped the woman, who might otherwise have been just a bit overwhelmed, but probably not defeated, who—as I here imagine it—went on to trim her nails, wash her hair, change the sheets, set the table, and plan a really tasty dinner.

---

16. Keller, *Apocalypse Now and Then,* 98, 102.

Let me be clear: I am not trying to romanticize meal preparation. Nor am I wanting to construct yet another dangerously misleading polarity by denying that there is in Augustine's text the trace of an intention to "counter" apocalypticism's simultaneous over- and under-investments in the demanding history of hungry bodies, to relinquish utopianism's potential for suicidal violence in order to make more visible the already-inbreaking possibility of a "felicity in history" not reducible to definition in terms of "drives and instincts."[17] What I *am* attempting to say—with Keller but in contrast to much scholarship on Augustine—is that Augustine's text fails most dramatically in the direction of these very intentions, that his strategies of displacement and deferral continue to inscribe a deep and deeply misogynistic mistrust of the flesh of history even while resisting the lure of asceticism's utopianism. These "failures" are not, moreover, accidental but inherent to the structure of his apocalypticism.

An effectively "counter-apocalyptic" reading of the *City of God* must locate itself at the edge of the text's possibilities—which is also to say, it must purposefully follow Augustine to the border of history and to the limit of the imagination. Straining to glimpse the Paradise that lies beyond both the past and the future, Augustine confronts us with a series of fantastic images—wiggling ears, musical (and odorless) behinds, and sweat and tears produced on command (14,24) are all offered as signs of still greater wonders, erections that are fully voluntary (14,26), meals consumed without hunger (13,22), and well-proportioned bodies that remain eternally "thirty-something" (as Paula Fredriksen puts it)[18] (22,15,19). Faced with such improbabilities, we may find ourselves breaking out into giggles. Nervously, we watch as the reality of carnal existence and human desire is unveiled and, in the same gesture, *re*veiled, *re*presented as a transgressive excess. We *almost* perceive the immensity of the suppression that is already partly realized, whose perfection beckons from beyond the boundary of what a mind can conceive. We want to go over the edge—and at the same time we want *not* to. Reading Augustine, reading with Augustine, we are caught between the fear of the flesh and the alarming absurdity of its notional loss. In other words, this book—crucially—produces not one but two horrors, matching its two loves. And if Augustine has succeeded

---

17. The reference here is to L. Irigaray, *I Love To You: Sketch of a Possible Felicity in History,* trans. A. Martin (New York: Routledge, 1996), a text whose very title hints at intriguing resonances with, and "counter-apocalyptic" resistances to, Augustine's *City of God.*

18. Fredriksen, "Apocalypse and Redemption," 166.

in bringing us to the borders of human tolerance, we may begin, giddily, to explore the zones that "exceed the limits even of *in*credibility," where the ground expands beneath our feet, time stretches, miracles proliferate, and the text itself seems to overflow all reasonable bounds, re-performing the abundance of feasts both consumed and disavowed. We cannot possibly take the measure of this capacious edge, of this book that audaciously constructs itself as the very site of exchange between finitude and infinity. Yet we may yet be able to discover—to create for ourselves as readers—momentary, localized, felicitous orderings, materializing within the productive chaos of Augustine's apocalyptic drama.

THE PLEASURE OF HELL IN
CITY OF GOD 21

Thomas A. Smith

"The Abominable Fancy"

The connection between pleasure and hell—certainly the positive connection—may not be obvious. Infernal images, deeply rooted in both pagan and Jewish soil, were firmly established in early Christian literature.[1] The fire and brimstone of the Psalms, with the unquenchable fire and undying worm of Isaiah 66, became Christian mainstays, established by some terrifying words of Jesus in the Gospels, and most famously by the *Apocalypse of John,* in which a "lake of fire and sulfur," where evildoers will be tormented "forever and ever," provides a riveting, sobering vision. In the final judgment, all, including the dead in Hades, are to be judged according to their deeds, and those whose names are not in the book of life will be sent to that lake of fire and its eternal torments.

Early on, the Christian imagination found in hell ample opportunity for exercise. Visions of hell were raised to new heights, or more properly, sunk to new depths, in second-century works like the *Apocalypse of Peter.* Here the

---

1. Instructive recent surveys of the development of doctrines of hell can be found in A. E. Bernstein, *The Formation of Hell: Death and Retribution in the Ancient and Early Christian Worlds* (Ithaca, N.Y.: Cornell University Press, 1993) and G. Minois, *Histoire des enfers* (Paris: Fayard, 1993).

horizon of eternal life fades from view in favor of lurid descriptions of punishment aptly described as "a form of self-righteous pornography."[2] In this work Jesus reveals to Peter and the apostles what will come to pass when he returns. Using the palm of his hand as a screen, Jesus unveils a scenario of unbridled vengeance for particular sins: in an atmosphere in which all the elements have been transmuted into fire, we find a panoply of torments. Some clearly connect crime with punishment: blasphemers are hanged by their tongues over a lake of fire; idolaters are burned along with their idols. Those who collaborated in sins are joined by their partners in crime: adulterous women, who style their hair to attract men, hang by that hair over a gurgling cesspool of muck, while their illicit lovers hang by what are delicately called their thighs, or by their feet, with their heads in the sewage. Murderers are thrown into a ravine full of beasts, and gnawed upon by a vast cloud of worms. Those who obtained abortions are sunk up to the neck in pools of bodily discharge, while aborted fetuses cast rays of destruction at them.[3]

Thanks to works like this, which went well beyond the fire, worms, and outer darkness of scripture, Christians by the mid-second century had within their imaginative grasp a fully equipped and thoroughly horrific hell. All future constructions, however elaborate, would be variations on an established theme. Hell was, to be sure, a place of justice, of the vindication of God's purpose, and also a kind of foil for the community, a delineation of the boundary not only between this world and the next, but also between the community of faith and a hostile, sin-filled world. More than that, though, hell became a place where every construction of human *dis*pleasure could be elaborately parsed.

The overwhelming majority of Christian writers of the first centuries, with particular concentration in the Latin west, held that the wicked were to be punished everlastingly. As one example among many, witness Tertullian, writing with typical curmudgeonly flair in the early third century. In the treatise *De spectaculis* he warns his readers off attending idolatrous public games such as gladiatorial combats and athletic contests; such events incite the passions, and do not encourage the religion of the savior. In the last chapter, he comforts the faithful with the cheery thought that in compensation they will have a chance to be in the audience for the greatest show of all:

> But there are other spectacles yet to come: that day of the Last Judgment with its everlasting issues . . . when the hoary age of the world and all its

---

2. A. Turner, *The History of Hell* (New York: Harcourt Brace, 1993) 85.

3. *Apocalypse of Peter* 21–25.

generations will be consumed in one fire . . . . What a panorama of spectacle on that day! What sight shall excite my wonder? Which my laughter? . . . Then will the tragic actors be worth hearing, more vocal in their own catastrophe; then the comic actors will be worth watching, much lither of limb in the fire; then the charioteer will be worth seeing, red all over on his fiery wheel; then the athletes will be worth observing, not in their gymnasia, but thrown about by fire . . . . What praetor or consul or quaestor or priest with all his munificence will ever bestow on you the favor of beholding and exulting in such sights? (*Spect.* 30)

Tertullian here discloses the secret of success of popular infernal literature, which had really lain behind works like the *Apocalypse of Peter*: reading them brings about a kind of pleasure. The pleasure of hell, or more precisely, the pleasure of being a spectator of hell, is a pious counterpart, or to wax slightly Freudian, a transference, of the enjoyment to be had in bloody public spectacles. This unseemly voyeuristic delight—famously referred to in the nineteenth century by Dean Farrar as the "abominable fancy"—was not unknown even in pre-Christian writings. Infernal tours featuring the tortures of Tartarus and the boiling mud of the Acheronian Lake were calmly described in Plato's *Phaedo* and elsewhere.[4] Still, Tertullian's remarkable frankness in confessing, indeed promoting, theological *Schadenfreude* is striking.

The chaotic and excruciatingly painful hell that brought such exquisite pleasure to its early Christian audience grew from an identifiably rigorist and vengeful mindset. Cyprian, for example, who echoed Tertullian's idea of the elect enjoying the tortures of the damned, did not mask an undercurrent of revenge against persecutors of the church.[5] The various portraits of hell were not rendered with the greatest consistency. The sole reliable and stable feature was bodily suffering, but the particular modalities of that suffering were concocted by the faithful without regard for systematic coherence. Two features, however, remain constant in this majority view: the fires of hell are real material flames, and the bodily torments of the damned last eternally. So Athanasius in *De incarnatione* 56 reflects a fourth-century consensus when he asserts that hell can begin only at the Last Judgment; a resurrected body is needed for the requisite suffering. Infernal fire is a somewhat more slippery topic, for its precise makeup remains mysterious. It affects both body and soul, and apparently requires no fuel, for it does not consume what it burns. Lactantius speaks of a pure fire that burns without smoking and runs like water.[6]

---

4. *Phaedo* 113–114c; *Republic* 10; Aristophanes, *Frogs* 145.
5. Cf. *Ad Demetrianum* 23–24; *De mortalitate* 14; *Ep.* 58,10.

Another Point of View

Though widespread, indeed dominant, this belief in an eternal hell replete with bodily sufferings was by no means universal. From the time of Clement, Alexandrian writers tended to regard the prospect with marked distaste. Clement brought his allegorical hermeneutic to bear, for example, on the fire of hell. Scriptural references to fire should be taken as referring to remorse for sin: fire, so-called, is that searing pain of the soul as one contemplates sins committed.[7] The inmates of hell also suffer the pain attendant on beholding the beatific existence of the elect.[8] Clement undercut the notion of hell's eternity as well. God does not simply punish, but corrects; God's actions must be remedial, so that the wicked are eventually brought to repentance.[9]

Clement was not systematically consistent, for in places his language suggests an eternal hell. But his intuitions were carried forward by Origen, who unambiguously asserted the provisional character of hell. The vision of the ultimate *apokatastasis panton* governs his discourse: the sufferings of the damned arise from their having placed themselves out of God's created harmony, into which they must finally return. If punishment were everlasting, reasoned Origen, God's express will to bring all things to their original unity would be frustrated. Surely no soul could be so wicked that God's power could not purify it. Souls must, rather, endure a purgative fire, whose length depends on the degree of the soul's taint. But eventually hell should be empty. Attacked for having hinted at the Devil's restoration, Origen adopted cautious language, but followers like Didymus the Blind seem to have followed his path to its universalist conclusion. Ambrose, though embracing Origen's allegorical view of hell's punishments[10] was more circumspect in his language about its duration: all Christians will be saved; some especially hardened sinners will experience purgative fire for a very long time; but only the impious and apostate will be in hell forever.[11]

---

6. *Institutiones divinae* 7,21.

7. *Stromateis* 7,6.

8. Ibid. 6,14.

9. Ibid. 7,12–16.

10. For Ambrose as well, the fire and worms were the remorse of the conscience; cf. *Expositio Evangelii secundum Lucam* 7,204.

11. *In duodecim Psalmos Davidicos* 36,26.

Jerome, characteristically perhaps, wishes to have it both ways. In the commentary on Ephesians he stands well clear of Origen, espousing a concrete hell featuring real fire and worms. In his Isaiah commentary he reveals more subtlety and more elitism: the ordinary faithful ought not to hear of an allegorical hell, nor of provisional punishment; a certain measure of fear is necessary to maintain good comportment. Gregory of Nyssa, meanwhile, unflinchingly took up the Origenian doctrine of *apokatastasis*: hell will disappear when all sinners have been cleansed. God and God's creatures cannot be eternally separated. The fires of hell are curative, and will eventually purify all.[12]

So by the late fourth century a considerable body of opinion posited an allegorical hell, and one whose punishments would end. Adherents to this current of thought found the literal, eternal hell of the rigorists not merely distasteful, but profoundly flawed, for it suggested a striking asymmetry in the spiritual architecture of the universe. John Chrysostom, who himself believed in an eternal hell, was aware of the perception of such imbalance, which became most acute when one compared the temporal and limited character of human sin to the profligate boundlessness of the penalty.[13]

The Prospect of Hell in Augustine's *City of God*

Certainly, then, we cannot speak of a single established doctrine of hell at the outset of the fifth century, when Augustine would take up the massive project of the *City of God*. Two broad streams of thought flowed toward Augustine: the one envisioned a raucous, heavily populated, eternal rigorist hell—some of whose authoritative advocates lay in the past of his African church—and the Alexandrian intellectuals' allegorical hell, whose population was smaller and decidedly transient. With the two hells came two kinds of pleasure. For the one, its power to transfix and to horrify with the unending, intimate violation of physical integrity dovetailed with the twin pleasures of voyeurism and vengeance; here was the "abominable fancy" in full flower. Its excessiveness was a part of its appeal.[14] For the other, pleasure came not from the contemplation of hell, but from looking through and considerably beyond

---

12. *Oratio catechetica* 26,26.

13. *In Epistolam ad Romanos homilia* 25,5–6 (PG 60.65–66).

14. One may note that the Vision (or Apocalypse) of Paul, a work whose scenes of cruelty rival those of the *Apocalypse of Peter*, is a product of the late fourth century. Cf. T. Silverstein, "The Date of the Apocalypse of Paul," *Medieval Studies* 24 (1962): 335–48.

it. Real pleasure was to be found in a harmonious, architectonically balanced divine economy. To fit into this theological aesthetic, hell must become a thing of gossamer, evanescent, destined to disappear. It exists, in the end, *hos me,* as if it did not. The contrast between these two kinds of hell was heightened by, on the one hand, increased animosity between Christian and pagan in the years following 410,[15] and on the other, an apparent revival of the Origenian denial of hell's eternity. So when Augustine turns his attention to hell in *City of God* 21 he is addressing an issue that is far from dead.

Quite understandably, the bishop of Hippo was predisposed to be a partisan of a hell of the strict observance, eternal and well populated, with bodily punishments. Yet despite the fact that much of *City of God* 21 is an apologia for that hell, Augustine still imbibed the same Neo-platonic instinct for unity and harmony that undergirded the Origenian view. Book 21 is an artifact of the collision between two imaginative worlds. It attempts to create a harmony, to fit a jarringly severe view of hell into the perfect balance and proportionality of the divine economy. As the book opens, Augustine shows himself aware of the patent difficulty of this task. He announces his intention to treat in detail the punishment due those of the Devil's city, prior to discussing the eternal felicity of the saints. As to why this should be so,

> it seems more incredible that bodies should endure in eternal torments than that they should continue, without pain, in everlasting bliss. It follows that when I have shown that this eternal punishment ought not to be thought incredible, this will be a great help to me by making it much easier to believe that the bodily immortality of the saints is to be exempt from any kind of distress.[16]

So a doctrine of eternal hell, properly understood, is a useful propaideutic; it enables, or at least buttresses, belief in eternal heaven.

Augustine's case for hell takes an ingenious turn in the second through eighth chapters, a perhaps underappreciated rhetorical *tour de force.* Augustine answers a series of possible objections to the eternal torments of hell by presenting something like a series of physics problems, with occasional forays into zoology and geology. The first of these, for example, considers the

---

15. A useful discussion of the intellectual context for Augustine's thinking about hell may be found in J. Le Goff, *The Birth of Purgatory*, trans. A. Goldhammer (Chicago: University of Chicago Press, 1984) 61–85, esp. 68ff.

16. *City of God* 21,1, trans. H. Bettenson (Harmondsworth: Penguin Books, 1972).

question whether a body could persist in fire without perishing. Surely, says Augustine, everyone is aware of the many animals who do this sort of thing all the time, not least among them those hardy worms who thrive in the boiling waters of hot springs. If these can live painlessly in such straits, is it less believable that others could subsist in fire with pain?[17] Still, unbelievers refuse to ascribe this marvel to the power of God.

The world is filled with wonders (*mira, miracula*) that speak eloquently of the power of God. Consider the salamander, who lives in fire, or the peacock, whose flesh resists putrefaction. Think of fire itself, and lime, and diamonds, and the remarkable lodestone, which Augustine himself had breathlessly witnessed as it attracted iron (*Civ.* 21,4). Yet despite all these marvels, the unbelieving mind will not admit to the great works God has yet in store, among them the inextinguishable fires of hell.

The rhetorical gain here for Augustine is twofold: he casts aspersions on those who harbor critical objections to the physics of eternal hell, suggesting that they have thrown in their lot with unbelievers. But more importantly, he invites the reader to adopt a new vantage point, namely, to consider the prospect of a person burning everlastingly not as a horror, nor as an affront to justice, but as a *miraculum*, a wonder wrought by God, akin to but far greater and more significant than those marvels catalogued here. The contagious sense of delight, of pleasure, that breathes through Augustine's prose is meant to attach itself even to the dolorous regions of Gehenna. Augustine's entertaining prolixity on the subject of fire and miracles is thus no detour, but serves his goal of bringing hell undiminished into an aesthetically satisfying framework.

Even within this framework, of course, the pains inflicted by fire and worm remain, and present an exegetical problem. Some, Augustine admits, take both fire and worm to refer to pains of the soul rather than the body, while others would see the fire as afflicting the body, as the soul is gnawed by the worm of sorrow. Though he concedes that the second interpretation is ostensibly more plausible, Augustine prefers the characteristic position of proponents of the popular, rigorist hell: both the fire and the worm of hell afflict the body. When the body is in pain, the soul, *ipso facto*, is tortured as well. In any case, the fire ought not to be explained away as mere metaphor, for, as he says,

> I have sufficiently argued that it is possible for living creatures to remain alive
> in fire, being burnt without being consumed, feeling pain without incurring

---

17. *Civ.* 21,2: *Mirabile est enim dolere in ignibus et tamen vivere, sed mirabilius vivere in ignibus nec dolere. Si autem hoc creditur, cur non et illud?*

death; and this by means of a miracle of the omnipotent creator. Anyone who says that this is impossible for the Creator does not realize who is responsible for whatever marvels he finds in the whole of the world of nature. It is, in fact, God himself who has created all that is wonderful in this world, the great miracles and the minor marvels which I have mentioned; and he has included them all in that unique wonder, that miracle of miracles, the world itself. (21,9)

Soon enough, Augustine notes, the saints' knowledge will teach them the truth about hell's pains, and speculation can be set aside. In the meantime, "The important thing is that we should never believe that those bodies are to be such as to feel no anguish in the fire."[18]

Demons, of course, who are to suffer in the same fire as condemned sinners, present a special problem, for their immateriality seems to argue against their being tormented by material fire. We cannot, of course, rule out their having bodies composed of thick moist air (21,10: *ex isto aere crasso atque umido*). But even if they are wholly immaterial spirits, they can still be tormented by fire. They will be in contact with material fires for their torment, and "this contact will be in a wondrous manner that cannot be described" (*miris et ineffabilis modis adhaerendo*). Augustine then turns to the point of greatest weakness for the rigorist position: the seemingly vast disproportionality between crime and punishment. How can an eternal sentence be meted out against temporal, even momentary, offenses? Augustine regards this question as revealing a misunderstanding even of human justice. In civil courts, magistrates do not apportion punishments in relation to the length of time taken to commit the offense. Indeed, hardly any punishment—except that of equivalent damages—could be conferred in the brief space it takes to perform a misdeed. And in fact a great many punishments, such as fines, exiles, and slavery, bear no prospect of end or pardon. Were it not for the fact that people die, such punishments would be eternal. Severity of punishment has to do not with the duration of an offense, but with its seriousness. And precisely here we see that the eternity of hell for the damned is an example of perfectly proportioned justice. What, after all, could be more serious than the sin of Adam? For in abandoning God, "he merited eternal evil, in that he destroyed in himself a good that might have been eternal" (21,12). Viewed in the light of God's eternal goodness, the eternity of hell and of its torments is entirely fitting. And indeed, the

---

18. *Civ.* 21,9: *dum tamen nullo modo illa corpora talia futura esse credamus, ut nullis ab igne afficiantur doloribus.*

fact that so many are released from these sufferings by God's mercy gives ample ground for thanksgiving (ibid.).

Augustine reserves some of his best venom for the Neoplatonic and Origenian notion of a purifying or corrective hell, an idea current among those whom he calls, with a voice dripping with sarcasm, "compassionate Christians." His relentlessly linear teleology has no place for the cycle of *exitus* and *reditus* that governed Origen's discourse. The free choice of higher or lower goods can be exercised only prior to the end of one's earthly life, that first death which is the separation of soul from body. Purgation and chastening occur only in this life, and those not sufficiently purified here will suffer unending adversity in the next life.[19] By contrast, Origen, who suffers at the hands of Augustine's unsubtle exegesis, would produce a universe of eternal instability, of "incessant alternations of misery and bliss, the endless shuttling to and fro between those states at predetermined epochs."[20] So the provisional, allegorical hell of Alexandrian coinage masks, behind its façade of compassion and harmony, a chaotic and confusing version of reality, in which the blessed are faced with the loss of their station, while the Devil and his legions may be introduced into the company of the angels. Far preferable is the pleasing architecture that has Christ as its foundation, where the lot of the blessed and that of the damned are sure and settled.

Piero Camporesi has recently suggested that Augustine bears responsibility for the furtherance of the abominable fancy.[21] It would be better to say that, stripped of the unseemly spectre of the abominable fancy,[22] hell takes on a peculiar aptness in the hands of Augustine: its chaotic and horrific aspects give way to an order, to an aesthetically pleasing symmetry. To read of hell in the *City of God* is not to be horrified or repulsed, but to take pleasure in one aspect of the architectonic perfection of the divinely ordered universe. Against those intellectuals who cannot find a pleasing harmony without making hell

---

19. *Civ.* 21,13. Some do endure temporal pains after death and do not face the eternal punishments that follow upon the second death.

20. *Civ.* 21,17: *alternantes sine cessatione beatitudines et miserias et statutis saeculorum intervallis ab istis ad illas atque ab illis ad istas itus ac reditus interminabiles.*

21. P. Camporesi, *The Fear of Hell: Images of Damnation and Salvation in Early Modern Europe*, trans. L. Byatt (University Park, Pa.: Penn State University Press, 1991) 53.

22. In *Civ.* 20,22 Augustine does treat, in passing, the question of the saints' knowledge of the torments of the wicked. These sufferings are known not by bodily presence or observation, but by intellection.

provisional and allegorical, Augustine strives not simply to supply a pallia-tive, but to make an eternally painful hell a *topos* of pleasure for the faithful. Yet this pleasure is not that of the sadistic voyeur watching bloodsport in a sun-drenched amphitheater, nor that of the vengeful moralist watching the wicked get their recompense. *Pondus meum amor meus*, he had famously writ-ten in the *Confessions*: "My weight is my love. Wherever I am carried, my love is carrying me. By your gift we are set on fire and carried upwards: we grow red hot and ascend" (13,9,10). In the *City of God* we are invited to see hell as a marvel of God's handiwork, the perfect erotic counterweight to that upward-soaring desire that lifts the saints to eternal beatitude. Hell is no longer a *res horribilis*, but a *res mirabilis*.

As a sequel one could point to St. Anselm in the late eleventh century, who conceived of a universal order governed by a God who is beauty, and who delights in the beauty of balance and symmetry. A reader of his *Cur deus homo* is struck by how often he refers to the beautiful or "fitting" nature of the di-vine economy. God's universe can admit of no ugliness. Even the will to disobey God must somehow be converted into some way of doing God's will and thus preserving the equilibrium of the universe.[23] If God is the greatest conceivable being, then any offense against God is infinitely great; it demands either infi-nite satisfaction or infinite punishment. Hell maintains the balance, the architectural beauty and symmetry, of the universe, a creation pleasurable to behold. Augustine's construction of hell thus prefigured and animated the la-bors of those scholastics who undertook to make hell a part of the elaborate edifice of Christian doctrine, just as their contemporary artisans painstakingly carved scenes of judgment, and the sufferings of hell, into the stone of cathe-drals that leaped toward heaven.

---

23. On this theme see F. B. Brown, "The Beauty of Hell: Anselm on God's Eternal Design," *Journal of Religion* 73 (1993): 329–56. The notion of punishment partaking of a larger good is not new; cf. Plato, *Gorgias* 471d.

Adapted Discourse: Heaven in Augustine's *City of God* and in His Contemporary Preaching

J. Kevin Coyle

This is an age when many would consider a strictly religious discourse on heaven to lack both appeal and reality. If Augustine, a bishop whose life straddled the fourth and fifth centuries, had an easier time selling an eschatological discourse than do its present-day promulgators—and that is not a given—he still would have faced the problem the utterer of any discourse must confront, which is that language proven effective with one audience will not necessarily work with others. In his case, the communication of an idea entailed choosing between at least three types of discourse: one at the more abstract level called for by his formal treatises; another, preaching, whose context was oral and liturgical; and a third dictated by the circumstances, content, and addressees of his written correspondence.

Ultimately, as Gerald Bonner has noted, the focus of Augustine's thought is always eschatological;[1] but it is a focus that has received sparse attention from scholars.[2] The studies that exist have dealt for the most part with Augustine's conceptualization of resurrection or, more precisely, of the characteristics of

---

1. G. Bonner, "Augustine's Thoughts on This World and Hope for the Next," *Princeton Seminary Bulletin*, Supplementary Issue 3 (1994): 86–87: "Augustine is eschatological in his thinking and concerned, first and foremost, with the next world, even while leading a vigorous life in this."

the resurrected body;[3] and no one has considered context as a determinant factor in the discourse employed.

In Book 6 of the *City of God* Augustine sets the stage for later books of that work when he says that "it is for the sake of eternal life alone that we are Christians."[4] This essay will demonstrate how Augustine's eschatological focus plays out in two different settings: sections of the *City of God*, and homilies Augustine was preaching during the time of their composition.

City of God 13 and Contemporary Homilies

Written in about 418, the thirteenth book of the *City of God* deals mainly with the concepts of life and death, and the relation between them; however, some attention is also given to the corporeal fate of the dead in the afterlife. Augustine is careful to underline the passing nature of this life (10), a theme that, as Henri-Irénée Marrou has remarked, "revient comme une obsession,"[5] and to which he brings a very Augustinian note: the stability of the life to come. Next, he takes issue with notions of "philosophers" (identified simply

---

2. B. Lohse, "Zur Eschatologie des älteren Augustin (De Civ. Dei 20,9)," *Vigiliae Christianae* 21 (1967): 221 n. 1, complained that up to his time only one general study had appeared on Augustine's eschatology. He meant that of H. Eger, *Die Eschatologie Augustins* (Greifswald: L. Bamberg, 1933). In addition, see D. J. Leahy, *St. Augustine on Eternal Life* (London: Burns, Oates and Washbourne, 1925) and É. Lamirande, *L'Église céleste selon saint Augustin* (Paris: Études Augustiniennes, 1963), esp. chapter 8 ("L'Église glorieuse"). It is true, though, that a thorough study of the subject has yet to be done.

3. G. Greshake and J. Kremer, *Resurrectio Mortuorum: Zum theologischen Verständnis der leiblichen Auferstehung* (Darmstadt: Wissenschaftliche Buchgesellschaft, 1986) 208–15; M. Alfeche, "The Basis of Hope in the Resurrection of the Body according to Augustine," *Augustiniana* 36 (1986): 240–96, esp. 280–96; idem, "The Use of Some Verses in 1 Cor. 15 in Augustine's Theology of Resurrection," *Augustiniana* 37 (1987): 122–86; and C. W. Bynum, *The Resurrection of the Body in Western Christianity*, 200-1336 (New York: Columbia University Press, 1995) 94–104.

4. Augustine, *De civitate dei* 6,9: *vita aeterna poscenda sit, propter quam unam proprie nos christiani sumus.*

5. H.-I. Marrou, "Le dogme de la résurrection des corps et la théologie des valeurs humaines selon l'enseignement de saint Augustin," *Revue des Études Augustiniennes* 12 (1966): 126 n. 72 (French version of *The Resurrection and Saint Augustine's Theology of Human Values* [The 1964 Saint Augustine Lecture, Villanova, Pa.: Villanova Press, 1965]). Compare, e.g., *Sermo Wilmart* 12, 5, in *Sancti Augustini sermones post Maurinos reperti*, ed. G. Morin, Miscellanea Agostiniana 1 (Rome: Tipografia Poliglotta Vaticana, 1930): 708, preached between 425 and 430, according to A. Kunzelmann, "Die Chronologie der Sermones des hl. Augustinus" in *Studi Agostiniani,* Miscellanea Agostiniana 2 (Rome: Tipografia Poliglotta Vaticana, 1931): 508 and 516. An improved edition of this homily was published by C. Lambot in *Revue Bénédictine* 79 (1969): 180–84.

as "Platonists") on what death is (16), and with their denial that the body can survive it (17). One of their main objections was that the body would be unable to rise (literally) and float upward to the land of the blessed; and so Augustine launches into a discussion (continued in *Civ.* 22,11) of the risen body's weight (18). This excursus includes the promise to "discuss in more detail, at the end of this work, if God wills, the belief in the resurrection of the dead and their immortal bodies."[6] For now, he satisfies himself with the simple declaration that at the resurrection the saved will possess the same bodies they had here, but without any disagreeable feature.

Then, suddenly, Augustine introduces the equation of "body" to "flesh" when speaking of the blessed. This terminological shift is not without interest, because "flesh" is not part of his usual vocabulary in this context. Following Paul (1 Cor 15,50: "flesh and blood will not possess the kingdom of God"), he long repudiated the notion that the flesh of the blessed could survive their death;[7] in them, it would transform into a "spiritual body."[8] Here, on the contrary, their flesh will "rest in hope" (see Ps 16 [15],9). Still, since the risen flesh of the saved will be "spiritual" (20), the resurrected will eat "only if they wish to" (22). These details are more than one will find in Augustine's contemporary preaching on the resurrection,[9] but certainly less than we will see in the final book of the *City of God*.

Thomas Camelot has characterized Augustine's preaching audience as "diverse" and his preaching style as "improvised."[10] By "diverse" he means that various ages, social classes, and walks of life—even pagans—figured in his audiences, and that Augustine the preacher faced the task of trying to reach them all. By "improvised" Camelot means that Augustine was not habitually working from a prepared text; that and the composition of his audience suggest

---

6. *Civ.* 13,18: *Sed de fide resurrectionis mortuorum et de corporibus eorum inmortalibus diligentius, si deus voluerit, in fine huius operis disserendum est.*

7. On the expression "flesh and blood" in Augustine, see M. Alfeche, "The Rising of the Dead in the Works of Augustine (1 Cor. 15,35–37)," *Augustiniana* 39 (1989): 72–84.

8. *De fide et symbolo* (composed in 393) 10,24: *illo tempore inmutationis angelicae non iam caro erit et sanguis, sed tantum corpus.*

9. Although that preaching mentions "equality with the angels," as in *Sermo Guelferbytanus* 11,3 (Morin, *Sancti Augustini sermones*, 475), preached during Easter week, in 416 or 417, according to Kunzelmann, "Die Chronologie," 485 and 516.

10. P.-Th. Camelot, "Saint Augustin, prédicateur," *La Vie Spirituelle* 140 (1986): 71–77. See also P. Charles, "L'élément populaire dans les sermons de saint Augustin," *Nouvelle Revue Théologique* 69 (1947): 619–50.

that he scrimped on the rhetorical niceties. Still, though he might have often been spontaneous, he was neither unprepared nor disorganized. He may have mounted the *cathedra* without notes, but never without reflection, experience, and prayer. The ideas conveyed in his preaching are no less authentic than those aired in other settings; they are simply expressed differently.

By the time Augustine composed this section of the *City of God* (ca. 418), some of his eschatological ideas were well established, while others remained in flux. In the lengthy Sermon 362, preached in 410–411,[11] he deals with two frequently asked questions: will there be a resurrection? and, what would resurrection be like? The first question receives scant attention (2–6);[12] the second is rephrased as: if bodies there are to be, what will they be like?[13] The highlights of the long answer to this are these: eating may occur in heaven, because Christ after his resurrection (7), the heavenly Jerusalem (8–9), and angels who appeared on earth (10–11) are said by Scripture to eat. Thus the resurrected retain the ability to eat and drink, but will have no need of such nourishment, and will not digest (12). Taking up Paul's assertion about flesh and blood not possessing the kingdom of God (1 Cor 15:50)—and contradicting the later *City of God* 13,20—Augustine argues that the flesh will endure only for those who die "in the flesh"; in those who rise "according to the spirit," it will be replaced by a transformed body, the *homo caelestis* (13–14), one uninterested in the carnal acts it knew in this life, such as eating, drinking, and sex. "With great speed" (17) the blessed will accede to "the life of angels" (see Lk 20,36), meaning to a life without risk of corruption (16–18)[14] of either body or spirit (20–22). To say that some rise "according to the flesh" implies that they have been marked for endless death (23); but Augustine is really more interested in the conditions awaiting those who achieve eternal life (24). The bodies of the blessed share the qualities of Jesus's risen body, in an angel-like existence (25), though details of the life of angels are unknown, except for their

---

11. On the date see P.-P. Verbraken, *Études critiques sur les sermons authentiques de saint Augustin* (The Hague: Abbatia S. Petri, 1976) 150.

12. *Sermo* 361, 2,2, preached in the same period (Verbraken, loc. cit.), begins with the same questions, but only the first is dealt with there, which is probably why it gets short shrift in *Sermo* 362.

13. *Sermo* 362, 7: *si corpora futura sunt, qualia futura sunt?*

14. See *De vera religione* 12,25, dating from about 390: *Inde iam erit consequens, ut post mortem corporalem, quam debemus primo peccato, tempore suo atque ordine suo hoc corpus restituatur pristinae stabilitati.* On the *pristina stabilitas* see also *De musica* 6,5,13. Augustine recants the idea of restoration to the "original stability" in *Retractationes* 1,11,3.

unsusceptibility to corruption (26). Then Augustine moves to two favorite themes in this context: service to Christ in the needy (27), and the eternal Alleluia: *Tota actio nostra amen et alleluia erit* (28). Lest listeners find the latter prospect uninviting, Augustine invokes a sub-theme: Amen and Alleluia will pour out of the fullness one enjoys, *insatiabili satietate*. Thus the life of the blessed will pass in rest and in contemplation of Truth itself (29). This is where Augustine employs his exhortatory powers to the full:

> We will rest, therefore, and see God as God is; and seeing, we will praise God. This will be the life of the saints, this the activity of those at rest, because we will praise without stinting. We will not praise for one day but, as that day will have no end as time is measured, so our praise will have no moment at which it ceases, and therefore we will praise for ever and ever.[15]

In Sermon 264, preached on the Ascension, probably between 413 and 420 (though its language suggests a date closer to the *City of God* 13),[16] Augustine, after dwelling at length on the reality of Christ's risen flesh, repeats (again, with reference to 1 Cor 15:53) that the flesh of the blessed "is changed and becomes a heavenly and angelic body. . . . When the flesh is changed, what does it become? It is then called a heavenly body, not mortal flesh. . . . The entire people of God will be equal to and associated with the angels."[17]

So here the flesh will not be immortalized, because it becomes something else, a "heavenly body," since the blessed enjoy "equality and association with the angels," who are in no way "carnal." Of course, they are not corporeal, either; but humanity has to retain something of the identity it possessed on earth. Augustine gives none of this explanation in Book 13. In fact, he seems to abandon this narrow perspective in the *City of God*, while retaining the idea

---

15. *Sermo* 362, 30,31: *Vacabimus ergo et videbimus deum sicuti est, et videntes laudabimus deum. Et haec erit vita sanctorum, haec actio quietorum, quia sine defectu laudabimus. Non uno die laudabimus, sed sicut dies ille non habet terminum temporis, ita laus nostra non habebit terminum cessationis; et ideo in saecula saeculorum laudabimus.* On the theme of the eternal Alleluia see Lamirande, *L'Église*, 226–29. On chanting the psalms in the liturgy as a prelude to the heavenly psalmody, see A. Becker, *De l'instinct du bonheur à l'extase de la béatitude: Théologie et pédagogie du bonheur dans la prédication de saint Augustin* (Paris: P. Lethielleux, 1968) passim.

16. For the dates see Verbraken, *Études*, 122. Alfeche, "The Rising," 79, places it between 393 and 396, which seems far too early.

17. *Sermo* 264, 6: *Caro . . . inmutatur, et fit ipsa corpus caeleste et angelicum . . . . Cum fuerit commutata, quid fiet? Iam corpus caeleste vocabitur, non caro mortalis, quia "Oportet corruptibile hoc induere incorruptionem, et mortale hoc induere inmortalitatem". . . . Erit omnis populus dei aequatus angelis et sociatus.*

of "equality with the angels"—probably his most consistent eschatological sub-theme.[18]

Since all of Augustine's theology ultimately has an eschatological orientation, it is surprising how seldom his homiletic discourses from this period pay direct attention to human resurrection.[19] Such sparse allusions as he makes appear mainly in the context of Easter or of martyr feasts, the two most privileged *loci* for his reflection on the ultimate destiny of faithful believers. His lengthiest such reflection from this period appears in a homily from Easter week of 418. It begins with the gospel passage on Martha and Mary (Lk 10,38-42), which introduces a favorite Augustinian theme, the "eternal Alleluia": "Hope sings it, love sings it now, love will also sing it then. Now love sings because it needs to; then it will sing out of pure enjoyment."[20]

But Augustine avoids details, for (as in Sermon 362) he wishes to sidestep notions he deems too materialistic:

> The fleshly soul, the soul addicted to flesh, embroiled in carnal lusts, its wings mired in the glue of wrong desires, says to itself: "What will there be for me to do in a state where I will not be eating, drinking, or sleeping with my wife? What kind of enjoyment is that?". . . . Recall the apostle and see what will be: "It is necessary for this corruptible being to put on incorruption, and for this mortal to put on immortality" (1 Cor 15,53). And we will be "equal to the angels" of God (see Lk 20,36) . . . . We will be filled, but with our God, and everything we desire here as having importance, God will be for us.[21]

---

18. As in *Civ.* 20,21. On this sub-theme see Lamirande, *L'Église*, 233–38.

19. His last 70 treatises on John's gospel may have been preached between 418 and 420—the dates are disputed (see J. W. Rettig's introduction to *St. Augustine, Tractates on the Gospel of John 1–10*, Fathers of the Church, 78 [Washington, D.C.: The Catholic University of America Press, 1988] 23–31)—but in any case contain little eschatological material, apart from treatises 83 (1) and 124 (5–7).

20. *Sermo* 255, 2 and 5: *Spes illam cantat, amor cantat modo, amor cantabit et tunc; sed modo cantat amor esuriens, tunc cantabit amor fruens.* On the dating see Verbraken, *Études*, 119. The eternal Alleluia theme also appears in another homily from the same Easter season, *Sermo* 256 (1).

21. *Sermo* 255, 7–8: *Dicit sibi anima carnalis, carni addicta, carnalibus cupiditatibus implicata, visco malarum cupiditatum involutas pennas habens, ne volet ad deum, dicit sibi, "Quid mihi erit, ubi non manducabo, ubi non bibam, ubi cum uxore mea non dormiam? Quale mihi gaudium erit?" . . . Recolite apostolum et videte quid erit: "Oportet corruptibile hoc induere incorruptionem, et mortale hoc induere inmortalitatem." Et erimus aequales angelis dei . . . . Pleni enim erimus, sed deo nostro, et omnia quae hic pro magno desideramus, ipse nobis erit.*

Another contemporary homily holds out Christ and the martyrs for imitation.[22] Indeed, their exemplary value seems to be the main eschatological emphasis in the preaching of this period.[23] Also briefly mentioned are the return of Christ in judgment, the winning of the crown, and the resurrection of the body;[24] but little stress is placed on the heavenly bliss that awaits, not even in Sermon 301, where the only answer to the question, "What awaits me in heaven?" (Ps 72 [73]; 25), raised no less than five times, is the curt "Incorruption, eternity, immortality, absence of sorrow, absence of fear, happiness without end."[25] The exhortatory elements could not be more terse.[26] Augustine prefers to dwell on the brevity of life (as in 11,9), a theme to which he often returns and which he shares with Stoicism and other philosophies of his age.[27]

City of God 19–22 and Homilies of Augustine's Final Years

The last four books of the *City of God* (ca. 426) are considered here together, because Augustine himself thought of them as a single, unified section.[28] Book 19's principal theme is "peace," for which all human beings yearn.[29] The opening chapters follow classical diatribe in describing the anxiety created by the insecurities of the present life. This prepares the way for the positive picture of a life where such insecurities will be unknown (10). After further rumination on this point (11), Augustine turns to a philosophically rooted reflection on peace,

---

22. *Sermo* 284, 4. The date is disputed: Kunzelmann, "Die Chronologie," 506 and 514, places it on May 8, 418; but see Verbraken, *Études*, 128.

23. See *Sermo Guelf.* 23–24 (ed. Morin, *Sancti Augustini sermones*, 516–527), preached between 416 and 420 (Kunzelmann, "Die Chronologie," 472 and 516).

24. As in *Sermo* 299, 4 and 8–10, preached on June 29, 418 (Kunzelmann, "Die Chronologie," 472 and 514).

25. *Sermo* 301 (Feast of the Maccabees = August 1) 9,8: *Quid enim mihi est in caelo? Incorruptio, aeternitas, inmortalitas, nullus dolor, nullus timor, nullus beatitudinis finis.* Preached ca. 417, according to Kunzelmann, "Die Chronologie," 476 and 514.

26. See *Sermo* 301, 8,7: *de vita futura cogitemus*; and *Sermo* 304 (St. Laurence = August 10) 4, preached after 417 (Kunzelmann, "Die Chronologie," 476 and 514): *ascendit Christus in caelum: sequamur eum.*

27. See A. di Giovanni, *Verità, parola, immortalità in Sant'Agostino* (Palermo: Palumbo, 1979) 132–58.

28. See his *Ep. ad Firmum presbyterum*, published by C. Lambot in *Revue Bénédictine* 51 (1939): 112–13; and *Retr.* 2,43.

29. On this theme see Lamirande, *L'Église*, 247–48.

culminating in the famous definition, "The peace of all things is the tranquillity of order,"[30] which he then applies to the heavenly city:

> In that final peace . . . our nature, healed by immortality and incorruptibility, will have no vices and none of us will be at odds, whether within oneself or with others. It will no longer be necessary for the reason to control the vices, since there will be no vices. But God will have mastery over the human being, [as will] the soul over the body, and there will be as much pleasantness and ease in obeying as happiness in living and reigning. . . . That is why the peace of this blessedness, or the blessedness of this peace, will be the supreme good.[31]

Although Augustine has now moved beyond simply pointing out the shortcomings of earthly existence to a note of future promise, he is still explaining the afterlife rather than instilling a longing for it. The remaining books move to redress this imbalance. Book 20 mentions the *pacatissimum regnum* (9), but is more concerned with the last days and the final judgment, which it handles in a framework of biblical references, largely from Revelation. Nonetheless, here we also find a long deliberation on the resurrection of the body (20), with a briefer one on the future life of the blessed, who are to become the perfect holocaust victims (26).[32]

Book 21 focuses on the pains that await the damned, not a subject to be treated here,[33] though it is the reverse side of the positive picture of the afterlife and the quest for it. The "delights" of the blessed are the topic of the final book, which relies mostly on New Testament references, even when Augustine is objecting to pagan conceptions of what awaits after death. The promise of eternal happiness was already made to Abraham and his descendants (3). This promise includes (as in 13,18)—again, against the objection that gravity

---

30. *Civ.* 19,13: *Pax omnium rerum tranquillitas ordinis.* On the sources for this definition see H. Fuchs, *Augustin und der antike Friedensgedanke: Untersuchungen zum neunzehnten Buch der Civitas Dei*, 2nd ed. (Berlin: Weidmann, 1965), esp. 55–60, 117–25, 139–54, and 182–223. See also J. Laufs, *Der Friedensgedanke bei Augustinus: Untersuchungen zum XIX. Buch des Werkes De Civitate Dei* (Wiesbaden: F. Steiner, 1973) 3–34.

31. *Civ.* 19,27: *In illa vero pace finali . . . , quoniam sanata inmortalitate atque incorruptione natura vitia non habebit nec unicuique nostrum vel ab alio vel a se ipso quippiam repugnabit, non opus erit ut ratio vitiis, quae nulla erunt, imperet; sed imperabit deus homini, animus corpori, tantaque ibi erit oboediendi suavitas et facilitas, quanta vivendi regnandique felicitas . . . , et ideo pax beatitudinis huius vel beatitudo pacis huius summum bonum erit.*

32. On the theme of perfect sacrifice in heaven see Lamirande, *L'Église*, 254–59.

33. See the essay by Thomas A. Smith in this volume.

would prevent it (see also 11)—the resurrection of the body (4), or (recalling *Civ.* 13,20, 20,20, and 20,26) of the flesh. It could be argued that Christ's flesh is meant here, rather than ours; but Augustine's point is precisely that the rising of the Lord's flesh presages the raising of our own (5).

After a long inventory of miracles (8–9), recounted because they witness to faith in Christ's resurrection (10), and after dealing with further arguments against the idea of a resurrected body (12–13), Augustine abandons his earlier reluctance[34] to speculate on how such a body would appear.[35] Each body will possess "the height of the fullness of the age of Christ" (Eph 4,13), since the "predestined" are "conformed to the image of God's son" (Rom 8,29). This goes well beyond merely figurative discourse: Augustine means *physical* stature (14). Each of the saints will be the same height he or she was at the age of 30 (Christ's age at his resurrection [15–16])—or would have been, if death comes prematurely. Resurrected women will retain their gender (17–18), an issue apparently still disputed in the fifth century.[36] But while maintaining the physical differences between the sexes, Augustine insists that there will be no "passion," the "cause of confusion" (*non enim libido ibi erit, quae confusionis est causa*).[37] From here on (19) his speculation is painted in even more graphic hues: hair and nails, though repeatedly clipped over one's lifetime, will be restored to their original location on the resurrected body, but only if they enhance it; otherwise, they will be absorbed into some other part of that same body, for "not a hair of your head will be lost" (Lk 21,18). Deformities will

---

34. See the same reticence in *De fide et symbolo* 10,24, repeated three years later (396) in *De agone christiano* 32, but retracted in *Retr.* 1,17 and 2,3.

35. See M. Pontet, *L'exégèse de saint Augustin prédicateur* (Paris: Aubier, 1945) 552: "Saint Augustin ne se montre donc pas rigoureusement fidèle à son propos de refuser toute représentation du Paradis: une harmonie lointaine et expirante, une brise musicale arrivant du ciel, il n'a pas su s'empêcher d'illustrer sa foi par ces images." More categorical (but less accurate) is F. van Fleteren, "Augustine and the Resurrection" in *Studies in Medieval Culture* 12, ed. J.R. Sommerfeldt and T. H. Seiler (Kalamazoo, MI: Cistercian Publications, 1978) 12: "Augustine is more interested in showing the fact and the reasonableness of the resurrection than in describing the state of the glorified body about which he quite rightly professes ignorance, since he has no experience to guide him."

36. See Marrou, "Le dogme," 128.

37. *Civ.* 22,17; see also 22,24. Here Augustine subscribes to a view that long antedates him: see B. Lang, "No Sex in Heaven: The Logic of Procreation, Death, and Eternal Life in the Judaeo-Christian Tradition," in *Mélanges bibliques et orientaux en l'honneur de M. Mathias Delcor*, ed. A. Caquot, S. Légasse, and M. Tardieu (Neukirchen: Neukirchener Verlag, 1985) 237–53.

disappear, and those who considered themselves over- or underweight in life will no longer be fat or thin. Scars will be retained if acquired in witness to the faith, but will be seen as signs of virtue rather than as flaws. Bodies destroyed by whatever means will be reassembled by the creator who, if able to make them in the first place, can surely remake them (20).[38]

If these musings appear trivial or fantastic to us, it should be remembered that an important component of Augustine's agenda is to emphasize that each human being regains his or her *own* body, in a clear affirmation of personal individuality and of continuity between earthly and post-earthly existences. The body will survive, and it will be the one we had on earth, albeit under altered conditions (through a *mutatio*, as Augustine likes to say).[39]

At the end of chapter 20, Augustine summarizes all these physical benefits before describing the miseries from which the blessed will be liberated (21–23)[40]—again, borrowing a *topos* from classical diatribe[41]—, affirming the good things they had known in this life (24), and further refuting deniers of the Lord's resurrection (25–28). "[The creator God] will raise up a flesh incorruptible, immortal, spiritual."[42] But what will the saints actually do with that flesh (or body)? They will enjoy the vision of God, perhaps even with their "spiritual" eyes (29), i.e., the eyes of their "spiritualized" bodies, and, with their whole being (body included), praise God, source of all good (30). The vision of God is both the consummation of human existence and the point of summation to which all of the *City of God* has been leading.

The reference to "eyes of the body" constitutes a shift from 408, when in a letter to Italica (*Ep.* 92, 6) Augustine firmly rejected the possibility of seeing God with the body's eyes, no matter how spiritualized. In ca. 413 he still held to that position,[43] intended perhaps to counteract the Manichaean belief that to see light and color was to gaze upon the divine substance itself.[44] Shortly thereafter, he seems to have become aware that overcompensation against one

---

38. These sections are still in response to non-Christian objections to bodily resurrection: in 22,12 and 22,26 Augustine explicitly refers to Porphyry's *omne corpus fugiendum*.

39. Some references in Marrou, "Le dogme," 123.

40. Another common theme in Augustine's preaching: see Lamirande, *L'Église*, 238–41; and J.-M. Girard, *La mort chez saint Augustin: Grandes lignes de l'évolution de sa pensée telle qu'elle apparaît dans ses traités* (Fribourg: Éditions Universitaires, 1992) 191.

41. See Marrou, "Le dogme," 132.

42. *Civ.* 22,26: *Ille igitur carnem incorruptibilem, inmortalem, spiritalem resuscitabit.*

43. See *Ep.* 147 to Paulina (= *Liber de videndo deo*).

unacceptable view creates the risk of tumbling into another: for eventually he declared himself willing to entertain reasonable arguments supporting a sensory vision.[45] By 415, then, he was allowing for sight involving the use of bodily eyes, alongside a purely spiritual vision.[46] The change may have been intended to ward off the impression of defending a "Platonizing" outlook that would pay no more than lip service to the idea of a resurrected body by robbing it of any meaningful function.[47]

The final chapter of the last book of the *City of God* then touches on some ancillary points: the happiness of the blessed in proportion to their merits; the benefits to be enjoyed in complete conformity with free will; evil known without being experienced; eternal rest in seeing God; and heavenly existence as the eternal seventh day after the world's six ages (30). Augustine's closing thought in the *City of God* about all this is that "there we will rest and we will see; we will see and we will love; we will love and we will praise. That is how it will be at the end without end. For what other end is there for us than that of reaching the kingdom which has no end?"[48]

The idea of "seeing, loving, and praising" is a direct echo of Augustine's preaching,[49] down to the poetry of its language, an oratorical indulgence rare in the *City of God*. If we have here, eschatologically speaking, an essentially

---

44. Augustine certainly has Manichaeism in mind in other parts of the *City of God*: see L. Cilleruelo, "La oculta presencia del maniqueismo en la 'Ciudad de Dios'," in *Estudios sobre la "Ciudad de Dios,"* vol. 1 (Madrid: Real Monasterio de San Lorenzo de el Escorial, 1955) 445–509; and J. van Oort, "Manichaeism in Augustine's *De civitate Dei*" in *Il De Civitate Dei: L'opera, le interpretazioni, l'influsso*, ed. E. Cavalcanti (Rome: Herder, 1996) 193–214.

45. *Ep.* 148 to Fortunatianus (= *Commonitorium*) 1,4.

46. *De Genesi ad litteram* 12,35–6. See also *Sermo Liverani* 8, 6 (ed. Morin, *Sancti Augustini sermones*, 394–95): "*Si diligeretis me, gauderetis, quod vado ad patrem: quia pater maior me est*" (Jn 14,28). *Hoc est dicere: ideo subtraho vestris oculis istam servi formam, in qua pater maior me est, ut ab oculis carnis servi forma remota dominum spiritaliter videre possitis.* Preached on May 16, 418 (Ascension), according to Kunzelmann, "Die Chronologie," 487 and 515.

47. See *Sermo* 277, 13–19, and *Retr.* 2,41; also the remarks of S. Poque, *Le langage symbolique dans la prédication d'Augustin d'Hippone: Images héroïques* (Paris: Études Augustiniennes, 1984) 373–74; Leahy, *Saint Augustine*, 95–104; K.E. Börresen, "Augustin, interprète du dogme de la résurrection: Quelques aspects de son anthropologie dualiste," *Studia Theologica* 23 (1969): 151–52; and Marrou, "Le dogme," 115–19.

48. *Civ.* 22,30: *Ibi vacabimus et videbimus, videbimus et amabimus, amabimus et laudabimus. Ecce quod erit in fine sine fine. Nam quis alius noster est finis nisi pervenire ad regnum, cuius nullus est finis?*

49. As in *Sermo* 254, 8, delivered in Eastertide, between 412 and 416: see Verbraken, *Études,* 119.

traditional view[50] (though garnished with Augustine's personal musings, particularly on the subject of risen bodies), it is one not usually declaimed in a manner calculated to set readers' hearts afire. That is not Augustine's intention in the *City of God*, which is rather, he says, to "prove."[51] So the eschatological component of the work, though it touches on "popular questions" such as the appearance of human bodies in heaven, is on the whole restrained, and displayed in rather dispassionate fashion.[52] By contrast, when orally addressing the flock, Augustine must find another language.[53]

As with Book 13, the final books of the *City of God* are compared here with Augustine's few contemporary homilies that can be described as overtly eschatological. Again, Eastertide and the feasts of martyrs are the usual occasions for preaching explicitly on an eschatological theme. In a homily for the Feast of Saint Laurence (August 10), preached in 425 at the earliest, Augustine again contrasts the uncertainties of the present life with future stability:

> The antichrist may threaten, but Christ protects. Death is inflicted, but immortality follows. The world is snatched from the slain, but paradise is presented to the revived. The temporal life is extinguished, but the eternal is received in exchange. How worthwhile, how sure, to leave with joy, to exit glorious amid the pressures and worries; to close for a moment those eyes with which humans and their world were viewed, and suddenly to open them where God can be seen by the person who has made that journey in blessedness![54]

---

50. B. Daley, *Eschatologie*, Handbuch der Dogmengeschichte, IV/7a (Freiburg: Herder, 1986) 193: "In den meisten Einzelheiten ist die Eschatologie des Augustinus durchaus traditionell."

51. The *Retractationes* state (2,43) that the last twelve books of the City of God are intended "to ward off the reproach that we have only refuted the ideas of others without proving our own" (*ne quisquam nos aliena tantum redarguisse, non autem nostra adseruisse reprehenderet*).

52. G. Bardy, "Introduction aux livres XIX–XXII" in Bibliothèque Augustinienne 37 (Paris: Études Augustiniennes, 1960) 20: "Saint Augustin lui-même parle avec émotion, dans plusieurs de ses sermons, de la béatitude du ciel. Par comparaison, les derniers chapitres de la Cité de Dieu semblent assez froids et ne sont pas aussi entraînants que nous le voudrions."

53. The *City of God* is not the only occasion on which Augustine addresses this issue in a work for the more sophisticated; for instance, there are passages in the *Enchiridion* (ca. 421) to which he probably referred as he composed the last section of the larger treatise. See Lamirande, *L'Église*, 37–41.

54. *Sermo* 303, 2: *Miniatur antichristus sed tuetur Christus, mors infertur sed inmortalitas sequitur, occiso mundus eripitur sed restituto paradisus exhibetur, vita temporalis extinguitur sed aeterna reparatur. Quanta est dignitas et quanta securitas exire hinc laetum, exire inter pressuras et angustias gloriosum; claudere in momento oculos quibus homines videbantur et mundus, aperire eos statim, ut deus videatur etiam feliciter migrando.* On the dating see Kunzelmann, "Die Chronologie," 507 and 514.

This says more about seeking the goal than about the goal itself, reflecting Augustine's usual approach in his final years.[55] The primary focus has become the need for a future free of this life's insecurities. A homily Augustine preached during his last three years, most likely after the first Vandal incursions into North Africa,[56] addresses the plight of hostages forced to pay "barbarians" in order to save their life. They may be thus buying a little more time on earth, says Augustine; but he prefers that they set their sights on life eternal:

> So that they can live a little [longer], they give away even that on which they could live always. . . . Why fear death unless you love life? Christ is that life. Why go after the insignificant and lose the sure? But perhaps it's not faith you have lost; are you to lose what you didn't have? Hold to that which lets you live always. . . . Don't you want to disdain those few days of life, and never die, and live in that endless day, protected by your redeemer and considered equal to the angels in the eternal kingdom?[57]

A third homily from the same period, delivered at a Sunday celebration of women martyrs, pursues the theme of misplaced values. To prolong their earthly life, hostages are willing to give up everything that makes even that life agreeable:

> If you hand [it] over to the enemy so you can live as a beggar, give something to Christ so you can live as one of the blessed . . . There is the enemy who took you captive, saying to you, "Give me everything you have," and, in order to live, you gave him all. Ransomed today, dead tomorrow; rescued by one, slaughtered by another. See how much people put up with at the hands of barbarians when it comes to the life which passes, and are disgusted at the thought of suffering something in view of the life eternal! . . . Ask your God and Lord, say to him, "Lord, I have brought to heaven what I had—or what I have, I have as though I did not have it. The kingdom of heaven is worth so much; how much is my inheritance?" It is beyond worth, for it is not truly something that can be "worth so much." Your Lord, whom

---

55. See e.g., *Sermo* 319, 2, preached on a feast of martyrs between 425 and 430, according to Kunzelmann, "Die Chronologie," 508 and 515. See also Verbraken, *Études*, 138.

56. The Vandals crossed in force from Spain in the early summer of 429. A year later they were at the gates of Augustine's episcopal city, Hippo Regius. See C. Courtois, *Les Vandales et l'Afrique* (Paris: Arts et Métiers Graphiques, 1955) esp. 155–71.

57. *Sermo* 344, 4–5: *Ut liceat illis paululum vivere dant etiam illud unde possent semper vivere . . . . Homo bone, quare timebas mortem, nisi amando vitam? Christus est vita. Quare adpetis parvam, ut perdas securam? An forte fidem non perdidisti, sed quod perderes non habuisti? Tene ergo unde semper vivas . . . et tu non vis ipsos paucos dies contemnere vitae, ut nullo die moriaris, et in sempiterno vivas die, a redemptore tuo protegaris, in aeterno regno angelis adaequaris?* On the dating see Verbraken, *Études*, 145.

you asked about "your inheritance" says: "You will live for a while, then you will die. In my kingdom you will never die, but live forever. There you will be truly rich, you will never be in need. . . . Are you really rich by having much, and is my angel then poor?". . . He who promises you the kingdom of heaven wishes to make you truly rich.[58]

So "equality with the angels" means no longer putting up with needs the angels have never known. But otherwise, the description of what awaits the faithful Christian is subdued. There is nothing of that detail seen in the *City of God*, nor even in earlier homilies; and even there the accent was more on the effort than on the prize.

Conclusions

1. In both his *City of God* and contemporary preaching, Augustine's favored scriptural texts are Luke 20:36 and 21:18, and 1 Corinthians 15:50, 53. Among his favorite themes are the brevity and insecurity of this life, the eternity and security of the blessed, and equality with the angels. Especially consistent in both types of discourse during Augustine's final years, when his world is sliding further into political and social chaos, is the contrast between the insecurities of a crumbling, earthly empire and the security of heaven.

---

58. *Sermo* 345, 1–2 and 5: *Qui das hosti ut vivas mendicus, da aliquid Christo ut vivas beatus . . . . Ecce inimicus qui te captiverat dicit tibi, "Quidquid habes da mihi," et ut viveres totum dedisti. Hodie redemptus, cras moriturus; ab isto redemptus, ab alio trucidandus. Ecce quanta a barbaris patiuntur homines propter vitam temporalem et piget aliquid pati pro vita aeterna . . . . Iam interroga deum et dominum tuum et dic illi, "Ecce iam migravi, domine, in caelum quod habui; vel quod habeo, sic habeo tamquam si non habeam. Tanti valet regnum caelorum, quantum patrimonium meum?" Carius valet. Non enim vere tale est ut tanti valeat. Hoc dicit dominus tuus quem interrogasti de patrimonio tuo: "Ad tempus victurus es et postea moriturus. In regno meo numquam moriturus, sed in aeternum victurus es. Verus ibi dives eris ubi numquam egebis . . . . Revera tu multa habendo dives es, et angelus meus pauper est?" . . . Divitem verum te facere vult qui tibi regnum caelorum promittit.* The dating is Kunzelmann's ("Die Chronologie," 509 and 520). Quoted sections are the same as *Sermo Frangipane* 3, 2 and 5 (ed. Morin, *Sancti Augustini sermones*, 203 and 206) which Kunzelmann (509 and 515) places "frühestens 428." The dating may be problematic, however, because that homily was preached on a Sunday, the Feast of the martyrs of Thuburbo—July 30, which fell on a Sunday during Augustine's priestly career only in 394, 405, 411, 416, and 422. Morin himself (201) thought Frangipane 3 must have been preached *post Romae a Gothis vastationem, aut etiam post primam Vandalorum inruptionem.* See Verbraken, *Études*, 145.

2. Augustine is essentially the pastor, seeking not just to inform but to motivate, and so his eschatological concern creates an urgency both real and persistent: How to convey that concern to others? In that regard, it is the fact of heaven that is the goal; its concrete details interest him far less, especially when he is preaching.

3. In the *City of God* the exhortation to seek the life of the blessed is missing, but details are present that appear nowhere else. In the homiletic discourses, Augustine does not discuss matters such as the body's weight, height, or hair, unless he is commenting on a germane scriptural verse. The one truly graphic description of risen bodies is in the *City of God*, presented there because Augustine wants to emphasize the physicality of the resurrected in heaven, an insistence intended to handle "Platonist" objections to any physical resurrection. His preaching, on the other hand, has a different aim: to offset unfettered speculation about what that physicality might imply. It would do no good in that context to speak of height, gender, hair, and fingernails, all the while assuring listeners that in heaven there will be food (but not because anyone needs it), and no sexual intercourse (because no one will want it).

4. Only occasionally in both the *City of God* and his preaching does Augustine overcome his reluctance to refer to immortalized flesh. In any case, his language on the afterlife always implies rebirth for the blessed of what he prefers to call their "spiritual (or heavenly) body." In fact, some homilies focus exclusively on belief in resurrection, arguing for it from faith in the resurrection of Christ's body.

5. The further Augustine delves into the subject of heaven, the more he seeks to counter the unchristianized Neo-platonist view of it. Again, this is true of both the *City of God* and the homilies seen here, even if an explicitly philosophical frame of reference is generally absent from the latter.

6. Perhaps most importantly, Augustine's homilies and the *City of God* hold in common that their author always speaks calmly and with hope of the future—a future where present disasters do not happen, because human minds are no longer able to frustrate the grand design of God. This is no escape mechanism, but an invitation to search for this life's true purpose and to await in God's good time the moment when this life and this being will be transformed.

AUGUSTINE AND THE ADVERSARY: STRATEGIES OF SYNTHESIS IN EARLY MEDIEVAL EXEGESIS

Kevin L. Hughes

Historians of Christian thought and students of apocalypticism have tended to divide the history of apocalypticism into three major epochs. First, breathing the volatile gases of Jewish apocalyptic thought, and in the wake of enthusiasm following the death and resurrection of Christ, the apostolic and subapostolic Fathers waited in joyful hope for the imminent return of the Lord. However, with the passage of time, this breathless anticipation seemed less and less credible, and, led by the great enemy of apocalyptic speculation, Augustine of Hippo, the later Fathers rejected a literal, millenarian vision of the end and began to interpret apocalyptic texts in a spiritual ecclesiological sense. The forecast of the end in apocalyptic texts was taken as an allegory of the church in the present. Such an authoritative rejection led to the early-medieval hegemony of anti-apocalyptic Augustinianism among the learned, until the coup d'état, if you will, of a new millennialism under the inspiration of Joachim of Fiore in the twelfth century.[1] The timeline of this account seems to imply

---

1. Thus S. D. O'Leary's engaging study of the rhetoric of apocalyptic, *Arguing the Apocalypse: A Theory of Millennial Rhetoric* (New York: Oxford University Press, 1994), still presumes that the "allegorical understanding of prophecy developed out of necessity in the centuries after the Apocalypse was produced" (72). O'Leary continues: "With the passage of time and the conversion of the empire to Christianity, however, [the Apocalypse] became more and more difficult to interpret as a set of historical predictions: the prophesied End had failed to materialize, and the former

that the apocalyptic world view cannot be sustained for very long. Faced by the frustration of its own claims, this charismatic phenomenon will eventually be re-tooled to fit a plodding institutional paradigm.[2] I have overstated the case, I am sure, but my purpose in this essay is really rather modest; it is to qualify the claims about the second epoch, the early medieval hegemony of anti-apocalypticism, and in so doing, to begin to question this underlying assumption. In essence, I wish to argue that the rumors of apocalypticism's early-medieval demise have been greatly exaggerated.

That rumor is rooted largely in the exegetical history of the Apocalypse, and may indeed be true for that particular exegetical history.[3] In the well-rehearsed tale of Apocalypse interpretation, the prevalent allegorical exegesis, in part filtered through Augustine's *City of God*, is disseminated throughout the early medieval world in the commentaries of Primasius, Caesarius, Bede, and Beatus, among others. The allegorical interpretation of the text is marked by a clear rejection of millennialism and an interpretive focus upon present ecclesiological realities as the church struggles with heresy and change. These marks became hermeneutical assumptions for early medieval interpreters of John's Apocalypse. Among the Carolingians, the commentary of Haimo of Auxerre faithfully recapitulates this Tyconian schema.[4] For Haimo, the Apocalypse is a statement about the "present and future Church." Its theme is the

---

Antichrist now convened ecclesiastical councils and used his troops to suppress heresy. . . . Under these circumstances, the drama of the End came to appear as an allegorical representation of theChurch's struggle against its enemies in all ages" (202). My intent is not to disparage in any way O'Leary's contribution to scholarship on apocalypticism. Rather, I have chosen to use his work as my example because its powerful argument about the internal logic of apocalyptic rhetoric presumes that this univocal, unidirectional development in the history of eschatology is self-evident, when it need not. My argument, I believe, could only help O'Leary's in the long run, since it contends for the persistence of both what he calls the "tragic" (realist) reading and the "comic" (spiritual) interpretation of Augustine throughout the tradition of theological reflection.

2. J. Gager's famous *Kingdom and Community* (Englewood Cliffs, N.J.: Prentice Hall, 1976) makes the point, and most sociological or anthropological treatments of apocalypticism echo this sense (see also K. Burridge, *Mambu: A Study of Melanesian Cargo Movements and Their Social and Ideological Background* [London: Methuen, 1960] for the anthropological locus classicus of apocalyptic movements).

3. And even this should be qualified, according to G. Bonner, *Saint Bede in the Tradition of Western Apocalyptic Commentary*, 1966 Jarrow Lecture (Newcastle upon Tyne: J. & P. Bealls, 1966), who argues that Bede "never allowed the allegorical interpretation of Holy Scripture to diminish his sense [of the] imminence of the Second Coming and the awful character of the Last Judgment" (12). One could also point to numerous instances in the writings of Gregory the Great where his faith in the imminence of the eschatological end is quite clear.

theme of every Christian's daily prayer, "Thy kingdom come."[5] As Ann Matter has noted, the early medieval interpretation of the Apocalypse of John is better described as anagogic—as disclosing the prayerful ascent of the Church toward the kingdom of God—not apocalyptic in the traditional sense of crisis—judgment—reward.[6] However, if we step away from the Apocalypse, we may find a different story. The history of exegesis of 2 Thessalonians, a brief but important letter in the Pauline corpus, testifies to the persistence of a literal, or what I have called "realist" interpretation of apocalyptic themes in the early Middle Ages in tandem with the Tyconian ecclesiological interpretation.[7]

2 Thessalonians

The roots of the exegetical tradition around 2 Thessalonians are split into two clusters. In the late fourth and early fifth centuries, Ambrosiaster, Pelagius, Theodore of Mopsuestia, and Jerome express a "realist" eschatology that represents the prevailing sense of the ancient Christian church. Each thinker has a distinctive portrait of Antichrist. For Ambrosiaster, Antichrist will be a person with supernatural powers who will revive Roman paganism and try to convert Christians away from worshipping the true God.[8] For Pelagius and Jerome, he is a Judaizing heretic.[9] For Theodore, he is explicitly a "false Christ."[10] None of these thinkers offers a timetable or predicts a date for the apocalyptic end, but all four share the general conviction that Antichrist will be a concrete individual acting in history, and that his coming will follow some specific historical event in the future.

---

4. Haimo does this by forging an "alloy" commentary from the works of Bede and Ambrose Autpertus. For further discussion, see E. A. Matter, "The Apocalypse in Early Medieval Exegesis," in *The Apocalypse in the Middle Ages*, ed. R. K. Emmerson and B. McGinn (Ithaca, N.Y.: Cornell University Press, 1992) 38–50.

5. *Ibique meruit videre hanc prophetiam de statu praesentis et futurae Ecclesiae. . . . Unde et quotidie in dominica oratione postulat suppliciter: Adveniat regnum tuum.* Haimo, *Expositio in Apocalypsin B. Iohannis* (PL 117.937–1220 at XX).

6. E. A. Matter, "The Apocalypse in Early Medieval Exegesis," 49.

7. For further discussion of this tradition, see K. L. Hughes, "The Apostle and the Adversary: Paul and Antichrist in the Early Medieval Exegesis of 2 Thessalonians," unpublished Ph.D. dissertation, University of Chicago, 1997.

8. Ambrosiaster, *Commentarius in Epistolam Secundam ad Thessalonicenses* 2,8,2 (CSEL 81[3].241).

9. Pelagius, *In Epistolam Secundam ad Thessalonicenses*, ed. A. Souter (Texts and Studies 9; Cambridge: Cambridge University Press, 1922) 443ff; Jerome, *Ep.* 121,11.

10. Theodore of Mopsuestia, *In Epistolas beati Pauli commentarii*, ed. H. B. Swete, vol. 2 (Cambridge: Cambridge University Press, 1882) 52ff.

Augustine of Hippo was apparently less confident than the rest when he read this brief Pauline letter. He gives sustained attention to 2 Thessalonians in two works. In the first, his famous Letter 199 to Hesychius, Augustine simply points out the impenetrable ambiguity of the text. 2 Thessalonians appears to Augustine as a cipher, and nothing more. The only "facts" he gleans from the text are that Antichrist will come and that Christ will kill him by the breath of his mouth; he can find no indication of who or what Antichrist will be or of any timetable whatsoever, and he concludes that it is better not to speculate. The second locus of his treatment of the text comes in Book 20 of the *City of God* as part of a thorough survey of eschatological texts from the Bible.

The *City of God* itself presents an interesting puzzle that complicates the traditional historiography of apocalyptic thought.[11] Book 20 of the *City of God*, taken as a whole, presents a rather straightforward rendering of the eschatological traditions of the church, without pause or hesitation. In fact, Augustine does not shy away from affirming that

> we have learnt that those events are to come about: Elijah the Tishbite will come; Jews will accept the faith; Antichrist will persecute; Christ will judge; the dead will rise again; the good and the evil will be separated; the earth will be destroyed in the flames and then will be renewed. All those events, we must believe, will come about; but in what way, and in what order they will come, actual experience will then teach us with a finality surpassing anything our human understanding is now capable of attaining. However, I consider that these events are destined to come about in the order I have given.[12]

In general, then, Augustine seems to endorse wholeheartedly the realistic and historical nature of the apocalyptic prophecies found in scripture. However, when he turns to specific texts like 2 Thessalonians, his endorsement seems less wholehearted.

After discussing passages from the Gospels, the Apocalypse, and the Petrine Epistles, Augustine at last comes to Paul. He prefaces his comments on 2 Thessalonians by acknowledging that he has left out many eschatological passages in the New Testament. "But I must not on any account pass over what the apostle Paul writes to the Thessalonians" (Civ. 20,19). He then quotes 2

---

11. My reflections upon the complexities of what we might call the "apocalyptic status" of the *City of God* are in large part the fruit of very provocative exchanges with Richard K. Emmerson at the conference in Vancouver. I thank him for his critical comments on my essay.

12. *Civ.* 20,30, trans. H. Bettenson (Harmondsworth: Penguin Classics, 1972) 963.

Thessalonians 2:1–12 and offers his exegesis. As he so often does, Augustine begins his exegesis by stating what we know for sure:

> No one can doubt that Paul is here speaking of Antichrist, telling us that the day of judgment (which he calls the Day of the Lord) will not come without the prior coming of a figure whom he calls the Apostate, meaning of course an apostate from the Lord God.[13]

For Augustine, the "rebellion" or desertion is Antichrist himself, the one who flees from God and resists him. He uses a variant Old Latin text that has *refuga*, "exile" or "apostate," instead of *discessio* and interprets it as follows: "*Unless first the Exile*, which no doubt is said of Antichrist, whom he certainly calls an exile from the Lord God. For if this is said of all the unjust, how much more can it be said of him?" Augustine thereby circumvents the traditional discussion of the fate of Rome—a topic he is perhaps eager to avoid in 427 CE. The *refuga* denotes the moral condition of this great sinner of sinners, not the apocalyptic—and perhaps too familiar—collapse of the Empire.

Augustine proceeds to discuss the reference to the temple. He considers the text somewhat opaque; its literal referent is unclear. He makes no attempt to decide whether Paul refers to the temple in Jerusalem or to the church; instead, Augustine cites a spiritual interpretation that supplements—or perhaps supplants—the literal sense:

> [S]ome people would have it that Antichrist means here not the leader himself but what we may call his whole body, the multitude, that is, of those who belong to him, together with himself, their leader. And they suppose that then it would be more correct to say, following the original Greek, that he "takes his seat as the temple of God" [*in templum*], instead of "in the temple of God" [*in templo*], purporting to be himself God's temple, that is, the Church.[14]

---

13. *Civ.* 20,19 (trans. Bettenson, 932): *Nulli dubium est eum de Antichristo ista dixisse, diemque iudicii (hunc enim appelabat diem Domini) non esse venturum, nisi ille prior venerit, quem refugam vocat, utique a Domino Deo.*

14. Ibid.: *Unde nonnulli non ipsum principem, sed universum quodam modo corpus eius, id est ad eum pertinentem hominum multitudinem, simul cum ipso suo principe hoc loco intellegi Antichristum volunt; rectiusqueque putant etiam Latine dici, sicut in Graeco est, non in templo Dei, sed in templum Dei sedeat, tamquam ipse sit templum Dei, quod est ecclesia.* Note that this really has little to do with the original Greek; instead, it has to do with Augustine's use of Tyconius, whose text reads *in templum*, in the accusative, and his explanation for this unusual form: *Tyconius, Liber regularum*, ed. and trans. W. Babcock (Atlanta: Scholars Press, 1989) 10.

For Augustine, Antichrist is present within the church now, as the body of potential schismatics, as much as he will come in the future as a historical figure seated in the church or restoring the Jewish temple cult. He seems to prefer discussing the former.

Augustine has not abandoned the uncertainty of his first attempt at the text in the letter to Hesychius. Twenty years later, he still finds most of the passages impenetrable. When he considers the meaning of verses 6 and 7, the restraining force and the mystery of iniquity, he points out first that Paul did not speak explicitly because his audience already knew his referent. But what they knew is now lost and Augustine confesses, "the meaning of this completely escapes me." Unable to offer his own exegesis, he reviews several prominent interpretations, which he calls "guesses." First he examines the traditional understanding of Roman imperial power as the "restraining force" in verse 6. Augustine recounts the theory that Paul wrote obscurely because he feared Roman persecution. He suggests that this theory implies that Nero is the "restrainer" of verse 7. This implication he connects to the Sibylline tales of Nero's escape or resurrection. Augustine expresses disdain for those who associate this passage with the Roman Empire (he may have Ambrosiaster specifically in mind here) and with the variety of speculations about the return of Nero. In coupling any speculation about Paul's obscure references to Rome with wild fantasies Nero's resurrection and return, Augustine places them all in the same category and dismisses them with a rhetorical flourish: "For myself, I am astonished at the great presumption of those who venture such guesses."[15]

Tyconius and the Antichrist

A better guess, in Augustine's eyes, is offered by certain "others" who seem to share Tyconius's perspective. These "others" think that the verse "refers only to the evil people and the pretended Christians who are in the church, until they reach such a number as to constitute a great people for Antichrist." This body of Antichrist is a "mystery of iniquity" because it grows in secret within the church. The second half of verse 7 is understood then as an exhortation to the faithful, saying, "Only let him who holds [faith] hold on, . . . until

---

15. Ibid. (trans. Bettenson, 933): *Sed multum mihi mira est haec opinantium tanta presumptio.* He admits that the verse could refer to the Roman imperial power, but only if it is understood as a tautology, "saying, in effect, let him who now reigns, reign until he is removed from the scene, that is, until taken away." But, understood in this fashion, the verse says little about anything, and Augustine can thus concede such an inconsequential reading.

the secret power of wickedness, now concealed, departs from the Church."[16] The "others" then refer to 1 John's declamation of the "many Antichrists" who have appeared, proving that "it is the last hour." For Augustine, this indicates that, just as in this first resurrection "many heretics are going out from the company of the church, in the same way, . . . at the actual time of the end there will go forth from the church all those who do not belong to Christ but to that last Antichrist."[17] Having given what I think is his "best guess" of these trouble-some verses, (although he does not claim it as his own) Augustine restates that there are many different possible interpretations of 2 Thessalonians, but he leaves the reader with little doubt as to which interpretation he prefers and which he finds "presumptuous." We cannot say simply that Augustine's position is "anti-apocalyptic": unlike Tyconius, Augustine never seems totally to deny or ignore the literal and realistic sense of the eschatological events.[18] Instead, Augustine remains agnostic about the time and events of the end and diverts attention toward the spiritual reality of Antichrist within the church of the present.

The *City of God*, then, seems to bequeath a mixed legacy to the early medieval church. Augustine has endorsed the historical reality of the eschatological events in general, but he has also subverted that endorsement in his spiritual readings of texts like 2 Thessalonians 2. On the one hand, Augustine is entirely

---

16. Ibid. (trans. Bettenson, 934): *ut in fide quam tenent tenaciter perseverent, . . . donec exeat de medio ecclesiae mysterium iniquitatis, quod nunc occultum est.* Note that this is a significant departure from Tyconius, whose thought is sectarian or, as J. Z. Smith might say, "utopian," so that for him the "removal" is of the saints from the mystery of iniquity. Augustine, on the other hand, requires that the mystery of evil be removed from the Church. See J. Z. Smith, *Map is Not Territory* (Chicago: University of Chicago Press, 1993).

17. Ibid.: *Sicut ergo ante finem in hac hora, inquiunt, quam Iohannes novissimam dicit, exierunt multi haeretici de medio ecclesiae, quos multos dicit Antichristos: ita omnes tunc inde exibunt, qui non ad Christum, sed ad illum novissimum Antichristum pertinebunt et tunc revelabitur.*

18. Tyconius's position on the reality of the eschatological events has been debated. I am persuaded by Paula Fredriksen that Tyconius did not anticipate an imminent apocalyptic end, and by Pamela Bright and Charles Kannengiesser that Tyconius's "mystic" meaning of scripture "is equal to divine, as opposed to human," unlike the larger tradition of exegesis (Origen, Ambrose, Augustine), in which the "mystic" sense "is equivalent to the spiritual sense as opposed to the literal sense." Thus, for Tyconius, Scripture has only one true sense, the divine, which, when properly understood, offered no forecast of an apocalyptic end. He may be the only truly "anti-apocalyptic" thinker in the patristic period. See P. Fredriksen [Landes], "Tyconius and the End of the World," *Revue des Études Augustiniennes* 28 (1982): 59–75, and C. Kannengiesser and P. Bright, *A Conflict of Christian Hermeneutics in Roman Africa: Tyconius and Augustine* (Berkeley: The Center for Hermeneutical Studies in Hellenistic and Modern Culture, 1989 [Protocol of the 58th Colloquy]) 83.

consistent with the majority of early Christian thinkers in the belief in a series of apocalyptic events that will take place at the end of time, including the conversion of the Jewish people, the persecutions of Antichrist, and the Last Judgment. On the other hand, his own particular exegesis of a text like 2 Thessalonians seems to discount the significance of these very events. It was the task of early medieval exegetes to make sense of this knotted tradition.

Early Medieval Exegesis

The early medieval exegetes of 2 Thessalonians followed the majority of the Fathers in reading the letter realistically. They therefore selected or combined particular details from the patristic tradition to arrive at an understanding of the signs of the end and Antichrist. To this primary reading, most of them added elements of the Augustinian interpretation, but always as yet another meaning of the text, not in opposition to the rest. Whereas Augustine's comments seem intended specifically to discourage speculation on the future coming of Antichrist and the end, early medieval exegesis dulls the rhetorical edge of Augustine's subtle polemic.

For example, the commentary of Rabanus Maurus, the ninth-century monk and bishop of Fulda, on 2 Thessalonians depends for its structure and much of its content on the fifth-century commentary of Theodore of Mopsuestia (whom he cites as "Ambrose"). Theodore's commentary assumes that the primary subject in the letter is the coming of Antichrist and the "Day of the Lord." Rabanus, for his part, maintains this emphasis upon the end and adds some excerpts from Jerome to pursue this apocalyptic line of thought. However, he also supplements this reading with selected texts of Augustine and Gregory the Great. After giving Theodore's interpretations of the "man of sin," and after carefully manipulating Theodore's version of "what restrains," Rabanus turns to Jerome for another account of the end, with the usual events all listed: the fall of Rome, the session of Antichrist in the temple or in the church, etc.[19] Then

---

19. (PL 113.565, 558). It is worth noting what Rabanus does not include from Jerome's letter. First, Rabanus only includes what Jerome says specifically about 2 Thessalonians, cutting all references to 1 Thessalonians and the synoptic "little apocalypse." This omission makes sense on the basis of Rabanus's pledge to include "only what is necessary" from the Fathers. Jerome's comments on other Scripture are better reserved for other commentaries. But second, and more suggestively, Rabanus cuts off his citation just before Jerome's notorious diatribe against the Jews. For Jerome, the discussion of Antichrist's "lying works" leads quite naturally into a discussion of the purpose of these deceptions, i.e., the just condemnation of the Jews. But Rabanus does not follow Jerome's line of argument this far. It is difficult to draw solid conclusions from this editorial action. Perhaps Rabanus felt that Jerome's animus against the Jews departed from the text and was therefore irrelevant.

Rabanus abandons Jerome for Augustine, and thus moves from the literal to the spiritual sense of 2 Thessalonians.

But it is significant that when he cites Augustine's treatment of the text from the *City of God*, he omits Augustine's summary dismissal of the Nero myth and other such speculation. Rabanus quotes only the portion of the text where Augustine discusses the connection between "what restrains" (verse 6) and the "mystery of iniquity" (verse 7). The mystery of iniquity is the number of "evil and false people" who are hidden in the church. They are restrained from appearing until they reach a critical number and make a "great people" for Antichrist. All this Rabanus culls right from Augustine's *De civitate dei* 20,19,[20] and it leads him to enrich the spiritual interpretation with an excerpt taken from Gregory's *Moralia*.

The "evil and false people" of which Augustine speaks are those to whom the Apostle John refers when he says that there are "many Antichrists now" (1 Jn 2,19). The excerpt from Gregory connects these various Antichrists to the "body of Antichrist," and gives the text a sharp moral edge:

> I may remain silent concerning the outwardly criminal people, for behold, someone envies his brother silently in his heart, and, if he had the occasion, he would try to supplant the brother. Whose member is he, if not the one of whom it is written "By the envy of the Devil, death entered the world" (Wis 2,24)?. Another one thinks himself to be of great worth, preferring himself, since his whole heart is swollen. He believes that all are inferior to him. Whose member is he, if not his of whom it is written, "He sees every high place and is the king over all the sons of pride" (Job 41,25)?[21]

Rabanus includes this moral, corporal sense from Gregory as the natural sequel to Augustine's interpretation. While he could have quoted more from each of these Fathers, he seems to include just enough to represent their spiritual, corporal exegesis. However, he clearly excludes any portion of Augustine's critique of apocalyptic realism, and he then returns to Theodore of Mopsuestia, his template, and his apocalyptic account of Antichrist and the end. This is but one example of several from the Carolingian period. In a similar fashion,

---

20. *Civ.* 20,19; Rabanus, *In Epistolam Secundam ad Thessalonicenses* (PL 113.572B).

21. Gregory, *Moralia* 29,7,15: *Ut enim de apertioribus criminibus taceam, ecce alius fratrem in corde suo tacitus invidet, et si occasionem reperiat, eum supplantare contendit, cuius alterius membrum est, nisi de quo scriptum est, "Invidia diaboli mors intravit in orbem terrarum"? Alius magni meriti esse se aestimans, per tumorem cordis cunctis se praeferens, omnes semetipso inferiores credit, cuius alterius membrum est, nisi eius de quo scriptum est, "Omne sublime videt et ipse est rex super universos filios superbiae"?* Rabanus, op. cit. (PL 113.572C–573A).

Sedulius Scotus more or less recapitulates the commentary of Pelagius (surviving under the name of Jerome), which also offers an apocalyptic realist account of Antichrist and the end. When he alters Pelagius, it is often to make the text more explicitly literal and political. Sedulius comments that "what restrains" in verse 6 is the Roman Empire, a point about which Pelagius was less specific. Yet, despite Sedulius's apocalyptic sympathies, he, too, folds into this realist account a tip of the hat to *De civitate dei* 20,19 on the "mystery of iniquity" when he comments that this is Antichrist working through his members.[22]

Haimo of Auxerre offers an interesting exception to this tendency among the Carolingians, since he makes no attempt in his 2 Thessalonians commentary to include an Augustinian perspective. Indeed, in Haimo's text, Augustine is conspicuous by his absence. Instead, Haimo offers only realist apocalypticism drawn from Jerome, Ambrosiaster, and Pelagius. Thus, in his Pauline commentary, he aims to present a thorough summary of the historical events and characters of the end, complete with an analysis of the theological issues that pertain to them. Haimo leaves no doubt in this commentary that Paul's *discessio* or "desertion" refers to the collapse of the Roman Empire and that this has already occurred.[23] When the Apostle speaks of "the man of sin, the son of perdition," he refers to a historical individual, fully human, who will come to persecute the elect and lead astray those who have already rejected Christ. That the former event has occurred and the latter has not yet come is due to God's providential decree that obscures the precise time of Antichrist's arrival from human eyes. Christ will slay Antichrist and give a brief respite to the saints before he comes in judgment. But, again, God in his providence alone knows how long this respite will be before Christ comes to reward those who have accepted the Gospel and condemn those who worship the devil.

Given this evidence, it would appear that we could place Haimo firmly within the apocalyptic realist camp. But such appearances can deceive. Haimo

---

22. Sedulius Scotus, *Collectanea in Epistolam Secundam ad Thessalonicenses* (PL 103.223B): IAM ENIM MYSTERIUM INIQUITATIS OPERATUR. *Antichristus per sua membra agit, ut Joannes dicit: "Multi antichristi facti sunt." In his ergo mysterium iniquitatis operatur, qui falsis doctrinis eius praevium faciunt iter, quos beatus joannes in mundum dicit exisse. Sicut enim Christus nunc per membra sua operatur, sic Antichristus.*

23. Haimo, *Expositio in Epistulam Secundam ad Thessalonicenses* (PL 117.780). For further development of this claim, see K. L. Hughes, "Apocalyptic Conservatism in an Age of Anxiety: The Exegetical Options of Adso of Montier-en-Der," in *The Apocalyptic Year 1000: Religious Expectation and Social Change, 950–1050*, ed. R. Landes and D. Van Meter (forthcoming).

also composed a commentary on the Apocalypse, and this commentary offers a decidedly different, and thoroughly allegorical, perspective. In the Apocalypse commentary, Haimo rarely refers to Antichrist without referring also to "his members," the heretics and sons of pride within the Church.[24] The contrast between the two expositions is so sharp that one might wonder if Haimo has attempted a deception of his own worthy of Antichrist!

But the source of conflict is far less insidious and it sheds some light upon Haimo's approach to Scripture. The *argumentum* to the 2 Thessalonians commentary gives a clear sense of Paul's purpose in writing: because the Thessalonians are afraid that the day of the Lord is at hand, Paul writes to them to dispel this fear, "and he shows them that the Roman Empire must be destroyed first."[25] For Haimo, Paul responds to the concrete fear of the Thessalonians with a concrete answer. He gives them what they need: evidence that the end will not yet come. The Apostle's purpose is to give them a literal, historical teaching. Haimo thus interprets this teaching in a literal, historical manner.

The Apostle John, on the other hand, receives the Book of Revelation as an "intellectual vision" as consolation for his imprisonment on Patmos. John's vision is one in which "such symbols [*sacramenta*] are revealed to him from heaven in his mind."[26] Paul relates events; John receives imagery. Thus from the Apocalypse, "nothing historical should be taken, because the words themselves, if they are examined carefully, are put forth to teach."[27] The difference between Haimo's expositions of 2 Thessalonians and the Apocalypse is not one of apocalyptic perspective, but of genre. It is the difference between historical and visionary literature.

For Haimo, then, both the Latin spiritual interpretation and the literal apocalyptic realism are true renditions of the apocalyptic tradition. But unlike his fellow exegetes, Haimo does not harmonize the two perspectives, but instead makes a careful distinction. Each is appropriate for its own genre and context. The "peaceful coexistence" of the two interpretations, so characteristic of early medieval apocalyptic thought, is organized rationally by the type of scriptural book. Haimo's commentary on 2 Thessalonians gives a thorough summary of

---

24. E.g., Haimo, *Expositio in Apocalypsin* (PL 117.1092D–1098D), where the first beast of Rev 13 is Antichrist and the second is his body.

25. . . . *et ostendit eis quod antea destruendum esset regnum Romanorum* (PL 117.777D).

26. . . . *divinitus sibi dum in mente tanta ostensa sunt sacramenta* (PL 117.940B).

27. *In hac autem revelatione nihil historicum est accipiendum, quod ipsa verba, si subtiliter inspiciuntur, docere probantur* (PL 117.938C).

the apocalyptic realist tradition because he understands the subject matter to be history and the genre to be catechetical, i.e., the teaching of doctrine to the Thessalonian community. In Haimo, as in Jerome before him, 2 Thessalonians becomes the authoritative New Testament resource on Antichrist and the events of the end, and Paul is its apostolic catechist.

For Rabanus, Sedulius, and Haimo, both the Augustinian spiritual interpretation of 2 Thessalonians and the literal apocalyptic realism of Jerome, Ambrosiaster, and Theodore are true renditions of the apocalyptic tradition. In the hands of Rabanus and Sedulius, the two could be knit together into one multivalent interpretation. Under the discriminating eye of Haimo, the two are distinguished, but neither is rejected. But for all of them, it is the apocalyptic realist perspective that generates theological reflection in 2 Thessalonians. If early medieval thinkers were somewhat chary of predicting an imminent arrival of Antichrist, they still had no doubt that, whenever the end might come, a single figure, an incarnation of human evil, would arrive upon the scene. And yet this literal, realist sense of Antichrist was complemented by the spritual interpretation of Tyconius and Augustine, so that Antichrist was both present and to come, both the immanent body of Antichrist and the future human person. In the context of this complementarity, the early medieval doctrine of Antichrist produced what Bernard McGinn has called a sense of "pyschological imminence" in which one's present actions could and should be understood *sub specie finis*, in light of the apocalyptic end.[28]

Conclusion

Thus Jaroslav Pelikan is only partly right to speak of "the apocalyptic vision and its transformation" in the early church as "nothing less than the decisive shift from the categories of cosmic drama to those of being, from the Revelation of St. John to the creed of the Council of Nicea."[29] The cosmic drama of

---

28. McGinn's argument is worth quoting: "In art and literature, as well as in theology, the centuries of the making of Christendom were obsessed with the theme of the coming judgment, though rarely with precise predictions for its coming. Although fear of judgment had been found in Christian texts from the beginning, I would suggest that the early-medieval rejection of predictiveness may paradoxically have allowed end-time anxiety a more pervasive, if necessarily somewhat diffuse, power." B. McGinn, "The End of the World and the Beginning of Christendom," in *Apocalypse Theory and the Ends of the World*, ed. M. Bull (Oxford: Blackwell, 1995) 63.

29. J. Pelikan, *The Christian Tradition*, vol. 1, *The Emergence of the Catholic Tradition* (100–600) (Chicago: University of Chicago Press, 1971) 123–132.

the *parousia* was less and less the focus of christology, sacramental theology, and other areas of theological speculation. But if the drama was no longer center stage, the set was never struck. The apocalyptic structure of history, the expectation of the Adversary, and the "psychological imminence" of the end became the backdrop against which these other theological elements were rehearsed. Haimo's Pauline commentary examines the doctrine of original sin and the doctrine of Antichrist with equal rigor. Rabanus Maurus was diligent in his pursuit of the Fathers' opinions on both grace and the end of time. Early medieval theologians, even as they addressed theological questions in the "categories of being," continued to "live in the shadow of the Second Coming"[30] and to wonder what that Second Coming might entail.

Antichrist was alive and well in the early Middle Ages, both as the immanent presence of evil and as the coming evil one. In the 2 Thessalonians tradition, apocalyptic realism provided the most fertile ground for debate and development, but it is always balanced or supplemented in some way by the Augustinian position. This "peaceful co-existence" between the literal and the spiritual, between the apocalyptic and the anagogic, is perhaps more characteristic of the early medieval attitudes toward apocalyptic themes than the traditional assumption of "Augustinian" anti-apocalyptic hegemony. It is at the fault line between the two fields—in the encounter between apocalyptic realism and a spiritual reading rooted in Augustine—that a distinctive early medieval apocalypticism was born.

---

30. I take the phrase from McGinn, "The End of the World and the Beginning of Christendom," 67. He, in turn, has adopted it from T. Weber's book about American millenarian thought, *Living in the Shadow of the Second Coming: American Premillennialism 1875–1982* (Chicago: University of Chicago Press, 1987).

III. THE SECULAR IMAGINATION

CIVITAS TO CONGREGATION:
AUGUSTINE'S TWO CITIES AND
JOHN BALE'S *IMAGE OF BOTH CHURCHES*

Gretchen E. Minton

In 1551, John Bale published a three-part work entitled *The Image of Both Churches*. This work, which was the first English commentary on the book of Revelation, was the fruit of Bale's years in exile, for he had fled to the continent in 1540 following the fall of his patron Thomas Cromwell. Bale had returned to England in 1547 when Edward VI was crowned, hoping for preferment. His previous writings as a Protestant (he had converted from Roman Catholicism in the 1530s) included numerous stage plays and anti-Catholic pamphlets. During his exile, Bale developed an interest in martyrs and in the Apocalypse that continued throughout the rest of his life. The *Image* reflects Bale's contention that "The very complete sum and whole knitting up is this heavenly book [Revelation] of the universal verities of the bible."[1] Bale sees the story of two radically opposed communities, exemplified by the cities of Jerusalem and Babylon, as the key to all history. He finds support for this view of history not just in the Bible, but in the fathers of the church. Bale states confidently on the second page of the *Image*: "And after the true opinion of St Austin, either we are citizens in the new Jerusalem with Jesus Christ, or else in the old superstitious Babylon with antichrist the vicar of Satan" (252). This

---

1. John Bale, *The Image of Both Churches*, in *Select Works of John Bale, D. D., Bishop of Ossory*, ed. H. Christmas (Cambridge: Cambridge University Press, 1849) 252. All references will be to page numbers in this edition.

comment, as well as Bale's title, has led many critics to suggest that Augustine's *City of God* influenced, or even inspired, Bale's idea of the two churches.

Bale's first modern biographer, Thora Blatt, is adamant: "It seems to me incontestable that at the basis of Bale's politico-religious creed we find St. Augustine, partly as he may have found his thoughts expressed at second hand in the Middle Ages, partly as he may have known them from his reading of *De Civitate Dei*."[2] This connection has been noted also in Leslie Fairfield's book on Bale,[3] and in the better known books about English apocalyptic, such as Paul Christianson's *Reformers and Babylon*[4] and Katharine Firth's *The Apocalyptic Tradition in Reformation Britain*. Firth posits that "[F]rom Augustine's two cities and the eternal opposition of the spirit and the flesh, [Bale] derived an earthly conflict between two sorts of men, the faithful and the unfaithful, and their two churches, of Christ and Antichrist."[5] Even the more reserved commentators on this subject, such as Peter Happé, allow that "There is a *distinct possibility* that St. Augustine's *City of God* was influential on Bale's division."[6]

If it is reasonable to suggest that there is a connection between the *Image* and the *City of God*, it is also important to note that the exact nature of this connection is difficult to discern. None of the commentators cited above has offered more than general assertions on this point. One of the main reasons for the lack of specific evidence adduced is that Bale rarely quotes Augustine within the text, and even in the marginalia that he includes in Part I of the *Image* he mentions Augustine only occasionally. Most of the references he does make to Augustine are included in a list of other authorities: Eusebius, Jerome, Joachim, Albertus Magnus, and many others, all of whom are cited as frequently as Augustine, if not more so. Nonetheless, by looking closely at the direct references, and then at the similarities between Augustine's model of the two cities and Bale's of the two churches, it will be possible to draw some more precise conclusions about the relationship.

---

2. T. Blatt, *The Plays of John Bale: A Study of Ideas, Technique and Style* (Copenhagen: Gad, 1968) 59.

3. L.P. Fairfield, *John Bale: Mythmaker for the English Reformation* (West Lafayette, Ind.: Purdue University Press, 1976) 83.

4. P. Christianson, *Reformers and Babylon: English Apocalyptic Visions from the Reformation to the Eve of the Civil War* (Toronto: University of Toronto Press, 1978).

5. K.R. Firth, *The Apocalyptic Tradition in Reformation Britain, 1530–1645* (Oxford: Oxford University Press, 1979) 58.

6. P. Happé, *John Bale* (New York: Twayne Publishers, 1996) 50, emphasis mine.

Bale Reading Augustine: The Textual Evidence

In the Introduction to the *Image*, Bale includes two references to Augustine in the margins. The first is beside the passage quoted above about Babylon
and Jerusalem, next to which Bale cites "Augustine," Revelation 21 (where
the new Jerusalem is described), and Jeremiah 1 (concerning the judgment of
the wicked, and Jeremiah's fortification of the city against them). The next
marginal reference to Augustine accompanies a passage about the theme of
exile in the book of Revelation:

> Of such a nature is the message of this book with the other contents thereof,
> that from no place is it sent more freely, opened more clearly, nor told forth
> more boldly, than out of exile. . . . In exile was it first written . . . , [i]n exile
> are the powers thereof most earnestly proved of them that have faith. (254)

Bale's reason for citing Augustine next to this passage cannot be certainly
determined, but it probably relates to the importance of peregrination and alienation in Augustine's concept of the *City of God*. Bale connects Augustine's
idea of alienation to his own situation as an exile, thus uniting the condition of
the Henrician exiles, John of Patmos, and the Augustinian *peregrini*.

Because Bale is attempting to elucidate the book of Revelation, his interest
in Augustine focuses upon this Father's comments on the Apocalypse. Interestingly, Bale lists Augustine as a commentator on Revelation in the year 420
(255).[7] This must be a reference to the *City of God*, because of the date and the
fact that Bale's only direct references to Augustine in the *Image* concern the
City of God. Whether or not the *City of God* is in fact primarily about Revelation,[8] it is clear that Bale *thought* it was. This citation of Augustine as a
commentator on the Apocalypse highlights the nature of Bale's use of Books
20–22 of the *City of God* as a source for his eschatology. Because Bale reads
the *City of God* as a commentary on Revelation, any reference he makes to
that work tends to be within an apocalyptic framework.[9]

Part I of the *Image* contains no direct quotations from Augustine, but Bale
mentions Augustine's name in seven different marginal references. The references serve to support some of Bale's points, and in these instances Augustine

---

7. "Saint Austin also, anno dom. 420."

8. See the essay by Harry O. Maier in this volume.

9. His only direct citations of the *City of God* are from Book 20, in which Augustine discusses
Revelation.

is included along with the relevant biblical passages and a list of other commentators on the subject (patristic, medieval, or Reformation). For example, Bale's first marginal reference to Augustine has him as a supporter of the doctrine of the trinity, along with Athanasius, Fulgentius, Revelation 1, and Isaiah 44. Bale also lists Augustine twice in connection with those who fought against heresies in the early church (316, 346). None of these citations is necessarily a reference to the *City of God*. However, the other marginal references probably are. One is about angels (368),[10] and two concern the nature of biblical secrets that are revealed only in part to God's people. Bale's cautious view of exegetical practice—"In the search therefore of godly mysteries, not the wit nor the learning of the man is to be sought, but rather the right meaning of God working in the man" (375)—echoes similar cautions throughout the *City of God*.[11] The other marginal notation accompanies Bale's explanation of the silence after the opening of the seventh seal, where he again mentions the relationship between God's secrets and the "inward working . . . reserved to spirit" (372). In both cases, Bale seems interested in Augustine's theories of exegesis, especially concerning the relationship between "inner" and "outer" significance.

After Part I of the *Image*, Bale abandoned the practice of including marginal references, claiming that "two cruel enemies have my just labors had on that behalf" (380–381). These two enemies are the sloppy printers and an unnamed "blasphemer" who had apparently used Bale's marginalia in order to prove him wrong and unlearned.[12] Because of this change of practice, it is more difficult henceforward to determine where Bale was using Augustine as a source or as a general authority in support of his own assertions. Part II is a particular problem, because Bale never mentions Augustine there at all. Whereas we could discern Bale's usage of Augustine from the marginal notes despite the absence of direct references in the text of Part I, in Part II we have neither notes nor references and are left entirely to conjecture.

Part III, by contrast, contains the clearest evidence of Augustine's influence upon Bale. There are six direct references to him, including two specific

---

10. Augustine is probably listed as an authority because of Book 12 of the *City of God*.

11. See, e.g., *City of God* 16,2, in which Augustine explains that all the hidden meanings of Scripture should interpreted "with reference to Christ and his Church, which is the City of God." My quotations follow the translation of H. Bettenson (Harmondsworth: Penguin Classics, 1972), here 652.

12. The identity of the blasphemer, whom Bale calls "Momus or Zoilus" (381), remains unclear.

references to the *City of God*. The first of these specific references is made in connection with Bale's reading of Revelation 20:4, where he notes:

St Augustine, in his twentieth book *De civitate Dei*, willeth by Gog to be signified the glorious hypocrites of the world, and by Magog the open enemies of righteousness. (570–571)

As the footnote in the Parker Society edition of the *Image* correctly points out, this is not exactly what Augustine says in chapter 11 of Book 20 when he discusses Gog and Magog. Instead, Augustine says that Gog and Magog respectively mean "the roof" and "from the roof," or "the house" and "the one who proceeds from the house." He interprets this etymology as a metaphor for the devil and those wicked men who proceed from the devil's camp. When Augustine goes on to describe these enemies in more detail, he refers the readers to his discussion of enemy nations in chapter 7,[13] in which he warned that the followers of the devil are shut up secretly, and cannot be discerned; this may be the source of Bale's idea of the connection between these evil characters and hypocrisy. Furthermore, in chapter 9 of the same book, Augustine gives his interpretation of the seven-headed beast as a representation of "the godless city itself." He then relates the "image" of the beast to its pretence and hypocrisy, which stands for those who put on an outward show of being Christians even though they are not. Thus, Bale read Augustine's general idea about two kinds of faithless people into his discussion of Gog and Magog as agents of the devil at the end of time. What holds these two ideas together is the emphasis on hypocrisy, on the difference between seen and unseen. Throughout the *Image*, Bale notes that there are two facets of the Antichrist—one that can be seen and one that cannot: "Therefore I do take [the beast] for one universal antichrist (as I did afore), comprehending in him so well Mahomet as the pope, so well the raging tyrant as the still hypocrite; and all that wickedly work are of the same body" (426). Like Augustine, who points out that "it is not only the open enemies of the name of Christ and his most glorious City who belong to this beast" (*Civ.* 20,9), Bale allows for a complex understanding of his two churches that goes beyond a simple dichotomy between "seen" and "unseen."

The other direct reference to the *City of God* in Part III of the *Image* reads: "For, as witnesseth St Augustine in his twentieth book and twelfth chapter, *De civitate Dei*, not only is this punishment to be referred to that latter judgment, but also to the extermination of antichrist's host by the word of God the world

---

13. *Civ.* 20,11: "according to our interpretation given above" (trans. Bettenson 920).

241

over"(576). This is indeed a paraphrase of this short chapter of the *City of God*, and Bale's direct citation at this point certainly suggests that he had a copy of the *City of God* to hand (or else was referring to the work of someone else who had), and used it as an authoritative commentary on the end times. The fact that both these direct references to the *City of God* concern Revelation 20 is no accident: this chapter is the only part of Revelation that Augustine discusses in any detail in the *City of God*. Moreover, Bale's use of the passage shows that he is looking for places in the *City of God* that suggest that some of these "apocalyptic" events have already begun.

Bale also uses Augustine when he would like to leave interpretation at a more general level than some other exegetes allow. When discussing Revelation 21:19–20, Bale lists several different opinions that commentators have given about the meaning of the various gems in the new Jerusalem. Rather than committing himself to one of these, Bale writes, "Enough is it for us to shew you, after the mind of St Augustine, these stones to signify the divers graces of the Holy Ghost" (609).[14]

One of the remaining three references that Bale makes to Augustine is a typical use of him in defense of the doctrine of grace: "Not our good works (Saith St Augustine), but his own mere gifts, doth the Lord crown in us" (631). The other two references are related, because they both include Augustine in a list of Christian writers and exegetes. In the first case, Bale lists Augustine as one of those Christians who "spoiled the Egyptians"[15] by bringing the glories of the pagan world into the heavenly City, in which there is no darkness (614). The final reference is a mention of Augustine in a list of commentators who have done no injury to the word by elucidating it for others: Bale is defending these commentators against the admonition to "put nothing, nor take any thing from, the Word" in Revelation 22:18–19 (637). In both cases, it is Augustine's practice as an *exegete* that Bale seeks to defend.

To summarize: in the marginal references, Bale includes Augustine along with other authorities in order to add weight to his general argument. He never gives the exact source in these citations, and they usually function as a supporting authority to his views against heresies, on the doctrine of grace, or upon other points of orthodoxy. All Bale's direct references to the *City of God* are to the last three books, which deal with the end times, and which Bale

---

14. I have been unable to determine to what work of Augustine's Bale is alluding in this instance.

15. A reference to *De doctrina christiana* 2,40,60–61.

seems to use as one of his many sources on the Apocalypse. Bale's direct use of Augustine is thus less extensive than might have been supposed, given the affinity of their projects. However, there are important patterns that can be detected from these direct references that make it possible to set up a discussion of the ways in which Bale may have been indebted to Augustine. For instance, it is evident that Bale was (in some sense) reading the *City of God*, that he believed it to provide a commentary on Revelation, and that he was interested in Augustine's theories of exegesis. Finally, perhaps the most striking point that emerges from this initial survey is that Bale saw his two churches as homologous to Augustine's two cities, and saw both paradigms as expressions of the apocalyptic struggle between the forces of Babylon and Jerusalem.

A Spiritual Community: *Civitas* to Congregation

Bale's title has led most critics to assume that the *City of God* was the major inspiration behind the *Image*. Paul Christianson argues that "Bale took St Augustine's idea of the two cities and transformed it into that of the two churches—one headed by Christ and the other by antichrist."[16] The nature of this supposed "transformation" deserves closer attention. Too often critics have been led by Bale's polemical attacks against the Roman Catholic church to believe that Bale identified it directly with the church of the Antichrist, and in turn identified the Protestant church with the true Christian church. As Blatt would have it, "Bale, of course, has a strong tendency to identify *civitas diaboli* with the papacy, which is as un-Augustinian as the attempt of the Church to monopolize *civitas dei*."[17] Indeed, a direct identification between either institutional church and the City of God or man *would* be un-Augustinian, and at points it is easy enough to understand why Bale can be read in this manner. He uses phrases such as the "proud church of hypocrites," the "rose-coloured whore," the "paramour of antichrist" and the "sinful synagogue of Satan" (251) to describe the Roman Catholic church. Nonetheless, it is important to note that, while Bale *did* identify the Roman Catholic church in this manner, his concept of the wicked church reached beyond the boundaries of this one institution.

Richard Bauckham, recognizing the complexity of this issue, observes that "[i]n Tudor Protestant thought the relationship between the 'church of the wicked' and the Church of Rome is often as difficult to pin down as that between

---

16. Christianson, *Reformers and Babylon*, 15.
17. Blatt, *The Plays of John Bale*, 128.

Augustine's *civitas Dei* and the visible church of Christ."[18] Bauckham's basic premise is correct, but his analogy between Bale's "wicked church" and Augustine's City of God confuses the issue, because it compares the negative community of Bale's model to the positive community of Augustine's model, suggesting that there is not a similar ambiguity in the other halves of Bale's and Augustine's models (which, of course, there is).

It is more fruitful to compare the relationship of Bale's "church of the wicked" and the church of Rome not with Augustine's City of God and the visible church, but with his earthly city and the "city" of Rome. Augustine consistently equates the earthly city with Rome, but sometimes he uses Rome as a negative apocalyptic symbol, as an embodiment of evil, while at other times he speaks of Rome as a more neutral realm that can be "used" by the pilgrims of the City of God while they are on earth.[19] While these two views may seem to create an ambiguous picture, one thing is clear: Rome may be neutral as a "city" of the earth, but Rome as a symbol of *the* earthly city is certainly not neutral—it is entirely evil. Similarly, in Bale the "church of the wicked" is entirely evil. However, despite the claims of critics such as Blatt, it is evident that Bale does not limit the citizenship of the wicked church to the Roman Catholic church any more than Augustine limits the citizenship of the earthly city to the "city" of Rome. Certain institutions (the Roman Catholic church or "the Turks" for Bale, and Rome for Augustine) may serve as resonant symbols for these negative communities, but they are merely a particular historical manifestation of a much larger concept. The entire human race, Augustine insists, can be divided into "two branches: the one consist[ing] of those who live by human standards, the other of those who live according to God's will. I also call these two classes the two cities, *speaking allegorically*."[20] By "speaking allegorically," both Augustine and Bale can construct ideas of communities that include, but do not limit themselves to, earthly institutions.

---

18. R. Bauckham, *Tudor Apocalypse* (Oxford: Sutton Courtney Press, 1978) 55.

19. The relative "neutrality" of the earthly city is by no means uncontroversial. The influential view of R. A. Markus in *Saeculum: History and Society in the Theology of St Augustine* (Cambridge: Cambridge University Press, 1970), which I follow here, has been contested by J. van Oort, *Jerusalem and Babylon: A Study into Augustine's City of God and the Sources of his Doctrine of the Two Cities* (New York: E. J. Brill, 1991). For John Milbank's critique of Markus's position, see the essay by Michael Hollerich in this volume.

20. *Civ.* 15,1 (trans. Bettenson 595), emphasis mine.

Like the earthly city, Augustine's City of God is a community that extends beyond institutional boundaries, and which exists on a symbolic level. Despite the fact that Augustine states explicitly in Book 18 and in other places that the City of God is not equivalent to the church, many have made that claim.[21] Part of the reason for this is that Augustine says, "the City of God, that is to say, God's Church" (*Civ.* 13,16), yet this church is not the institutional Catholic church, but an eschatologically defined community that is synonymous with the heavenly city. When Bale discusses the heavenly city or church, he shows himself attuned to Augustine's spiritual/metaphorical description of this city. When he speaks of the holy city, he often cites the verse from Psalm 87 ("Glorious things are spoken of you, O City of God"), which was the basis of Augustine's title. And Bale makes it clear that the heavenly city is not the earthly Jerusalem, but a city "grounded upon the strong foundation of the apostles and prophets, even upon the hard rock-stone, Jesus Christ" (385). Bale sees this city not only as an eschatological realization, but as a "living generation of them which fear, love, and seek their Lord God in faith, spirit and verity, and not in outward shadows." Like Augustine, he views the pilgrims on this earth as "children of promise, the true offspring of Abraham, the chosen house of Israel, and the kingdom of the Holy Ghost" (386). Thus, when he says, "City of God, or the holy congregation" (574), we should not take it any more literally as a reference to the Protestant church than we take Augustine's phrase "God's church" as a reference to the Catholic church of his time.

Bauckham argues that "the doctrine of the two churches has its deepest roots in Augustine's doctrine of the two cities, and though Augustine never used the terminology of churches, early sixteenth-century writers had no hesitation in calling their doctrine his."[22] What does this shift in terminology imply? Augustine did of course use the term "church," but when speaking of both communities together, he always used *civitas*, a more rhetorically powerful term, both because of the scriptural dichotomy between the cities of Babylon and Jerusalem, and because of the historical importance of the "city" of Rome. In Protestant rhetoric, however, the true and false cities had been overlaid with

---

21. See J. J. O'Donnell, "The Inspiration for Augustine's *De Civitate Dei,*" *Augustinian Studies* 10 (1979): 79: "In that misreading of Augustine's work, it became possible to identify official, ecclesiastical Christianity—the church in this world and even a Christian state—with the heavenly city itself and to indulge in a kind of Christian imperialism which thought that an earthly society could become that which was in Augustine's view really only possible in heaven."

22. Bauckham, *Tudor Apocalypse*, 55.

true and false churches. And just as Augustine could also call the City of God a church, Bale could also call the church of God a congregation. The term congregation was the preferred one for Protestants, because it emphasized the communal but non-institutional identity of believers. Thus, despite the shift in terminology, Bale's use of Augustine's scheme of the two cities remains more faithful to the original idea than medieval writers such as Otto of Freising had been.[23]

Although both men privilege the spiritual and symbolic significance of the city or church of God, they do not ignore the literal or temporal level, because without the original form of an earthly institution, there would be nothing to reflect, and therefore there would be no image of what is to come. It is the movement from the temporal to the eternal, from the literal to the spiritual, that structures Augustine's and Bale's models. A related point that is absolutely integral to Augustine's paradigm is the idea that the membership of the City of God is divided between citizens of heaven and pilgrims on earth. Augustine identified pilgrimage as the natural state for members of the City of God who are still on earth. As noted above, Bale identified Augustine's themes of pilgrimage and alienation with the themes of persecution and exile as described in the book of Revelation, and with his own situation. Although Bale could not quite see himself as a martyr, he did see himself as an exile throughout most of his life. When he wrote the *Image* during his first exile on the continent, he remarked:

> I have exiled myself for ever from mine own native country, kindred, friends, acquaintance, (which are the great delights of this life,) and am well contented for Jesus Christ's sake, and for the comfort of my brethren there, to suffer poverty, penury, abjection, reproof, and all that shall come besides. (260)

Thus he felt particularly prepared to provide a commentary on the book of Revelation. Bale's sense of alienation informed not only his understanding of the Apocalypse, but also his framework of the two churches. The citizens of the true Christian church are often sent into exile, and persecuted, for they are strangers to life here on earth whose "reign is not of this world." Bale believed that persecution was a sign of election, and used martyrs as the symbol of these strangers on earth—people such as John Oldcastle, Anne Askewe, and even himself as he escaped, like St. Paul, from torments on the sea.

---

23. See Firth, *Apocalyptic Tradition*, 2–3, for a discussion of Otto's use of Augustine. See also G. J. Lavere, "The Two Cities of Otto, Bishop of Freising: A Study in Neo-Augustinian Political Theory," *Augustinian Studies* 13 (1982): 55–65.

Katharine Firth contends that "In Part II of the *Image*, Bale had made a point of the importance of martyrdom in his history of the church, and had hinted at the transformation of the two cities, represented in the Apocalypse by Jerusalem and Babylon, into two kinds of people and two churches, one dedicated to the spirit and one to the flesh."[24] This dichotomy between the spirit and the flesh is certainly emphasized by Bale in many places, most notably when he says, "In the church is evermore variance and strife without ceasing betwixt the Spirit and the flesh, the good and the bad, the faithful and the unfaithful. . . . Continued hath this battle from the first beginning, and so shall still to the latter end" (411). However, a closer look at Bale's views on flesh and spirit shows that he was not setting up a simple dichotomy between the two in terms of good and evil. He says of the godly church,

> In spirit and verity shall they worship him, and not in dumb ceremonies nor outward shadows. Speared is God's temple, when his true worshipping is hid; and opened it is again, when that is clearly seen. Till Christ's coming in the flesh nothing thereof appeared: with the key of David opened he the mysteries thereof; whereby through faith the conversation of many is now and hath been ever since in heaven. (403)

The first sentence is a distinction between two kinds of worship, and does indeed associate the godly people with spiritual and unseen truths. Yet Bale's emphasis on the Incarnation shows that there is an integral relationship between flesh and spirit, and that there is a good flesh as well as a bad flesh. In this case, it is Christ's flesh that leads to the spiritual understanding which God's pilgrims may glimpse partially during this life, and fully in the next. Like Augustine, Bale sets up a binary model that does not allow for a separation of flesh into one realm and spirit in another. For Augustine, the essential event at the Last Judgment is the perfect union between the spirit and the flesh— for both the saved and the damned. In like manner, Bale sees the resurrection, and the community of believers, as a combination of spirit and flesh.

The most important feature of the two cities for Augustine is that they are intermingled here, but separated at the end. The eschatological orientation of these two cities determines the way Augustine views history and interpretation, which are both necessary only because of the Fall.[25] And so we may ask: if Bale adopts the general paradigm of the two cities, and if his use of the term "church" does not

---

24. Ibid., 44.

25. On history as a result of the fallen condition, see Markus, *Saeculum*, 10.

essentially alter this scheme, does this model inform Bale's methods of historiography and hermeneutics in the same way that it does Augustine's?

The Two Churches as a Model for Historiography

Bale's contribution to English Protestant historiography is widely recognized. Already his dramas from the 1530s posit a Protestant view of history that is derived from Augustinian ideas. For instance, in his play *Three Laws*, Bale presents history as an evolution from natural law to the law of Moses to the law of Christ, echoing Augustine's threefold scheme of before the law, under the law, and under grace. When he wrote the *Image*, Bale followed Augustine's combination of this threefold scheme with the seven ages of history that he outlines at the end of the *City of God*.

As R. A. Markus has noted, this division of history into seven ages has the effect of draining significance from the sixth age, between the Ascension and the Parousia.[26] But while it is true that Augustine believed there could be no more decisive turning points in history after the Ascension, he does not leave the sixth age devoid of all meaning. Although the sacred history narrated in the Bible usually concerns the first five ages, Revelation and other prophetic books provide clues for the unfolding of the sixth age. Thus Augustine turns his attention to prophecy and revelation in Books 19–22 of the *City of God* and cautiously interprets what the Scripture seems to say about the ends of the two cities. Markus observes that for Augustine "[t]here is no sacred history of the last age: there is only a gap for it in sacred history."[27] For Augustine this gap is not a major concern, but for Bale, who is interested primarily in the history of the sixth age, it becomes central. There are important differences that arise from these diverging emphases, to which we shall return in a moment. In principle, however, Bale's objective was not so very different from Augustine's: to trace the origin, development, and destined end of the two cities.

Because Bale sees Revelation as the "complete sum and whole knitting up ... of the universal verities of the bible" (252), he combines his understanding of the Apocalypse with other scriptural sources in order to explain the origin and development of the two cities/churches. Like Augustine, Bale equates the beast of Revelation 13 with the earthly city, and he explains in the *Image* that

---

26. Ibid., 20–1.
27. Ibid., 23.

[f]rom the world's beginning hath this beast risen up in Cain, the first murderer, in the fleshly children of men, in Cham the shameless child of Noe, in Ismael and Esau, in Jannes and Jambres, in Balaam and Baal's prophets, in the Benjamites and Bel's chaplains, in Phasur and Semeias, in Judas, Annas and Caiphas, in Bar-jesu and Diotrephes; and now, since their time, most of all in Mahomet's doctors and the pope's quiresters. (437)

The genealogy of the beast, or wicked church, is traced by Bale in the same way that Augustine traces the genealogy of the earthly city, even using the same biblical characters for support. This listing of members not only relates individuals to communities, but also locates historical people and events within the larger framework of history. Although Bale does not comment extensively on pre-Ascension matters in the *Image*, this passage certainly calls into question Firth's assertion that "Bale limited the universal antichrist to the history of the Christian church from the Ascension."[28] Indeed, Bale is adamant that "[t]he execrable beast or carnal kingdom of Antichrist, which thou hast seen here in mystery, was as concerning his beginning in Cain first of all, and so continued forth in the fleshly children of men" (499). While Bale assigns a preeminent importance to the Incarnation, he clearly believes that the opposing churches had their origin in the garden. Bale sees the pregnant woman of Revelation 12 as the growing body of the righteous who

waxed . . . bigger and bigger, till the fulness of her time was come that she should be delivered: which was such time as Christ appeared to the world, taught, and was conversant here among men. And this course hath she kept ever since, and shall do to the latter day in them that believe. Thus hath she had Christ in her womb since the beginning. (405)

Although Augustine does not discuss this passage from Revelation 12 in the *City of God*, Bale's reading of it is strikingly similar to Augustine's interpretation of Revelation 21, which reads:

This City is said to come down from heaven because the grace by which God created it is heavenly. . . . This City has been coming down from heaven since its beginning, from the time when its citizens began to increase in number as they have continued to increase throughout the period of this present age. (*Civ.* 20,17)

Thus both men consider the two cities/churches as products of a history that had its beginning in the garden (or before then, in Augustine's case), and that continues until the end of time.

---

28. Firth, *Apocalyptic Tradition*, 53.

Both Bale and Augustine, after explaining the origin and development of the two cities/churches, must describe, to the best of their ability, the destined ends of these two communities. Bale's reading of Revelation emphasizes the opposing ends of the two churches, showing how the wicked lament for Babylon: "Oh, that city, that city, that sometime was so mighty and strong, so fair and beautiful, so glorious and holy, is now become waste and desolate!" (525). He then assures the faithful citizens of the other city/church of their promised felicity: "No longer are ye strangers and foreigners, but citizens of heaven and the very household children of God" (545). The Augustinian themes of pilgrimage and citizenship dominate Bale's understanding of both communities. Like Augustine's *peregrini*, Bale's faithful pilgrims wander as exiles in this world because they are members of a heavenly community that they cannot enter until the end of time.

The major difference between Bale's historiography and Augustine's is that Augustine emphasizes the intermingled quality of the two cities throughout history, whereas Bale, who is more interested in the moment of separation between the two churches, reads his eschatological understanding back into secular history in a way that Augustine is reluctant to do. It is true that Bale interprets many of the events of Revelation as if they had happened in the past, whereas Augustine considers all of these events as part of the future. However, this is not to say, as Avihu Zakai does, that

> [t]he great difference between Bale, and indeed Protestant historiography in general, and Augustine, is that while in Augustine's thought the struggle between the two cities marks the essence of profane, secular history, and will be resolved beyond time and history, according to Bale the apocalyptic struggle between the two churches is inherent in providential history and is played out and resolved within time. It is in history (now redefined as "providential history"), Bale argued, that "the two churches" receive their due fate.[29]

First of all, any suggestion that Augustine thinks that the struggle between the two cities is exclusively the domain of "profane, secular history" is clearly a misunderstanding of the *City of God*. Secondly, it is unclear how Zakai imagines that Bale's concept of "providential history" is any different from Augustine's account of "sacred history."[30]

---

29. A. Zakai, *Exile and Kingdom: History and apocalypse in the Puritan migration to America* (Cambridge: Cambridge University Press, 1992) 28.

30. See Markus, *Saeculum*, ch. 1 ("History: Sacred and Secular").

Moreover, for Augustine these apocalyptic events are not resolved "beyond time and history"; instead, they actually constitute the end of time and history. Zakai goes on to argue that

> in sharp contrast to Augustine's pessimistic view of history as devoid of any sacred or human progress, and his resultant concept of alienation from the world, Bale and other Protestant historians developed a sense of history as the arena in which the drama of salvation is unfolding, a realm in which sacred, and hence human, progress is made from divine promise to its fulfillment. In sharp contrast to Augustine, Protestant historiography perceived history as rich in immanent meaning.[31]

It is not fair to label Augustine's caution about interpreting history as "pessimism," or to say that he viewed history as completely devoid of meaning. Zakai and Firth are right to contend that there is a difference between Bale's and Augustine's historiography. Yet this difference is not one of kind so much as it is one of emphasis. Both Bale and Augustine see the Incarnation as central. Even though Augustine views the Incarnation as the decisive moment after which history as a cosmic evolution has nothing more to accomplish, that does not mean that he believes the sixth age has no meaning. The last age of history exists to make up the number of saints, and this goal gives contemporary history a content that cannot possibly be seen as "devoid of any sacred or human progress."

Augustine consistently emphasizes education throughout the *City of God*, for "[t]here is a process of education, through the epochs of a people's history, as through the successive stages of a man's life, designed to raise them from the temporal and the visible to an apprehension of the eternal and the invisible" (*Civ.* 10,14). Like Bale, Augustine is a preacher, and there are deep pastoral concerns within the theological fabric of his historiography. Caught in a secular world between the Incarnation and the Last Judgment, the pilgrims of the City of God must make sense of history by becoming part of a community of believers that reenacts the story of human salvation on a microcosmic level. In Augustine's narrative of history, there are hermeneutic spaces that can be filled by what we might refer to as "the secular imagination." In the *City of God*, Augustine gestures toward the meaning of Revelation cautiously, yet tantalizingly, leaving room open for conjecture and imagination. For Bale, the story of this last age comprises a space that becomes cosmic in

---

31. Zakai, *Exile and Kingdom*, 28.

its significance. It is this hermeneutical gap that Bale, as the citizen of a world 1100 years older, cannot but attempt to fill.

The Two Churches as a Model for Exegesis

For Bale and Augustine alike, all interpretive acts begin with the words of Scripture. Augustine believes that all answers lie in the Bible—not just the answers to explain the past, but also the present and the future: "All this was foretold and promised in the Scriptures. We see the fulfilment of so many of these promises that we look for the fulfilment of the rest with the confidence of a devotion rightly directed" (*Civ.* 10,32). However, because of the fallen condition, the words of the Bible are unclear to us, and must be interpreted carefully and painstakingly. Augustine's belief that Scripture holds all the answers, coupled with his belief that we can see only dim reflections of the truth of God's word in this saeculum, creates an unattainable desire for perfect hermeneutical understanding. Thus his exegesis moves, like his desire, from the literal to the spiritual level of signification. Even in his interpretation of Revelation, where he is reluctant to be historical, he still begins with the literal level of the text—by which I mean, at the word itself. After quoting one passage, he often quotes several others that seem related, and from there he begins to construct a spiritual interpretation. The whole of Augustine's exegesis in the *City of God* points to the idea of the two cities: as the governing principle of interpretation laid down in the *De doctrina christiana* was charity, so in the *De civitate dei* it is the absolute opposition between the two cities.

Similarly, Bale structures his entire exegesis of Revelation around the idea of the two churches—churches that can be glimpsed not by their reality, but by their "images." Bale also begins with the words of Scripture, insisting that the "literal interpretation of the biblical text must underlie all historical application."[32] Throughout the *Image*, he attempts to provide a model Protestant exegesis that moves from the literal level to the spiritual, underlining correct interpretation while accusing his chief adversary, the Roman Catholic church, of bad interpretation. In fact, Bale relates the beast of the earth to the problems with the corruption of the Word, interpreting the beast's two horns as

the corrupted letter of the two testaments, falsely interpreted, and for a carnal purpose alleged. And therefore it is but apparent, hypocritish, and deceitful; yea, and clean repugnant to the Lord's meaning, not having the judgment of his

---

32. J. N. King, *English Reformation Literature* (Princeton: Princeton University Press, 1982) 62.

Spirit. This letter without the Holy Ghost is dead, and nothing pertaineth unto Christ: he is the verity and life; this is but a fable or fiction. (437)

This statement makes it clear that Bale was not a "literal" interpreter of Scripture, as some have alleged. There must be a perfect interlocking between the letter and the spirit, and an exegete must be able to move from one to the other. The Word of God is the key of David "which openeth the kingdom of God to them that faithfully believe, and that speareth it up also from them which dwelleth in unfaithfulness. . . . The word speareth and openeth, looseneth and bindeth, saveth and damneth" (389–390). In contrast, the other church says, "Interpret the scriptures at your own lusts and pleasures, as your law-master of Rome hath done afore your time" (444). When Bale complains about the two enemies who corrupted Part I of the *Image*, he cites two different types of corrupters—those who visibly erred (the printers) and the mysterious blasphemer who corrupted the text. Thus Bale finds both a literal and a spiritual corruption in his own text, which parallels the double working of the Antichrist as typified in the workings of Mohamet and the Pope.

Bale's emphasis upon the unseen nature of the beast—the spiritual corruption of Satan's church—explains in part why he used the term "image" to describe both churches. Both churches have a literal or carnal side, and they also both have a spiritual side. Bale describes the false spirituality of the wicked city/church:

For spiritually is their city called. A glorious name usurp they, as though they were none of the world. They will be called the holy church. . . . And therefore the Spirit of God doth judge here this great city not to be called Jerusalem, but stinking Sodom, and most miserable Egypt. (392–393)

As noted above, Augustine speaks of the image of the beast as standing for pretence, and when Bale speaks of the "image" of the Antichrist's church, he is often describing the false ceremonies and shows of the Roman Catholic church, or the superstition of the Jews. At the same time, however, the church of God has an image. This is not associated with pretence, of course, but with the dim reflection that is all we are able to see, because of the difficulty of discerning truth here on earth. This dim reflection of God's church is seen most clearly not through the model of earthly institutions, but through the text of the Bible itself.[33] In the *Image* Bale presents an arena for controlled interpretation —for a

---

33. Ibid., 63. King explains Bale's use of the term *image*: "The title implies that the problem of discrimination between images of truth and falsehood is central to the Reformation. Guided by faith, the elect Christian reader should see in Revelation his own individual history and the history of mankind. The scriptures offer an image of the divine, an image of past human history, and an image of one's own personal condition."

progression from the letter to the spirit that will provide for the people of God the clearest possible image of the glory to come.

Yet Bale's efforts in the *Image* betray his fear that it is difficult to understand the nature of Revelation at all, and he notes several times, as does Augustine (e.g., *Civ.* 20,17), that John's language is difficult, and that he often repeats in a different way something he has already said. And even when Bale attempts to present his readers with a proper interpretive text, he is besieged by problems with the printers and enemies, which he uses as evidence that both the seen and the unseen elements of the beast are at work at all times to frustrate the efforts of honest Christians.

Bale's view of exegesis is often misunderstood because of his seemingly inconsistent view toward prophecy. Paul Christianson writes that

> Holy history provided the framework for [Bale's] exegesis, but the mystery of unlocking sacred tropes preserved Bale from too direct an application of specific prophecies to individual historical events. The chronology mattered most, not the minute details. . . . [C]aught up in the task of convincing his compatriots that they lived under the mantle of the false church, Bale sometimes ignored his own dictum and descended to specifics.[34]

This statement fails to recognize that there is an essential difference between the way that Bale views past history and future history. He is very cautious when interpreting Revelation in terms of future events—a caution no less marked than Augustine's in Book 20 of the *City of God*. Only when interpreting events of the past does Bale "descend to specifics," and this use of specific historical events to support his theories is all practiced under the mantle of the two churches, where any number of historical moments can be used to support the view that there have been two churches from the beginning, progressing through time toward the destined end that is suggested in Revelation, but never quite understood because of the limited nature of interpretation on earth.

The problems that Bale himself faced while attempting to spread the Word of God are, in his view, typical of the human condition. The difficulty in interpretation is a product of the fallen world and of the history that results. Bale, like Augustine, is ambiguous on the point of how much is legible in this saeculum, but both men speak of the enjoyment of heaven in terms of the revelation of hidden meaning (a model taken from Revelation itself). Bale describes heavenly felicity as an exegetical revelation for the saints:

---

34. Christianson, *Reformers and Babylon*, 16.

Their senses were opened, and great knowledge had they in the scriptures. The figures and prophecies that were hid to others were manifest and open unto them. The dark veil was removed from Moses' face, and the light of the laws appeared. They could then discern good from evil, light from darkness, and sweet from sour. The yoke was then taken from them, and no longer were they subject to strangers. Dead men perceived the secrets of the book. (565)

In this passage, Bale uses allegory to explain the revelation of hidden meaning after the judgment, just as he had used the symbol of the key of David earlier to explain the role of exegesis. Bale's method of exegesis informs his practice as a writer in general—specifically his use of allegory. Many critics have had occasion to propose that Bale's own use of language was divided between "figurative" and "plain." Andrew Hadfield writes that a

> binary opposition between "true" and "false" is stated as the key to Bale's reading; language can be divided as easily as martyrs, governors and the church. But whilst Bale fulminates against the use of "figurative speech", he is seemingly blind to his own use of metaphor to establish the distinction between the literal and the figurative, i.e., the key of David opening the door.[35]

I would agree with Hadfield that Bale divides language as he does everything else, but would emphasize that Bale's division is not in this case a simple distinction between "figurative" and "plain" language. Because both churches have spiritual components, Bale distinguishes between two types of spiritualities and interpretations. Allegory can be used effectively if it is directed toward the purpose of educating the true believers on the nature of their church. Bale is opposed to the employment of allegory that does not clarify the message but instead obscures it, yet the key of David is just the opposite—it is the sort of allegory of which Bale approves because he divides his language not between figurative and plain, but according to how each church uses each type of language.

Hadfield calls Bale's project in the *Image* an attempt to "produce a text that, in Roland Barthes's terms, has been 'already read' because all answers are known in advance; all meaning has become confined to an allegorical code which cannot be challenged."[36] This allegorical code directs the reader toward two stable signifieds—which are the two churches. Any of Bale's exegetical movements can be reduced, or enlarged, to fit into this paradigm. Yet the very

---

35. A. Hadfield, *Literature, Politics and National Identity* (Cambridge: Cambridge University Press, 1994) 67.

36. Ibid., 68.

difficulty of Bale's project suggests that he knew only too well that language resists stable signification that could help to identify these still intermingled churches. Indeed, he takes the very multiplicity of the beasts as a sign that meanings are multiple, and not completely discernible by human comprehension. Therefore, no matter what Bale does interpret, he is careful not to stray far from the letter, and so when he provides a commentary on Revelation, he includes the entire text, verse by verse. In the Augustinian scheme, this movement from letter to spirit is the pilgrimage of the faithful, who still live in the world where both cities are intermingled. And despite Bale's rather different interpretation of Revelation, he does remain true to Augustinian thought in his practice of an exegetical method that looks for a movement from the letter to the spirit throughout an entire history that can be read as a seamless story of two opposing communities in a drama directed by Providence.

THE *CITIE OF GOD* (1610) AND THE LONDON VIRGINIA COMPANY

Mark Vessey

Introduction: An English *City of God*

That most glorious society and celestiall Citty of Gods faithfull, which is partly seated in the course of these declining times, *wherein he that liueth by faith,* is a Pilgrim amongst the wicked; and partly in that solid estate of eternitie, which as yet the other part doth paciently expect, vntill *righteousnesse be turned into iudgment,* being then by the proper excellence to obtaine the last victorie, and be crowned in perfection of peace; haue I vndertaken to defend in this worke: which I intend vnto you (my deerest *Marcellinus*) as being your due by my promise, and exhibite it against all those that prefer their false gods before this Cities founder: The worke is great and difficult, but God the maister of all difficulties is our helper.

The making of this sentence English, and with it the twenty-two books that follow to the author's final Amen, was virtually complete by spring of the year 1610. A few months later the printed sheets for a volume in folio came off a press in London's Fleet Lane, a stone's throw from the city wall. The title page read:

For invaluable help in the research for this essay and many a detective hint I warmly thank my friend and former student Doug Brigham, now of the University of British Columbia Library.

St. / AVGVSTINE, / OF THE CITIE OF GOD: / WITH THE LEARNED / COMMENTS / OF / IO. LOD. VIVES. / Englished by J. H. / [Emblem] / Printed by GEORGE ELD. / 1610.[1]

The emblem depicted a face skied in cloud, from which rays shot down to a troubled sea, with the legend: SIC. AVGVSTINVS. DISSIPABIT. A similar device had appeared on a medal struck thirty years earlier to commemorate the dispersal of the Spanish Armada; there, the cloudy power was identified by the tetragrammaton and a verse with biblical overtones: FLAVIT ET DISSIPATI SUNT ("[The Almighty] breathed and they were scattered").[2] Turning the page, the reader of this new volume found the following letter of dedication:

> To the Honorablest Patron of Muses and Good Mindes, Lord William Earle of Penbroke [sic], Knight of the Honourable Order, &c.

> Right gracious and gracefull Lord, your late imaginary, but now actuall Trauailer, then to most-conceited *Viraginia,* now to almost-concealed *Virginia*; then a light, but not lewde, now a sage and allowed translator; then of a scarse knowne nouice, now a famous *Father*; then of a deuised Country scarse on earth, now of a desired *Citie* sure in heauen; then of *Vtopia,* now of *Eutopia*; not as by testament, but as a testimonie of gratitude, obseruance, and hearts-honour to your Honor, bequeathed at hence-parting (thereby scarse perfecting) this his translation at the imprinting to your Lordships protecting. He, that against detraction beyond expectation, then found your sweete patronage in a matter of small moment, without distrust or disturbance in this worke of more worth, more weight, as he approoued his more abilitie, so would not but expect your Honours more acceptance.

> Though these be *Church-men,* and this a *Church-matter,* he vnapt, or vnworthy to holde trafique with either; yet heere *Saint Augustine,* and his Commenter *Viues*; most sauour of the secular: and the one accordingly to *Marcellinus,* the other to our *King Henry,* directed their dedications; and as translators are onely tyed, to haue, and giue, true vnderstanding: so are they freer then the authors to sute themselues a Patrone. Which as to *Scipio,* the staffe and stay, the type and top of that *Cornelian* stemme, [marginal note: *Cic. in Brut.*] *in quam, vt plura genera in unam arborem, videtur insita multorum illuminata sapientia,* your poore *Pacuuius, Terence,* or *Ennius,*

---

1. *A Short-Title Catalogue* [hereafter STC] *of Books Printed in England, Scotland, and Ireland and of English Books Printed Abroad 1475–1640,* ed. A. W. Pollard, G. R. Redgrave and K. F. Pantzer, 2nd ed. (London: Bibliographical Society, 1976–91) no. 916. I have used a reproduction by University Microfilms Inc. of a copy in the Cambridge University Library (Syn 4.61.27).

2. C. Martin and G. Parker, *The Spanish Armada* (London: Hamilton, 1988) 14. Cf. Ps 17,15 (LXX): "et intonuit de caelo Dominus et Altissimus dedit vocem suam . . . et misit sagittas et dissipavit eos."

(or what you list, so he be yours) thought most conuenient to consecrate. Wherefore his legacie laide at your Honours feete, is rather here deliuered to your Honours humbly thrise-kissed hands by his poore delegate,

Your Lordships true-deuoted,

Th. Th.[3]

This preface contains several puzzles, some of which, as we shall see, can be solved by referring to other publications of the time. The biggest puzzle is what it omits. For the obsequious dedicator gives no clue why anyone would wish to publish an English version of Augustine's *ingens opus,* with an elaborate apparatus of notes, in 1610. The London presses were hardly groaning under the weight of patristic translations in the early years of King James I. Far from it. The only substantial work of the kind then in print was Meredith Hanmer's rendering of Eusebius and other Greek ecclesiastical historians, first published in 1577 and recently reissued. A small-format edition of Gregory the Great's *Dialogues* in English with other texts appended (including the chapter on miracles from Book 22 of *De civitate dei*) began circulating in Recusant circles in 1608, but that was no more a publishing precedent for the present work than the labored version of the *Enchiridion ad Laurentium* issued in London in 1607. No major work of Augustine had appeared in England in English since the mid-sixteenth century, and there was to be no significant Latin edition of any of his writings made in that country until 1631. When the *Confessions* came out in English in 1620, it did so by the offices a Recusant translator, Tobie Matthew, and from an overseas press. In sum, there was nothing in the record of English publishing of the Fathers before 1610 to prepare the way for the *Citie of God* or to make it likely that a printer would now lay out money on such a venture.[4]

George Eld had acquired various stock since setting up shop in 1604.[5] He had invested in play-texts by Christopher Marlowe, Thomas Middleton, and William Shakespeare, and in a series of histories of modern European nations.

---

3. Sig. B1r-v.

4. W. P. Haugaard, "Renaissance Patristic Scholarship and Theology in Sixteenth-Century England," *Sixteenth Century Journal* 10 (1979): 37–60; M. Vessey, "English Translations of the Latin Fathers, 1517–1611," in *The Reception of the Church Fathers in the West,* ed. I. Backus, 2 vols. (Leiden: E. J. Brill, 1997) 2.777–835; *Augustinian Studies* 24 (1993) 164–66. An edition of Augustine's *De haeresibus* was published at Oxford in 1631 as an appendix to the *Commonitorium* of Vincent of Lérins (below, n. 21).

5. STC iii.58.

From time to time he printed sermons. Augustine was a new undertaking for him. Whether he profited by it is impossible to say at this distance; even if quickly bought up, a property as singular as the *Citie of God* would be unlikely to generate sequels. Probably the first edition sold steadily over the years. In 1620 Eld and his partner Miles Flesher were ready, or induced, to bring out a second, in view of which (we are told) J. H.'s translation was "compared with the Latine Originall, and in very many places corrected and amended."[6] Close collation of the two editions would perhaps bear out this claim; on a cursory inspection I find nothing to support it. The whole text was, however, reset and the riddling preface of 1610 replaced by a much longer, more earnest letter of dedication, addressed jointly to William Herbert, his brother Philip, Earl of Montgomery, and his brother-in-law Thomas, Earl of Arundel. The writer, William Crashaw, loses no time in justifying the project: "As Man amongst creatures, and the Church amongst men, and the Fathers in the Church, and S. *Augustine* amongst the Fathers, so amongst the many precious volumes, and in the rich store-house of his workes, his bookes of the City of God, haue a speciall preheminence . . . for as in his other labors, he went before other men, so in this he exceeded himselfe; in so much as not onely for excellency of Diuinity, but for variety of all learning, it is called and esteemed A Storehouse of knowledge." Crashaw celebrates Augustine as a slayer of heretical monsters. His own doctrinal errors are "few, and not fundamentall." Where he seems to give comfort to the Papists, it is likely that the texts have been "forged anew" in the "Romish forge"—in other words, fraudulently altered. His biblical scholarship is sound, excellent in fact for his time, his holiness beyond doubt. And so to business:

> His Workes are of such excellent matter, as some of them are not onely translated into many vulgar tongues, but which is rare, and the like seldome knowne, into Greeke also. This worke of the *Citie of God* was long ago translated into French. I saw not therefore any reason why it should be denied to our English people, so many desiring it as did daily: Wherefore I set one about it, who if he had time enough (for he is now with God) wanted not I am sure, neither will nor skill to doe it well. And now that our Brittish World hath it, seeing many in France thanked *Maldonat* though a Iesuit, for perswading *Gentian Hervet* to put it into French, I neede not doubt but many in this Island will thanke him that was the meanes of putting it into English.[7]

---

6. *Saint Augustine of the Citie of God: with the learned comments of Io. Lodovicus Vives. Englished first by J. H. And now in this second edition compared*, etc. (STC 917).

7. Sig. ¶3r-v.

On this evidence, the motives for publishing an English *City of God* were two: esteem for Augustine's works (especially the *De civitate dei*) as a repository of humane learning and correct divinity, and a patriotic desire to make English for a Protestant nation what was already accessible in the vernacular to those under the Roman yoke. While there is no reason to impugn the sincerity of either motive, we may doubt whether they fully account for the anomaly of the 1610 edition. Enlarging on hints from the 1620 preface, the present essay offers a more circumstantial view of the matter.

"The Authors Owne Booke": Of Romish Forgeries and English Reformation

When Jean Mabillon presented the Maurist edition of the *Opera Augustini* to Louis XIV in 1679, he gave the impression that the *City of God* had been the apanage of French monarchs from the time of Charlemagne,[8] conveniently forgetting that the best previous edition of that work had been dedicated by a Spaniard, Juan Luis Vivès, to Henry VIII of England. Vivès's edition, undertaken at the prompting of Erasmus and published by Johannes Froben at Basel in 1522, was equipped with philological and antiquarian notes, the fruit (as the editor complained) of infinite pains.[9] It is Vivès, in his preface to King Henry,[10] who speaks of the *De civitate dei* as a "treasury" or "storehouse" of ancient learning, commending its author as a "light . . . and pillar to the Christian Commonwealth" (*specimen columenque reipublicae Christianae*) and assimilating his cause to Henry's as defender of the faith against Luther: "For as you wrote for that better Rome against Babilon, so Saint *Augustine* against Babilon defended that ancient, christian and holier Rome."[11] Text and commentary were reprinted many times. In 1572 both appeared in a French translation by Gentian Hervet, an accomplished humanist and editor of the Greek Fathers who had assisted Cardinal Pole at the Council of Trent.[12] By

---

8. *Sancti Aurelii Augustini Hipponensis episcopi operum tomus primus* (Paris, 1679) sig. ã4r-v.

9. See the notice on Vivès in *Contemporaries of Erasmus: A Biographical Register of the Renaissance and Reformation,* ed. P. G. Bietenholz and T. B. Deutscher (Toronto: University of Toronto Press, 1985–87) 3.411–12.

10. Conveniently repr. in PL 47.435–38.

11. Ibid., 437–38, as translated in the 1620 edition of the English *Citie of God,* sig. A1r.

12. *Saint Augustin de la Cité de Dieu . . . Illustrée des commentaires de Iean Louis Viues ... Le tout faict Françoys par Gentian Heruet . . . Et enrichy de plusieurs annotations . . . par François de Belle-Forest* (Paris, 1572). The prefatory matter in this and subsequent editions is programmatically anti-Protestant. On the "Maldonat" named by Crashaw as inspirer of the translation, i.e.,

then the commentary was subject to censorship, its author's impatience with scholastic theology having earned it a place on the *Index Expurgatorius*. How far the censor's proscriptions were followed in this case need not concern us here. It is sufficient to note that in the eyes of one English theologian of a Calvinist turn of mind, zealous to uphold the Reformation in his country after the turn of the century, the purging of Vivès's Augustine represented a gross instance of "Romish" forgery.

William Crashaw of Handsworth, near Sheffield, deserves better than to be remembered as the father of a poet capable of rhyming "they say" with "Teresia."[13] Neglected by the *Cambridge Bibliography of English Literature* and *Oxford Dictionary of the Christian Church* alike, he survives in his writings as a resourceful and energetic, if at times longwinded, member of the distinguished band of Protestant divines whose works helped pave the broken way from Thomas Cranmer to John Milton. Crashaw graduated Bachelor in Divinity from St. John's College, Cambridge, in 1603 and was soon afterwards appointed preacher at the London Inns of Court. His first printed work, dedicated to the Societies of the Inner and Middle Temples and published in London in 1606, is entitled in English: "The first booke of the first tome" of *Romish forgeries and falsifications: together with catholike restitutions* "obserued, collected, and now discouered for the vse and honour of the Catholike Church, and to the iust rebuke of the Romish Sinagogue . . . set forth in Latine and English for the use of the English Reader, whether he be a true Catholike or a Romish."[14] An epigraph from the Apocalypse and a facing Latin epigram comparing the pope to the emperor Nero set the tone. The dedication and two "large" prefaces announce "the beginning of a great Worke,"[15] in which, by painstaking collation of printed editions, it will be shown how the "Romish" party has "corrupted all the Authors of this last two hundred years"— notably those from which Protestants might otherwise prove the catholicity of

---

the Spanish Jesuit scholar Juan de Maldonato, see the notice in the *Dictionnaire de théologie catholique* and, for the Erasmian quality of his humanism, J. W. O'Malley, *The First Jesuits* (Cambridge: Harvard University Press, 1993) 259.

13. Richard Crashaw, "The Flaming Heart: Upon the book and picture of the seraphical Saint Teresa, as she is usually expressed with a seraphim beside her," lines 5–6, in *Steps to the Temple*, published in 1646 shortly after the author's reception into the Roman Catholic church. On the father see the *Dictionary of National Biography* and P. J. Wallis, "The Library of William Crashawe," *Transactions of the Cambridge Bibliographical Society* 2.3 (1956): 213–28.

14. STC 6014.

15. Sig. ¶3r.

their doctrines—"yea and razed the records of higher antiquitie reaching vp to some that liued 500. and 800. years ago, taking out words and whole sentences, adding to, and altering at their pleasure in some one booke four or fiue hundred places," with the result, says Crashaw, affecting to address his "beloued Countreymen, the seduced Papists of England," that "you good soules haue a book so gelded, and clipped, and chopped, thrust vpon you as the Authors owne booke, who if he liued would refuse it as none of his."[16] The 800-year limit comfortably excludes the period of the Church Fathers as the English Reformers since Jewell had defined it.[17] Although Crashaw is in no doubt that the Papists are also guilty of adulterating patristic texts, he is content to leave that demonstration to others.[18] His own immediate concern is with the *recentiores,* especially writers of the previous century. This first book of his projected first tome will deal with the "falsification and restitution" of the commentaries of the German theologian Johannes Ferus[19] on the First Epistle of St. John. Books 2 through 5 would take up Ferus's other commentaries on the New Testament, Books 6 through 9 certain works by other writers, and Book 10 *"Ludouicus Vives* his Comment. vpon Augustine *de Ciuitate Dei."* That is as far as Crashaw commits himself, "not doubting but others (whose leasure is as much, and Libraries larger, and reading greater then mine) will go on, and annexe a second Tome, and so forward, till in our *restoring* we haue ouertaken them [i.e., the Papists] in their *corrupting."*[20]

Even in an age of electronic text-processing, Crashaw's scheme for unexpurgating the library of modern Christian classics sounds alarmingly grandiose. Small wonder that he got no further than the restitution of Ferus on 1 John. A contemporary and parallel enterprise by Thomas James, first Bodleian librarian, for a large-scale collation of printed editions of the Fathers against ancient manuscripts, similarly foundered for want of manpower and financial

---

16. Sig. E3v.

17. S. L. Greenslade, *The English Reformers and the Fathers of the Church* (Oxford: Clarendon Press, 1960).

18. "See what cause we haue to suspect that they haue corrupted the *Fathers* also, seeing that they haue not spared some as ancient as some Fathers" (sig. Cr), i.e., according to a more generous definition of the patristic age.

19. Johann Wild, 1494–1554, a Franciscan of Mainz, known for his preaching and biblical exegesis. Crashaw collates the text of his commentary on 1 John printed at Antwerp in 1556 with the "expurgated" Roman edition of 1577.

20. Sig. B3v.

support.[21] Like James, Crashaw seems at one time to have hoped for royal support. A manuscript headed "A discoverye of popyshe corruption requiring a kingely reformation," now in the British Library, is said to contain a prospectus for further work along lines sketched in the *Romish Forgeries* and an appeal to the King for a royal commission to undertake it.[22] Nothing came of the initiative. Thus was the English public deprived of the bulk of Crashaw's castigations of the "Romish" editions of Ferus and the rest, to be blessed instead, a year or two later, with a vernacular edition of the *De civitate dei* containing a full and (presumably) unexpurgated set of the notes that should have been the subject of Book 10 of the first tome of the *Romish Forgeries*.[23]

But by what logic could the abandonment of one project have led to the prosecution of the other? The issuing of an English version of the "original" of Vivès's notes on the *City of God* was clearly consistent with Crashaw's desire to lay the authentic records of Catholic Christianity before his compatriots. Yet there is no hint in the *Romish Forgeries* that the Spaniard's (antiquarian, historico-philological) commentary on a patristic text was to take precedence over theological commentaries on Scripture, such as those of Ferus and others, or that the doctrinal content of the *City of God* itself was so important

---

21. See James's *Treatise of the corruption of scripture, councels, and fathers, by the prelats, of the Church of Rome* (1611) and the *Explanation or enlarging of the ten articles in the supplication of doctor James, lately exhibited to the clergy of England* (1625), with N. R. Ker, "Thomas James's Collation of Gregory, Cyprian, and Ambrose," *Bodleian Library Record* 4 (1952–53): 16–30. In preparation for this work, James compiled a catalogue of the manuscript collections of Oxford and Cambridge, the *Ecloga Oxonio-Cantabrigiensis,* to which Crashawe refers in the *Romish Forgeries* (sig. Cv). The edition of Augustine's *De haeresibus* mentioned above (n. 4) is a product of his Oxford atelier.

22. Wallis, "Library of William Crashawe," 216–17. The petitioner "claimed to prove 5000 falsifications in ten authors, but complained that he had insufficient time and means to complete his list" (217). The document (MS Royal 17.b.ix) is undated; Wallis places it ca. 1609.

23. Traces of Crashaw's project of textual restitution can also be found in his *Sermon preached at the crosse* (St. Paul's Cross in London) on February 14, 1607/8, printed with full apparatus of citations in 1608 and again the next year (STC 6027–6028). Taking for his text Jer 51,9 ("We would have cured Babel, but shee would not be healed"), he sets out to show "[t]he XX. wounds found to be in the body of the present Romish religion, in doctrine and in manners." In a preface to the reader, he flatters himself that he has "forged no new Author . . . falsified none . . . corrupted none ... to [his] knowledge misalledged none" (sig. *1r). When he claims (59) that the situation of the Romish Babylon is "the worse because [the Pope] hath razed out manie sentences, and passages out of manie Authors, wherin he thought himselfe and his seate to be wronged," a marginal note lists "Ludou. vives: Ferus, Erasmus, Stella, Oleaster[,] Espencaeus and infinite others." There is a similar list at *Romish Forgeries,* sig. ¶4v. Oleaster, Vivaldus and Erasmus are cited severally in the *Sermon,* but not Vivès .

to the anti-Roman party as to require a full translation. In the 1620 preface Crashaw claims that the Papists had misrepresented Augustine's teaching on purgatory,[24] but it is hard to believe that the huge labor of the 1610 translation was designed merely to set the record straight on that score. Why then, in the words of the same preface, did Crashaw see fit to "set one about" the task of translation? And why, if it is true, were there "so many desiring it as did daily"? At this point it may be helpful to return to the preface of 1610 and try to solve some of its puzzles.

"Your Late Imaginary Travailer": The Adventures of J. H.

The name of William Crashaw does not appear in the preliminaries to the 1610 edition, responsibility for which is shared by the obscure translator (J. H.), the noble patron (W. H.), and the pun-loving intermediary (Th. Th.). No mystery need here surround William Herbert, Third Earl of Pembroke. Nephew of Sir Philip Sidney, he was (in Aubrey's words) "the greatest Maecenas to learned men of any peer of his time or since" and the recipient of literary dedications from all and sundry.[25] Th. Th. is the London stationer Thomas Thorpe, publisher in the previous year with George Eld of William Shakespeare's *Sonnets,* cryptically dedicated to their "onlie begetter" Mr. W. H., who has sometimes been identified with the third Earl of Pembroke.[26]

---

24. Sigs. ¶3r-v. Note esp. the following insinuation: "But to doe right to this holy Father, and the truth it selfe; it is more likely hee is wronged, and his workes corrupted, and altered since he died, for else it is impossible so wise a man as he should be so contrary to himselfe." In the same year as the first edition of the *Citie of God,* Thomas Morton, Dean of Gloucester, published an *Encounter against M. Parsons* (Robert Parsons, the Jesuit controversialist) in which he handled inter alia "the generall fraude of [the Roman Catholic] church, in corrupting of authors," and offered "a performance of the challenge, which Mr. Parsons made, for the examining of sixtie Fathers, cited by Coccius for proofe of purgatorie; to shew thirtie one of them to haue beene either apocrypha, or corrupted, or wrested" (title-page). Both Crashaw and James are known to have assisted Morton during this controversy; P. Milward, *Religious Controversies of the Jacobean Age: A Survey of Printed Sources* (Lincoln: University of Nebraska Press, 1978) 82–86, 154–56.

25. M. Brennan, *Literary Patronage in the English Renaissance: The Pembroke Family* (London: Routledge Press, 1988) 152–76.

26. The case is now powerfully put by K. Duncan-Jones in her Arden edition of the *Sonnets* (London: Thomas Nelson, 1997) 53–69 . The dedication reads: "TO. THE. ONLIE. BEGETTER. OF. / THESE. INSUING. SONNETS. / Mr. W.H. ALL. HAPPINESSE. / AND THAT ETERNITIE. / PROMISED. / BY. / OVR. EVER-LIVING. POET. / WISHETH. / THE. WELL-WISHING. / ADVENTURER. IN. / SETTING. / FORTH.// T.T." Noting that the *Sonnets* were entered in the Stationers' Register in the same week that the Earl of Pembroke was incorporated as a member of the Virginia Company of London, Duncan-Jones expounds the text thus: "While

Thorpe's main business of the decade to 1610 had been with English poetry and plays by the likes of Christopher Marlowe, John Marston, Ben Jonson, and George Chapman.[27] From 1609 onward he also seems to have had a stake in the writings of a certain John Healey, J. H. of the title page of Augustine's *Citie of God.*

A rendering by Healey of Joseph Hall's utopian satire *Mundus alter et idem,* englished as *The discovery of a new world, or a description of the South Indies,* was entered for publication in the Stationers' Register by Thorpe in January of 1609 and printed, like the *Sonnets* and *Citie of God,* by George Eld;[28] it is the context for many of the lesser riddles of the first paragraph of the preface to the latter work. In a prefatory letter signed "I. H." Healey had dedicated the *Discovery* to the Earl of Pembroke, and spoken of himself as a "traueller that neuer trauelled."[29] Hall's fiction took its narrator to a *terra australis incognita,* one of whose regions, ruled over by women, appeared on the latest maps as Viraginia or New Gynia, "which others incorrectly call Guinea."[30] In Healey's version this country became "[t]he new discouered *Womandecoia,* (which some mistaking both name and nation call *Wingandecoia,* & make it a part of *Virginia*) otherwise called *Shee-landt.*"[31] Hall apparently took offence at Healey's translation of his work, a fact which may explain Thorpe's later reference (in the 1610 preface to *The Citie of God*) to "detraction beyond expectation" and the "sweete patronage" extended by the Earl of Pembroke.[32] Healey seems to have wished Pembroke to receive the dedication of other translations of his,

---

Thorpe was an "adventurer in setting forth" in the sense that he made an investment, and took a risk, in "setting forth", or publishing, "THESE. ENSUING. SONNETS.", Herbert was committed to a much more exciting kind of "setting forth"'"expeditions to explore and colonize the New World."

27. STC iii.168; L. Rostenberg, "Thomas Thorpe, Publisher of 'Shake-Speares Sonnets'," *Papers of the Bibliographical Society of America* 54 (1960): 16–37. Thorpe and Eld were also responsible, in 1612, for the printing of *A Funeral Elegy* by W.S., recently (and controversially) attributed to Shakespeare.

28. STC 12686; ed. in quasi-facsimile by H. Brown (Cambridge: Harvard University Press, 1937).

29. Sig. ¶3v.

30. Quoted from the modern (and more accurate) translation of J. M. Wands, *Another World and Yet the Same* (New Haven: Yale University Press, 1981) 57. The best critical treatment of Hall's satire and Healey's version of it is R. A. McCabe, *Joseph Hall: A Study in Satire and Meditation* (Oxford: Clarendon Press, 1982) 73–109, 321–30.

31. Sig. G8v.

32. See also Healey's preface "To the Readers" in the second ed. of the *Discovery* (1613/14), repr. by Brown, 145–49, with McCabe, 329–30, who records that "[t]he *Mundus* itself was virtually disowned by Hall and deliberately excluded . . . from all editions of his collected works."

including one of Epictetus's *Encheiridion* and another of the so-called *Table of Cebes.*[33] In the event, both those works were published by Thorpe (and printed by Eld) in 1610, with a dedication to John Florio, translator of Montaigne's *Essais.*[34] Thorpe implies that Florio had won Pembroke's protection for the *Discovery* and urges him to do so for the new pieces. In the same breath, he hints that some greater work is in the offing: "This *Manuall of Epictetus,* though not *Saint Augustines Enchiridion,* now by hap is the hand, or rather the hand-maide of a greater body of *Saint Augustines.*"[35] We can assume, I think, that this is a reference to the *Citie of God,* by then entrusted by Healey to Thorpe and perhaps already in the press.

Of John Healey, first English translator of the *De civitate dei,* we regrettably know nothing besides what can be gleaned from his published writings and their prefaces. By the time his Augustine appeared in print he had sailed to Virginia; so much we infer from the prefaces of 1610. How long he spent in the new colony is not certain; his name does not appear in any of the extant lists of early planters. He was apparently still alive (and in London?) in 1613/ 14 when he signed a new preface to a second edition of the *Discovery,* but dead by 1616 when Thorpe dedicated a new edition of his Epictetus and Cebes to the Earl of Pembroke as "the bequest of a deceased Man."[36] Most modern summaries of Healey's curriculum vitae are misleading, if not fanciful, and none conveys the least idea of why he should have translated the *City of God.*[37] Four or more years after the translator's death, William Crashaw could publicly claim to have "set [him] about it." Yet, as we have seen, the record of

---

33. So much is stated by Thorpe in his dedication of the second edition of these works (with Healey's translation of Theophrastus's *Characters*) to Pembroke in 1616.

34. *Epictetus his manuall. And Cebes his table. Out of the Greeke originall.* See Rostenberg, "Thomas Thorpe," 25–33, for speculation on Florio's role as a procurer of manuscripts for Thorpe. It is not clear why she takes the *Manuall* to have been published after *The Citie of God.*

35. Sig. A3v.

36. Above, nn. 32–33.

37. The author of Healey's notice in the *Dictionary of National Biography* mysteriously infers that he "was ill, according to a statement of his friend and printer, Thomas Thorpe, in 1609, and was dead in the following year." Others, with no more reason, relate that he died in Virginia. In an article on Hall's *Mundus alter et idem* in *The Gentleman's Magazine* 281 (1896): 82–84, E. A. Petherick tried to identify John Healey the translator with another of that name, son of a Recusant, Richard Healey, servant of Lord Sheffield. This John Healey was held on suspicion of complicity in the Gunpowder Plot: *Calendar of State Papers (Domestic), James I, 1603–10,* 295, 301, 310–13. The translator's connections with the Earl of Pembroke and, more tellingly, with William Crashaw rule out such an identification.

Crashaw's personal interest in Augustine's work scarcely accounts for the commission and in any case his name is not visibly associated with the 1610 edition. Although Thomas Thorpe has sometimes been held to rival Shakespeare's Autolycus as a snapper-up of unconsidered merchandise, that imputation may be unjust.[38] Besides, the English *Citie of God* was no "trifle." Patristic texts were not in George Eld's usual line of business. And there is nothing in John Healey's other works to suggest that he himself was specially devoted to Augustine. To put the riddle again: What possible *interest* could Healey, Eld, Thorpe, Crashaw, or anyone else have had in procuring a translation of the *De civitate dei* at this time? Having exhausted other lines of inquiry, let us glance after our "now actuall Trauailer . . . to almost-concealed Virginia."

"The Erecting of a Great Cittie" and the Printing of John Smith's *True Relation*

After an abortive attempt to plant a colony during the reign of the Virgin Queen herself, the English settlement of Virginia was put on a new footing under James I with the granting in April 1606 of a charter setting up two companies under the direction of a royal council.[39] At the end of the year, the London Virginia Company sent out an expeditionary fleet commanded by Captain Christopher Newport. "[A]fter many crosses in the downes by tempests," wrote one of those on board,

> wee arriued safely vppon the Southwest part of the great Canaries: within foure or fiue daies after we set saile for Dominica[.] [T]he 26. of Aprill [i.e., in 1607]: the first land we made, wee fell with Cape Henry, the verie mouth of the Bay of Chissiapiacke, which at that present we little expected . . . . And arriuing at the place where wee are now seated, the Counsell was

---

38. See now Duncan-Jones (above, n. 26) 36.

39. Though in some respects superseded, the fullest calendar and edition of documents relating to the activity of the Virginia Company in its first decade remains that of A. Brown, *The Genesis of the United States: A Narrative of the Movement in England, 1605–16,* 2 vols. (London: Houghton, Mifflin & Co., 1890). Also still valuable, subject to caution, is the narrative in his *The First Republic in America* (Boston: Houghton, Mifflin, & Co., 1898). Critically superior, but less comprehensive even for the years it covers, is P. L. Barbour, *The Jamestown Voyages under the First Charter 1606–1609,* 2 vols. (Cambridge: Cambridge University Press, 1969). A useful selection of documents can be found in *New American World: A Documentary History of North America to 1612,* ed. D. B. Quinn (New York: Arno Press, 1979) 5.159–358. The works of Captain John Smith are now to be consulted in the edition by P. L. Barbour, 3 vols. (Chapel Hill: University of North Carolina Press, 1986).

sworne . . . [and there] was made choice for our scituation, a verie fit place for the erecting of a great cittie.[40]

The "great cittie," then and long afterward little more than a fort, was named for King James. The writer of this account, the first *printed* narrative of the new settlement, was Captain John Smith, a future president of the council in Virginia and one of the infant colony's most colorful and controversial figures. In later years Smith would carefully supervise the printing of his own version of events,[41] but he was still thousands of miles away in the autumn of 1608 when the lines just quoted were sent to press by William Welby, a London stationer who in years to come would run up quite a list of publications for the Virginia Company. Variants of the title-page of the *True Relation,* as it was called, show that the publishers initially mistook the author's identity. The muddle is explained in a preface "To the Courteous Reader," in which Smith's first editor (as in effect he was) compares himself to "an vnskilful actor . . . hauing by misconstruction of his right Cue, ouer-slipt himselfe, in beginning of a contrary part."[42] This person claims to have "happen[ed] vpon th[e] relation by chance" and to have published it at the prompting of "diuers well willers of the action."[43] Almost certainly he was "acting" for the Virginia Company, at whose behest he cut Smith's narrative in several places where it spoke of difficulties, and added a suitably ringing conclusion.[44] Thus we hear that when the ship carrying the original text of the *True Relation* sailed for England, it left the author and his fellow colonists

---

40. *A true relation of such occurences and accidents of noate as hath hapned in Virginia since the first planting of that collony, which is now resident in the south part thereof, till the last return from thence* (1608) sig. A3r (STC 22795). For publication details see *Complete Works of Captain John Smith,* ed. P. L. Barbour, 1.116–17. Barbour prints a facsimile of the 1608 edition with facing transcription. I have followed his punctuation of the passage quoted above, but have not marked the excisions he suspects in the text of Smith's original letter.

41. K. J. Hayes, "Defining the Ideal Colonist: Captain John Smith's Revisions from *A True Relation* to the *Proceedings* to the Third Book of the *Generall Historie,*" *Virginia Magazine of History and Biography* 99 (1991) 123–44; M. C. Fuller, *Voyages in Print: English Travel to America, 1576–1624* (Cambridge: Cambridge University Press, 1995) 106–40; D. D. Hall, "The Chesapeake in the Seventeenth Century," in his *Cultures of Print: Essays in the History of the Book* (Amherst: University of Massachusetts Press, 1996) 134–3.

42. Sig. ¶1r.

43. Ibid.

44. This is the opinion of Barbour, which (pace Fuller, 107) I see no reason to dispute. On the editor as constructor of a "transatlantic bridge between writer and reader," see W. C. Spengemann, "John Smith's *True Relation* and the Idea of American Literature," in his *A New World of Words: Redefining American Literature* (New Haven: Yale University Press, 1994) 51–93 at 68.

in good health, all our men wel cõtented, free from mutinies, in loue one with another, & as we hope in a continuall peace with the Indians, where we doubt not but by Gods gracious assistance, and the aduenturers willing minds, and speedie furtherance to so honorable an action in after times, to see our Nation to enioy a Country, not onely exceeding pleasant for habitation, but also very profitable for comerce in general, no doubt pleasing to almightie God, honourable to our gracious Soueraigne, and commodious generally to the whole Kingdome.[45]

The same commercial, nationalist, and religious inducements are listed at the close of the preface, only with greater emphasis on religion. The "end" of the "action" is there said to be "the high glory of God, to the erecting of true religion among Infidells, to the ouerthrow of superstition and idolatrie, to the winning of many thousands of wandring sheepe, vnto Christs fold, who now, and till now, haue strayed in the vnknowne paths of Paganisme, Idolatrie, and superstition."[46] The preface closes with a prayer to "the mighty Iehovah to blesse, prosper, and further" the present enterprise "with his heauenly ayde, and holy assistance."[47]

The note of religious zeal sounded by these editorial additions of 1608 is heard repeatedly in the printed propaganda issued thereafter on behalf of the Virginia Company. In the words of Perry Miller, the literature as a whole exhibits "a set of principles for guiding not a mercantile investment but a medieval pilgrimage."[48] To contemporary eyes, he writes, "the colonizing of Virginia could be no ordinary commercial transaction; it was an act in the economy of redemption, a special and supernatural summons, a maneuver which the wisdom of God had made inevitable from the beginning of time and was now carrying to its foreordained completion."[49] The first and earliest text cited by Miller in support of these generalizations is the one quoted above from the preface to the *True Relation*. In an essay on "Religion and the Virginia Colony, 1609–10," John Parker likewise speaks of a "great crusade."[50] Reviewing the

---

45. Sig. E4v.

46. Sig. ¶1v.

47. Sig. ¶2r.

48. P. Miller, "The Religious Impulse in the Founding of Virginia: Religion and Society in the Early Literature," *William & Mary Quarterly*, 3rd ser., 5 (1948): 492–522.

49. Ibid., 504.

50. J. Parker, "Religion and the Virginia Colony, 1609–10," in *The Westward Enterprise: English Activities in Ireland, the Atlantic, and America 1480–1650*, ed. K. R. Andrews, N. P. Canny, and P. E. Hair (Liverpool: Liverpool University Press, 1978) 245–70, at 270.

documentary evidence for religious motivation among promoters and planters of the colony in the eighteen months after the grant of the first charter, he observes that "[n]o published statement made public the Company's plans or intentions in 1606 or 1607," adding: "That changed in 1608 with Captain John Smith's *A True Relation*."[51] According to Parker, the new public insistence on the religious aspect of the Virginia colonization anticipated a change in the way the Company's work would be advertised after its privatization under the second charter of May 1609. In fact, the crusading spirit seems to have been abroad well before then.

The man who, like an "vnskilfull actor," first delivered John Smith's lines to the London public, signed himself "I. H." Editing the *True Relation* for the Hakluyt Society in 1969, Philip L. Barbour developed a suggestion already made by other scholars and identified I. H. as John Healey. The grounds for the attribution, considered by Barbour to be "all but conclusive," were (1) "Healey's interest in the New World, as shown in his translation of Bishop Joseph Hall's *Mundus Alter et Idem*," (2) his travelling to Virginia himself in 1610, and (3) his association with Thomas Thorpe, a known supporter of the colony.[52] To these we may now add (4) Healey's association with the Reverend William Crashaw, one of the most fervent of the Virginia colony's many clerical promoters, and (5) his translating the *City of God*, probably at Crashaw's prompting.

It is likely that William Crashaw was already interested in the Virginia enterprise by the time of the first expedition of 1606–1607. One of the original planters, auspiciously named Ralegh Crashaw, may have been a relative of his. The name of "William Crashaw, Clerk, Batchelor of Divinity" appears in a class of its own, immediately after those of the noblemen, knights, doctors, captains, and the sheriff of London, ahead of the esquires, in the list of persons receiving the charter of 1609.[53] He therefore had a financial stake in the colony. In February 1610 he preached a sermon for the Company in the presence of the newly appointed Governor for Virginia, the text of which was duly printed by William Welby; it contains a strenuous apology for the religious and patriotic aims of the settlement.[54] He is also thought to have had a hand in another

---

51. Ibid., 250.

52. Barbour, *Jamestown Voyages*, 1.168.

53. Brown, *Genesis*, 1.214.

54. Below, n. 77.

publication of the Company from the same year, entitled *A true and sincere declaration of the purpose and ends of the plantation begun in Virginia.* "At any rate," remarks Louis B. Wright, "shortly afterward Crashaw was serving as a sort of director of publicity for the company."[55] He wrote prefaces for two pamphlets published to promote the colony in 1613[56] and assisted in the preparation of John Smith's 1612 *Map of Virginia.*[57] His involvement with the Company's affairs can be traced as late as 1620.[58]

"Our Brittish World": Augustine's City in England's Empire

By triangulating the several kinds of circumstantial evidence adduced so far, it is possible to suggest a more precise, albeit still hypothetical, location for Healey's *Citie of God.*

In an effort to reach a fuller understanding of the work's appearance in 1610 than its enigmatic preface would seem to promise, we first took bearings from two other texts: the 1620 preface to the second edition, where William Crashaw offers the new translation as a general boon "to our English people" and the same writer's 1606 *Romish Forgeries* where he speaks of collating editions of Vivès's commentary "vpon Augustine *de Ciuitate Dei.*" Although lines drawn from each of those texts could be seen to intersect in the area of the 1610 *Citie of God,* it was not obvious that they led to its conceptual centre. We therefore took a third sighting, this time on Virginia, and found that John Healey and William Crashaw both had interests there as early as 1608, as did Thomas Thorpe. We saw, moreover, that Crashaw and Healey were both engaged on behalf of the London Virginia Company in a campaign to persuade potential investors and planters that English colonial expansion in the New World was an affair not only of state and commerce but also, even fundamentally, of Christian religion. Combining these data, and considering the potential for neo-imperial readings of the *De civitate dei* in a time of this-wordly

---

55. L. B. Wright, *Religion and Empire: The Alliance Between Piety and Commerce in English Expansion 1558–1625* (Chapel Hill: University of North Carolina Press, 1943; repr. New York, 1965) 100. Wright's chapter on the Virginia colony, entitled "A Western Canaan Reserved for England," anticipates the position taken by Miller in his 1948 article (above, n. 48).

56. Silvester Jourdain's *A plaine description of the Barmudas* (STC 14816) and Alexander Whitaker's *Good newes from Virginia* (STC 25354).

57. Barbour, *Jamestown Voyages,* 2.464.

58. Wallis, "Library of William Crashawe," 215, citing S. M. Kingsbury, *The Records of the Virginia Company of London* (Washington, D.C.: Government Printing Office, 1906–35) 1.370.

utopianism and European colonial expansion,[59] we may now ask whether Augustine was not in some sense coopted by the London Virginia Company. Is it conceivable that among those reputedly "desiring" an English translation of Augustine's "great and difficult" work, some—including perhaps a few of the more influential—thought it a book to stir the hearts or loosen the purse strings of any as yet unwilling to adventure to or for Virginia? Should the *Citie of God,* in other words, be added to the list of works drawn up by John Parker under the title of *Books to Build an Empire?*[60]

So much, I think, can be shown to be not only conceivable but likely. Perry Miller's analysis of the religious arguments for new-world colonization advanced by English preachers and pamphleteers, from John Healey in 1610 to John Donne in 1622, already strongly suggests why a promoter of the Virginia Company might consider that he, and it, had an interest in promulgating Augustine's vision of the society of God's elect on its earthly pilgrimage. The Virginia tracts stress both the visibility of God's design in reserving a country for Protestants and its inscrutability, evinced by the sufferings of the would-be colonists. They make much of biblical precedents for migration and mission, routinely assimilating Virginia to the land of Canaan and the travails of Englishmen to those of the Apostles. They imagine the American wilderness as belonging to the Devil, a realm of evil spirits who delight to sow discord among settlers. They evoke vast narratives of the human race from the time of Adam and Eve, and expound a philosophy of history that "followed as an inevitable corollary from the doctrine of providence."[61] Finally, for all their concern with the practicalities of the present, their perspective is relentlessly eschatological.

Of course, these emphases required no special support from Augustine in 1609; nor indeed were they necessarily consistent with the teaching of the *City of God.* It is perhaps significant that while Miller in his classic study of *The New England Mind* refers consistently to "Augustinian" models of thought and action, in his article on the early preaching of Virginia he speaks only of

---

59. For signs of "political" Augustinianism in the discourses of early modern European colonialism, see A. Pagden, *Lords of All the World: Ideologies of Empire in Spain, Britain and France c. 1500–c.1800* (New Haven: Yale University Press, 1995) passim, and, for the longer tradition of thought, J. W. Schulte Nordholt, *The Myth of the West: America as the Last Empire,* trans. H. H. Rowen (Grand Rapids, Mich.: William B. Eerdmans, 1995).

60. J. Parker, *Books to Build an Empire: A Bibliographical History of English Overseas Interests to 1620* (Amsterdam: N. Israel, 1965). See esp. the chapter on "Preachers and Planters" (192–216), which surveys the major publications on Virginia.

61. Miller, "Religious Impulse," 510.

the workings of Protestant or "Puritan" piety, of "intellectual affinities" with Calvin on the one hand and Loyola on the other. In a more recent and ambitious study, Avihu Zakai places the early propaganda of the Virginia Company in the context of trends in historical and apocalyptic thought that had emerged in the course of the sixteenth century in the writings of such English Protestants as John Bale (author of the *Image of Bothe Churches* and of a "literal" commentary on the Apocalypse) and John Foxe (ecclesiastical historian of the English nation in his *Acts and Monuments*). For Zakai, the keynote of this tradition was a more—that is, less—than Augustinian belief in the possibility of applying biblical prophecy to events of the present age:

> The ultimate achievement of the apocalyptic tradition in England [he writes] was undoubtedly the deep-seated conviction among Protestants and Puritans alike that prophetic revelations constitute the very essence of history. History, therefore, was placed within the sacred dimension of time and prophetic revelations situated within the dimension of history. Consequently, the accepted Augustinian view that an essential gulf divided sacred and profane history, or prophecy and history, was totally abolished in the English apocalyptic tradition. Prophecy became history, and history became prophecy. In other words, historical events were interpreted as the realization of prophetic revelation while divine prophecy was seen as the source for explaining the progress of history.[62]

Some such theory of the interlegibility of history and prophecy can be seen to underwrite the insertion of "America" into English ecclesiastical history.

> [T]o a large extent, the justifications for and the vindications of the Protestant settlement of Virginia and the Puritan migration to New England were based upon the premises of the apocalyptic tradition or upon the apocalyptic interpretation of history. Indeed, it is hard to conceive of the English colonization of America without the apocalyptic dimension according to which the settlement of America was seen as a divine duty to spread the Gospel in remote corners of the world. In the apocalyptic struggle between Christ and Antichrist, or between the true Protestant Church of England and the false Catholic church of Spain and Portugal, the battlefield spread across the Atlantic Ocean to America. The New World increasingly became the stage upon which the rivalry between the European forces of Reformation

---

62. A. Zakai, *Exile and Kingdom: History and Apocalypse in the Puritan Migration to America* (Cambridge: Cambridge University Press, 1992) 56. Zakai's reconstruction of this English "apocalyptic" tradition of historiography is not without problems, e.g., with regard to his understanding of Augustine's theory of prophecy; see the remarks of Gretchen E. Minton at n. 29 in her essay in this volume.

and Counter-Reformation took place. With the migration of the apocalyptic struggle between Christ and Antichrist to the New World, America gradually began to occupy a unique role in the course of sacred, providential history.[63]

Against this background, the conjunction of Crashaw's proof of Romish forgeries with his commission of a *City of God* for "our English people" and "our Brittish World" begins to make sense, as does the patterning of the title page emblem of Healey's translation after a medal commemorating the defeat of the Spanish Armada.

The studies of Miller, Zakai, and others demonstrate that the preaching of the Virginia colony after 1608 created, or rather *presupposed,* a climate of opinion among learned supporters of the enterprise in which a person acquainted, if none too familiar, with Augustine's *City of God* might think of arranging for its translation. And that is probably as much as we need to grant in order to solve the main historical problem posed by the English edition of 1610. We do not have to suppose that the Reverend William Crashaw or any of his associates had expert knowledge of Augustine's theology of history and society, let alone of his complex exegesis of John's Apocalypse. Few people in any age, it is safe to say, have fully assimilated the teachings of the *De civitate dei.* We know Crashaw had made some study of Vivès's commentary by 1606, but that would not oblige him to read Augustine's work in its entirety or even at great length. Though bristling with arguments interestingly comparable to Augustine's, the sermon he preached for the Virginia Company in February 1609 betrays no textual knowledge of the *City of God,* despite the fact (if we take him at his word) that by the time he delivered it he had already set John Healey on his herculean task of translation. The *De civitate dei* may indeed have looked, to some, beguilingly like a book on which to "build an empire." To argue, however, that it served in any direct way as an engine of early English colonialism would be to exceed our information. Rather, it appears that the ideological interests of colonialism were what first brought the

---

63. Ibid., 61. Zakai distinguishes between a "*Genesis*-type" of narrative, in which America counts as a "sacred place in the history of salvation only so far as it is connected with the sacred center of England as the elect nation," and an "*Exodus*-type" in which the new land is "established . . . as an independent and autonomous sacred place in providential history, which necessarily and indeed intentionally entailed the severing of ties with England which the Puritans no longer considered a sacred center" (99). Discourse of the Virginia colony is of the former type, that of early New England of the latter (see esp. ch. 3 of *Exile and Kingdom,* "The Eschatology of the Protestant Settlement of Virginia"). Although both narratives are equally apocalyptic in their inflection, the *Exodus*-type would seem to have the more natural affinity with the *City of God.*

work to an English-reading public. Talk of an earthly city of God was music to the ears of English Protestants at the beginning of their nation's overseas expansion, for reasons that had little to do with Augustine.[64]

Acts and Monuments of the London Virginia Company, 1607–1610

If the foregoing arguments are substantially correct, we may imagine events in England during the period 1607–1610 unfolding as follows:[65]

8 October 1607. Captain Newport sails with the First Supply to the Virginia Colony, under strict instructions to fetch better warrants of the mineral wealth of the region than he had brought at his last return thence. Otherwise, as one interested party remarks, "Oure newe discovery ys more Lyke to prove the Lande of Canaan then the lande of Ophir."[66] He is expected back in England "before the myddle of January next."[67]

Early 1608. Newport has been delayed. Disappointed in their expectation of quick and easy profits from the new colony, the leaders of the Virginia Company in London consider other ways of maintaining public support. Plans are laid for a larger expedition to Virginia, to be commanded by Sir Thomas Gates. Among those privy to the counsels of these men is William Crashaw, B.Div., preacher at the Inner Temple, noted champion of the English Protestant

---

64. Consider, e.g., a pair of passages from a sermon preached in London by Daniel Price' on 28 May 1609. First he urges "this Honourable City" to persevere in its support of the new colony, assuring his listeners that they "will make *Plutarches* PONEROPOLIS [*Moralia* 520b], Athenaeus['] OURANOPOLIS [*Deipnosophistae* 3,98] a Sauadge country to become a sanctifyed Country." A moment later, he turns the trope around: "I will ende with one word of exhortation to this City[:] many excellent things are spoken of thee, as sometimes of the City of God. Hither the Tribes come, euen the Tribes of the Lord, herein is the Seate of iudgement, euen the seate of the house of *Dauid*[.] Peace bee within thy walles, plenteousnesse within thy Pallaces. Yet remember how manyfold infections hence as from a fountaine haue issued out . . . . London . . . should be *Ierusalem* the City of God, and it is become Murthers slaughter-house, Thefts refuge, Oppressions safety, Whoredoms Stewes, Vsuries Banke, Vanities Stage, abounding in all kind of filthinesse and prophanenesse." *Sauls prohibition staide* (1609) sigs. F3r-v (STC 20302).

65. My narrative depends on Brown, *Genesis* and *First Republic,* and Barbour, *Jamestown Voyages.* For the chronology of events in Jamestown see *Complete Works of Captain John Smith,* ed. Barbour, 1.15–22, 127–30.

66. Letter of Sir Walter Cope to Lord Salisbury, 13 August 1607; Barbour, *Jamestown Voyages,* 1.111.

67. Letter of Sir Thomas Smythe to Lord Salisbury, 17 August 1607; Barbour, *Jamestown Voyages,* 1.112.

("Catholic") church, and perhaps a relative of one of the planters in Virginia. Crashaw's own projects of this time include a collation of editions of Vivès's commentary on the *De civitate dei,* for which he has recently sought (or will shortly seek) material assistance from King James I.

3 May 1608. In the Stationers' Register, under this date and against the name of the printer George Eld(e), is entered "for his copie . . . A book called. *The Cittie of GOD. 22. bookes* wrytten by Saint AUGUSTINE. With *ye Learned Commentaryes* of JOHN LUDOUICK VIUES ... . vjd."[68] If Crashaw's statements in the preface to the 1620 edition of this work are reliable, the task of translation has been committed by him to John Healey, a London freelance with as yet no publications to his name.

21 May 1608. Newport returns with news of famine, disease, and death in the colony, but no gold. With him comes Edward Maria Wingfield, first president of the ruling council in Virginia, deposed by his fellow colonists. At the close of a discourse to the London court of the Virginia Company, in which he answers charges made against him, Wingfield "reioyce[s] that my trauells & daungers haue done somewhat for the behoof of Ierusalem in Virginia."[69] Written accounts of the progress of the colony and of the quality of the country and native inhabitants of Virginia begin to circulate in manuscript.

Shortly before 7 July 1608. The *Phoenix* under Master Francis Nelson returns from Virginia, carrying a letter from one of the colonists (John Smith) addressed to a friend in England. The Company decides to make public an edited version of the text. The work is entered in the Stationers' Register for 13 August as *A true relation of suche occurrences and accidentes of note as haue happened in Virginia synce the first plantinge of that Colonye which is nowe resident in the south parte of Virginia till master Nelsons comminge away from them etc.*[70] It is published shortly afterward, not without some confusion over the authorship. The preface, signed "I. H.," is by John Healey, who had been charged with making the necessary adjustments to the text. The result is an odd blend of Smith's disabused narrative of places, people, and events with the Company's high-flown rhetoric of conquest, commerce, and—more especially now—Christian conversion.

---

68. *A Transcript of the Registers of the Company of Stationers of London; 1554–1640 A.D.,* ed. E. Arber (London: private printing, 1875–77) 3.377.

69. Barbour, *Jamestown Voyages,* 1.233.

70. *Transcript,* ed. Arber, 3.388.

Early 1609. In January Newport returns from delivering the Second Supply. A new royal charter is drawn up, under which control of the affairs of the southern colony will pass to a private corporation of subscribers (the "new" Virginia Company) with its own executive council. The charter confirms that "the principall effect" desired and expected "of this action is the conuersion and reduccion of the people in those partes vnto the true worshipp of God and Christian religion."[71] It will be signed and granted on 23 May, at which time the council will formally deliver its instructions to Sir Thomas Gates, first governor of the colony. Meanwhile, every effort is made to drum up subscribers. In a pamphlet called *Nova Britannia,* published in late February or early March, Robert Johnson proclaims Virginia another Promised Land "by diuine prouidence offered to our choice."[72] In April the Spanish ambassador writes to Philip III that the promoters of the colony "have seen to it that the ministers, in their sermons, stress the importance of filling the world with their religion, and of everyone exerting themselves to give what they have to so great an undertaking."[73] Several such sermons were printed and survive to this day.[74] At the beginning of June a fleet under Sir Thomas Gates and Admiral Sir George Somers leaves Falmouth for Jamestown, carrying with it the legal instruments for a refoundation of the colony.

Late 1609. Toward the end of November, news reaches London of the loss of Gates's flagship, presumed wrecked off Bermuda. The remainder of the fleet is reported to have reached Jamestown safely; however, in the absence of the new governor, affairs in the colony are in disarray. On 14 December, with a view to reassuring anxious investors, Lord De La Warr and other leading members of the Council for Virginia enter for publication *A true and sincere declaracon of the purpose and endes of the plantacon begunne in Virginia.*[75] The work is published early the next year. Its (unnamed) author reaffirms that

---

71. *New American World,* ed. Quinn, 5.211.

72. *Nova Britannia. Offring most excellent fruites by planting in Virginia. Exciting all such as be well affected to further the same* (London [for Samuel Macham], 1609), sig. E2r (STC 14699). Wright, *Religion and Empire,* 94; Parker, "Religion and the Virginia Colony," 252–54; Zakai, *Exile and Kingdom,* 100–102.

73. Barbour, *Jamestown Voyages,* 2.259. A few weeks earlier the same ambassador had sent his master a copy of *Nova Britannia,* parts of which were translated into Castilian by an English Jesuit.

74. Wright, *Religion and Empire,* 90–99; Parker, "Religion and the Virginia Colony," 254–62; Zakai, *Exile and Kingdom,* 104–13.

75. *Transcript,* ed. Arber, 3.425.

The *Principall* and *Maine Ends* [of the Virginia plantation] weare *first* to preach, & baptize into *Christian Religion,* and by propagation of that *Gospell,* to recouer out of the armes of the Diuell, a number of poore and miserable soules, wrapt vpp vnto death, in almost *inuincible ignorance*; to endeauour the fulfilling, and accomplishment of the number of the elect, which shall be gathered from out all corners of the earth; and to add our myte to the treasury of Heauen, that as we pray for the comming of the kingdome of glory, so to expresse in our actions, the same desire, if God haue pleased, to vse so weak instruments, to the ripening and consummation thereof.[76]

De La Warr is named Lord Governor and Captain General for Virginia, and preparations are made for a relief expedition under his command.

21 February 1610. William Crashaw delivers a farewell sermon for De La Warr in the presence of his lordship "and others of his Maiesties Counsell for [Virginia], and the rest of the Aduenturers in that Plantation . . . wherein both the lawfulnesse of that Action is maintained, and the necessity thereof is also demonstrated, not so much out of the grounds of POLICIE, as of HUMAN-ITY, EQUITY, and CHRISTIANITY."[77] The preacher appeals to the opinion of "the primitiue fathers" against the Roman interpretation of Christ's words to Peter in Luke 22:32, which he has chosen for his text ("But I haue praied for thee, that thy faith faile not: therefore when thou art conuerted strengthen thy brethren"), reminds his audience that "the end of this voiage is the destruction of the diuels kingdome, and propagation of the Gospell," then launches into an elaborate defence of the enterprise against its detractors.[78] "[L]et no wise man obiect," says Crashaw, "that our fleete was dispersed and sore shaken by *a storme*; for he cannot but know that such as saile by sea must as well expect *tempests of winde,* as trauellers on the land *shewers of raine.*" God will send his angels to preserve the general and his company "by land and sea, at home and abroad, from the diuell and all other enemies." Later ages will celebrate them as "the first beginners of one of the brauest and most excellent exploits . . . attempted since the Primitiue times of the Church."[79]

---

76. *A true and sincere declaration of the purpose and ends of the plantation begun in Virginia* (London [for I. Stepneth], 1610) sig. A3v (STC 24832). Wright, *Religion and Empire*, 103; Parker, "Religion and the Virginia Colony," 264–65.

77. *A sermon preached in London before the right honorable the Lord Lawarre,* etc. (London [for W. Welby], 1610) title-page (STC 6029). Wright, *Religion and Empire,* 99–102; Parker, "Religion and the Virginia Colony," 265–68; Zakai, *Exile and Kingdom,* 113–15.

78. *A sermon . . . ,* sigs. A1v, B4r.

79. Ibid., sigs. E1v, I4v, K3r.

1 April 1610. De La Warr's fleet sets sail from the Isle of Wight. Among those taking passage to Virginia is John Healey, a man who only a year earlier had called himself a "traueller that neuer trauelled."

Between 1 April and 1 September 1610. Thomas Thorpe dedicates Healey's translation of the *City of God* to the Earl of Pembroke, a fellow officer of De La Warr's on the Royal Council and a prominent supporter of the Virginian enterprise since its inception. Since Thorpe speaks of the translator as an "actuall Trauailer . . . to Virginia," without implying that he knew of his safe arrival there, it is likely that the dedication was written before De La Warr's return to England in September,[80] at which time (for all we know) Healey may have come home too. Why it should have fallen to Thorpe instead of Crashaw to make the dedication remains a puzzle. The somewhat grudging tone of the latter's reference to Healey in the 1620 preface may indicate that the two had fallen out, or that there had been some other upset between the translator and persons associated with the Virginia Company.[81] Thorpe's plea on Healey's behalf for Pembroke's acceptance "without distrust or disturbance in this worke" may point in the same direction. Whatever accidents had befallen the undertakers, George Eld either had too much already invested in the book or too firm a hope of its good reception to be deterred by them.

Conclusion: The "King James Version" of the *City of God*

Obvious though the choice of Pembroke was as dedicatee for the 1610 *Citie of God,* given both his previous favors to Thorpe and Healey and his prominence in the Virginia Company, we may wonder whether this book, with its ostentatiously reprinted exchange of courtesies between Vivès and Henry VIII, was not designed at some stage for an even more illustrious patron. Despite the apparent difference of objects, already remarked upon, between his program for restoring the authentic texts of "Catholic" authors and the

---

80. The returning fleet brought news of the miraculous survival of Gates and his crew, who had wintered comfortably in Bermuda and then sailed on to Jamestown to arrive there a few weeks before De La Warr. Written reports of the wreck and its sequels soon began to circulate in London and one of them, Silvester Jourdain's *A discouery of the Barmudas, otherwise called the Ile of Divels* (STC 14816), was printed before the end of the year, providing material for Shakespeare's *Tempest.*

81. In the preface to *Philip Mornay, Lord of Plessis his teares* (1609) Healey speaks of himself and his friend John Coventry as two "who haue thus long sayled in a deepe, darke sea of misfortunes" (sig. A3r); it is possible that some further mishap impelled him to try his luck in Virginia.

promotion of the Virginia settlement, it is not impossible that Crashaw conceived of an English *City of God* that would be conducive to both. Viewed *sub specie aeternitatis,* or in the light of the apocalyptic hope of certain English Protestants at the beginning of the seventeenth century, the civilization of the American savage as a good "Catholic" (i.e., Protestant) Englishman and the promulgation of a pure, English printed text of Christian literature were two means to the same divinely appointed end.[82] If James I were gratified by an association with his predecessor Henry VIII, defender (in Vivès's terms) of "that better Rome against Babylon," might he not then look more warmly on a project for the "kingely reformation" of latterday Romish corruption? Such arguments are purely conjectural, of course. There was to be no "King James Version" of the *City of God.* It does appear, however, that His Majesty received a copy of Healey's translation, and that it was placed in his library.[83] And within a few years there would be at least one copy of Augustine's great work in a library of the new colony in Virginia.[84]

---

82. In the Epistle Dedicatorie to Alexander Whitaker's *Good newes from Virginia* (1613), Crashaw construes as triple "demonstrations of Gods all gouerning prouidence" his witholding until recent times of the art of printing, the use of a compass for navigation, and the discovery of "the new world of America." Printing he describes in terms reminiscent of the *Romish Forgeries* as "an inuention so excellent and so vsefull, so much tending to the honour of God, the manifestation of the truth, propagation of the Gospell, restoration of learning, diffusion of knowledge, and consequently the discouerie and destruction of Poperie, that the Pope and Popish Politicians wish it had neuer been" (sig. A2v). Whitaker was the minister who baptized Pocahontas; C. Porter, "Alexander Whitaker: Cambridge Apostle to Virginia," *William & Mary Quarterly,* 3rd ser., 14 (1957): 317–43. A letter of his to Crashaw, dated from Jamestown, 9 August 1611, was printed by Brown, *Genesis,* 1.497–500.

83. In its autumn 1994 catalogue, Simon Finch Rare Books Ltd. of London advertised a copy of the 1610 *Citie of God,* bound in "[c]ontemporary vellum over boards . . . with the royal arms of James I stamped in gilt in the centre." It quickly sold for £650.

84. Kingsbury, *Records of the Virginia Company,* 3.567: "At the . . . Quarter Court [held the 30. of *Ianuary* 1621] a small Bible with a Couer richly wrought, a great Church-Bible, the Booke of Common Prayer, and other bookes were presented to be sent to *Virginia,* in the name of a person who had the yeare before sent for the vse of the Colledge at *Henrico*; *S. Augustine De ciuitate Dei,* Master *Perkins* his workes [i.e., the works of the influential Puritan theologian William Perkins], and an exact Map of *America*: the giuer is not known, but the books are valued at £10.0.0." On the College at Henrico, founded "for the trayning and bringing vp of Infidells children to the true knowledge of God and vnderstanding of righteousnes," see Kingsbury 1.220–21. W. S. Powell, "Books in the Virginia Colony before 1624," *William & Mary Quarterly,* 3rd ser., 5 (1948): 177–84, at 180; Hall, "Chesapeake" (above, n. 41) 131.

Is the Augustinian Heaven Inhuman? The Arguments of Martin Heidegger and Hannah Arendt

Peter J. Burnell

Both Martin Heidegger and Hannah Arendt began their philosophical careers with studies of Augustine. Their work on him has now become more accessible to the public than before. Arendt's study was a Master's thesis at the University of Heidelberg, on Augustine's concept of love; that work, translated by E. B. Ashton at Arendt's behest and subsequently revised by her, has recently been published.[1] Heidegger's was a series of seminars given at the University of Freiburg soon after the First World War; a detailed summary of those seminars has recently appeared.[2]

Both Arendt and Heidegger argue, though on different grounds, that Augustine by holding a notion of a perfectly serene and secure heaven is philosophical and Platonic rather than authentically theological and Christian. Does Augustine say and mean what Arendt and Heidegger respectively say he says and means? Arendt's criticism is discussed first, since it is concerned with the desire for heaven, Heidegger's with heaven itself.

---

1. H. Arendt, *Love and Saint Augustine*, ed. and with an intepretive essay by J. V. Scott and J. C. Stark (Chicago: University of Chicago Press, 1996).
2. T. Kisiel, *The Genesis of Heidegger's Being and Time* (Berkeley & Los Angeles: University of California Press, 1995) 192–219.

Arendt

Of the three notions of love that Hannah Arendt specifies in Augustine's thought, she particularly criticizes one: love of God in the form of a single-minded craving for a heavenly future. To contemplate eternity in that way, she argues, is to turn it into a desired commodity, so that the only difference between charity and lust is the object of the craving, not any quality in the love itself; in this sense such a love may be said to be too worldly.[3] In another sense she regards such a love as too other-worldly: an excessive, procrustean rejection of the world, because the heaven that it desires is (that unresolved oxymoron) an absolute future, in reference to which all else must be treated as nothing; this, she argues, precludes any real love of neighbor, since amid the "all else" is one's neighbor; and though there may be room elsewhere in Augustine's moral theology for a real love of neighbor, that love of neighbor would still not, according to Arendt, have anything to do with this love: the craving for the "absolute future" of heaven.

The problem arises most clearly, as Arendt is aware, in Augustine's famous division of reality into what must be enjoyed and what must be used: ultimately only God is to be enjoyed; all else, used with a view to that fruition.[4] And since full enjoyment of God cannot be had in this world, only in the next, our attention must all be on that future reality. Despite Augustine's attempts to guarantee a place for love of neighbor in this framework, Arendt argues that a logical exclusion of that love is in the final analysis inescapable; what is enjoined here, she says, is not charity, but hope, in the furtherance of which one's neighbor can only be incidental. That, says Arendt, amounts to fundamental "lack of concern with the particular entities being arranged" in this order of love, "standing in flagrant contradiction to the very essence of love in all its forms";[5] for to love something is, as Augustine points out elsewhere, to desire it for its own sake.[6] Hence even in Arendt's final synthesis of Augustine's notions of charity, which allows for a socially originated love of neighbor, there is no place for any idea of using one's neighbor in such a way.

---

3. Arendt, *Love and Saint Augustine,* 16–17.

4. Augustine, *De civitate dei* 15,22, but especially *De doctrina christiana* 1,22,20–1,23,22 and 1,25,26–1,27,28.

5. Arendt, *Love and Saint Augustine,* 42.

6. *De diversis quaestionibus octoginta tribus* 35,1.

Augustine does not, however, apply *usus* to love of neighbor with complete bluntness; in Book 1 of *De doctrina christiana*, rightly noted by Arendt as the classic text in point, Augustine asks specifically about our treatment of ourselves and each other whether it should be a matter of enjoyment or of use;[7] in other words, despite the absolute restriction he has already made of *frui* to relationship with God, he still asks the question again about love of human beings as distinct from other beings because, he says, although a human being, unlike God, is a thing, this thing, unlike any other, is made in God's image. In answering the question he first reasserts his main point: if one aims at the enjoyment of something, one loves it for its own sake, and God is the only absolutely suitable object of enjoyment. Then a subtlety (of which Arendt was aware) emerges: there are some beings that, though they are to be used, are also to be loved: angels, other people, and ourselves (together with our bodies which, however, are not completely distinct beings). All these, says Augustine, unlike all other non-divine beings, should be loved as well as used because they are one with us in a common relationship to God; and we can know this, he says, because the moment one tries to find self-fulfillment in oneself, enjoyment of oneself, one finds one's own condition, together with the attempted self-fulfillment, to be impaired by the very attempt. In other words, the failure to direct all one's desire ultimately to the enjoyment of God prevents full self-enjoyment. To criticize a form of behavior, even for the sake of argument, by saying that it frustrates the attainment of a particular end is to assume that in itself the particular end is worthy. In this case the end is enjoyment of self. And, says Augustine, what is said morally about love of oneself must equally be said about love of neighbor, in accordance with the second great command.[8] Arendt regards this notion of a middle category of beings usable in a loving way as an incongruous intrusion into the distinction between use and enjoyment, and as inexplicable in terms of it. In her view Augustine does not, by this method, succeed in finding room for a genuine love of any being other than God for that being's own sake. He still maintains, she argues, a "sublime indifference," a "basic lack of concern for the particular entities" purportedly loved in this way.[9] Similarly, Oliver O'Donovan regards the proposed middle group of beings as a false conceptual step: an abortive attempt to treat use as

---

7. *De doctrina christiana* 1,22,20. Cf. J. Burnaby, *Amor Dei: A Study in the Religion of St. Augustine* (Norwich: The Canterbury Press, 1991; first published 1938) 105. Cf. *Civ.* 19,13–14.

8. *De doctrina christiana* 1,22,20–21.

9. Arendt, *Love and Saint Augustine*, 40, 42–43.

capable of being a form of love and to give an objective ontological basis for an irreformably positivistic idea.[10]

But the implications of Augustine's position absolve him from Arendt's and O'Donovan's criticisms. In order to desire one's own good without mad egotism, one must desire God primarily, desire an intimacy with God the primacy of which, as an end, gives meaning to the very notion that one's own good could be an end; not desire one's own good as if it could exist as an absolute. And in order to love one's neighbor for one's neighbor's own sake, without a mad idolatry from which that person would do well to run screaming, one must desire intimacy with God vicariously for one's neighbor, not desire that individual's good as if it had the same status as the very reality whose absolutely primary status alone can make sense of such a notion as one's neighbor's good. These implications are a sound basis for Augustine's proposed middle category of beings. Legitimate "use," in the case of such a being, means treating that being's sake as secondary to God's, whom one loves for his own sake absolutely speaking. Legitimate enjoyment of such a created being makes that being's good an end, though in reference to God. Although initially, as O'Donovan says, he expresses the notion of use in strictly positivistic terms, of values placed, that is, rather than of determinative principles, Augustine has succeeded in propounding, as a matter of principle rather than of choice, a notion of the use of human beings that is also ordered to the enjoyment of them. Thus Augustine forbids loving a human being for that being's own sake simply speaking, but not in every respect. His point is that there must be no area of human allegiance left unengaged by God, for if any area were, some other being than God could become its sole end; but short of that, the enjoyment of a human being—oneself or another—is a legitimate end. Thus the criticism by Arendt of this one of Augustine's accounts of charity does not quite rightly characterize that account of charity; for what he says stands in contradiction not so much to the very essence of love, as to idolatry.

One may go a step further. The last words of the 1966 edition—the so-called "new edition"—of Arendt's *Origins of Totalitarianism* are:

Initium ut esset homo creatus est—"that a beginning be made, man was created," said Augustine. This beginning is guaranteed by each new birth; it is indeed every man.[11]

---

10. O. O'Donovan, *The Problem of Self-Love in St. Augustine* (New Haven: Yale University Press, 1980) 26–29.

In effect her claim here is that Augustine's statement (from Book 12 of the *City of God*) anticipates her own concept of "natality": the constant presence, in every new human being, of a capacity for the unprecedented, for the uniquely fresh and unpredictable. There is indeed a trace of that notion in the Augustine text. The Latin actually reads: *Hoc [initium] ergo ut esset, creatus est homo, ante quem nullus fuit* ("So that there might therefore be this beginning, a human being was created, before whom none was"). Thus the idea of a radical newness comes as part of a larger argument, which Arendt has pruned from the quotation. That argument asserts the utter permanence of heaven. Augustine is rebutting the doctrine of the "everlasting return": the inescapable, endless recycling of human souls in one earthly life after another. His contention is that, regardless of whether the total number of human souls is fixed or not, they all pass through this world and out of it forever, and therefore have to have had an absolute beginning (not a mere recommencement). His main argument in support of this contention is that no doctrine as depressing as the endlessly repeated return could possibly be true; for in particular it makes love more shallow than befits a human being. Where separation is always in prospect, where there can be no ultimate prospect of complete and eternal intimacy, love freezes: for then one will always withhold something in the giving of one's love, deterred by being aware that the relationship has a term. This, he says, is true of human love for human beings, and pre-eminently true of human love for God. Underlying this argument is the premise that human love in this world can be fully itself only where one has in view an absolutely inviolable, future union with the beloved. It must therefore be the case, he argues, that each soul is created to enter the world once, to confront evil, and to be freed from it for eternity.

In this argument each soul's "absolute future" is logically prior to its "natality." Augustine's reason for believing in the utterly new creation (as opposed to recycling) of each human soul is the belief in its heavenly future; and that future is even the purpose of the soul's utterly new creation. Moreover his argument that there is such a heavenly future rests in turn on a more fundamental basis: the observation that only such a heavenly future allows human love to have an appropriately humane depth.

---

11. H. Arendt, *The Origins of Totalitarianism* (New York: Meridian Books/World, 1958) 479; cf. *Civ.* 12,21 (final sentence); see also the comments of Joanna Vecchiarelli Scott at n. 11 in her essay in this volume. Except for the one quoted here, which is Arendt's, all translations from Augustine in this essay are the author's.

This orientation profoundly affects his view of politically constituted society. His position is not that affairs of state are independent of heavenly considerations, but vice versa, heaven being the purpose of human activity. This conditions his attitude to plurality in political institutions. For him innovation in this area of life is properly the handmaid of grace and has the pull of heaven as its discipline. Though he has a notion of "natality," then, it is so directed by eschatological considerations as to be different in kind from Arendt's. There is reason to take a different view of this matter from that taken in Professor Scott's essay. She describes both Augustine and Arendt as worldly political philosophers who celebrated plurality in governmental practices. But although, as she implies, Augustine does not give us anything resembling a single, blueprinted governmental constitution, he is not, as is Arendt, inclined to rejoice in the variety of such institutions to be found in the world. He was aware (none better) of the fundamentally religious character of politically constituted societies, and constantly described them in religious terms. His chronological survey of the earthly city in Book 18 of the *City of God* is a picture of a theological tower of Babel, while the more detailed account (in Book 3) of the changes in Roman political institutions over time is rather a narrative of over-hasty damage control in a theologically errant society than a testimony to endlessly fresh potential for political creativity.

Heidegger

Heidegger's disagreement with Augustine on heaven is part of a more comprehensive disagreement with Platonic philosophy. His main point is that it is an intellectual disaster to abstract from the concrete immediacy of things or to arrange them in an intellectually conceived hierarchy if one wants to grasp their true reality; for that reality, their being, is intimately hidden in their physical actuality, and one must never abstract from that if one is to gain a true intuition of being.

This view is concerned with things and is part of Heidegger's later philosophy. It is, however, analogous to a notion of human experience developed in the Augustine seminars he held as a young man. In these he maintains that troubledness, worry, is essential to human experience. Thus even if one could opt out of that mental struggle, one would be abandoning something essential to one's humanity by doing so; in particular any truthful account of the human relationship with God will, according to Heidegger, include *cura*: *Bekümmerung*. In Augustine, Kisiel tells us, Heidegger claims to find traces of this notion in the vivid descriptions of a human soul's turmoil, from Book 10 of the *Confessions*:

> I am a burden to myself; joys that should be wept over contend with griefs that I should really be happy about; and which side gains the victory I do not know.[12]

The thesis that some such state of mind is natural, fundamental to human life is Heidegger's, and his divergence from Augustine on this point no doubt devolves largely into irreducible philosophical differences. But implicit in what Heidegger says there is also an interpretation of Augustine. He claims to find two quite different approaches to God in Augustine's thought: facing God authentically, and therefore with the experience of insecurity; and treating God theoretically, evaluating the things of the world by reference to a concept of that highest reality: an attitude that Heidegger saw as ignoring the fundamental terms of one's existence by withdrawing from a crucial part of experience. The criticism is that in Augustine these two approaches to God were wound together inextricably but not really integrated.[13]

Heaven comes into the argument because according to Heidegger both these purportedly ill-assorted notions reappear in Augustine's eschatology: heaven as the quintessence of what has been the character of our relationship with God in this life and entailing, therefore, the purification, not the abolition of the troubledness itself, and heaven as perfect security from the possibility of harm, of sin, of being separated from God. That the latter view of heaven is Augustine's is incontestable: it is the *non posse peccare* of the final chapter of the *City of God*. But only the former notion of heaven is acceptable to Heidegger, assuming that human beings will remain human in heaven; he implies, then, that even in heaven the blessed will remain terrified of falling away from God again. Is he right to attribute to Augustine this very different idea of heaven also?

His main Augustinian text in support of this view is from the ninth Homily on St. John's First Epistle.[14] In this part of that great disquisition on the love of God Augustine distinguishes between unchaste and chaste fear of God. Unchaste fear of God is like an adulterous wife's attitude to her husband: fear that he might come home; this, says Augustine, is the kind of fear that perfect

---

12. *Conf.* 10,28,39.
13. Kisiel, *Genesis,* 201–206.
14. Kisiel, *Genesis,* 216; Augustine, *In epistulam Iohannis ad Parthos tractatus decem* 9, 5–8.

love casts out. Chaste fear of God is like that of a faithful and virtuous wife: fear that her husband may become absent, desire for him to be at home. This kind of fear, says Augustine, lasts in *saeculum saeculi*; it will persist even when the embrace of the heavenly bridegroom has become a full reality, for then the wife (the pious soul) "will be vigilant and watchful to avoid iniquity of her own, for fear she may again sin: not for fear that she may be consigned to the fire, but for fear that she may be deserted by him."

This illustrates Heidegger's point. "For fear she may again sin" presents a certain contrast with the "being unable to sin" of the *City of God*. But also the text is surprising by itself; for even as Augustine concludes that this fear lasts forever he says that the chaste soul in heaven "fears, but without insecurity": *timet, sed securiter*. What is this fear, then? (Though undoubtedly awe is entailed, this state is implicitly defined not as awe, but as an everlasting fear of being deserted by God and of sinning again.) And what is the nature of Augustine's distinction between fear of being thrown into the fire (which this fear is not) and fear of sinning again and being deserted by God (which this fear is)?

The text and its entire context are about the nature of love, and its crucial aspect specified here is desire. The contrast between the wives is between two desires: negative and positive. The unchaste wife, for example, stretches out as it were to grasp at her husband's absence; she is smitten with the potential delight of adultery. The chaste fear of God's absence is the desire for the continuance of his presence; and in heaven the perfection of that chaste fear will be the complete and utter desire for that continuance. But, as Augustine says near the end of the homily, "love is God" (his famous converse of St. John's dictum), and "all my good is to cleave to God freely."[15] Hence the desire for God is God and its presence is God's presence. In other words, the desire for the continuance of God's presence effects that continuance. The only possible obstacle to such a desire's fulfillment is failure of the desire itself; so the more one felt fear defined in this way the more secure one would have reason to feel. Such a fear, if it could ever be perfectly unadulterated, would therefore be the experience of perfect security. Thus the possibility of falling away from God when in heaven is only a logical one. Since there can be no question of God's gratuitously deserting someone in heaven, this eternal fear of sinning again and so being deserted by God is, far from being fear of damnation, the experience of the consciously perfect and permanent absence of sin.

---

15. Ibid., 9,10.

But this experience converges exactly with heaven as Augustine projects it at the end of the *City of God*: in heaven, human free will be freer than before, by being "liberated from the delight in sinning, even to the point of an indeclinable delight in not sinning" (*usque ad delectationem non peccandi indeclinabilem*).[16] As the emphasis on *delectatio* implies, in this passage too the heavenly inability to sin is defined in terms of desire. That inability is the result not of losing the innate potentiality for sin, but of gaining the inalienable desire not to sin. This, as Augustine explicitly points out, is naturally a divine, not a human characteristic. But, as he goes on to imply, it is human in the larger and more profound sense of being a divine characteristic that each human being is designed to receive; for our original ability not to sin and our ultimate inability to sin are the first and second degrees of one divine gift (*gradus divini muneris*). This gift really consists not of an ability and a contradictory inability, but of two abilities: free will, and the capacity, fully engaged, to be utterly free from temptation. Both here, then, and in the Homily on St. John's Epistle what is described as heaven for a human being is the indefectibly efficacious desire to be with God.

Furthermore, Heidegger's general criticism—that Augustine presents the human relationship with God as essentially intuitive but also as intellectual and axiological without integrating the two—has considerable philosophical interest but again does not fairly represent Augustine's position; for in Book 10 of the *Confessions* (the text under discussion for Heidegger) Augustine in the end describes his perception of the hierarchy of being not as the fruit of explicable philosophical estimation, but as a shocking, God-given realization of the absolute superiority of God to nature:

> You were inside; I was outside; I was looking for you there and rushing, ugly, into the beautiful things that you had made. You were with me, I was not with you. Those beautiful things held me far from you, even though they would not have existed if they had not existed in you. You called, shouted, broke through my deafness. You gleamed, shone, routed my blindness. You gave off a fragrance; I breathed it in, and now I pant after you.[17]

His climactic discovery that nature is contingent on God is presented here not as the product of Augustine's own reasoning (though plenty of that had preceded this climax), but as a supernaturally given intuition; furthermore he shows an intimation of his perilous relation with God to be part and parcel of that

---

16. *Civ.* 22,30.
17. *Conf.* 10,27,38.

divine disclosure. That is, in one and the same discovery he realizes that it is false to think God part of nature and that to cling to that falsity is to cling to the curse of separation from God. Thus in his memory, at least, the perception that to be trapped in mere nature is a horror and the perception that that horror comes about precisely because the wellspring of all happiness utterly transcends nature are essentially one perception.

Conclusion

Two general conclusions may be drawn. It is not correct to say that Augustine's notion of charity as desire for heaven precludes loving people for their own sake; rather the fullness of such desire positively implies such loving, though not for their own sake absolutely. Nor is it correct to say that Augustine's conception of heaven itself implies the shearing-off of the essential human ability to fall from grace; rather it implies that that ability is an inferior form of the freedom to cleave to God, the fullness of which, entailing the fulfillment of our humanity, is the freedom to cleave to God with perfect security.

Hannah Arendt's Secular Augustinianism

Joanna Vecchiarelli Scott

As intellectuals in the United States bid a somewhat reluctant adieu to the Cold War, we note with unexpected regret that things were a lot simpler when the world was Manichaean, and when the Evil Empire confronted the Free World. Many of our icons from that dear dead era are making a rather rocky transition to the unsettling environment of postmodern uncertainty. The shades of Hegel and Marx are growing silent, but then too so is the dour ghost of Adam Smith. We dig up de Tocqueville on a regular basis, but his venerable corpse is losing its luster as civil society becomes distinctly less civil. Other French thinkers, Derrida, Foucault, Lacan, and the PoMo glitterati fill in some gaps. They amuse and "transgress" but ultimately leave the reader as unsatisfied as a visually elegant but unfilling meal, appropriately "nouvelle."

We comfort ourselves by declaring victory in the war of historical progress which ended in 1989. Our team won by virtue of being the last one left standing. Academics and "public intellectuals" rush off to Central and Eastern Europe to lecture on democracy and free enterprise. But they have no nostrums for the crime, violence and political extremity mushrooming through the cracks of the former Soviet Empire. We jostle for photo opportunities with Vaclav Havel and extol the virtues of eighteenth-century revolutions or their "velvet" equivalents. Eyes cast resolutely backwards we chant, "Let entrepreneurial crime bosses, nationalist political parties and a thousand McDonald's franchises, bloom." It will all sort itself out in the end and the world will have been made safe for democracy and the IMF.

Much more at ease in the new, disquieting, post-everything world are two ghostly icons, Aurelius Augustinus and Hannah Arendt. Judging by the rapidly expanding list of their works in print and of secondary commentaries, they are still very much with us. I have added to the list with the first English edition of Arendt's doctoral dissertation on Augustine (with Judith Stark).[1] Augustine was a maverick in his century just as Arendt was an "avant-gardiste" in hers. Both chose life on the frontier over safer venues. They migrated from native soil to foreign climes, and from established mentalities to heady visions of freedom and transcendence. Immune to easy categorization, Augustine and Arendt are claimable by all ideological advocates, and by none. Indeed, Augustine fits almost too easily into our current self-portraits. Consider this eerily ageless satire on materialism triumphant produced more than 1500 years ago in the late Roman equivalent of our own times—sans McDonald's:

> This is our concern, that every man be able to increase his wealth so as to supply his daily prodigalities, and so that the powerful may subject the weak for their own purpose. Let the poor court the rich for a living, that under their protection they may enjoy a sluggish tranquillity; and let the rich abuse the poor as their dependents. . . . Let the people applaud not those who protect their interests, but those who provide them with pleasure.[2]

Perhaps Augustine's long-term endurance and Arendt's relatively short-term perseverance are a function of the fact that both of them were attuned to change—a kind of change associated with beginnings and not ends, with contingency and not historical culminations. While Augustine needs no introduction to classical and patristic scholars, Arendt may. Born in 1906, she completed her doctoral research on Augustine under the influence (in more ways than one, some would argue) of Martin Heidegger and Karl Jaspers. Under threat of arrest for Zionist activities in newly Nazified Germany, she escaped with her mother and husband to France in 1933 where she worked for Jewish emigré organizations until 1940 when she was detained in a Vichy camp for undocumented emigrés. Her second escape took her over the Pyrenees, in the company of her husband and Walter Benjamin, and eventually to New York City, in 1941. By 1951, with the publication of *Origins of Totalitarianism*, she had

---

1. Hannah Arendt, *Love and Saint Augustine*, ed. and with an interpretive essay by J. V. Scott and J. C. Stark (Chicago: University of Chicago Press, 1996).

2. Augustine, *De civitate dei* 2,20 (trans. M. Dods [New York: Modern Library, 1950] 59).

become a star in the firmament not only of that constellation often termed the "New York Intellectuals" but also of the international republic of letters.[3] She never fell from the heavens, even though she was often the subject of vehement, personal criticism. When she died in 1975 she was eulogized by everyone who was anyone on the front page of *The New York Times*. It is said that Woody Allen wrote a satire about the intellectuals' reaction to her death for *The New Yorker*, but I can't find a trace of it. It was probably suppressed.

Without doubt, Arendt is one of the most widely read, debated and cited political scientists of this century. Her impact, however, extends well beyond the usual suspects in the academic world of political theorists and philosophers—to include a broad range of informed readers interested in the triumphs and atrocities of the twentieth century, their genealogy in the crisis of the tradition of western political thought, and the prospects for human freedom in the new age before us. Like her "old friend"[4] Augustine, she believed there was no going back to a golden age of the perfect polity.

While Arendt used the Athenian *polis* as her touchstone in defining what she termed the "lost treasure" of political experience, her political theory was never intended as an academic version of *Raiders of the Lost Ark*. Freedom for her was a state of mind, an experience of creativity in the public world and not identified with a particular set of institutions, laws or customs. Even more than Augustine's *civitas dei*, the Greek *polis* she so frequently referenced was an ideal type useful as an analytic frame but not achievable in the twentieth-century *saeculum*.

As scholars such as Jean Elshtain, Peter Iver Kaufman and Robert Markus have noted, Augustine also strategically undercut the "world we have lost"

---

3. Of the many intellectual histories of the New York Intellectuals and Arendt, the following are particularly useful: A. Bloom, *Prodigal Sons: The New York Intellectuals and Their World* (New York: Oxford University Press, 1987); C. Brightman, *Writing Dangerously: Mary McCarthy and Her World* (New York: Clarkson Potter, 1992); R. Boyers, *The Legacy of the German Intellectuals* (New York: Shocken Books, 1972); T. A. Cooney, *The Rise of the New York Intellectuals: Partisan Review and Its Circle* (Madison, Wisc.: University of Wisconsin Press, 1986); G. Dorrien, *The Neo-Conservative Mind: Politics, Culture and the War of Ideology* (Philadelphia: Temple University Press, 1993); A. Gleason, *Totalitarianism: The Inner History of the Cold War* (Oxford: Oxford University Press, 1995); M. Jan, *Permanent Exiles: Essays on the Intellectual Migration from Germany to America* (New York: Columbia University Press, 1986); A. Wald, *The New York Intellectuals: The Rise and Decline of the Anti-Stalinist Left from the 1930s to the 1980s* (Chapel Hill, N.C.: University of North Carolina Press, 1987).

4. I am indebted to Jerome Kohn, New School for Social Research, for this remembrance of Arendt's affection for Augustine.

argument of his Roman contemporaries.[5] The Old Romans harkened back to an exceptionalist model of the early Republic in order to attack the christianized and badly weakened Empire of their own lifetimes. But Augustine's riveting, colorful chronicle of murder and mayhem, punctuated by the short-lived interventions of virtuous Romans, let it be known that the past provided no escape from the present.

Augustine's and Arendt's most widely read works today, the *City of God*, the *Confessions*, *Origins of Totalitarianism*, the *Human Condition* and *Eichmann in Jerusalem*, were written in the heat of battle and uncertainty.[6] They wrote to expose and explain human motivation and the multifaceted, brilliant, beautiful and dangerous world humans had constituted. These texts were prepared for immediate public consumption not only by specialists (or the already converted) but by a broadly informed and engaged readership. They were stimulated by, and consciously addressed to, rapid, violent shifts both in conceptual paradigms and in the very foundations of cultures and institutions.

Not surprisingly the authors' sensibilities, in the one case profoundly religious and in the other deeply secular, had a great deal in common: first, they shared a commitment to the victory of creation over death, to human freedom over the determinisms of class, ethnicity and nationality; second, they both insisted on the responsibility to act in the *saeculum* despite its ethical ambiguities, and despite the tragic inevitability of unintended outcomes. Stoic silence was not an acceptable option. Third, they also agreed on a hermeneutic methodology characterized by a confident, cheerful deconstruction of received truths and texts.

Arendt's techniques have been described by her fans as "trawling the past with a question for a net"[7] and by her detractors as being that of a "café intellectual," a "popularizer."[8] Augustine, too, cuts and pastes Sallust and Cicero until they are contradicting not only each other but themselves and making his

---

5. See J. B. Elshtain, *Augustine and the Limits of Politics* (Notre Dame, Ind.: University of Notre Dame Press, 1995); P. I. Kaufman, *Redeeming Politics* (Princeton: Princeton University Press, 1995); R. A. Markus, *Saeculum: History and Society in the Theology of St Augusine* (Cambridge: Cambridge University Press, 1970).

6. H. Arendt, *The Origins of Totalitarianism* (New York: Meridian Books/World, 1958); *The Human Condition* (Chicago: University of Chicago Press, 1958); *Eichmann in Jerusalem: A Report on the Banality of Evil*, rev. ed. (New York: Penguin Books, 1964).

7. E. Young-Bruehl, "Reflections on Hannah Arendt's *The Life of the Mind*," *Political Theory* 10 (1981): 285–86.

8. T. L. Pangle, *The Spirit of Modern Republicanism: The Moral Vision of the American Founders and the Philosophy of Locke* (Chicago: University of Chicago Press, 1988) 49.

case against the Roman "good old days" for him. By the end of his life in his last great battle with Julian, Augustine accuses his opponent of being an elitist philosophical aristocrat, out of touch with the existential reality of human suffering and sin. Instead of the traditional Constantinian portrait of the Christian as Roman citizen, rational, just and free, Augustine counterpoises images worthy of Dante's *Inferno*.[9] The African mentalité trumps the Roman in Augustine's rhetoric, while the Holocaust trumps the Weimar mandarins in Arendt's great works.

Their differences are also evident and significant. Arendt distrusted any determining factor outside the individual as free agent. The givenness of cultural context could never undo in her mind the need for judgment informed by independent reason as the basis for "natality" in the world. Hence her ready adaptation of Augustine's notion of *consuetudo* to her Eichmann study. The so-called "banality" of thoughtlessly enacted evil was her direct, contemporary application of Augustine's epistemology. However, the accompanying argument for divine grace and predestination, which Augustine developed over a lifetime, clashed with Arendt's own journey as an emergent philosopher of freedom. She even tried to argue in her Aberdeen Gifford Lectures (which were published posthumously as *The Life of the Mind*) at the end of her own life that Augustinian *caritas* can authentically be defined as a spontaneously occurring, entirely internal, healing power which puts an end to what Augustine termed the monstrosity of the will's divided impulses. In the context of her efforts to focus exclusively on the mental faculties of thinking, willing and judgment, Arendt relegated grace to an offstage presence, effectively substituting love for grace.

> [T]he healing of the will, and this is decisive, does not come about through divine grace. At the end of the *Confessions*, [Augustine] returns once more to the problem and relying on certain very different considerations that are explicitly argued in the treatise, *On the Trinity*, he diagnoses the ultimate unifying will that eventually decides a man's conduct as *Love*.[10]

"Divine grace would not help," she argues, once Augustine discovered that the monstrosity of the divided will was the "same for the evil and for the good will." Augustine's Catholic panorama of providential grace and redemption linking the individual soul to a cosmic order is concentrated, internalized and

---

9. P. Brown, *Augustine of Hippo: A Biography* (Berkeley: University of California Press, 1969) 383–97.

10. H. Arendt, *The Life of the Mind: Thinking and Willing* (New York: Harcourt Brace Jovanovich, 1978) 95.

rendered almost solipsistic in this last of her published works. The inward gaze of The *Life of the Mind* was hard to recognize as Arendtian political theory when it was published after her death. Also in disguise was the Augustine of Arendt's dissertation and of his various cameo appearances throughout her work until 1975.

Arendt's 1929 Augustinianism, which she reiterated in the text she prepared for publication in the early 1960s, centered on a vision of the pilgrim soul in the *saeculum*. Her agenda was, however, never theological. Instead her chosen images are drawn from the secular world of plural loves and institutions. The contested soul of Augustine's citizen in the late Roman world is capable of free choice and the enabling power of *caritas*, which results from an unmerited, wholly contingent injection of grace. As such, the pilgrim soul is an apt metaphor for the modern individual. In Arendt's first encounter with Augustine, love stands for an empowerment which is not conditioned by class, religion, ethnicity, nationality or any of the other constraints she saw around her in Weimar Germany. Augustine's pilgrim could be George Grosz, the avant-garde satirist of bourgeois values; or Karl Mannheim, the sociologist arguing for a "platform" from which to engage yet critique the world; or a young, brilliant Jewish woman in the male, largely Christian world of the German university in the 1920s, who was trying to make a respectful, but determined declaration of independence from her overpowering mentor, Martin Heidegger.

The existential reality of modernity, she tells us as early as 1929, is one of radical alienation punctuated by social and political engagement. In Arendt's hands, mortality as a "limit condition" is the efficient but not the final cause of the search for Being. Instead, her central metaphor for the search throughout her works, both in Germany and in America, was "natality" or "new beginnings." Not the inevitability of dying but the promise of giving birth to the unexpectedly new was Arendt's refuge against an overly determined world.

She claimed to have derived the term "natality" directly from Augustine's argument against cyclical conceptions of history in the *City of God*, specifically Book 12, chapter 21. The term was her own but the idea was Augustine's. "New beginnings" and "natality" became an Arendtian mantra repeated throughout her career. In Book 12 Augustine wanted to vindicate God's power to "create new things never before created," including human souls, while retaining the order of Providence. A beginning must be posited for the universe, its inhabitants and their behaviors, he argues, and "this beginning never before existed. That this beginning, therefore, might be, the first man was created." For her part, Arendt's agenda did not include rescuing God from classical determinists. But it did include defending the possibility of human freedom by invoking Augustinian creativity rather than the dangerous implications of Nietzschean or Heideggerean willfulness.

A typical extrapolation of the Augustinian text can be found in her essay "What Is Freedom?" collected in *Between Past and Future*. Arendt observes a "new beginning" in Augustine's own writings, a shift from the definition of freedom as *liberum arbitrium* to "an entirely differently conceived notion" which emerged in "his only political treatise," *De civitate dei*. Freedom emerges "not as an inner human disposition but as a character of human existence in the world." The individual literally is freedom, rather than being the possessor of it.

> His coming into the world is equated with the appearance of freedom in the universe; man is free because he is a beginning and was so created after the universe had come into existence; *initium ut esset, creatus est homo, ante quem nemo fuit.*[11]

Arendt's work, like Heidegger's, was obsessed with time. He called *Being and Time* the most important work he ever wrote. Arendt had attended the lectures that eventually comprised the text. She invoked historical temporality in the *Origins of Totalitarianism*, and again in *Men in Dark Times*, and an eternal present time in *Between Past and Future*.[12] In her dissertation, as in *Being and Time*, time is the context for the "throwback" to Being. But Arendt's understanding of the backward search, influenced more by Augustine than by Heidegger, takes the form of memory (*memoria*). As a mental faculty, memory provides the means by which future and past meet in the mental *nunc stans*, or "space" of memory. Internally, *caritas* bridges reason and judgment in the space provided by memory. Projected forward and outward in her later works, the locus of encounter will be transformed into the "public space" where immortal acts of word and deed take place—the founding of the American Republic, revolutionary Soviets, student rebels at Columbia University. It is *caritas* and its paired mental faculty, free will, which transforms Heidegger's anxiety-producing "they" into the community of "neighbors" in the world who are loved both for themselves and for the sake of their common source in the phenomenological Creator.

---

11. H. Arendt, *Between Past and Future: Eight Exercises in Political Thought* (New York: Penguin Books, 1977) 167.

12. *Eichmann in Jerusalem* (n. 6 above); *Between Past and Future* (New York: Penguin Books, 1977); *Men in Dark Times* (New York: Harcourt, Brace and World, 1968).

Reading Augustine through Arendt poses the same challenges as looking for the "real" Virgil and Cicero in Augustine's Christian polemics. Indeed, there is an ironic justice in Arendt's selective secularization of her primary source since Augustine himself played fast and loose with his classical interlocutors in order to adapt them to the changed context of emergent Christianity and Roman imperial decline. Georg Gadamer in *Truth and Method* describes this approach as the "fusion of horizons," or the creative appropriation of a past debate into the changed terminological and historical context of the contemporary questioner.[13] For him, the conscious "application" of this enlarged past consciousness to contemporary understanding is "the central problem of hermeneutics."

I would argue that in comparing Augustine to Arendt, using not only her dissertation text but also her explicitly political writings in America, a crucial image comes through this reflective and refractive process intact. It is their shared determination to balance personal self-determination and community obligation—*libertas and auctoritas*—using the normative force of either God (Augustine) or the fulfillment of human potential (Arendt) to justify each imperative. This they accomplish while accepting as an unchanging given the murky mixture of conflicting loves in the real world.

Theirs was a worldly social philosophy; that is, a celebration of what Arendt termed, following Augustine, the "plurality" of life (customs, languages and political practices) even while lamenting the tendency of this mixture of "loves" to degenerate into *libido dominandi* (Augustine), violence (Arendt) and the rapid escape from the responsibilities of freedom. Living in but not "of" the world of the *saeculum*, then, was the existential challenge both posed to their successors who had to cope with the end of empires and of certainties. Augustine's and Arendt's hope was derived from their shared belief that amidst the determinisms which constrain freedom of judgment there is always "natality."

Arendt inserted the idea of "new beginnings" in the last line of the last page of the most cited chapter of *Origins of Totalitarianism*, "Ideology and Terror," which she added in 1958. The idea, it is important to note, was also present in the original version of her doctoral dissertation written in 1929 and remained in the text of the dissertation throughout its multiple revisions which she began in the early 1960s in New York while she was completing and revising her other major political commentaries, including *On Revolution, Eichmann*

---

13. H.-G. Gadamer, *Truth and Method*, 2nd rev. ed., trans. J. Weinsheimer and D. G. Marshall (New York: Seabury, 1975) 306.

in Jerusalem and the essays in *Between Past and Future*.[14] It is also present in her phenomenological study, *The Human Condition*, which was published in the same year as the chapter on ideology and terror.

The dissertation, *Love and Saint Augustine*, takes two Augustinian premises—freedom and love of neighbor—and links them intimately. Opening the portal between thought or belief and external, collective life in the *civitas* while at the same time preserving the independent integrity of each poses a central problematic in both of their writings. Arendt opens her dissertation with a question, which she explicitly derives from Augustine, about the relevance of the neighbor to a theology of personal salvation. The "neighbor" is the necessary witness and partner in the exercise of love-enhanced free will, and not simply an expendable minor actor in the pilgrim soul's drama.

The pivotal paradigm of natality and its linkage to *caritas* binds Arendt's thought to Augustine's with a force which no amount of Heideggerean or Nietzschean deconstruction can weaken. The linkage is undeniable and compelling. The Augustinian citation at the end of the "Ideology and Terror" chapter is probably the most frequently cited part of a very frequently cited book. Building up to her final salvo, Arendt agues that totalitarian rulers depend on mobilizing masses by resorting to an "inner compulsion," the "tyranny of logicality" inherent in ideological non-thought. Thus is born a tragic dyad of the "self-coercive force" of deterministic thought matched externally by "total terror . . . which, with its iron band, presses masses of isolated men together and supports them in a world which has become a wilderness for them." This double bind is only possible when people have lost contact with their fellows and have, as Arendt argued, "lost the capacity of both experience and thought."[15]

And yet though today the term totalitarianism itself has been consigned to the gnawing criticism of the mice (and political scientists) and had already come under academic attack even during her lifetime, Arendt insisted until she died, in 1975, that Augustine's categorical imperative of natality still held, and that its dark inverted image as the politics of compulsion and the "banality" of thoughtlessness was still a force in the world. She concluded the "Ideology and Terror" chapter in both an Augustinian and postmodern fashion with the these words:

---

14. *On Revolution* (New York: Penguin, 1963); nn. 6 and 12 above.
15. *Origins of Totalitarianism*, 473–74.

But there remains also the truth that every end in history necessarily contains a new beginning; this beginning is the promise, the only "message" which the end can ever produce. Beginning, before it becomes a historical event, is the supreme capacity of man; politically it is identical with man's freedom. *Initium ut esset homo creatus est*—"that a beginning be made, man was created," said Augustine. This beginning is guaranteed by each new birth; it is indeed every man.[16]

This striking thematic and substantive congruence between Augustine's great work and Arendt's make *Origins* a twentieth-century secular recapitulation of the *City of God*.

Two expanding academic cottage industries are flourishing devoted to the works and the contemporary influences of Augustine and Arendt, in North America, in Europe and in Asia. In the late 1980s when I discovered an unpublished, and heavily annotated English translation of Arendt's dissertation among her papers in the Library of Congress, the fact that there was an Augustinian connection in Arendt's thought was not known among Arendt scholars. Indeed, not only was it a revelation, but it was also definitely not a welcome one. Reactions from those who were the keepers of the Arendtian flame were almost uniformly incredulous and, in some cases, actively hostile. They asked why the romantic enthusiasms of a Heidelberg student should be taken seriously, whether they were directed at a dead saint of the Catholic church or a very alive and notorious professor of German philosophy. After all, she was a Jew whose future career as a political theorist began not with her dissertation on Christian existentialism but with her experiences in the Holocaust.

Our edition of the dissertation, together with an extensive interpretive essay, answers these concerns by demonstrating that Arendt's entire orientation to the life of the mind and the world did not change drastically after she left Germany in 1933. Her continuing encounter with Augustine is a window through which the reader can glimpse the continuity of what Arendt would term her "thought trains." Throughout her career Augustine was for her purposes "no theologian"[17] but instead a philosopher of the human condition. The eternal return which attracted Arendt was not Nietzsche's but Augustine's, the return from the "vast camps of memory" where the creature remembers Creation

---

16. Ibid., 479. Arendt takes her Latin text from *Civ.* 12,21. The translation is her own. See also the comments of Peter J. Burnell at n. 11 in his essay for this volume.

17. Letter from Arendt to Karl Jaspers, July 13, 1955. Cited in E. Young-Bruehl, *Hannah Arendt: For Love of the World* (New Haven: Yale University Press, 1982) 74.

and comes into the presence of its source. The return is to the "world consti-tuted by" human beings consisting of communities bound by their multiple, conflicting loves. When one has understood one's own being by making it "explicit," as she wrote in her dissertation extrapolating on Augustine, then "the other person's being becomes explicit as well." Only when this inner journey is reversed and becomes an outer journey into the world, can "the other become my brother." Out of this equally "explicit tie of brotherliness grows *caritas*."[18]

Being "carried off to God," as Augustine expressed it, when translated into Arendt's secular idiom means "estrangement from the world." It is a recurrent modernist metaphor, appearing in the guise of "radical alienation," "the stranger" and other descriptions in the literature of philosophy, sociology and the arts in the early decades of the century. In Germany, the problem of "van-tage point" or "distancing" can be found in the writings of Weber, Simmel, Mannheim, Kafka, Arendt's friend Walter Benjamin, and also in the art of the German expressionists. Indeed, Peter Gay says, "the term political expres-sionism is, I think, Hannah Arendt's."[19]

Arendt repeatedly used the terms "radical," "estrangement" and "alienation," alone and in combination. Her dissertation is larded with them, and her revi-sions did nothing to alter their number or contextual meaning. From 1929 to 1975 she stuck to the same fundamental theme, one she shared with many of her generation and with her "old friend" Augustine. On the other hand, the obligations entailed in being a creature not only of a transcendent Creator but also of an historical, experienced, man-made community cannot be cast aside. Friendship, love and citizenship are all manifestations of *caritas*—ties that bind. However, the *saeculum*'s call does not preclude 'new beginnings' mani-fested in the founding of new communities and polities of like-minded individuals. Arendt makes the point that:

> "[I]n estrangement from the world, divine grace gives a new meaning to human togetherness—defense against the world. This defense is the foun-dation of the new city, the city of God. Estrangement gives rise to a new togetherness, that is to a new being with and for each other that exists be-side and against the old society."[20]

---

18. Arendt, *Love and Saint Augustine*, 108.

19. P. Gay, *Weimar Culture* (New York: Harper Torchbooks, 1968) 121.

20. Arendt, *Love and Saint Augustine*, 108.

The believer, she writes in her gloss on Augustine, relates to other individuals by virtue of their common ontological source and their common danger—death and sin. Arendt terms this relationship an "indirectness," and uses the triangular model (person-God-neighbor) later on in her American works to build an argument for individuality, collectively expressed as plurality, as the basis of political freedom. The fusion of the many into one, which is characteristic not only of totalitarianism but of all mass phenomena in this century, eliminates both personal life and civil society as independent levels of existence. It destroys the distinctiveness and separateness of individuals which are essential to political discourse and action in the public realm. So the foundation of new communities, whether the *civitas dei* or other *civitates* within the *saeculum*, depends, Arendt writes, on the "indirectness of mutual relations . . . which allows each to grasp the other's whole being." In the more usual understanding of communities of interest "the being of the human race, but not that of the individual" is presupposed. Bureaucracy, political parties, philosophies of historical determinism or progressive liberalism, she says, all speak of aggregate units, whether classes, masses, nations, voters or the oppressed.

Arendt's allergy to collective discourse was pronounced. Not suprisingly, like Augustine she is often claimed as "conservative," but she refused political categorization and preferred to hide in plain sight, at a safe distance. It was a favorite paradox of hers, inspired by her reading of Augustine, that the individual as such can only be grasped through the denial of selfhood, and community understood only through the odyssey of the individual pilgrim soul. Foregrounding the self and community, in other words, is achieved by a willed spiritual abstraction from the interpersonal context of inherited customs and roles, and ultimately in an "isolation in which the believer stands before" the Creator in the mind's memory.[21]

The plurality of "indirectness" is the only legitimate basis for understanding the meaning of equality in Arendt's political thought. Augustine has given "a new meaning" to the term equality, she writes, based not on sameness of condition but of potential for natality and *caritas* derived from a common source in the Creator. This form of equality retains individual "explicitness" and does not sacrifice it to historical kinship. "The explicitness of equality is contained in the commandment of neighborly love." Even more important for Arendt's reading of Augustine is that the answer to the question of the relevance to the

---

21. Ibid., 111.

neighbor "is not tied to Christianity." She cites Augustine's injunction to "extend your love over the whole earth if you will love Christ."[22] This does not mean universal conversion, she thinks, but rather making the world into a neighborhood of brotherly love. "The binding power of the common faith in Christ is secondary," she rather surprisingly concludes in her dissertation, since its function is to "redeem the past" and specific communities have specific pasts. The primary binding power is the common ontological source of creation. "The fact that people belong to each other is no longer determined by generation and geographic proximity but by imitation," by a freely willed, explicit choice.[23]

Thus, Augustine's pilgrim souls abolish the *civitas terrena* as such, but they do so only by fighting it and not simply by radical alienation from it. "The past remains at work in the impossibility of complete isolation for the believer who cannot act by himself, only with others or against them," Arendt writes. The believer is a grounded, contextualized citizen of the world. And so, "Salvation is made to depend on the conduct of the world or rather, on its conquest." This dynamic "return" is natality in action. It is "through freedom of choice" that the individual is "recalled" from the world and breaks previous social ties, but learns in the process that "the equality of all people, once posited, cannot be canceled out." Existential equality is the basis of a new *caritas* in the world. As a result, Arendt writes, the "coexistence of the people in their community" also changes. It ceases being "inevitable and matter of course" and becomes "freely chosen and replete with obligations."[24]

In the end, for Arendt love is the source of both individuation and collectivity. It is an existential link between past and future and the basis upon which natality can "appear" in the world of Arendt's later political writings as the founding of new public realms. Augustine's *caritas* allows Arendt to redefine Heidegger's veiled Being as a transcendent Creator and at the same time to engage Being directly in the human condition, thereby overcoming a fundamental tension in her mentor's work. The effect of Arendt's appropriation of Augustine's *caritas* is to merge, and even to transcend, both Jasper's "factual-life-in-process" and Heidegger's "question of Being."

---

22. Ibid., 107 and n. 38. Arendt's quotation is taken from the *Homilies on the First Epistle of John* 10,8.
23. Ibid., 107 and in general, 93–112.
24. Ibid., 102.

The journey from the inner world of *caritas* binding the divided will to the outer world of *caritas* binding communities and nations is the journey from theology to political theory in Arendt's writings. By the time she publishes *Origins* and becomes an American "covergirl," the dynamics of inner grace quietly drop out and there is a dramatic shift of scene to the *saeculum,* the realm of Augustine's *City of God,* and from there to the contested play of "words and deeds" in a political world under siege. But making the transition intact are Arendt's central concepts of natality as free will, plurality, foundation, and *caritas.* In America, they were transformed into political theory.

It must be admitted, however, that while her other Augustine-derived terms are clearly secular, *caritas* does still seem to exude an otherworldly penumbra. Depending on one's perspective, that eminence might be identified either as Christian theology or a German *Gemeinschaft* romanticism. Of course, Arendt did not see it that way, claiming the term and ignoring the content that did not work for her own rhetorical purposes. Acknowledging its source in Augustine, she nonetheless did not hesitate to adapt it to political science, just as Augustine had retrofitted Cicero's definition of a *res publica* for a value-neutral, contextual argument about the origins and purposes of political institutions.

By making a distinction between structural/functional meaning and the normative standard of justice, Augustine was able to propose what would in this century be termed a "realist" reading of the ebbs and flows of empires and states. Similarly, Arendt separated moral content from the operational meaning of *caritas* in order to demonstrate its existential reality. Cleverly avoided in both cases is the need to schematize, rank-order or engage in the sort of normative morphology which has been the hallmark of the canonical texts of political science from Plato to the Cold War and beyond. For Arendt and Augustine, the point is not the moral weight of government, its laws and structures, but the shifting socio-political consensus that drives it, and the dynamic process by which that consensus is reached. Arendt focused on the public realm of political discourse and action and showed how these "spaces" could be continuous or discontinuous with existing governmental institutions. Augustine's social philosophy looked at the formation and degeneration of communities of like-minded individuals within and beyond the boundaries of the state. Both saw "love" as, in Tolkien's terms, "the one ring to bind them all."

In *The Human Condition*, *caritas* makes a sudden and startling appearance. Arendt's resort to Augustine as *deus ex machina* is particularly shocking to those political theorists who prefer to understand Arendt's definition of politics exclusively rather than inclusively. Arendtian scholars such as Margaret Canovan recognize the tension in Arendt's works between an Aristotelian politics of formal equality and an underlying socioeconomic and moral complexity. But none connects her perspective to the multilayered, nuanced political observations of late Roman writers such as Augustine. Instead, Arendt is portrayed as a nostalgic Athenian *polis*-admirer who is fearful of the threats to freedom resulting from state-imposed equalities of class, race and gender of the Platonic sort. Jean Elshtain once famously termed this a bad case of *"polis* envy." In modern terms, public life is essentially about negative rights, constitutional procedures, and issues of public import which citizens ought to debate as equals. It is not in essence about the economics, education or family values.[25]

It is important, however, to observe that what Arendt does *not* say speaks as eloquently as her spoken exclusions. That is, she does not say that politics has no connection to the moral dynamics of consensus or Augustinian "loves." We can conclude from the sum total of her work that for Arendt communities of shared values animate the social realm and constitute its plurality. They set the scope and limits, though they cannot wholly determine the substance, of political debate in the state. In fact, Arendt is only demarcating public, social and private realms of discourse for the purposes of analysis. She always operates on the assumption that the public institutional realm encompasses many moral *civitates* and is reflective of their "loves."

Indeed, this demarcation of zones sounds immediately familiar to the Augustinian scholar. The state is not co-extensive with any *civitas* of the spirit, whether *dei* or *terrena*, nor for that matter is the church. Augustine argued that the providential role for institutions of state is, at minimum, to maintain the peace "among a rough population" by whatever means necessary and, at maximum, to encourage and reward civic virtue among a people so inclined. As with Arendt, the political realm responds to the values and needs of the people but is not to be confused with the *populus* itself. Even Christian rulers must use force, and even pagan Roman rulers can be virtuous.[26]

---

25. M. Canovan, *Hanah Arendt: A Reinterpretation of Her Political Thought* (Cambridge: Cambridge University Press, 1992); Elshtain's remarks were made at the American Political Science Association panel on Arendt in September 1993.

26. On this point, see my "Augustine's Razor: Public vs. Private Interests in *The City of God,*" in *The City of God: A Collection of Critical Essays*, ed. D. F. Donnelly (New York: Peter Lang, 1995) 151–68.

Augustine is present in at least twelve different locations in *The Human Condition*. We find him discoursing on the mysterious, undefinable essence of human nature ("I have become a question to myself"); on the obligatory "burden" of public life imposed by the imperative of *caritas*; on the "natality" of man as a newcomer capable of *initium* in the world; and on *caritas* as the "Christian political principle." All of these references, despite the passage of almost 30 years, are either direct citations of or extrapolations upon her 1929 dissertation. The difference is that they are being woven into a text which is not about Augustine at all, but about the precarious legitimacy of the public realm under conditions of modernity.[27]

Here *caritas* is not the bonding agent of communities abstractly rendered, as in 1929, but of concrete counter-*civitates*. *Caritas* is the Christian political principle, she writes. It was, she reminds her audience, "Augustine who proposed to found not only Christian `brotherhood' but all human relationships on charity." This *caritas* is "like the world . . . between men," linking them together yet maintaining their separateness.

> This surprising illustration of the Christian political principle is in fact very well chosen, because the bond of charity between people, while it is incapable of founding a public realm of its own, is quite adequate to . . . carry a group of essentially worldless people through the world, a group of saints or a group of criminals.[28]

Caritas is not sufficient to create kingdoms or polities, but it is certainly a necessary precondition—a "prepolitical" foundation. Be careful what you love, Augustine warned. And Arendt took him seriously.

After she wrote her Eichmann report first for *The New Yorker* and then in book form, an avalanche of criticism and outright hatred descended upon her—precisely at the time (the late 50s and early 60s) when she had planned to publish the dissertation. Diverted by the Eichmann affair, the rest of the decade was largely devoted to damage control. Only the Vietnam War and student protests were sufficiently riveting to partially divert the attention of her American detractors. Arendt, too, shifted gears and began a series of commentaries on American political values and behavior.

But in the heat of defending her position on the "banality" of evil and the complicity of Jewish elders in the deportation of their flock, Arendt took on a

---

27. *The Human Condition*, 10, 12, 14, 53, 60n., 74n., 177, 229n., 252n., 317n., 318n.
28. Ibid., 53.

towering figure in the international Jewish community, Gershom Scholem. Former President of Hebrew University and once her close collaborator in the movement for a Jewish-Arab federated homeland, Scholem turned on Arendt in 1964 and publicly denounced her work as traitorous. There was "little trace" in her book of the "love of the Jewish people" which was required of any Jew. Instead there was a "flippancy," a disrespect for the dead. Arendt shot back that her Jewishness was a fact, a given that was, as she termed it, "pre-political."

> You are quite right . . . . I am not moved by any "love" of this sort, and for two reasons: I have never in my life "loved" any people or collective, neither the German . . . nor the French . . . nor the American people, nor the working class . . . . I do not "love" the Jews, nor do I "believe" in them; I merely belong to them as a matter of course, beyond dispute or argument.[29]

In other words, *caritas* as the glue holding communities together does not destroy the individual's capacity for disinterested judgment. Indeed, belonging becomes the consequence of free will and not a "fact" of biological inheritance or historical contiguity. Arendt refuses to be understood as a "daughter" of the Jewish people, if that entails prescribed behavior and speech. The language of familial or group identity cannot be transferred unthinkingly to the public realm because, as Scholem invokes it, Arendt's Jewishness makes critical distance from Jewish history impossible. For Arendt, the price of membership does not have to be complicity. Translated to the public space, *caritas* empowers. It makes "new beginnings" possible, including choosing other identities than those determined by birth, though it does not directly build political institutions or write laws. For Arendt there is an implicit normative injunction in *caritas* which legitimates the simultaneous love of one's own people, and of all people, of the rights of one's own people and justice for all.

And so, the intertwined paths of Augustine and Arendt carry us into the new beginning of a post-Cold War, postmodern world. It is a world where, inexplicably, ideological barriers between peoples fall only to be replaced by "new" ones, some of which are very old indeed—race, nationality, ethnicity. That evil persists in the modern world of laws, technology and communication demands an explanation—one that Arendt did not live to deliver. She "changed her mind," as she publicly said, between writing *Origins* and the Eichmann report about the "radical" nature of evil actions. Though she does not cite Augustine, she summons his spirit to assist her in a final response to Scholem.

---

29. "'Eichmann in Jerusalem': An Exchange of Letters between Gershom Scholem and Hannah Arendt," *Encounter*, January 1964, 51–56.

Arendt insists that evil can never be radical in the sense of achieving a hyperreality. It is "only extreme (and) possesses neither depth nor any demonic dimension." She prefers a different metaphor than "radical," a term she associates with fundamental thinking and action. Evil "can overgrow and lay waste the whole world precisely because it spreads like a fungus on the surface." Evil acts defy thought and judgment because they "try to reach some depth, to go to the roots." But there are no roots, "there is nothing," only "banality." And so, to be a radical thinker is to plunge beneath the surface of complexity and doubt and to approach the good which lies at the foundation of the world constituted by humans and which is reborn every day with each "new beginning."[30]

---

30. Ibid.

JOHN MILBANK, AUGUSTINE, AND THE "SECULAR"

Michael J. Hollerich

I

When Robert Markus's *Saeculum: History and Society in the Theology of St Augustine* was first published in 1967, it was welcomed as an authoritative statement on what an older generation of scholarship had called Augustine's "theology of history."[1] Markus built his interpretation on certain commonly accepted features of Augustine's thought on the two cities, the *civitas terrena* and the *civitas dei*. It had long been recognized that Augustine distinguished two different sets of meanings in these terms. On the one hand, *civitas terrena* and *civitas dei* referred to historical, sociological and empirical realities, which could appropriately be identified as "state" and "church." On the other hand, Augustine used the two cities to indicate eschatological realities which could not be neatly identified with actual earthly institutions. In the latter sense they expressed the communities of the saved and the damned, to which all humans (and angelic beings as well) belonged, depending on the objects of their loves. Those who loved God above all things, even to the contempt of self, were citizens of the heavenly city; those dominated by *amor sui* belonged to the

---

1. R. A. Markus, *Saeculum: History and Society in the Theology of St Augustine* (Cambridge: Cambridge University Press, 1970). A revised edition of 1988 reprinted the original book along with a new introduction. The revised edition is cited here.

earthly city. But since the ordering of love in any individual soul was a mystery ultimately knowable by God alone, the ultimate destiny of human beings was lost to us so long as this world lasted. In this sense it was not wrong to say that the earthly and the heavenly cities were "invisible." Many who were inside the church as baptized Christians would fail to be among the elect; and many who presently appeared to be outside the church would yet prove to be among the saved. The church was therefore a mixed body in which saints and sinners co-existed, like the wheat and tares of the parable, not to be separated until the last judgment.

So much was commonly granted by scholars. Disagreement tended to focus on such matters as the precise valuation Augustine put on politics and the secular order, or on whether there could be members of the city of God who remained outside the boundaries of the sacramental communion of the church. Markus made an important contribution in showing how Augustine's thought on the two cities was given its enduring form as a consequence of a roughly datable change in his estimation of the role of the Roman Empire in God's plan for human history. Up to the years 400 or 401, Augustine shared the religious enthusiasm of many of his Christian contemporaries for the *tempora Christiana*, the post-Constantinian phase of Roman history (ch. 2). Subsequently, however, he grew disenchanted with this "sacralization" of the empire (ch. 3). Instead he came increasingly to see the Roman Empire in a coldly "secular" light as simply one of the many contingent—and disposable—instruments God had used throughout human history to advance his purposes, which, apart from his revelation in the canonical scriptures, were unknown to us. Such a "secularization" of politics, Markus proposed, was the ultimate conclusion Augustine drew from his reflections on divine theodicy following the fall of Rome in 410. Henceforth the sphere of the political was to be construed as a field of activity in which ultimate loyalties and commitments had no place. The political realm was the area of the overlap of the two cities and could be identified with neither one. It was now neutral territory, "secular" in an almost modern sense. Christians were obliged to seek the limited kind of peace appropriate to the earthly city, even though in doing so they might have to cooperate with unbelievers who did not share their religious faith (ch. 4).

One difficulty for this interpretation, Markus realized, was Augustine's defense of religious coercion, which he came to advocate in dealing with the Donatist schism. There was a contradiction, or at least an inconsistency, in saying that the Roman Empire as a political institution played no essential role in salvation history, while at the same time advocating that a now Christianized government should use force to repress dissent and schism. Part of the purpose of his book, Markus wrote, was to do something that had not previously been done: to learn how the "secularization of politics," if such it was, co-existed in Augustine's mind with religious coercion.[2]

The solution which he proposed held that, although Augustine rejected all notions of a divine sanction for the empire and its social order as institutions, he continued to hold that individual office holders and magistrates should actively and forcefully promote Christianity's welfare. They did so, however, not as servants of a Christian state but as members of the Christian church. Augustine's preference for thinking in terms of personal and individual conceptions of agency and responsibility, his virtual atomizing of any idea of the state as an objective and collective institution, underlay this appeal to the Christian magistrate's religious duties and loyalties. It was therefore, ironically, the same intellectual habit which enabled him to focus clearly on the eschatological character of the two cities that also enabled him to justify religious coercion.

In the last chapter of his book, Markus tried to draw out more systematically some of the theological implications of Augustine's concept of the *saeculum* (ch. 7). Here he put his theological cards on the table, invoking such bellwether names from the nineteen-sixties as Hans Küng, Dietrich Bonhoeffer, Harvey Cox, and Jürgen Moltmann. They were his preferred guides for a new understanding of the church's relation to the modern secular world. The world for which Augustine's attack on the sacral interpretation of the empire was really intended was our own: "His 'secularization' of the realm of politics implies a pluralistic, religiously neutral civil community."[3] Only in our time, he argued, have Christians faced fully what it means to live without the social and political props of "Christendom."[4] The church, too, had to submit to a measure of "secularization" like that to which Augustine had subjected the state. The church could not claim a direct institutional continuity with the city of God, or the kingdom of God. At best its role was to be the sign of that kingdom's yet-to-come character; in the meantime, it was no more than the world insofar as it had been reconciled to God.

---

2. Ibid., 31–2; for the resolution, see esp. 139–53.

3. Ibid., 173.

4. Ibid., 162–6.

II

Saeculum has held its place as a standard interpretation of Augustine's thought on history, society, and politics.[5] To one such as the present writer, whose own scholarly specialty is in the writings of Eusebius of Caesarea, who is so often set as a foil for Augustine, it seems indisputable that Augustine's mature treatment of the Roman Empire represents something new and important in early Christian thought on the state. Nevertheless, the book bears the mark of the times in which it was written. Certain unsatisfying features of Markus's interpretation have assumed clearer shape in the past generation. I am thinking especially of the benign and expansive interpretation he gives to the concept of the secular, and the effect this has on his treatment of the church and its relation to the world.

In recent years numerous articulate "modernity-critics"[6] have made us more critical of the philosophical liberalism underlying modern notions of "the secular." One of the most aggressive and original of these critics is the British theologian John Milbank, whose *Theology and Social Theory: Beyond Secular Reason* appeared in 1990. Although the book was commissioned for a series on theology in dialogue with non-theological disciplines, *Theology and Social Theory* is hardly an exercise in intellectual ecumenism. From the first page to the last, it sustains a furious attack on the very idea of an objective social science which theology can claim to use as an acceptably neutral tool kit for expounding Christian faith in the contemporary academy. Milbank's deconstruction of the "secular" flatly contradicts basic assumptions of Markus's book:

> Once, there was no "secular." And the secular was not latent, waiting to fill more space with the steam of the "purely human," when the pressure of the sacred was relaxed. Instead, there was the single community of Christendom, with its dual aspects of *sacerdotium* and *regnum*. The *saeculum*, in the medieval era, was not a space, a domain, but a time — the interval between fall and eschaton where coercive justice, private property and impaired natural reason must make shift to cope with the unredeemed effects of sinful humanity. The secular as a *domain* [emphasis added] had to be instituted or *imagined*, both in theory and practice.[7]

---

5. As noted most recently in O. O'Donovan's *The Desire of the Nations: Rediscovering the Roots of Political Theology* (Cambridge: Cambridge University Press, 1996) 7.

6. The phrase is from O'Donovan, *The Desire of Nations*, who sketches their criticisms of liberalism on 271ff.

In Milbank's reading, there is no supposedly neutral public sphere in which people can act politically without reference to ultimate ends. Those ultimate ends cannot be bracketed either for methodological purposes, in the name of a putatively objective social science, or for political purposes, for the sake of constructing a political order shorn of ontological presuppositions. The assertion that there is such a domain is merely a social construct with a definable history, one which it is the task of his book to unmask and deconstruct.

The book is divided into four parts. The first deals with the foundations of liberalism in early modern philosophy and political economy, whose roots Milbank finds in a voluntarist and nominalist notion of individual *dominium* and a "neo-pagan" celebration of passion and desire (what traditional Christianity had criticized as the *libido dominandi*). The second part deals with the rise and development of a positivist science of society from Malebranche to Weber, culminating in a critique of the sociology of religion, including remarks on the sociological study of Christian origins. Part three, on theology and "dialectics," mainly discusses Hegel and Marx but concludes with a fascinating discussion of their courtship by modern Catholic theology. The fourth and final section, "theology and difference," takes leave of the Enlightenment-inspired universalism of both positivist social science and Marxism and focuses on "postmodern" attention to difference and pluralism, and the challenges they present to theology. The final two chapters of the book return to the ancient period, for a re-reading, first, of the classical literature on virtue and the *polis*, in critical dialogue especially with Alasdair MacIntyre, with whom Milbank has much in common, and then of Augustine's *City of God*, a chapter which Milbank says consummates the argument of his whole book.

The rest of the present essay focuses on this last chapter. It will present the substance of Milbank's re-reading of Augustine, noting those places where he differs most directly from Markus.

---

7. J. Milbank, *Theology and Social Theory: Beyond Secular Reason* (Oxford: Blackwell, 1990) 9. For critical reaction, see the July 1992 issue of New Blackfriars (vol. 73), which is devoted entirely to discussion of the book. For a self-description, see Milbank's "'Postmodern Critical Augustinianism': A Short Summa in Response to Forty-Two Unasked Questions," *Modern Theology* 7 (1991): 225–37.

III

Milbank's presentation of "theology as a social science" seeks to restore theology's traditional status as the queen of the sciences. Such a theology will have to develop its account of human society from its own, historically specific resources, not from those of some ostensibly neutral, rational account. It will also be a species of ecclesiology, based on the actual practice of the historic Christian church. Telling the story of the church will provide the narrative by which to measure the stories of all other societies and institutions. "The *logic* of Christianity involves the claim that the 'interruption' of history by Christ and his bride, the Church, is the most fundamental of events, interpreting all other events. And it is most *specifically* a social event, able to interpret other social formations, because it compares them with its own new social practice" (388).

Milbank's sketch of such a social and critical theology is executed in three stages: a "counter-history" which tells the story of all of human history in terms of the emergence of the church, a "counter-ethics" which describes the different practice of the society of the church (in particular how it differs from pre- and post-Christian ethics), and a "counter-ontology" which lays out the difference of Christianity from all other cultural systems, which it regards as so many roads to nihilism.

Such a program explains the appeal of Augustine and of the *City of God*. In Milbank's view, Augustine provides the most successful Christian example of a "metanarrative realism" which can criticize both secular society and the church itself on the basis of resources provided entirely from within the Christian tradition. Augustine, he argues, is in fact the originator of the very notion of such a critique. The Enlightenment and its modern offspring are actually "abridgements and parodies" of Augustine's accomplishment, an insight he credits to Nietzsche. It was also Nietzsche who correctly identified the unique feature of Christianity's tradition of practice, the thing which separated it from other societies. He called it the "celebration of weakness," though Milbank prefers to describe it as "peaceful reconciliation."

This emphasis on peace and peaceful reconciliation is central to Milbank's project. He argues that Christianity transcends every type of postmodern philosophy of "difference" in its refusal to grant an original or ontological priority to the conflictual antagonism which (he says) is presumed by such philosophies and whose explicit and unavoidable end is nihilism.[8] However, his

---

8. See ch. 10, "Ontological Violence or the Postmodern Problematic."

insistence on the preeminent importance of the peaceful way of life of the city of God has to reckon with another important strand in Augustine's thought. Along with giving peace a central and fundamental role in the *City of God*, Augustine also recognizes the apparently inescapable necessity of *power* in human life. On this basis, for example, he legitimated the use of violence by the state (now administered by Christian magistrates), rationalized the participation of Christians in a just war, and sanctioned the use of religious coercion by Christian magistrates against schismatic fellow Christians. Augustine's pessimistic anthropology has had a significant impact on numerous modern appropriations of his social and political thought, from the realism of Reinhold Niebuhr to Jean Bethke Elshtain, whose recent *Augustine and the Limits of Politics* recommends an Augustinian tonic for American democracy.[9] Augustine's awareness of the power of sinful human self-interest, and the necessity of a greater power to counteract and restrain it, has struck a responsive chord not just with conservatives, as one might expect, but with certain facets of modern liberalism. In Milbank's view, this selective affinity with modern liberalism has led to significant misreadings of Augustine's thought on the church and on society. We will return to this affinity in a moment.

Despite Augustine's recognition of the baleful effects of original sin, his most fundamental contribution is not a modern-style shrewdness for dealing with the abuse of power, but an assertion of the *absolute priority of peace over violence and antagonism of every kind*. Milbank argues that this is clear from his historical narrative of the two cities, and from the ontology of peace and violence which is grounded by the narrative. The deepest hallmarks of the earthly city are precisely its sinful self-interest and love of self-assertion, to the denial of God and of others: the *libido dominandi*. In the case of the history of Rome, Augustine demonstrates this by appealing to the brutal facts of the always fragile peace won by Roman arms (e.g., *Civ.* 3,14), to the unconditional character of ownership, which allows the owner to do as he likes with his property (*Civ.* 2,20), and to the patricians' oppression of the plebs (2,18). Such systemic violence was perpetually inscribed through pagan myth and ritual, for instance by the cult of Jupiter Stator, whose staying hand spared Romulus' men from reprisals for having raped the Sabine women (3,13). Over against such a brutal world Augustine posits the self-donation of a God who creates out of nothing, rather than by mastering a previous violent chaos, in

---

9. J. B. Elshtain, *Augustine and the Limits of Politics* (Notre Dame, Ind.: University of Notre Dame Press, 1995).

the manner of Jupiter Stator. The heavenly city is Jerusalem, the "vision of peace," in the etymology long known to Jews and Christians, which comes down to earth to restore the peace which God had intended in the beginning, before the onset of pride and domination. Not Romulus' murder of his brother but the memory of the murdered Abel is the founding act of the heavenly city's earthly pilgrimage; this inauguration establishes its character as the society marked by the forgiveness of sins. "Instead of a peace 'achieved' through the abandonment of the losers, the subordination of potential rivals and resistance to enemies, the Church provides a genuine peace by its memory of all the victims, its equal concern for all its citizens and its self-exposed offering of reconciliation to enemies" (392).

IV

Such is the "counter-history" narrated by Augustine. The "counter-ethics" which Milbank discerns in the *City of God* begins, as did the counter-history, with an account of ecclesiology, for the distinctive ethos of Christianity is rooted in the new type of community of the church. The true character of such a "counter-ethics," however, is obscured by those modern interpreters of Augustine who tend to see Christianity as the "cradle of liberalism." Here is where Milbank's disagreement with Markus comes out most directly, for Markus is certainly to be numbered in their company. Such interpreters see Christianity as a turning away from the "creative politics"[10] of classicism, that is, from the notion that the *polis* or the state was the most comprehensive setting for the full development of human life. For them, Christianity continued to exist within the boundary of the ancient city, while expressing its full churchly character in its sacramental life and as the community of the elect known to God alone. But this, in Milbank's view, is to underestimate the degree to which Christian communities maintained their own social practice, within their own households, before Constantine's conversion and even in some measure afterwards.

The modern liberal reading of Augustine therefore seeks to define Augustine's greatest accomplishment as *arriving at an individualist conception of both church and state*. There are thus two poles to the interpretation: "on the one hand, [Augustine] interprets the state as merely a compromise between individual wills for the satisfaction of material conveniences, and, on

---

10. The phrase is taken from the seminal study of C. N. Cochrane, *Christianity and Classical Culture* (Oxford: Clarendon Press, 1940) 29, 83, 106, 249 and passim.

the other, he understands the true Church, the *civitas Dei*, as the collection of elect true believers known only to God" (400).

1. In speaking here of Augustine's understanding of the state, Milbank is referring to the passages in the *City of God* in which Augustine redefines the definition of a commonwealth which Cicero attributes to Scipio in his *Republic*, namely, that a *res publica* was "an association united by a common sense of right and a community of interest" (*Civ.* 2,21, trans. H. Bettenson). Augustine rewords this to say that "a people is the association of a multitude of rational beings united by a common agreement on the objects of their love" (*Civ.* 19,24). The point of his reformulation is usually seen as an interpretation of the state in terms not of justice but simply of whatever it is that brings the citizens or subjects together as a commonality. The theological payoff of this change then becomes the conception of a neutral state in which Christians are free to participate so long as their religious allegiances are not violated. Not only free to participate but obliged to do so, since the state exists for the limited but necessary, and divinely willed, end of securing earthly peace. Christians' purposes for acting thus will differ from those of their non-believing fellow citizens, since for them earthly peace must be used or referred to the ultimate peace of the heavenly city. But at the level of this-worldly performance they can, and must, collaborate with unbelievers in practical matters, while bracketing questions of ultimate ends.[11]

To Catholic ears such a line of argument sounds as though it had been lifted from the pages of John Courtney Murray, who famously argued for full Catholic participation in modern liberal democracies. Murray stressed that particularly in America stable government was founded on agreement on the common good at the level of performance, sparing us the divisive experience of unresolvable and ideologized debate over ends.[12] Milbank construes the liberal account of Augustine's achievement in the same way, but only to reject it as a tendentious and apologetically motivated concession to the secular state. Such a reading of Augustine, he argues, overlooks an important aspect of his revision of Scipio's definition of the state. Throughout the *City of God*, Augustine does not offer us a picture of some hypothetical state in which people might be joined in pursuit of basically neutral, limited ends. Rather, his subject is the Roman Republic in its actual existence as a state dominated by perverted passions

---

11. Cf. Markus's own sketch of this reading of Augustine, *Saeculum*, 100–104.

12. J. C. Murray, S. J., *We Hold These Truths: Catholic Reflections on the American Proposition* (Kansas City, Mo.: Sheed and Ward, 1960) 73.

and misdirected desires and loves. What its members shared in common was no more than a conception of *dominium* devoted to selfishly individualist ends. In such a state one naturally expects, says Augustine sarcastically, that "the laws should punish offenses against one another's property, not offenses against a man's personal character. No one should be brought to trial except for an offense, or threat of offense, against another's property, house, or person; but anyone should be free to do as he likes about his own, or with his own, or with others, if they consent" (2,20). There is an obvious affinity between such a description and the modern liberal theory of the state as dedicated to the maximization of personal freedom, the protection of private property, and the sanctity of contract.

Is it fair to impute such a political subtext to Markus's reading of Augustine? In one sense, no. It seems clear from Markus's book that he himself inclines towards a redistributive and activist mission for the state that is far from the Lockean liberalism which Milbank has targeted. Certainly Markus's theological *periti* (Moltmann, Cox, and company) speak for welfare liberalism and social democracy more than Ciceronian or Lockean defenses of the rights of property.[13] And yet his actual account of the secular state seems cast in terms drawn entirely from modern individualist liberalism, in which the state is founded on contract and consent, not on our nature as social beings, and which lacks any transcendental legitimation or attachment.[14] Such a state must necessarily be secular, open, pluralistic, and religiously neutral—freedom plus groceries, as one admirer has described the goal of the liberal state.[15]

2. The modern individualist misunderstanding of Augustine has even graver consequences when applied to his conception of the church. Here the tendency is to maximize the gap between the visible, historic Christian church on the one hand, and the city of God on the other, by emphasizing the eschatological character of the *civitas dei*: the heavenly city of the elect will be revealed in its fullness only in the next world. In the meantime here below, the church is a "mixed body," a *corpus permixtum*, blended like the wheat and the tares in the parable, and not to be visibly separated until the final judgment. Augustine of course commonly *speaks* of the institutional church on earth as the "city of God," but his fundamental assertion is that the true church, the community of

---

13. E.g., *Saeculum*, 171–72.

14. Ibid., 174–78 and Appendix B. Note the comparison with John Stuart Mill (!) on 101, at least so far as the character of the *saeculum* as the domain appropriate to intermediate ends is concerned.

15. Ibid., 173. The phrase is Max Lerner's, as cited in J. P. Diggins's review of a new book on Lerner's life, in *The New Republic*, November 16, 1998, 44.

the saints, is known to God alone. Markus proposed that Augustine did not take his "secularization" of the church far enough, and that we needed to assert more explicitly that the institutional church was merely a signpost on the way to the eschatological reality of the city of God: "And this City is not the Church, though it will exist within the Church as well as outside it. The path of its pilgrimage is hidden, its working is anonymous. . . . The Church is not this Kingdom, even in its germ or its chrysalis."[16]

Milbank charges that this suggests that institutional adherence only held some sort of secondary status in Augustine's mind. That would be a grave underestimation of the critical importance Augustine attached to the actual public life of the church. The Donatist controversy is revealing on this score. Even though Donatism was the catalyst which stimulated Augustine's most profound reflections on the church as a mixed body, his obsessive campaign to re-establish sacramental communion and to end the schism makes little sense unless we take him at his word and understand that the unity of the church was not a peripheral by-product of redemption but its very substance. The bishop who sought by such strenuous efforts to bring the schismatics back into the fold could not have been so committed to a narrow conception of interiority as we are sometimes tempted to think. In fact, Milbank reminds us, Augustine would accuse the Donatists of being more committed to the priority of the attitudinal, on which they were willing to make the very efficacy of the sacramental system depend.[17]

The most serious consequence of what Milbank stigmatizes as the "individualist" misunderstanding of Augustine is that *it fails to recognize the degree to which Augustine sees the church itself as a "political" reality which strives to embrace the whole of our social life and whose inclusivity therefore far exceeds that of the ancient polis* (403). Here Milbank appears to have hit on a serious shortcoming of Markus's book, which has always left me uneasy because of the way in which the church, in which Augustine was a prominent and aggressive leader, threatens to disappear from view. It is true that Markus's research concentrated on the role of history and society in Augustine's theology, and that he did not intend to treat the church extensively.[18] And yet the reader

---

16. *Saeculum*, 180–81.

17. Prof. J. Partout Burns suggested to me in discussion that Augustine should not be taken at face value on this point. The emphasis on the interior attitude in sacramental efficacy which he imputed to the Donatists may have been primarily a self-serving invention.

18. *Saeculum*, xxi.

is certainly left with the impression that the church and everything connected with it (sacraments, ministry, discipline, community life) occupied a reduced and even discretionary space in human life, an impression that the book's last chapter did nothing to dispel. The real "action" was not in the church but in the world (i.e., the *saeculum*). The source of this mistake, in Milbank's view, was Markus's reliance on such dichotomies as "inner and outer," "historical and eschatological," "visible and invisible," and the like, which are predicated on what he regards as arbitrary and imaginary oppositions.[19] The whole thrust of his massive book is to deconstruct such dualities as self-inflicted wounds theology has suffered in a futile effort to win intellectual respect. Augustine saw no radical distinction between the church and the city of God, even though he conceded that not all baptized Christians were likely to be saved, and that not all those who were going to be saved were already baptized Christians. But the significance of this awareness on Augustine's part does not consist in a relativization of the importance of the church. The church was nothing but the community of salvation insofar as its social practice, replicating its narration of the story of Jesus, embodied the forgiveness of sins and realized the bond of charity among its members. The church's *raison d'être* was the extension of its practice into the whole of human life, not excepting a putatively "political" realm reserved for the competency of "the state." The peace of the city of God was to be realized in practice, and realized in all spheres of life: the life of the individual (the "soul"), the life of the household, and the life of the *polis*. Milbank argues that Augustine's unique insight into the ontological priority of peace over violence equipped him to give expression to a comprehensive vision of human life at all levels of association, ordered and harmonized in right desire as a series of "mediations" connecting parts to whole.

> Augustine's Christian ontology . . . implies both that the part belongs to the whole, and that each part transcends any imaginable whole, because the whole is only a finite series which continues indefinitely towards an infinite and unfathomable God. This series is nothing but a sequence of mediations between individuals, households and cities. The "whole" is Christ, the mediator, and he articulates his body and conveys this mediation as an endless series of new mediations which interpellates human "persons."[20]

---

19. Markus's careful account of Augustine's gradual detachment from Platonic and metaphysical notions of "inner and outer" or "earthly and heavenly" as levels of being, in favor of a more biblical conception of human life under sin vs. under grace is found in chapter 4 of his book, on the foundations of political authority. The account reads persuasively—and yet seems to point more toward Luther on the "Two Kingdoms" than to Augustine the Catholic bishop.

20. *Theology and Social Theory*, 405. See 403–408 for the full statement of this "Christian ontology."

This rhapsodic evocation, with its allusion to the "social logic" of the Christian Middle Ages, leads Milbank to his master thesis and, at the same time, his central conundrum. "All 'political theory,' in the antique sense," he says, "is relocated by Christianity as thought about the Church. The difficulty, for patristic and medieval thought, was how and whether to conceive of a political structure in addition to that of the Church" (405). There is no problem of "church and state" because there is, properly speaking, no state in the sense of an independent, sovereign political realm outside the true commonwealth of the church. Beyond the church is simply the realm of sin *tout court*, dominated by self-love, violence, and wrongly-directed desires. The *civitas terrena* is not the state but simply the phase of history in which human society used wrongly the finite goods of this world. Government in the sense of the earthly city, with its coercive apparatus, is virtually indistinguishable from slavery. Nonetheless, so long as the heavenly city is on pilgrimage in this world in its fallen condition, it too must make use of the same coercive instruments provided by God to curb the effects of sin.[21]

V

It is at this point, concedes Milbank, that Augustine's social thought becomes most problematic. For the heavenly city's use of instruments such as coercion, slavery, property, and economic competition, puts it in the risky position of using the *instruments* of sin to control the *effects* of sin. As much as possible, these instruments, above all governmental coercion, will be used with pastoral intent and not for the love of power. Similarly, it will be remembered, Markus recognized that Augustine's defense of religious coercion was the most resistant evidence to the thesis of *his* book. His solution was to propose that Augustine expected the magistrate to impose coercive measures not in the name of a Christian *state* but as a member of the Christian church. In this way, Markus thought, we might better understand how in Augustine's own mind he could arrive at an essentially "secular" notion of the Roman Empire, while still expecting the state vigorously to enforce Christian principles.

---

21. Markus's account of the state (*Saeculum*, ch. 4) is similar, for he too denies that Augustine's mature thinking recognized an ontological grounding of "the state" in the order of nature; indeed that is a major point in his reading of Augustine. What he does not say clearly enough is that Augustine's dethroning of classical conceptions of "creative politics" is a consequence of his shift to the church as the primary society to which Christians belonged.

The final section of this essay compares the way in which Milbank and Markus fit Augustine's endorsement of coercion into their overall interpretations. It should be noted, to begin with, that there is a good deal of agreement in their approaches. Both recognize that Augustine has, properly speaking, no political theory, no true sense of the state as a natural institution in human life. Both also recognize that Augustine understood coercion as essentially a *pastoral* instrument, employed on behalf of the church for the sake of human beings' religious welfare.[22] What really separates them are their understandings of exactly why Augustine's defense of coercion is incompatible with other elements of his thinking. For Markus, the problem was Augustine's failure to follow his most original insights to their logical conclusion, not merely the "secularization" of the state but of the church as well. For Milbank, the problem is Augustine's betrayal of his "ontology of peace" by excessive and dangerous concessions to the sway of force and violence. I would like to conclude this essay with a brief statement of his case.

Milbank begins by noting that Augustine's thought contains some significant hedges against abuse of power. For one thing, his blurring of the boundary between what we would call church and state is part of a "social ontology" or "social logic" that does not concentrate power at the top of a hierarchical construction, but envisions, as stated, an interlocking or nested series of communities, an apparently parochial array of corporations with a variety of mediations and overlapping connections. Since "the religious" is not clearly demarcated from "the political," there is no opportunity for a single social formation, either state or church, to arrogate to itself a determinate sphere of life as specially its own—precisely as would happen during the High Middle Ages, when the course of modern secularization was first charted: "Better, then, that the bounds between Church and state be extremely hazy, so that a 'social' existence of many complex and interlocking powers may emerge, and forestall either a sovereign state, or a hierarchical church" (408).

Furthermore, and perhaps more importantly, Augustine can envision a church which makes actual progress towards achieving justice and virtue, unlike the dismal performance of the earthly city. Why is it that justice cannot exist in the earthly city? We all know Augustine's answer to that, hearkening back to his rejection of Scipio's definition of a commonwealth: because the earthly city, by definition, lacks the love of God above love of self. But Milbank reminds

---

22. *Saeculum*, 140ff.

us that the earthly city's fatal defect is not just a failure of "religious" practice, for love of God necessarily entails love of others as well. "That is why," Augustine writes in *City of God* 15,6, "so many precepts are given about mutual forgiveness and the great care needed for the maintenance of peace, without which noone will be able to see God." And again:

> And yet it is we ourselves—we, his City—who are his best, his most glorious sacrifice . . . . It follows that justice is found where God, the one supreme God, rules an obedient City according to his grace, forbidding sacrifice to any being save himself alone; and where in consequence the soul rules over the body in all men who belong to this City and obey God, and the reason faithfully rules the vices in a lawful system of subordination; so that just as the individual righteous man lives on the basis of faith which is active love, so the association, or people, or righteous men lives on the same basis of faith, active in love, the love with which a man loves God as God ought to be loved, and loves his neighbor as himself. (*Civ.* 19,23; cf. also 10,5–6)

In this account—despite the language of the soul "ruling" the body in the text just quoted—charity is not grounded, as was antique virtue, on the forceful suppression of the passions within the soul, but on the redirection of desire, so that the peace of the heavenly city is not at risk from barely suppressed, turbulent forces, but rests securely on a genuine and heartfelt consensus. This is why it is so important, in Milbank's view, to recognize that for Augustine divine perfection is not approached by our virtuous excellence but only through forgiveness.

> Augustine's real and astounding point [he writes] is this: virtue cannot properly operate except when collectively possessed, when all are virtuous and all concur in the sequence of their differences . . . . [T]he only thing really like heavenly virtue is our constant attempt to compensate for, substitute for, even short-cut this total absence of virtue [i.e., in a human life dominated by conflict and violence], by not taking offense, assuming the guilt of others, doing what they should have done, beyond the bounds of any given "responsibility." Paradoxically, it is only in this exchange and sharing that any truly actual virtue exists. (411)

What then of Augustine's defense of coercion, not just by government for its ordained purposes, but also by government on behalf of the church? First, it must be remembered that the two are different, both as to ends and also as to means: government's coercive restraints of the consequences of sin serve a different purpose from the church's pastoral intentions in employing governmental aid to coerce the Donatists back into communion. The latter efforts were undertaken in the name of saving the sinner from himself, for the sake of the peace of the heavenly city, whereas the former were purely and simply the exercise of power in the name of restoring an always shaky balance of power which *had* no higher end. The means too were different: potentially lethal on the one hand, only disciplinary or remedial on the other, using the instruments of chastisement familiar to parents, teachers, and bishops alike.

Milbank identifies several problems here. First, it is obvious that the church risks being ensnared directly in the exercise of a coercion that can easily cease to be remedial. Second, the very brutality of the means which government must use are all but indistinguishable from sin itself, and therefore will always bear an inevitably tragic character. This "precarious" distinction, as Milbank calls it, always threatens to disappear and thus to confuse church and government, with the deadly effect of sacralizing government and its coercive authority.

Finally, and in Milbank's view most seriously, Augustine's real mistake was to betray his own most revolutionary insight, namely, the "ontology of peace" which refused to grant any ontological priority to sin and evil and regarded them only as privations of being: all forms of power for their own sake were hereby depreciated in the most fundamental way. His justification of coercion, however pedagogical or remedial in intent, occluded the violent and arbitrary moment in any and all punishment and gives some forms of it a divine validation (420). But, argues Milbank, appealing here to ideas of Eriugena's and ultimately of Origen's, punishment is incompatible with God's nature, and all punishment for sin is properly *self*-punishment, in the form of the knowledge of the sinner's estrangement from reality. Far from punishing *us*, God "permits us to judge *him* and to condemn *him* to death here on earth," so that Jesus' trial and punishment is really the condemnation of all punishment (421). The most consistent position, therefore, is for the sinner to be denied social peace by experiencing estrangement from the community which his sin provoked, while at the same time being extended the forgiveness that is the very *raison d'etre* of the community of the *ecclesia*.

In sum: this essay has argued that John Milbank's reading of Augustine provides us with a valuable corrective to Robert Markus's classic study. The corrective does not invalidate the still persuasive account Markus has given of Augustine's disenchantment with a Christian legitimation of the Roman Empire. It does, however, reject that account's time-bound assumptions about "the secular," and the de-emphasis of Augustine's churchmanship associated with it.

INDEX OF PASSAGES CITED
FROM THE *CITY OF GOD*

Book 3	3,6	120
	3,7	63
	3,9	64
	3,13–14	317
	3,14	68, 164
	3,15	49
	3,17	63–5, 114
	3,18	63, 153
	3,29	66
Book 4	4,1–2	62
	4,2	87, 107
	4,3	52, 87, 164
	4,4	53
	4,5	88
	4,7	65, 71
	4,33	154
	4,34	62
Book 5	praef.	61
	5,1–11	54
	5,8-9	65
	5,12–19	52
	5,12–20	125
	5,12	61, 71–2
	5,15	62
	5,16	71
	5,17	73, 88
	5,18	63, 70, 74
	5,19	73, 154
	5,20	73
	5,22	62–3
	5,23	69, 72
	5,24	30, 53, 73, 108
	5,25	108, 120
	5,26	32–3, 53, 66, 99
Book 6	6,1	64
	6,9	206